CW00330328

The Problem with Interreligious Dialogue

Bloomsbury Advances in Religious Studies

James Cox and Steven Sutcliffe

This ground-breaking series presents innovative research in theory and method in the study of religion, paying special attention to disciplinary formation in Religious Studies. Volumes published under its auspices demonstrate new approaches to the way religious traditions are presented and analysed. Each study will demonstrate its theoretical insights by applying them to particular empirical case studies in order to foster integration of data and theory in the historical and cultural study of 'religion'.

Appropriation of Native American Spirituality, Suzanne Owen
Becoming Buddhist, Glenys Eddy
Community and Worldview among Paraiyars of South India,
Anderson H. M. Jeremiah
Conceptions of the Afterlife in Early Civilizations, Gregory Shushan
Contemporary Western Ethnography and the Definition of Religion,
Martin D. Stringer
Cultural Blending in Korean Death Rites, Chang-Won Park
Globalization of Hesychasm and the Jesus Prayer, Christopher D. L. Johnson
Innateness of Myth, Ritske Rensma
Levinas, Messianism and Parody, Terence Holden
New Paradigm of Spirituality and Religion, Mary Catherine Burgess
Post-Materialist Religion, Mika T. Lassander
Redefining Shamanisms, David Gordon Wilson
Reform, Identity and Narratives of Belonging, Arkotong Longkumer
Religion and the Discourse on Modernity, Paul-François Tremlett
Religion as a Conversation Starter, Ina Merdjanova
Religion, Material Culture and Archaeology, Julian Droogan
Spirit Possession and Trance, Patrice Brodeur
Spiritual Tourism, Alex Norman
Theology and Religious Studies in Higher Education,
edited by D. L. Bird and Simon G. Smith
Religion and the Inculturation of Human Rights in Ghana, Abamfo Ofori Atiemo
UFOs, Conspiracy Theories and the New Age: Millennial Conspiracism,
David G. Robertson

THE PROBLEM WITH INTERRELIGIOUS DIALOGUE

Plurality, Conflict and Elitism in Hindu–Christian–Muslim Relations

Muthuraj Swamy

Bloomsbury Academic
An imprint of Bloomsbury Publishing Plc

B L O O M S B U R Y
LONDON · OXFORD · NEW YORK · NEW DELHI · SYDNEY

Bloomsbury Academic

An imprint of Bloomsbury Publishing Plc

50 Bedford Square	1385 Broadway
London	New York
WC1B 3DP	NY 10018
UK	USA

www.bloomsbury.com

BLOOMSBURY and the Diana logo are trademarks of Bloomsbury Publishing Plc

First published 2016
Paperback edition first published 2017

© Muthuraj Swamy, 2016

Muthuraj Swamy has asserted his right under the Copyright, Designs
and Patents Act, 1988, to be identified as Author of this work.

All rights reserved. No part of this publication may be reproduced or transmitted
in any form or by any means, electronic or mechanical, including photocopying,
recording, or any information storage or retrieval system, without prior
permission in writing from the publishers.

No responsibility for loss caused to any individual or organization acting on
or refraining from action as a result of the material in this publication
can be accepted by Bloomsbury or the author.

British Library Cataloguing-in-Publication Data
A catalogue record for this book is available from the British Library.

ISBN: HB: 978–1–4742–5640–7
PB: 978–1–3500–4859–1
ePDF: 978–1–4742–5641–4
ePub: 978–1–4742–5642–1

Library of Congress Cataloging-in-Publication Data
A catalog record for this book is available from the Library of Congress.

Series: Bloomsbury Advances in Religious Studies
(Continuum Advances in Religious Studies)

Typeset by Deanta Global Publishing Services, Chennai, India

To

Amma & Appa

CONTENTS

Preface   ix
Foreword   xi
Acknowledgements   xiv
Abbreviations   xvi

INTRODUCTION   1

Part I
THE PROBLEM: THE CONCEPT AND
PRACTICE OF DIALOGUE

Chapter 1
DIALOGUE IN POST-COLONIAL INDIA: A BRIEF SURVEY   23

Chapter 2
THE PRACTICE OF DIALOGUE: A CASE FROM KANYAKUMARI DISTRICT   48

Part II
LIMITATIONS OF RELIGIOUS PLURALITY,
CONFLICT AND ELITISM

Chapter 3
'RELIGION' AND 'WORLD RELIGIONS': SOME CONTEMPORARY
APPROACHES   71

Chapter 4
RELIGIOUS PLURALITY AND DIALOGUE   94

Chapter 5
ARE RELIGIONS IN CONFLICT?   110

Chapter 6
DIALOGUE AND THE MYTH OF RELIGIOUS CONFLICTS:
A CASE STUDY   128

Chapter 7
DIALOGUE AS ELITIST   145

Contents

Part III
MULTIPLE IDENTITIES AS A CHALLENGER

Chapter 8
RELIGION, MULTIPLE IDENTITIES AND EVERYDAY RELATIONS
AMONG ORDINARY PEOPLE   163

Chapter 9
AFTER DIALOGUE   183

CONCLUSION   206

Bibliography   211
Index   228

PREFACE

Two interrelated questions are increasingly receiving serious attention in the contemporary context in the study of religion. The first is whether religion is a distinct entity different from others such as secularism, politics, economics and so on; the second is whether the 'world religions' category – where each religion is assumed to be a neatly developed, homogenized, complete system that is different from another similar system – is an appropriate framework to understand, define and interpret how religion is understood and practised among common people. The heavily Western-, colonial- and Enlightenment-influenced notions of religion as a distinct unit and of world religions and their influences on contemporary societies are continually examined and critiqued by various studies undertaken by scholars of religion. This book attempts to join the discussion by critically looking at interreligious dialogue, an enterprise that uses the aforementioned categories uncritically. While carrying out its proclaimed objective of working for a peaceful, non-violent and harmonious society, where 'religion' can contribute to the welfare of 'society,' interreligious dialogue crystallizes these notions. In the process, dialogue neglects how ordinary people understand and integrate religion with other aspects of their life, and how they live with multiple identities among which religious identity is only one – also not always based on 'world religions.' Such realities among common people and common life-situations often go unnoticed or are intentionally ignored in elite theories of life. This book attempts to discuss some of them as a way of challenging interreligious dialogue as well as the world religions category.

This critique of interreligious dialogue is rooted in the fascination for dialogue that I held for several years, since the beginning of my theological education, and my subsequent realization of its limitations when I closely interacted with common people who are invited to dialogue. Of course, as a theological perspective on Christianity's relationship to other religions, dialogue has given rise to open attitudes among followers of religions challenging the fundamentalist and exclusivist perspectives prevalent among some sections of religions that claim others are false. But the serious problem with dialogue is that it is accelerating the problem it wants to solve: namely the conflicts and tensions among people, which, most often, dialogue associates, solutions included, with religion explicitly or implicitly.

It is true that interreligious dialogue has undergone various changes during the last few decades, in the light of changing contexts as well as in the process of responding to the challenges posed to it by its critics. In the process there are a number of suggestions and perspectives directed at dialogue to be more effective, more participatory, non-elitist and so forth. However, the basic assumptions in dialogue about the plurality of religions and religious conflicts as well as attitudes to ordinary forms of relating (and negotiating) in everyday living have seldom changed, or even been challenged, which makes dialogue only more problematic.

This book analyses these problems, keeping in the background the past seventy years of dialogue activities in India. The whole body of thinking and writing on dialogue as well as the practical dialogical activities are immense, both in India and outside of it. However, for my purpose in this book I am selective in using the materials available for discussion even while attempting to offer a bird's-eye view on dialogue in India in the first part of the book. Insights received from fieldwork in rural South India are discussed to show how dialogue is oblivious to grassroots ways of relating and negotiating when dialogists still talk *about* dialogue at or *for* the grassroots. Towards the end, this book explores how multiple identities based on everyday ordinary living situations can be a challenger to interreligious dialogue based on the world religions category and fixed religious identities, without attempting to idealize and essentialize the former: the fundamental problem that is addressed is how dialogue just ignores or considers inferior and secondary the everyday relations among common people in their ordinary life situations.

The research for this book was originally undertaken as part of my PhD work – which included a year's fieldwork in rural South India – and submitted to the University of Edinburgh in 2012. I have revised the material and updated it wherever possible.

FOREWORD

Far from dying out in the face of the rapid socio-economic and educational changes of recent times, changes accompanied by explosive increases in migration between and especially within most countries, interest in and practise of a usually ritual-filled relationship to the less visible – commonly called 'religion' — is not diminishing. A negative reason for this comes from the links currently made between religion and violence, attributed to the assumption that 'religion gives the strength that simple ethnic polarisation does not because it … presents itself as a total world view with a total effect on people'.[1] There is truth in this. There is, indeed, often a gap between 'religion' as a 'total singular entity' in the view of those speaking for it and those followers silenced by such an exclusive view – people for whom religion may rather present one variable element in contextualized, and commonly therefore multiple, identities. Further, and more generally, we must always be cautious in accepting that actions designated by actors as coming from 'their religion' are indeed 'religiously' motivated, and not the actions of ruthless gangsters such as those identifying with 'Islamic State,' who validate evil while insisting on their so-called Islamic credentials. 'Religion' has often been a muffling blanket thrown over problems by governments to cover violence which may derive as much or far more from relative economic marginalization or sheer poverty: the Hyderabad riots between Muslims and Hindus of the 1990s, disputed national identity in Myanmar between militant Buddhists and Muslim Rohingas, historical remnants of colonization affecting Christians in Northern Ireland or, the topic of this book, tensions between caste groups which erupted in fighting in the 1990s in southern Tamil Nadu.

Religion may thus be brought into the discussion and analysis of certain social issues to the advantage of those in power, rather than a more accurate but politically demanding term such as poverty, or corruption, to enable a secular elite to wash its hands of the problem. On the other hand, researchers in the field of religious studies, and to an extent it seems in the corps of interreligious dialoguers, may support such views by carving out their own subject matter, pristine religion, from the totality of human thought and action. One outcome, the main theme of this book, is that where interreligious dialogue specialists become part of the solution to what certain, perhaps rather partial, authorities label as religious violence, their work may merely smooth over or altogether miss underlying socio-economic caste problems. Moreover, lack of interest in dialogue shown by people with multiple identities, especially those for whom scraping a living dominates, may be taken as a sign of intransigence or resistance rather than of the irrelevance of what is offered. In social science, field research is less a matter of discerning answers to questions, for many a bored or kindly informant will give answers, than of slowly working out what the key questions are.

I have already touched on the internal divide in any tradition (least evident in locally limited or 'indigenous' traditions) between the few with specialist knowledge and the right to perform certain collective rites, and the legion with neither. This leads to a problem of representation: is the 'religion' used in discussing interfaith issues or attributing blame for interreligious violence defined by the trained leaders, or the masses? This is crucial. Researchers within religious studies commonly reflect on the thoughts, meanings and actions attributed to a particular tradition they study, and it seems the norm to start from the scripturally trained elite practitioners rather than build up a picture of the tradition from praxis of the ordinary person, whose interest waxes and wanes, and whose knowledge and sense of commitment may be slight.

The outcome perhaps inadvertently strengthens the view of religions as so many discrete entities, and while those who take the subject further may hear that challenged, not all take heed. The ensuing rigidity may well dissuade researchers and practitioners from delving into the complex tensions between global and local in so-called universal traditions. Still less do they, or teachers in seminaries, madrasa and the like, respectfully and sensitively explore the immense differences between two equally valid representations of the tradition: an often scripturally and philosophically based religion of the elite, which define the tradition for both insiders and outsider researchers, and the practices of people concerned primarily with living appropriately in their visible and less-visible context by performing whatever is deemed necessary to manage life or indeed death. One outcome of this essentializing of elite-defined religions as specific tiles in a world religions mosaic is that these clearly bounded scriptural 'religions' which are the usual subject of the 'interreligious' discussions are not particularly relevant to the average non-specialist person who may identify in some way with one or more locally embedded traditions. Thus what is being discussed and compared exists more in the discussion than in ordinary life. A similar problem is evident in the growing field of intercultural theology which, while it may give lip service to anthropological writing on culture, is still working with predetermined tiles fired in a central kiln with little hope of an outcome relevant beyond ivory towers.

It is for these reasons, among others, that Muthuraj Swamy's book is a welcome addition to literature on interreligious and interfaith studies, and more generally to the study of the multiple religious traditions of southern India. His personal and family background in the Hindu tradition and his subsequent training in the Christian tradition, alongside his experience in interfaith dialogue in the wake of the Kanyakumari riots of the 1980s and 1990s and reflection on that within religious studies, have given him the necessary breadth of understanding to approach the topic dispassionately, exploring the processes of and problems with interreligious dialogue seen from the varied viewpoints. Moreover, the patient care with which he conducted fieldwork with a wide cross-section of people, political and church leaders, fishermen and clusters of working women, both in the immediate area and further afield, enabled him to build up the understanding necessary to begin to know what questions addressed the concerns of otherwise silenced peoples. His conclusion, that 'multiple identities and everyday relations of people from the bottom need to be learned and understood by those at the top rather than delivered in the reverse direction through elite discourses such as dialogue based on world religions', is one that all concerned should take to heart. This could contribute to the future of southern India and all other places where conflict linked (whether appropriately or not) to religion is seen as the province of interfaith dialoguers. Just as important, in questioning the assumptions of dialoguers not only about the normal proper tension between a universal creed and all local expression thereof but also the actual place of what is called religion in ordinary people's lives, Muthuraj offers the religious studies community and that of interfaith exponents a valuable text with which to reflect and possibly reform.

Rev Dr Elizabeth Koepping
Heidelberg, 2015

Note

1 Chandra Muzaffar, *Universalism of Islam* (Penang: Aliran 1984), 123.

ACKNOWLEDGEMENTS

As often stated, a book in the making has hundreds and thousands of people behind it. Yet, while everyone is thanked, some names are acknowledged, perhaps rightfully. I sincerely thank a number of people who have been supportive, but I must acknowledge some who have offered scholarly support, moral support and financial support (including those who helped in exploring grants) for this work at various stages: Dr Elizabeth Koepping for supervising my research, that forms the central part of this book's content, at the University of Edinburgh, and writing a foreword as well, and Dr Jeanne Openshaw, the co-supervisor of the research; Dr Sathianathan Clarke, Dr J. Jayakiran Sebastian, Dr R. Sahayadhas, Dr Eric Lott, Dr Israel Selvanayagam, Dr Duncan B. Forrester, Dr Robin Boyd and Dr Adrian Bird with whom I discussed this work at various stages and who offered their valuable suggestions; Rev Canon Roger Simon, Bishop G. Devakadasham, Rev Justin Devadasan, Dr Jonathan Gnanadasan, Rev Dr D. Chellappa, Mr Ian McCafferty, Dr David Manohar and Dr Christina Manohar, for offering support at various levels including support related to funding; all my interviewees, both from the community of dialogists and from Gramam village, especially Rev C. Rajamony and Dr Samuel Dhasan; the community of Union Biblical Seminary (UBS) where I have been teaching for the last five years, especially Dr David Samuel, Mr David Muthukumar, Dr Asish Thomas Koshy and Mr Richie Varghese, who have helped in various stages of revising my writing for this book and encouraging for publishing it; Dr John V. Sundaram, Rev Mrs Jessie Nesakumar, Bishop Sam Yesudhas, Mr Isaac Rethinamony, Mr R. Selvanathan, Mrs P. Grace Victory Bai, Rev A. Paul Sundar, Rev M. Immanuel Kinson Bell, Mrs I. Sobana, Mr James Wesly, Mr D. Martin, Dr Sathya Velmurugan, Rev Boosa Moses, Mrs Ruth Angoove, Rev Peter Clarke and Mrs Janice Clarke, Rev Margaret Macgregor, Rev Roy Pape, Dr John Joshvaraja and Mrs Rachel Joshvaraja for their support and encouragement in various ways; the College of Humanities and Social Sciences as well as the School of Divinity of the University of Edinburgh for offering me postgraduate scholarship awards to pursue my research leading to this book; St Augustine Foundation, Canterbury, for supporting much of my stay, along with my wife and children, in Edinburgh during my research period; the Fellowship of St Thomas in Scotland, Friends of United Theological College (UTC) in the United Kingdom and Friends of Church in India in England; the libraries of the UTC, Bangalore, UBS, Pune, Christian Institute for the Study of Religion and Society (CISRS), Bangalore, Henry Martyn Institute (HMI), Hyderabad, St Colms International House, Edinburgh and New College and University libraries, Edinburgh.

I thank the Bloomsbury publishing house for accepting my manuscript for publication and the series editors of the Bloomsbury Advances in Religious

Studies, Dr James L. Cox, Dr Steve Sutcliffe and Dr Craig Martin, as well as the commissioning editor for Religious Studies, Dr Lalle Pursglove, for their kind encouragement and support thorough the process.

As acknowledged in several cases, the family also suffers along with the author/ researcher. This is true in my case too, and my family has been very supportive for writing this book, even though I might not have gratefully acknowledged it always. My wife Mahiba spent more time in taking care of our daughters Mona and Mano through all these years to provide me with more time to concentrate on my research. I thank my family members who have been supportive and encouraging through this journey, especially my parents-in-law, Y. Gnanabai and Paul Thurai. My parents, S. Saraswathi and Swamy Nadar, who did not have formal education but always envisioned their children's education, extended all the support they could offer to me for my education in spite of their very difficult living conditions as well as the constraints in resources available to them: with a grateful heart I dedicate this book to them.

ABBREVIATIONS

BJP	Bharatiya Janata Party
CIRSJA	Centre for Inter-faith Relations, Studies and Joint Action
CISRS	Christian Institute for the Study of Religion and Society
CPJ	Centre for Peace and Justice
CREED	Centre for Rural Employment and Education for Development
CSI	Church of South India
ECI	Election Commission of India
GoI	Government of India
GoTN	Government of Tamil Nadu
HMI	Henry Martyn Institute
IMC	International Missionary Council
MEET	Multi-religious Education by Extension in Tamil
PASA	People's Association for Social Action
PWDS	Palmera Workers Development Society
RSS	Rashtriya Swayamsevak Sangh
TTS	Tamil Nadu Theological Seminary
UTC	United Theological College
VHP	Vishwa Hindu Parishad
WCC	World Council of Churches
WPR	World Parliament of Religions

INTRODUCTION

1 The Problem with Interreligious Dialogue

Interreligious dialogue[1] (hereafter I will use simply 'dialogue', except where the full phrase is required for a better understanding of the ideas expressed) in contemporary society is an attractive topic of discussion as well as an act practised in many parts of the world, especially among religious leaders, thinkers and theologians. It is undertaken to create better relationships between people belonging to different religions by bringing them together: it thus aims to establish peace and harmony in a society which has been devastated by conflicts between religions. There is much information regarding interreligious meetings and gatherings, conferences, seminars and workshops and invitations to interreligious collaborations. The vast amount of materials produced during the last few decades brings home the fact that there seems to be an increasing interest in this field. There are many institutions, mostly non-governmental organizations (NGOs) – churches, ashrams and centres of spirituality as well as academic centres and institutes – committed to carrying out dialogue activities in different parts of the globe.[2] One often notices that government and state institutions, which normally proclaim the separation of religion from the public sphere, are also sometimes involved in encouraging their citizens to maintain dialogue in order to avoid what they perceive as religious conflicts and to maintain law and order.

There are limitations in the assumptions behind dialogue as well as the method and process of how dialogue is carried out, which is the focus of this book. The central argument of this book, drawing on predominantly Christian-initiated dialogue in the post-colonial Indian context over the last seven decades, is that dialogue, in spite of its arguably positive contributions to society by offering less aggressive Christian attitudes to other religions and redefining the Christian mission within inclusive and pluralist paradigms, is still limited. At least three limitations can be pointed out. First is the perception of the plurality of 'world religions' between which dialogue should occur: this involves the assumption and endorsement of fixed religious identities for people. Further, there is also a silence in dialogue concerning how, where and why 'religion' and 'religions' were constructed; rather there is an uncritical acceptance of these essentialized categories in dialogue. In other words, Western constructions of 'religion' and its plural 'religions', religion as a distinct entity opposed to 'secular', 'world religions' category and the European colonial creation of religious identities for people in many colonies including India, have seldom been questioned in dialogue. Second, there is also an uncritical reception and interpretation of 'religious conflicts' or 'conflicts in the name of religions', which fails to appreciate that religious conflicts are often more than 'religious' and, in many cases, not even 'religious' conflicts at all, 'religion' having become a useful peg on which to hang the violence. Third is to do with the elite nature and method of dialogue. In dialogue, grassroots people (and their life and issues) are silent objects of elite discussions and only passive listeners to whom the 'knowledge' of dialogue should be passed on by the elites. Accordingly, the elitist dialogue has ignored the actual living relationships among people in ordinary situations – having different religious identities as well as multiple community identities. While these lacunae are still not addressed, there are increasingly wider appeals inviting people to live in dialogue. This book critiques dialogue for these limitations by making use of the insights available on how grassroots and common people understand religion(s), use religious and other identities in ordinary situations, perceive 'religious' conflicts and relate and negotiate with their neighbours from other communities. Especially important are the multiple identities exercised in grassroots living that include intra-religious and multireligious identities as well as identities other than religious.

Interest in this current research derives from two sources. First, it stems from my appreciation of dialogue, especially for its underlying objectives of reducing conflicts between people and creating better relationships, and the less aggressive attitudes it has offered for Christians to approach other religions,[3] and from my involvement in dialogue activities for the last many years, which includes six years of full-time work with interreligious organizations in South India. Secondly, and at the same time, it emerges from my perception of dialogue's limitations in terms of its assumptions about the plurality of world religions and the manner in which it is carried out. While in my undergraduate thesis in 2001, I evaluated the work of some interreligious organizations in South India,[4] in this book I have attempted to investigate the aforementioned limitations which I started to realize amid my post-2001 involvement in dialogue activities.

My involvement with dialogue started in 1998. I had completed my under-graduate degree in theology and had been involved in church ministry for a year. My undergraduate degree from the Senate of Serampore College, also known as Serampore University, in India, had courses involving dialogue (one such course was 'Christians and People of Other Faiths'), and they had generated a lot of enthusiasm in me: I was convinced that dialogue was a better model compared to the other models available for Christianity's relationship with other religions. To be involved in dialogue activities was in my thoughts for some time, and I opted to join the Centre for Peace and Justice (CPJ), an interreligious organization in my district, Kanyakumari, in Tamil Nadu, South India. My major work at CPJ was visiting villages and forming youth groups consisting of young people from different religions. In addition, I also assisted in organizing dialogue meetings and multireligious celebrations of religious festivals in villages. My interest in dialogue activities prompted me to upgrade my undergraduate degree to Bachelor of Divinity (BD) at the United Theological College (UTC), Bangalore, where the study of religion and efforts for dialogue was popular during that time. My enthusiasm for dialogue encouraged me, as already noted, to write my BD dissertation in UTC on dialogue. After my BD, I again returned to full-time work in dialogue and joined the Centre for Inter-faith Relations, Studies and Joint Action (CIRSJA).[5] My work with CIRSJA helped me to continue my earlier work such as visiting villages and arranging multireligious celebrations of festivals locally, in addition to being involved in national-level dialogue programmes. These activities helped me to gain some in-depth experience in dialogue programmes and to realize some of the limitations of dialogue, especially when I met people in villages for follow-up meetings after the dialogue programmes.

During such meetings I started to realize that there are some fundamental problems with dialogue. In my conversations with ordinary village people, it was becoming clear that they looked at the interreligious meetings and celebration of religious festivals in their villages as occasional and political: that is, as some outsiders coming and conducting some programmes for village people in the presence of many political leaders. My conversations with people helped me to observe that religion was neither the primary nor the only factor causing conflicts between them. People's capacity to maintain peace and harmony in spite of their apparent lack of knowledge of dialogue; the different reasons for conflicts among them; how they resolved those conflicts – all these things I learnt in my interactions with the people in villages. These were not really new to my own life situation, but my interactions with people helped me realize how ignorant I had been to this reality and how inadequate dialogue programmes/organizations and theological education were on this point. This motivated me to study and evaluate the assumptions of dialogue in India and to record common people's understanding of religion(s) and religious conflicts and their relations and negotiations with each other in ordinary everyday life situations. This book is the result.

My experience and observations during my work with interreligious organizations led me towards the following questions: Do people at the grassroots look at religions as they are presented by their elite leaders, thinkers and theologians? Are differences between religions the only cause of conflicts among them? Can religions be put into single unified systems and differentiated from each other? Why are conflicts between religions often spoken about and uncritically accepted in the dialogue circles? If there are many causes for conflicts, why is religion claimed as the prime cause? Why and how does one talk about the ability of religion or religions to solve conflicts in a (bad) society? What are the different ways people at the grassroots understand and perceive relationships between religions, and how do they live their everyday life in such contexts, and how are these different from elite conceptions of religion and dialogue? These questions will be discussed throughout this book.

Theoretically, the discussion of the limitations of dialogue in the present context may be started by observing the ambiguities in dialogue. First, etymologically speaking, dialogue means conversation between two or more people, and therefore, interreligious dialogue means conversation between people belonging to different religions. Applied in this sense, any conversations between people with different religious identities, both in the past and in the present, could be considered as interreligious dialogue. In such interactions the goals of dialogue vary from polemics and apologetics to understanding and learning from each other, or just an exchange of information. Moreover, the conversation does not need to be just about religion, but it can be on any issue or concern. It is simply dialogue – conversation – between people with different religious identities.

But in the contemporary period, interreligious dialogue is not simply any conversation between people with different religious identities. Rather it is presented as an important step in understanding one's own religion and one's neighbours' religions, and thus a step towards better understanding and relationships between people of different religions.[6] The presupposition is that dialogue helps to eliminate religious conflicts and tensions because religions have the potential to further the cause of world peace, if the process is explicated through dialogue. Dialogue is presented as an approach in which positive attitudes and openness to other religions are implied, the view being that such positive attitudes between members of different religions are necessary to create better relationships among humans in society. This positive attitude varies from showing mutual openness and mutual sharing among the participants while keeping the distinctive features of their respective religions, to affirming and acknowledging the differences between religions while emphasizing the unity of aim or intention of all religions, even though the latter is sometimes criticized in dialogue circles. Such dialogue, it is observed, is not just a practical activity; it has become a sort of 'ideal stance' which is different from the 'actualities of dialogue'.[7] In this approach, the dialogue promoters write about it or articulate it purely in terms of theory and principle.

My focus in this book is to critique dialogue as it is understood by its proponents. In formal dialogue, it is more than an ordinary two-way conversation, for dialogue refers to particular types of conversation, or conversation with particular attitudes. As a result, the term dialogue has been conceptualized, essentialized and imbued with ideas which refer to meanings beyond conversation, such as positive attitudes and tolerant approaches. While I would like to keep the term 'interreligious dialogue' or 'dialogue' to refer to formal dialogue, I would prefer to use different terms such as interreligious interactions or relations to refer to what normally happens outside of formal dialogue.

The second type of ambiguity in dialogue is related to the history or the past of dialogue: the different ways in which the various pasts of dialogue are talked about. There are generally two perspectives in this regard. First, whatever interreligious interactions happened in the past (especially before the end of the colonial period) were not *genuine* dialogues, for they were implicitly based on or had aspects of apologetics or polemics. Therefore *new* dialogue, which is a *genuine* dialogue or dialogue with a *positive* attitude, breaks with the 'tainted' interreligious interactions of the past. According to this perspective, the new version is appropriate for the contemporary context. The alternate perspective, and one which rejects this 'tainted and pure' dichotomy, links contemporary formal dialogue to the various interreligious interactions of the past, discerning common assumptions and intentions.[8] The two perspectives are not absolute, indeed often the two poles touch, when the past (otherwise rejected) is called to add strength and validity to the present. For instance, while introducing his book *Hindu-Christian Dialogue*, Harold Coward says,

> Hindu-Christian dialogue has had a long and checkered history. Up until the beginning of this [20th] century most Hindu-Christian interaction took place in India. The first half of this century saw the expansion of Hindu-Christian discussion to Europe and North America. Worldwide pluralism in the decades since the fifties has resulted in a gradual intensification of this interaction at both the lay and scholarly levels. But there has been no broad and sustained Hindu-Christian dialogue.[9]

Coward here uses different terms such as 'dialogue', 'discussion' and 'interaction' to talk about his subject. This indicates the tensions involved in relating the present dialogue with the past interreligious interactions. On the one hand, he talks about the 'history' of dialogue, and on the other hand, he differentiates, but does not explicate, the 'broad and sustained Hindu-Christian dialogue' from the interactions of the past. Thus, one can see both the perspectives indicated in his words – relating the present dialogue with the past interactions as well as making the dialogue serve new purposes. Coward continues to talk about early contact between India and the Greco-Roman world, Mughal Emperor Akbar's summons to Jesuit Christians to take part in theological debates, the exchanges between European missionaries and Hindu reformers like Raja Ram Mohan Roy, Dayanand Saraswati, Keshab Chander Sen, Vivekananda and Radhakrishnan within a framework of the past Hindu–Christian dialogue,[10] which he nevertheless then downplays.

But dialogue, or precisely the *awareness of* and the *emphasis on* it, is a very new development in the global context and in India. The idea that followers of different religions *should* participate in dialogue activities in order to understand the religions of each other and to create healthy relationships among them is a relatively new trend. While a general understanding of interreligious *relations* is that people with different religious identities *are* meeting, interacting and relating with each other in various ways (as in the past), the advocated dialogue is mostly associated with the imperative, 'ought'. In other words, the ideas of interreligious links are: there *should* be dialogue; the *urgency* of the time demands it; people of different religions *must* come together in dialogue to overcome religious conflicts – commonly with the unspoken pressure that failure to engage in dialogue may contribute to, or even cause, violence; and proper *preparation* is necessary for taking part in dialogue. A striking feature of formal dialogue is the assumption that *it is not happening* among ordinary people and that this is the cause for religious conflicts and violence in society, solved only when the grassroots are educated about dialogue. This approach may also imply that ordinary people are the perpetrators of 'religious conflicts'.

Of course, it is true that dialogue, as articulated by its exponents, is not happening among many common and ordinary people but is restricted to the formal dialogue programmes, which are mostly attended by elites. But what is ignored here is the fact that people belonging to different religions, at various places, times in history and levels, *were* and *are* in continuous interaction. While many times these everyday interreligious relations are ignored, sometimes they are also treated as superficial and shallow, as not theologically grounded or as done by unsophisticated villagers.[11] Against the 'ordinary', 'familiar' and 'local' interreligious relationships in everyday living contexts, people are encouraged to take part in *faithful* and *genuine* dialogue.[12] This book therefore critiques the assumptions and ideas behind this 'new dialogue', and the nature and methods of its practical execution, and in so doing, describes and discusses the relations among ordinary people with different religious identities.

Dialogue is found in academic and non-academic fields in various parts of the globe. It has acquired a significant place in the field of theology, particularly in Christian theology, and in religious studies – universities have departments and centres of dialogue and offer programmes and courses in it,[13] and there are a number of centres and programmes outside university institutions as well that are widely endorsed and spoken about by churches and church-related organizations, governments and NGOs. This is mainly because of the assumption that the world is perceived as divided on the basis of religions, and hence efforts for dialogue are necessary to bridge chasms. Discussion of common themes and the notion of 'religions together for the common welfare' of human beings are some important aspects of dialogue among its advocates. One common assumption appears to be that just as cultures are said to do this or that, so too religions are said to dialogue. Neither of these abstract nouns such as religion or culture actually *do* anything, of course: rather, people with this or that ethnic or religious label (accurate or not) act in certain ways.

This kind of formal group-to-group dialogue has dominated the Indian context, especially Indian Christian thinking, since the post-independence period, and it continues to do so in spite of criticisms aimed at it from Christian fundamentalists, conservatives and sometimes evangelicals who fear syncretism, relativism, dilution and compromise of Christian truth.[14] In India, dialogue was proposed as a viable tool for relationships among followers of different religions after independence, when the question of the relationship of religious minorities in India such as Christians and Muslims with Hindus, Buddhists and Sikhs became vital,[15] and against the background of the violent partition in which Hindu and Muslim identities were involved. The initiatives for dialogue were taken mainly by Christian thinkers, but people from other religions also joined them. Indian nation-building was put forward as a common platform where people belonging to different religions could come together and relate with each other.[16]

The 1960s and 1970s witnessed many such efforts taken in India through churches, NGOs, ashrams and research centres.[17] Moreover, in the same period the Roman Catholic Church officially supported the need for Christianity's relationship with other religions in the Second Vatican Council (hereafter Vatican II), held between 1962 and 1965, and the World Council of Churches (WCC), on the side of Protestant Christians, made many efforts for dialogue and produced the already mentioned document 'Guidelines on Dialogue' in 1979. These attempts had much influence on the promoters of dialogue in India, who in turn also contributed to the dialogue programmes of the WCC, the Vatican and other international bodies by participating in them and appropriated them in the Indian context.

Since the 1980s, especially after the demolition of Babri Masjid in 1992 and the subsequent violence, dialogue in India has concentrated on the issue of 'religious conflicts', commonly referred to in India as communal conflicts. Believing that mostly it is the misunderstanding of religions among people that leads to conflicts, dialogue claims that religious conflicts can be eliminated when people of different religions come together in dialogue. One common notion in dialogue is that the level of religious misunderstanding is high especially among ordinary people or people at the grassroots, and because of this they are vulnerable to getting involved in religious conflicts. Therefore, it is claimed, these people have to be educated about dialogue to ensure the maintenance of communal harmony in the contemporary Indian context.

In Kanyakumari district in the state of Tamil Nadu in India – where I conducted fieldwork for this research – one can find this type of dialogue as it is found elsewhere in India. Officially, Hinduism, Christianity and Islam are the three major religions followed in this district, and there are a number of dialogue activities in the district. In the 1960s and 1970s, the efforts of Vatican II and WCC influenced the dialogue programmes there.[18] However, dialogue was posed as an urgent need after 1982 when, it is claimed, religious clashes were occurring between Hindus and Christians in the district.[19] Many initiatives were taken by churches in the region, especially the Roman Catholic Church, to create better relationships among people. NGOs were established after this period to work for communal harmony and peace in society, and existing NGOs were also involved in promoting this purpose.

This book is concerned with critiquing these trends in dialogue in the Indian context over the last seven decades. As mentioned earlier, I limit my analysis to picking up three aspects that I consider as the limitations of dialogue. First is how religion as a distinct unit or entity or system is used in dialogue. As it is obvious, dialogue is preoccupied with religions and religious plurality. Very often one can hear about the dialogue between 'world religions'. But what does it mean to talk about 'religion' (and its binary, 'secularism'), 'religions' and 'world religions' in the modern context? How have these categories been constructed? What was the context in which these categories were created? What were their locations? Are these concepts familiar to people all over the world and in each Indian village? Answers to many of these questions lie in discussing how these categories have been constructed in the context of Western Enlightenment and Christianity and how they have been passed on elsewhere through European colonialism particularly from the eighteenth century. The role of Western Orientalists, Christian missionaries, travellers and colonial administrators in creating religions and religious identities for the colonized people is an important aspect which nevertheless has been paid little attention in dialogue.

In the Indian context, one consequence of these forces was the imagination or construction of 'Hinduism' through the Western notions of 'religion'. While there are a number of traditions within what is known as Hinduism, the Western intellectuals and administrators during the colonial times, in their observations and interpretations, simplistically made Hinduism a singular entity.[20] Moreover, in the process, the brahmanical traditions were selected to represent the whole of Hinduism for people in the West, which also spilt over into Indian understanding. The 'science of religion' or the comparative study of religions, established in the West during the nineteenth century, crystallized this process.[21] As a result, Hinduism became a 'world religion' or a 'major religion' as did Christianity, Islam, Judaism, Confucianism and others. In relation to the Indian context, the imagination or invention of Hinduism is important to this study — for this notion is uncritically used in, among others, dialogue. This is discussed in detail in Chapters 3 and 4.

The second limitation compels us to investigate and understand what are termed 'religious conflicts', which are claimed to be crucial to the context of dialogue. As mentioned earlier, the purpose of dialogue, as often claimed, is to do away with 'religious conflicts' (or communal conflicts) and create communal harmony, peace-building and a non-violent society. In the global context of terrorism, especially since the attacks on the World Trade Center in New York in September 2001 (9/11 as it is often referred to by many, including contemporary dialogists), this gains even further significance. The assumption that 'religion' or 'religions' contribute to violence (directly or indirectly), and the uncritical acceptance of this notion has, in fact, set many limitations for dialogue. It is almost always overlooked that what is claimed as 'religious violence' usually stems from the socio-economic and personal struggles of people, and from the political intervention which plays with the religious identities of people in order to boost vote-bank politics. For instance, in India, what are termed 'religious conflicts' have been, at the roots, mostly a social issue involving caste domination and oppression, or economic struggles between people or groups, or manipulations by the political class for power or even the personal problems of a few individuals, which erupt into larger inter-community problems. Questions such as how they evolve into 'religious conflicts' and how and why they are projected or named as such, and how these economic, political and social realities are overlooked in dialogue, need serious attention. Convenience and benefit to power holders apart, Chandra Muzaffar's comment with regard to Malaysia may be relevant here: 'Religion gives the strength that simple ethnic polarization does not because it ... presents itself as a total world-view, with a total effect on people.'[22]

Moreover, while talking about religious conflicts, dialogists also simply accept that religion, in one way or other, has been instrumental in creating conflicts among people, and they rush to propose what has to be done instead of analysing critically why and how these conflicts have occurred. As Elizabeth Koepping comments, responses to the issue of religious conflicts 'easily slip into generalizations based on what *ought* to be the case according to power-holders – whether political, religious or academic – rather than working from what actually is the case in local daily life'.[23] Unfortunately dialogue promoters work as 'power holders': they may well need the theme of religion or the designation of 'religious conflicts' in order to propose dialogue as a solution to eliminate them. Koepping continues:

> While remaining at the level of reality as lived and observed over time risks drowning the observer in data, extrapolating too readily from the theoretical macro to some assumed micro-level risks labelling conflict or tension as religious in nature when other issues are more relevant. Not only do many such assumptions put religion in an unreasonably bad light, but the resulting misapprehensions may make the resolution of tensions all but impossible.[24]

Dialogue runs into exactly this problem: first, it either labels conflicts among people as religious or uncritically accepts such labelling, which is really done by power seekers such as politicians and other elites, and second it then offers dialogue as a solution to do away with 'religious conflicts'.[25] This trend in dialogue needs critical evaluation, and this book attempts such an evaluation.

Discussing the third limitation brings out the elite nature of dialogue and its consequences. The nature of formal dialogue programmes, the participants, the locations of the programmes, their content and themes and their attitude to and impact on people who do not participate in these programmes need critical study. Often dialogue activists express the idea that dialogue should 'reach' or should be passed on to ordinary people, ignoring the everyday relationships of people. Does dialogue, which claims its concern is for building communities, take seriously the experiences of the grassroots people in relating with their neighbours?

> Dialogue cannot be reduced to the act of one person's 'depositing' ideas in another, nor can it become a simple exchange of ideas to be 'consumed' by the discussants ... because dialogue is an encounter among women and men who name the world, it must not be a situation where some name on behalf of others. It is an act of creation, it must not serve as a crafty instrument for the domination of one person by another. The domination implicit in dialogue is that of the world by the dialoguers. ... How can I dialogue if I always project ignorance onto others and never perceive my own? How can I dialogue if I record myself as a case apart from others – mere 'its' in whom I cannot recognize the other 'I's? How can I dialogue if I consider myself a member of the in-group of 'pure' [wo]men, the owners of truth and knowledge, for whom all non-members are 'these people' or 'the great unwashed'? *How can I dialogue if I start from the premise that naming the world is the task of an elite and that the presence of the people in history is a sign of deterioration, thus to be avoided?*[26]

These words of Paulo Freire, a Brazilian educator, have been uttered in relation to the 'Pedagogy of the Oppressed', but they are also very relevant to interreligious dialogue in India as they bring challenging insights to it. If dialogue separates itself from the silenced non-members of the dialogue, it is no longer a dialogue at all. Because what is then implied is that knowledge – knowledge of how to relate with people of other religions – is found or achieved only through dialogue done by a tiny minority. In dialogue or conversation, contrary to the world view, there are not merely two kinds of partners. There is always a group of people, an audience, who may not participate in dialogue but who are still important, because the implications of dialogue are always addressed to them. They are not people who lack knowledge, experience and any glimmer of a capacity for thought, which is how they inevitably have to function in 'dialogue' as the passive recipients of knowledge. It is here that the most crucial limitation of dialogue becomes identifiable. One anthropologist of religion, in a different context, thus says: 'We tend to presume that everyone is as concerned with ideology, language, and thought as we are. We expect that the discourse of religion, especially, takes place on a sophisticated and high plane – "different" from the everyday and common'.[27] I shall be arguing that it does not. Yet dialogue mostly functions on the basis of this kind of illusion, which needs to be critiqued.

2 Note on Fieldwork

I undertook fieldwork in Kanyakumari district in India for four months in 2007 and eight months in 2008 to study specifically how dialogue is practised among the proponents and promoters of dialogue who are mostly elites, and how relationships are maintained among people at the grassroots. My fieldwork was more of a reflexive ethnography. According to Charlotte Aull Davies, who has produced an outstanding work on reflexive ethnography, it is 'a process of self-reference ... in which the products of research are affected by the personnel and the process of doing research'.[28] For, 'it is possible to make comprehensive and positive use of this reflexivity while still avoiding the inward-looking radical reflexivity, associated with postmodernist critiques, which undermines our capacity to do research intended to produce valid and generalisable knowledge of other people, and not merely of oneself'.[29] In my field research, I have used reflexive ethnography for many reasons that I discuss next.

I was born in this district and have lived here for more than thirty years. As I mentioned earlier, Kanyakumari is a district where people with different religious identities live. Hinduism, Christianity and Islam are the major religions in the district. This district is multireligious in the sense not only that more than one religion exists, but also more than one religion is professed in the same family. That is, people following different religions live in one household. This trend could be found in the district for more than a century and continues to be the case even today. I too come from such a family, and I have lived in this reality from my childhood. My family was originally a Hindu family, and I am a converted Christian. While some of my family joined Christianity later, the rest continue to follow Hindu traditions. But we have continued to live in the same household. While living within this reality I never came to know anything about either 'dialogue' or 'religious conflicts' and solutions. We just lived it. Even today many people in villages in this district do not know what exactly religious dialogue is, but they live in harmony with their neighbours from different religions – I found this reality in my field research, which will be discussed in detail in Chapter 8.

My fieldwork in Kanyakumari district consisted of three primary stages. The first stage was to study and understand the 'religious' conflicts in the district, which are claimed by the dialogue promoters to be the context that necessitated dialogue. I was revisiting the 'Mandaikadu religious conflict' or 'Mandaikadu Hindu-Christian conflict' (locally known as *Mandaikadu matha kalavaram*) of 1982 and its impact on the whole district for the subsequent years.[30] The purpose of doing this was to understand and study the conflicts not only within the religious context, but also within various other interlinked factors, including socio-economic and political ones.[31] While this conflict involved multiple factors and was primarily between fisherfolk and inland people, for the last more than three decades it has been projected as a religious conflict. This will be presented in detail and analysed in Chapter 6. The data regarding the Mandaikadu religious conflict were collected primarily through four methods. First, the primary and publically available written document regarding the Mandaikadu religious conflicts is the report of the commission headed by Justice Venugopal, appointed by the state government of Tamil Nadu to investigate the events. This is generally known among people in Kanyakumari district as the Venugopal Commission report.[32] This report has been both welcomed as well as criticized by people in the district. To be more precise, since the report held both the Christians[33] and the Hindus[34] in the district responsible for the clashes and proposed solutions that favoured as well as challenged them, both groups endorse it where it favours their cause and criticize it where it does not. Naturally, the report has some shortcomings, which will be discussed later. Nevertheless, this is the only document publicly available which provides people with a somewhat detailed report and analysis of the clashes, notwithstanding whatever limitations and conclusions it has. Secondly, I could get information regarding print media circulating at the time of the clashes which were used by both groups to attack each other. Wall posters, small notices and declarations in local newspapers were used as a means to incite violence. The third method is the studies and reflections concerned with the clashes after they were over. These include unpublished dissertations and other writings.[35] Finally, I interviewed people who have knowledge about the clashes and who directly witnessed them. In addition to studying these clashes, I also collected data regarding some of the recent conflicts in the district, which are often claimed to have their roots in the Mandaikadu religious conflicts and are thus classed as 'religious'. In this regard, I wanted to interview some politicians in whose discourse religious conflicts occur quite often. I approached three district-level politicians, but only one responded – from Bharatiya Janata Party (BJP).[36] I also interviewed some local social scientists and historians who approach the society and history of local people from different perspectives and who have published materials pertaining to it. While discussing the information collected through interviews in the field research, I also make use of the insights I have received from my experience while working with dialogue organizations.

The second stage of fieldwork was interviewing people associated with churches and NGOs who posited dialogue as the solution for the 'religious clashes' in the district. I studied what has been done both at the official levels and at the local church levels in the Church of South India (CSI), the Roman Catholic Church and other churches. This involved studying the official declarations of the churches on communal harmony, and interviewing the pastors, priests and lay leaders who were involved in dealing with finding solutions for these clashes. As well, I interviewed people who were involved in dialogical activities in the district.

In total I was able to interview twenty-nine people involved in dialogue activities – seven Protestant Christians (five clergy, two lay people), five Roman Catholic Christians (four clergy and one lay person), eleven Hindus (all lay people), and six Muslims (all lay people); twenty-seven men and two women – both the women are from Hindu tradition; twenty-one people above the age of fifty, four each in their forties and thirties; fifteen subjects working in church or government or other institutions, eleven retired from such work and three running business, and the minimum education qualification of all twenty-six people who were working or were retired was an undergraduate degree. The issue discussed was how the promoters of dialogue understand religion(s) and their plurality, the relationship between them and Mandaikadu religious clashes and other subsequent conflicts together with their efforts for offering solutions. Specific information was gathered about the nature of the dialogue programmes, the methods and means they follow, the locations and the participants. The major purpose in this stage of field research was to study and understand how the dialogue promoters understood the context and definitions of 'religious clashes' and the extent to which their activities remain at elite level.

The third stage was studying how the ordinary people look at the Mandaikadu religious conflict and how they relate (and negotiate) with each other irrespective of these clashes. I carried out this part of my field work in a village, Gramam (pseudonym). The word *gramam* literally means village. Gramam is near my native village and familiar to me – the familiarity helped me as a starting point in carrying out the field research among the people in this village with ease and helped the respondents to freely discuss issues. First, participant observation methods helped me to observe, understand and study how people at the grassroots relate with each other irrespective of religious differences. This included observing and studying their attitudes and the symbols and stereotypes that are used in relating with/ separating from each other, and studying how their memory of the past in terms of interreligious relationships has been formed. Secondly, there is a custom in the villages in South India called *Thinnai Pecchu* (veranda talking). People (mostly male who are not formally educated), irrespective of religions and any other classifications, gather in some public places in small numbers (nowadays tea shops are usually used for this) and discuss various issues including religion, politics, society and day-to-day issues. They are mostly spontaneous, and these informal gatherings help researchers to collect data by participating in their discussions. Thirdly, I also conducted two formal focus-group interviews where Hindus, Christians and Muslims in the region came together and discussed issues related to religions, violence and interreligious relationships. In addition to informal talks with many people in the village, for formal interviews I could approach forty people in the villages from all religions (fifteen Hindus, fourteen Christians and eleven

Muslims), both genders (twenty-three men, seventeen women) as well as people who are young – in their twenties and thirties – and older adults (nineteen young, twenty-one older adults): ten people working in/retired from government or other institutions, six people doing small business or shop keeping, eleven people either farmers and masons or doing some coolie work or working in companies and thirteen housewives. The ten who work in government or other institutions have at least passed SSLC (ten years of study in school from the age of six), whereas the education level of those who are in business and are working in companies varies from schooling to postgraduate degree. Farmers, masons and others who are doing coolie work have no formal education at all or have some schooling at the primary level.

In addition I could also arrange two focus-group interviews. The first was arranged in the premises of the Hindu temple in the village. Five people (all men) turned up – two Christians (one young, one adult); one Hindu (young); and two Muslims (one adult, one young). The second was arranged for another group in the CSI church premises. This time eight people turned up – three Christians (adult men), three Hindus (one young man and two adult women) and two Muslims (two adult men). In addition to the formal focus-group interviews, some of the interviews I had with people in Gramam turned out to be 'informal' focus-group interviews where, when I was doing a formal interview with a person, their neighbours also came and joined in. They listened to the interactions between me and my interviewees and gradually participated in the discussions by expressing their views as well. This is a normal custom in villages, and most often for research purposes this is productive rather than destructive. The main purpose of this stage of my fieldwork was to collect data to study how grassroots people look at religions and religious conflicts and relationships between religious followers and how they relate with each other in their everyday lives, and this information has been used in critiquing the elite nature of dialogue.

A word about the use of names of my interviewees in my field research. Some of my interviewees in the dialogue promoters group have published literature on dialogue. Since I use their writings as well as information from interviews with them in this book, I use their real names, except where they have asked for confidentiality, in order to avoid confusions in discussion. But for my interviewees in villages I use pseudonyms, since some information they shared was sensitive. They include both women and men, Hindu, Christian and Muslim. For the Hindu interviewees I use common names of Hindu gods and goddesses, for Christians I use Bible names, for Muslim men I use the common Muslim male names and for Muslim women I use common Muslim female names.

3 Structure of the Book

The book is structured in such a way as to first briefly offer a background of theoretical trends and practical manifestations of dialogue; then critically analyse its problems in terms of religious plurality, religious conflicts and its elitist nature; then record and discuss the realities at the grassroots in order to show how they bring a critique to dialogue; and, finally, to utilize these insights to construct and test an alternative to dialogue. Although a critique of dialogue for its limitations is the central focus of this book, nevertheless it follows this order of presentation-critique-alternative for the purpose of setting the background of the fieldwork in the early part of the book.

The first chapter surveys the concept and practise of dialogue carried out especially through Christian dialogists in Protestant and Roman Catholic circles in India since the 1950s. The ideas and perspectives of prominent dialogue thinkers are discussed in detail. The influence of global dialogue activities on Indian dialogists is also discussed. How dialogue has been conceived, formulated and practised in India in relation to plurality of religions and scriptures; Christian approaches to other religions, secularism, socio-economic realities, contextual theologies and ecumenism and religious and communal harmony and how the nature, objectives and the imperativeness of dialogue have been laid down are discussed in this chapter and will be evaluated in later chapters.

Chapter 2 records and analyses the fieldwork materials which pertain to dialogists. In the light of the field research done in Kanyakumari district, this chapter discusses the practice of dialogue undertaken through dialogue centres in churches, mainly in the CSI and in the Roman Catholic Church, government institutions (local district administrations) and NGOs in the region. The background of dialogue activities in the district during 1970s and 1980s is explained, and the different types of dialogue programmes and dialogue meetings are outlined.

How 'religion' and 'world religions' are viewed in contemporary scholarship is the focus of Chapter 3. In order to explicate the problem of religious plurality and religious identities in dialogue in the later chapters, this chapter attempts to offer a background to understand the construction of the very idea of religion in the colonizing West. Incorporating the insights from postcolonial criticism in the current scholarly works, this chapter discusses the idea of religion, which has undergone various changes in the West, especially during the Enlightenment, and been passed on to many parts of the colonized world including India. How the idea of religion has been constructed in distinction from secularism; singular and homogenous religious identities constructed for people in India; a unified Hinduism projected as the religion of India; and how the 'world religions' category has come to dominate the thinking about religion, which in turn would shape the dialogists' notion of religious plurality, are discussed in this chapter.

Developing further the perspectives discussed in the previous chapter, Chapter 4 deals with how the idea of religion and world religions developed in the West has been appropriated by elites in the once-colonized countries, among which one of the groups is dialogue activists. The way that the colonial forms of knowledge, approaches and methods have been uncritically accepted and developed in promoting dialogue in India is discussed in detail. The dialogists' uncritical use of religious-secular distinctions, world religions category and single and fixed religious identities for people are examined and critiqued.

The assertion in dialogue that religions (or religious misunderstanding) are both the root causes of the conflicts in society and solutions to those conflicts is questioned in Chapter 5. The way that dialogue ignores and undermines wider socio-economic and political contexts and the power relations involved in actual violence and conflicts are discussed. The dialogue proponents interpreting conflicts primarily, if not only, in terms of religious differences may merely aggravate the tensions in society, thus they and their ideas become implicated in conflicts and violence that they want to undo. This chapter highlights different perspectives and frameworks available through which conflicts among people in India can be understood and interpreted in their contexts, and discusses how conflicts which have little to do with religion are often labelled as 'religious'.

Continuing the previous discussion, Chapter 6 attempts to show through a case study how the discourse of Hindu–Christian conflict is necessary for dialogists to argue their point and carry out their activities. Examining the 1982 clashes in Kanyakumari district, which have come to be termed 'religious conflicts' for the last three decades, the case study unearths the socio-economic and political factors operative in the clashes in addition to 'religious fanaticism'. The various identities of people involved in the actual conflicts, the political processes by which these clashes were reduced solely to 'religious' clashes and the different ways in which they are discoursed among dialogists, religious extremists and ordinary people in the district are discussed. The fallacy of dialogists' assumptions that religion, in one way or other, is a reason for every conflict is refuted.

Chapter 7 explains how elitism is being exercised among those who promote dialogue – religious leaders, theologians and dialogue activists – over the ordinary people at the grassroots who, without even knowing the principles of elite dialogue, relate and negotiate with their religious neighbours in their everyday lives. The dialogical elitism that is found in elite descriptions of imperative dialogue and the prerequisites of dialogue, dialogue based on written scriptures and theological concepts, elite apprehensions about relativism and syncretism, the search for defined common platforms for dialogue and an appeal to reaching the grassroots with the perceived aim of converting people from 'absence-of-dialogue' to 'only-dialogue' situations are discussed; and that way that all these activities are built on the notion of world religions is pointed out and critiqued.

The grassroots realities researched through fieldwork in Gramam village in Kanyakumari district are discussed in Chapter 8. The notion of religious plurality and its theoretical constructions used in dialogue is challenged in the light of how ordinary people in villages perceive and practise religion mostly in terms of its expressed and lived forms. This chapter discusses how fixed religious identities are overcome by people in their everyday lives, where relating and negotiating between religious adherents occur with different rhythms; it shows how the everyday relationships among the ordinary people at the grassroots are spontaneous, ordinary and familiar but work better than formal dialogue on many occasions. Further, the multiple factors involved in people's negotiations with each other and the multiple identities that are exercised in their relationship; the positive ways in which the ordinary people perceive and deal with communal tensions and violence, which dialogue aims to overcome but does not often succeed; and the challenges that the relationships among grassroots people pose to formal dialogue are explicated.

Raising three fundamental questions about dialogue for its usefulness, necessity and possibility, the last chapter constructs and proposes an alternative model – 'multiple identities of common people in the ordinariness of everyday life' – for understanding and dealing with religion, religious identities and everyday relations among common people. This model appeals for the examination of the life of people in terms of multiple and fluctuating identities, of real-life conflicts – conflicts in their often complex context caused by multifarious factors and result in numerous consequences – and of understanding how ordinary people relate and negotiate with each other, rather than of coercing them into submitting to elitist interreligious dialogical discourses. In developing this model, the insights gained from the fieldwork on multiple identities and everyday relations of common people, as well as some theoretical discussions on multiple identities and ordinariness of everyday life from contemporary thinkers in different disciplines, are critically utilized.

My approach in this book, primarily, is not based on any theme/issue in dialogue, but rather has more to do with the general assumptions and methods of dialogue: I am more concerned with a critique of the notions behind dialogue, and the ways in which it is carried out, rather than looking at any particular theological issue within actual dialogue or between two particular religions. Of course, theological and other issues related to dialogue are mentioned, but only as examples and when necessary. I will be concentrating on the Hindu–Christian–Muslim dialogues which are popular in South India, the location of my field research. As far as my field research is concerned, my aim is to critique what is going on under the aegis of dialogue in Kanyakumari district in Tamil Nadu in India today. However, this is not unrelated to conceptualizing dialogue in India. Hence, to critique today's practical activity of dialogue in Kanyakumari district is also to critique the theoretical and wider historical situations that have prompted this.

This book interrogates the 'world religions' category that ascribe monolithic identities to people. However, due to the non-availability of alternative terminologies, I make use of the available terms. There are also limitations regarding defining 'elites' and 'grassroots'. While these two terms are ambiguous and relative, and there is no clear line of difference, nevertheless in relation to my research elites are the advocates of dialogue – mostly religious leaders, thinkers and activists – who think that formal dialogue should be propagated because it can bring better relationships among people; and the people at the grassroots are those who maintain relationships (and negotiations) between each other irrespective of having multiple identities. One can also note that the elite proponents of dialogue, outside their formal dialogue activities, maintain relationships with their neighbours in their everyday life, like other ordinary and common people, but my main contention is that non-elites are often targeted by elite dialogue activists to follow their directives for dialogue, which needs a critique.

Notes

1 In this book, I use 'dialogue' to refer not just to the act of dialogue between religions, but also as a widespread movement involving many thinkers, perspectives and organizations.

2 For instance, Marcus Braybrooke, *Interreligious Organizations, 1893–1979: An Historical Directory* (New York and Toronto: The Edwin Mellen Press, 1980) provides details of many organizations working for dialogue worldwide. See also his book *Pilgrimage of Hope: One Hundred Years of Global Interfaith Dialogue* (London: SCM Press, 1992). For a recent writing on information on the last 100 years of dialogue, see Marina Ngursangzeli Behera, ed., *Interfaith Relations after Hundred Years: Christian Mission among other Faiths* (Oxford: Regnum Books International, 2011). *A note on footnoting*: while footnoting a book/article for the first time I provide the full reference, and while using it again, I just give a short form of it with authors' surnames. The abbreviation *ibid.* has been used wherever appropriate.

3 By 'less aggressive' I refer to the Christian approaches in the past two centuries, which claim to take other religions 'seriously' and study them with interest, rather than treat them with disdain as 'heathen', 'pagan' and irrelevant, and exercise a positive approach.

4 S. Muthuraj, 'The Contributions of Peace Trust in Interreligious Relations in Kanyakumari District', BD thesis, United Theological College Bangalore, 2001.

5 By now CPJ, with which I worked earlier, was renamed CIRSJA.

6 Various dialogue agencies and people define dialogue this way. For instance, see World Council of Churches, *Guidelines on Dialogue with People of Living Faiths and Ideologies* (Geneva: WCC, 1979), 10–11; revised in 2002 as *Ecumenical Considerations for Dialogue and Relations with People of other Religions* (Geneva: WCC, 2003). For a more recent work on dialogue, see Catherine Cornille, *The Wiley-Blackwell Companion to Inter-religious Dialogue* (Malden, MA: Wiley-Blackwell, 2013): several essays in this book take a 'dialogue for better understanding' approach. See also, Aasulv Lande, 'Recent Developments in Interreligious Dialogue', in *The Concept of God in Global Dialogue*, ed. Werner G. Jeanrond and Aasulv Lande (Maryknoll, New York: Orbis Books, 2005), 32–47.

7 Eric J., Sharpe makes this observation in his assessment of dialogue. Sharpe, 'Hindu-Christian Dialogue in Europe', in *Hindu-Christian Dialogue: Perspectives and Encounters*, ed. Harold Coward (Maryknoll, New York: Orbis Books, 1989), 110. See also his essay 'The Goals of Inter-religious Dialogue', in *Truth and Dialogue: The Relationships between World Religions*, ed. John Hick (London: Sheldon Press, 1974), 77–95.

8 One such approach is found in the already-mentioned book by Behera, *Interfaith Relations after Hundred Years*, a volume published in relation to Edinburgh 2010 (Edinburgh 2010 was the first centenary of the World Missionary Conference held in Edinburgh, Scotland, in 1910). Many articles in this book trace dialogical attitudes to Edinburgh 1910 and some (for instance, K. P. Aleaz 'Christian Dialogues with Hinduism', 79–104) even beyond that. See also Israel Selvanayagam, *A Second Call: Ministry and Mission in a Multifaith Milieu* (Madras: CLS, 2000), especially chapter 2; *A Dialogue on Dialogue: Reflections on Interfaith Encounters* (Madras: Christian Literature Society, 1995). Also Martin Forward, *Interreligious Dialogue: A Short Introduction* (Oxford: Oneworld, 2007).

9 Harold Coward, 'Introduction', in *Hindu-Christian Dialogue: Perspectives and Encounters*, ed. Harold Coward (Maryknoll, New York: Orbis Books, 1989), 1.

10   Coward, 'Introduction,' 1–7. In the same book Richard Young discusses the interactions between Francis Xavier and Saivite Brahmins in South India in the sixteenth century within a 'Hindu-Christian dialogue' framework: 'Francis Xavier in the Perspective of the Saivite Brahmins of Tiruchendur Temple,' 64–79. See also in the same book John C. B. Webster, 'Gandhi and the Christians: Dialogue in the Nationalist Era,' 80–99; Richard Taylor, 'Current Hindu-Christian Dialogue in India,' 119–128. See also S. Wesley Ariarajah, *Hindus and Christians: A Century of Protestant Ecumenical Thought* (Grand Rapids, MI: William B. Eerdmans Publishing Company, 1991).

11   When I was sharing my ideas about going to undertake field study for this research, one reputable theologian of dialogue from South India asked me: 'What do the grassroot people know about dialogue, and why do you want to do research among them?' This indicates how ordinary villagers and their knowledge are perceived among dialogists. Since it was an informal chat, I maintain confidentiality.

12   WCC, *Guidelines on Dialogue*, 10–11.

13   To mention a few from the Western world, the *Cambridge Interfaith Programme* in the University of Cambridge (http://www.interfaith.cam.ac.uk/), *Interreligious Studies* in Irish School of Ecumenics, Dublin (http://www.tcd.ie/ise/study/), *Dialogue Institute* in the Temple University, Philadelphia, (http://institute.jesdialogue.org/programmes/temple/graduate/). In the Indian context, Serampore University dialogue is an important topic in courses in religion and theology since 1970s, and UTC, Bangalore, and the Tamil Nadu Theological Seminary (TTS), Madurai, give importance to this theme.

14   Some such criticisms are found in M. Bage, R. Hedlund, P. B. Thomas, Martin Alphonse and George David, *Many Other Ways: Questions of Religious Pluralism* (Delhi: ISPCK, 1992), which was a response to Paul Knitter's, *No Other Name? A Critical Survey of Christian Attitudes toward World-religions* (Maryknoll, New York: Orbis Books, 1985); Ken Gnanakan, *The Pluralistic Predicament* (Bangalore: Theological Book Trust, 1992), and its modified version, *Proclaiming Christ in a Pluralistic Context* (Bangalore: Theological Book Trust, 2002); Matthew Philip, *The Unique Christ: Dialogue in Missions* (Bangalore: Centre for Contemporary Christianity, 2006); Lesslie Newbigin, *The Gospel in a Pluralist Society* (London: SPCK, 1991). Some of these may not reject dialogue outright but criticize what they perceive as syncretism and dilution of faith in dialogue.

15   In this perspective, P. D. Devanandan is considered to be the pioneer of dialogue through his work as the founder-director of the Christian Institute of Study of Religion and Society (CISRS), and his attitudes to dialogue will be discussed in detail in Chapter 1.

16   P. D. Devanandan and M. M. Thomas undertook various efforts to work for nation-building through dialogue. M. M. Thomas, *Christian Participation in Nation-Building* (Bangalore: NCCI & CISRS), 1960.

17   They include various dioceses of the CSI, CISRS, Henry Martyn Institute (HMI) in Hyderabad, Dialogue Centres in UTC (Bangalore and TTS), Madurai. There are also many Roman Catholic ashrams such as Santivanam in Tamil Nadu for dialogue activities.

18   C. Rajamony, Interview, Nagercoil, 10 July 2008. Rajamony is a retired CSI presbyter and dialogue activist. Also, Antony Tobias, Interview, Nagercoil, 22 June 2008. Tobias is a retired Catholic priest and former secretary, the Dialogue Commission, Kottar Diocese, which is one of the dioceses of the Roman Catholic Church in Kanyakumari

district. *A note regarding footnoting interviews*: when I first footnote an interview
I provide the name of the interviewee, the place and the date of the interview.
Thereafter when referring to the same interview again, I just use the format – 'Name,
Interview' – to avoid redundancy.

19 Abdul Salaam, Interview, Nagercoil, 13 July 2008. Salaam is a Muslim and a dialogue
     activist.
20 There are several works currently available on the invention or imagination or
     construction of Hinduism in India. For a critical study of this, see Richard King,
     Orientalism and Religion: Postcolonial Theory, India and 'The Mystic East' (London
     and New York: Routledge, 1999). See also Sharada Sugirtharaja, *Imagining Hinduism:
     A Postcolonial Perspective* (London: Routledge, 2004); Geoffrey A. Oddie, *Imagined
     Hinduism: British Protestant Missionary Constructions of Hinduism, 1793–1900*
     (New Delhi: Sage Publications, 2006); Esther Bloch, Marianne Keppens and Rajaram
     Hegde, *Rethinking Religion in India: The Colonial Construction of Hinduism* (New
     Delhi: Routledge, 2011); Timothy Fitzgerald, 'Hinduism and the "World-religion"
     Fallacy,' *Religion* 20, no. 2 (1990): 108–18. Will Sweetman, 'Colonialism all the way
     down? Religion and the secular in early modern writing on south India,' in *Religion
     and the Secular: Historical and Colonial Formations*, ed. Timothy Fitzgerald (London
     and Oakville: Equinox Publishing Ltd., 2007), 117–34.
21 Fitzgerald, 'Hinduism and the "World-religion" Fallacy.' For a detailed discussion
     of comparative religion, see Sharpe, Eric J., *Comparative Religion: A History* (1975;
     London: Duckworth, 2003).
22 Chandra Muzzafar, ed., *Universalism of Islam* (Penang: Aliran, 1984), 123.
23 Elizabeth Koepping, 'Family, State and Religious Conversion: Multiple Discourses
     from Malaysia and South Australia,' *Bulletin of the Royal Institute for Inter-Faith
     Studies* 2, no. 2 (2000): 141.
24 Koepping, 'Family, State and Religious Conversion,' 141–2.
25 For instance, see Stanley Samartha, *One Christ – Many Religions: Towards a Revised
     Christology*, rev. edn (Bangalore: South Asia Theological Research Institute, 2000), 7,
     57–9.
26 Paulo Freire, *Pedagogy of the Oppressed* (1970; New York: Continuum, 2003), 88–90.
     Emphasis added.
27 Melinda Bollar Wagner, 'The Study of Religion in American Society,' in *Anthropology
     of Religion: A Handbook*, ed. Stephen D. Glazier (Westport, CT and London: Praeger,
     1997), 97.
28 Charlotte Aull Davies, *Reflexive Ethnography: A Guide to Researching Selves and others*
     (London and New York: Routledge, 2008), 2.
29 Davies, *Reflexive Ethnography*, 272.
30 Mandaikadu is a small village near the seashore in the western part of Kanyakumari
     district where the conflict is said to have originated.
31 An often-expressed idea regarding studying past conflicts is that such research
     may rekindle people's feelings and memory of conflicts. In my own fieldwork, I
     was confronted by some interviewees who claimed that researchers contribute to
     continuing violence (I discuss this in some detail in Chapter 8). Balarasu, Interview,
     Swamithoppu, 2 July 2008. Balarasu is a dialogue activist and teacher in his forties
     living in Swamithoppu, which is a semi-town near Gramam where I conducted
     fieldwork among grassroots people. However, in my research, I need to revisit the
     1982 clashes, because of the way the events are projected by researchers and dialogue
     promoters as well as those with vested interests, especially in the political arena.

32   Government of Tamil Nadu, *Venugopal Commission Report* (Madras: GoTN, n.d.).

33   Christian fundamentalists who were criticizing other religions, particularly
     Hinduism, *Venugopal Commission*, 239–41.

34   Mainly the Rashtriya Swayamsevak Sangh, which was attacking other religions,
     particularly Christianity and Islam. *Venugopal Commission*, 238.

35   D. Austin Edwin Richard, 'A Research on Mandaikadu,' BD thesis, TTS, 1986; George
     Matthew, 'Hindu Christian Communalism: An Analysis of Kanyakumari Riots,'
     Social Action 33, no. 3/4 (1983): 49–66; Susan Bayly, 'Christians and Competing
     Fundamentalisms in south Indian Society,' in *Accounting for Fundamentalisms*, vol. 4,
     ed. Martin E. Marty and R. Scott Appleby (Chicago: The University of Chicago Press,
     1994), 726–69; A. Maria David, *Beyond Boundaries: Hindu-Christian Relationship and
     Basic Christian Communities* (Delhi: ISPCK, 2009), especially chapters 1 and 2.

36   Velan, Interview, Kanyakumari, 12 July 2008.

Part I

THE PROBLEM: THE CONCEPT AND PRACTICE
OF DIALOGUE

Chapter 1

DIALOGUE IN POST-COLONIAL INDIA: A BRIEF SURVEY

Discussing the history of dialogue is a herculean task, given the large amount of literature on it involving many trends, perspectives and people. Further, as I discussed in the introduction, there are also ambiguities about the past of the dialogue – ambiguities in locating the exact origins of dialogue. However, in order to provide a theoretical and historical background for the subsequent discussions, I shall present a brief outline of the developments in the concept of dialogue. In doing so I shall limit myself to the context of India, and locate the beginning of the contemporary forms of dialogue more in the post-colonial or post-independent India.

Broadly speaking, there are at least five major developments in dialogue over the last seven decades. First, during the 1950s and early 1960s, dialogue in Christianity in India, especially among Protestants, primarily aimed at bringing adherents of different religions together for Indian nation-building and common community. Second, the predominant theme then especially among Roman Catholics in India was the dialogue between West and East, or Western and Eastern religions, on the basis of common spirituality and contemplative experience. Third, with the increasing efforts for dialogue within the WCC and in Vatican II and with the rising awareness of the plurality of religions, dialogue from the 1970s was increasingly becoming the model for Christian approaches to other religions, replacing earlier models primarily based on the universality and supremacy of Christianity. In this regard various theologies of religious plurality and dialogue were developed, and in the process, the nature, method and objectives of dialogue were laid down. Fourth, the 1970s started to witness liberation theologies worldwide, and since the 1980s, theologies such as Dalit theology in India began to challenge the Christian theological links to the dominant Hindu brahmanical traditions in India, hence they also challenged dialogue with such links. This then led dialogue to accommodate the concerns of liberation and the welfare of the poor and the downtrodden. Fifth, since the 1990s, especially after the demolition of Babri Masjid in Ayodhya in 1992 in the Indian context, and the attacks on the World Trade Center in September 2001, which influenced dialogical efforts at the global level, dialogue has been increasingly related to religious harmony, peace and reconciliation in the context of religious conflicts. These developments are not strictly confined to the above time frames or denominations/organizations involved, as dialogue in India has multiple dimensions in terms of its nature and purpose and is believed to have responded to the changing contexts in India through the last seven decades.

Each of these major trends in dialogue will be discussed in some detail in this chapter, although the aim is not to discuss Indian theologies of dialogue in depth or to construct a history of dialogue in India. Rather I will provide a brief outline of the major trends: the specific limitations in dialogue mentioned in the Introduction which are the focus of this book will be discussed and analysed in Part II. As mentioned earlier, discussing trends and developments in a single chapter is a mammoth task given the multifarious perspectives on dialogue in India, the many thinkers reflecting on this theme and various agencies rushing to promote dialogue in India. Hence the major dialogical thinkers/theologians and key perspectives in dialogue will be selected for discussion in order to provide the general outlook of dialogue in India.[1]

The primary focus is on major Indian Christian writings on dialogue, which are involved in constructing theologies of dialogue. Contributions to dialogue from other religious groups in India such as Hindus, Muslims, Buddhists, Sikhs and Jains, which are scattered in the many writings on dialogue,[2] and from Westerners writing about dialogue activities in India,[3] cannot be discussed in detail here, though they will be noted wherever possible. I will be primarily discussing Indian Christians developing the concept of dialogue in India or in the international circles[4] – such as P. D. Devanandan, M. M. Thomas, Herbert Jai Singh, Russell Chandran, Stanley Samartha, Thomas Thangaraj, K. C. Abraham, Israel Selvanayagam, K. P. Aleaz, and David Immanuel Singh from the Protestant Christianity, Amalorpavadoss, Sebastian Kappen, Michael Amaladoss, Samuel Rayan and Felix Wilfred from Roman Catholic Christianity, and Paul Verghese (also Paulose Mar Gregorious), Geevarghese Mar Osthathios from the Orthodox Christianity; and Westerners adapted to Indian context and engaged in dialogue in India for longer periods such as Swami Abhishiktananda, Murray Rogers, Bede Griffiths, Klaus Klostermaier and Raimon Panikkar.[5] Wherever necessary, I shall also make use of Asian theologians on dialogue such as Sabapathy Kulandran, D. T. Niles, Aloysius Pieris, Wesley Ariarajah, R. S. Sugirtharajah and Peter C. Phan, who emphasize the significance of Asia in dialogue which includes the Indian situation. I will discuss the works of theologians and trends in dialogue not separately but simultaneously, as one trend is dealt with by more than one theologian, and one theologian has contributed to more than one trend.

1 Christian Initiatives for Dialogue in Early Post-Independent India: Interreligious Cooperation for Nation-Building

The beginning of formal dialogue in the post-colonial India can perhaps be attributed to the activities of the CISRS, which was founded in Bangalore in 1957.[6] A prominent person associated with CISRS was Paul D. Devanandan who was its founder-director. An ordained minister of the CSI, Devanandan developed CISRS along with many other thinkers interested[7] in religion and dialogue, arranging dialogue programmes between people of different religions in India. Since 1957, CISRS has organized a number of consultations, seminars, workshops and conferences where priests, leaders and thinkers from different religions gathered for dialogue. Its journal, *Religion and Society*, has provided a strong platform to carry out the dialogue activities of CISRS,[8] publishing many of the papers that were presented at the interreligious conferences. Even though based in Bangalore in South India, CISRS has been involved in organizing interreligious programmes in different parts of India.

Devanandan's primary work was on the necessity of dialogue for Christians in post-independent India.[9] He invited Christians to take initiatives to relate with Hinduism, their mother religion, from which they or their forebears converted to Christianity. Writing in 1961, Devanandan advised Indian Christians thus:

> The fact remains that when we became Christians, as a rule, we decided to opt out of Hindu society. Therefore, to recover our lost position within the community and reclaim affinity, it is for us to take the initiative by establishing identity in cultural interests and social concerns, in what may be called the secular context of our national life.[10]

In the third general assembly of the WCC in New Delhi in 1961, Devanandan was one of the speakers who spoke about Christian witness in India, emphasizing the urgency and necessity of dialogue for Christians in India.[11]

Another prominent theologian closely associated with Devanandan and CISRS was M. M. Thomas, a lay theologian from the Marthoma Church, who became the director of CISRS (1961–76) after Devanandan.[12] Devanandan and Thomas primarily emphasized the urgency of dialogue in the newly independent India. Maintaining that 'a genuine desire to seek and find ways of effecting a real sense of national solidarity'[13] is the need of the hour for Indians in the immediate post-independent period, Devanandan wrote,

> Our main concern is to work for and achieve a real sense of national solidarity, an integrated community of people bound together by lasting ties of kinship, a closely welded group of men and women that work together for common ends and mutual good.[14]

This was the immediate post-independence period when the ideas of the first prime minister of the independent India, Jawaharlal Nehru, that promoted progressive space for all religions in secular India were positively accepted, unlike the situation in her neighbour Pakistan under Islamic rule. The context in India also involved a renascent Hinduism growing stronger and a minority consciousness among Indian Christian community becoming stronger. In this context, Devanandan and Thomas thought that Christians coming together in dialogue with their neighbours from other religions for nation-building would serve the nation and the wider community.[15]

Devanandan and Thomas believed that in secular India not only people from all religions but also from secular ideologies were expected to contribute to the welfare and the development of the nation.[16] In order that Indian Christians could work for nation-building activities, Devanandan and Thomas emphasized ideals such as 'common humanity', 'secular humanity' and 'community' that served as helpful bases for people of different religions coming together in dialogue and cooperation.[17] Such ideals indicate that all people share the same humanity, and people of different religions and secular faiths can come together for working for 'humanization'.[18] Of course, the ideal of community or humanity derived from the belief that Jesus Christ was the foundation of this community, the 'new creation' on which the community could be built.[19]

This was the framework within which Devanandan and Thomas developed the idea of Christians participating with their neighbours from different religions and secular ideologies for nation-building and the other common welfare issues in society. The attention they paid to this theme is evidenced by the numerous researches they undertook and the reflections they made to the wider audience through CISRS. Clearly in post-independent India, attempting to bring together various religious communities, undergoing different transitions, through dialogue was a challenging task, and the work of Devanandan and Thomas and of CISRS must be related to that time, even as it has continued to be one of the dominant platforms for dialogue in the Indian context. Thomas Thangaraj, a contemporary proponent of dialogue from South India,[20] has also highlighted the importance of this:

> If we, as citizens of this country, are to be meaningfully involved in the life of this nation, we need to be in constant and continuous dialogue with each other so that our faiths may provide us with both the ethos and impetus for action.[21]

K. C. Abraham,[22] Michael Amaladoss[23] and Felix Wilfred[24] are some of the other Christian theologians continuing this theme of inviting people of different religions to participate in dialogue for the welfare of the nation and wider society. Moreover, the dialogue for the welfare of the nation and society has also been stressed in the last few decades due to the arrival of liberation and political theologies in India focusing on political participation and socio-economic liberation for the poor, which will be discussed later in this chapter. Also in today's context, Christian involvement in nation-building and cooperating with people of other religions in dialogue is discussed within the framework of public theology.[25]

2 Meeting of the West and the East in Spirituality

While Protestant Christians' efforts for dialogue in India in the 1950s and 1960s were predominantly found in the work of CISRS, there were various efforts taken by Roman Catholic Christians mainly centred on Christian ashrams,[26] despite Vatican opprobrium.[27] One of the earliest ashrams to encourage dialogue activities was *Saccidananda Ashram* in Tamil Nadu, also known as *Eremus Sanctissimae Trinitatis* (Hermitage of the Most Holy Trinity), *Shantivanam* (Grove of Peace),[28] founded in 1950 by Fr Henri Hyacinthe Joseph Marie Le Saux, or Henri le Saux, a French Benedictine monk who came to India and took an Indian name Swami Abhishiktananda because of his appreciation for the Indian life and advaitic tradition, and Fr Jules Monchanin,[29] another priest from France who was working in Indian villages. This ashram became a centre for contemplation and spirituality, encouraging dialogue between religions on the grounds of common spiritual experience.

Abhishiktananda, influenced greatly by the advaitic traditions in India, interprets dialogue, in his case the Hindu–Christian dialogue, in terms of inner spiritual experience, or dialogue between people 'for whom religion is something personal ... the very centre of their being'.[30] Maintaining that the Hindu–Christian meeting point is 'within the cave of the heart' (personal spiritual experience), he said that 'the most essential qualification for a fruitful dialogue is not so much an acute mind, as a contemplative disposition of the soul'.[31] He says thus:

> Dialogue may begin simply with relations of mutual sympathy. It only becomes worthwhile when it is accompanied by full openness ... not merely at the intellectual level, but with regard to [the] inner life of the Spirit. Dialogue about doctrines will be more fruitful when it is rooted in a real spiritual experience at depth and when each one understands that diversity does not mean disunity, once the Center of all has been reached.[32]

Inviting Christians to take part in dialogue with Hindus, Abhishiktananda emphasizes that they should be prepared before coming to dialogue. Maintaining that they should dialogue with 'genuine representatives of Hinduism,' he warns that any 'superficial acquaintance with the religious folklore of India' may not help much in dialogue.[33] For him,

> The Christian who desires to enter into contact with the Scriptures and the mystical tradition of India needs above all else an inward disposition – what the schoolmen called a *habitus* – of recollection and contemplation. He needs the 'knowledge' of those ultimate depths of the self, 'the cave of the heart,' where the Mystery revealed itself to the awareness of rishis. ... At any other level religious dialogue with India will necessarily remain superficial and unfruitful.[34]

Some other Roman Catholic thinkers in India who held similar perspectives on dialogue were J. A. Cuttat,[35] a Swiss ambassador to India who interpreted West–East dialogue in terms of spiritual experience. Cuttat was concerned with the dialogue of the West and East and said that 'East and West should meet like two spiritual persons'.[36] Murray Rogers, associated with Abhishiktananda on dialogue activities, also followed a similar approach to dialogue centred on the spiritual experiences of the partners who need to have inner dialogue before having external dialogue.[37] This direction in dialogue continued in the works of Bede Griffiths,[38] a Benedictine monk who came to India in 1955 and spent the rest of his life here. Influenced by *Shantivanam*, he founded an ashram in Kerala in 1958, and later became the Acharya of *Saccidananda Ashram*. Having been convinced that dialogue between Western Christianity and Eastern religions was urgent and that it was possible only at the level of spirituality, Griffiths says that

> above all the sense of the presence of god in nature and the soul, a kind of natural mysticism which is the basis of all Indian spirituality ... therefore ... if a genuine meeting of East and West was to take place, it must be at this deepest level of their experience and this ... could best come through the monastic life.[39]

This approach to dialogue has continued to be significant during the 1960s and 1970s. Klaus Klostermaier, a German who has spent years in India dialoguing with Hindus in North India, observed that the dialogue groups were becoming 'less and less concerned with "comparative religion" or with "theology" and centred more and more on spirituality'.[40] Pointing out that such a principle 'seemed to be the only basis for a true encounter',[41] he says that the actual dialogue 'could take place only at the level of spirituality, not on that of formulated theological systems'.[42]

As noted, the emphasis on one's personal spiritual experience through contemplation becomes the most important aspect in this form of dialogue, and ashrams in India served as good places for executing dialogue activities. This approach in early post-independent India was further strengthened by an awareness of the need for dialogue between West and East in an increasingly multicultural world. However, such dialogue represents a very limited approach, limited to those who see contemplation or meditation as the most important aspect of religious life, even though it is presented as the most significant approach by those who are involved in it. That how in reality such perspectives on dialogue may not go well with the understanding of religion and religious experiences of ordinary people in everyday living situations will be spelt out later in this book.

3 Towards Developing Theologies of Dialogue in India Since 1970s

(a) Dialogue and Ecumenical Movements

The two evolving attitudes to dialogue among both Roman Catholics and Protestants in India, discussed in the previous sections, are closely connected to the two major international developments in the field of dialogue in the 1960s and 1970s – one Protestant and one Roman Catholic – which both influenced and were to an extent affected by the efforts for dialogue in India. One is the initiatives for dialogue within the WCC based in Geneva, Switzerland, which led to the formation of a sub-unit for dialogue in the council, and the other was the endorsement given by Vatican II for dialogue. The efforts of the sub-unit of dialogue in WCC had a strongly Indian contribution as the first director of the sub-unit was Stanley J. Samartha, a prominent Indian Christian thinker who worked for much of his life in this field.[43] Likewise, Vatican II opened ways for the Roman Catholics in India to dialogue with their religious neighbours through forming units for dialogue in local dioceses and many centres for the study of religions. I am not going to discuss them here as there are plenty of materials on these two movements that give accounts of the dialogue activities of these or assessments of them. It suffices to mention here that there are connections and links in multifarious ways between these movements and dialogical thinking and activities in India.

(b) Dialogue and the Plurality of Religions

It is an obvious fact that the emergence of dialogue is fundamentally related to the affirmation of plurality of religions or at least the *awareness* of plurality, and dialogue emphasizes respect for plurality of religions. It should be noted here that for the last several decades both in India and at the global level, theology of religions has been seen in terms of three types — exclusivism, inclusivism and pluralism[44] — even though such a strict approach is challenged in the contemporary times. In the Indian context, while the awareness of plurality may be a new reality, there is a strong emphasis in writing on dialogue in India on the age-old religious and pluralist nature of India/Asia against the opposite of the West.[45] For instance, Felix Wilfred, a contemporary Roman Catholic dialogue proponent, holds that 'pluralism has been the hallmark of Asian life, and without it, Asia loses all hopes for its future.'[46] Noting that pluralism is seen by many as a bête noire, he invites Asian Christians to broaden the 'outlook on the issue of pluralism, or better, plurality, and see it through Asian eyes, not simply as an issue of contemporary Occidental discussion' which is a necessary understanding for any dialogical activity between religions.[47] Arguing that there are limitations when approaches to dialogue are considered from a Western perspective, Wilfred emphasizes that the location of dialogue should be moved to the context of Asia.[48] According to him, changing the location means changing the fundamental question about dialogue. 'The question has to shift from how can Christianity relate to other religions to what is the *place* of Christianity itself in a religiously pluralistic Asian world,' he says.[49] While the first question is Christianity-centred, where other religions are looked from a Christian point of view and with which genuine dialogue with other religions cannot take place, Christianity as one of the religions among many in the Asian context will offer a better platform for dialogue.[50] Further, emphasizing the importance of the Asian context in dialogue often goes along with another reality in Asia, namely the socio-economic and political context, which also cannot be neglected in dialogue. Wilfred thus says,

> As long as the point of departure does not change, we will be concentrating on such questions as salvation in other religions, because we have spiritually and theologically transported ourselves to the perspective of European and North American Christianity and its history with all its discussions concerning *vera et falsa religio*. For us, the point of departure for dialogue is the concrete socio-political and historical context of Asia.[51]

Thus one can see quite often the importance of the Asian context in general and Asian religiosity in particular in the deliberations of dialogue. While people belonging to different religious traditions and identities have long existed in Asia/India, an overemphasis on the religiosity and spirituality of India or Asia is questionable, especially given the colonial-Orientalist constructions of the 'secular West versus religious East' (or enlightened West vs. mystical East), which I will be discussing in detail in Chapters 3 and 4.

Secondly, dialogue affirms the importance of a plurality of religions, because without that dialogue cannot proceed. What is understood as inclusivism[52] also opens ways for dialogue, but unlike inclusivism, which believes in the final fulfilment of all religions in one religion, pluralism believes in the validity of multiple ways (or religions) that lead to the Reality, identified as Absolute, Mystery, Ultimate Truth and God. Pluralism is of the view that different religions of the world consist of different responses to the one Ultimate Reality or God. Samartha argues that exclusivism and inclusivism are not very useful in a pluralist context as they in one way or the other affirm the superiority of one religion over other religions.[53]

Thirdly, however, such affirmation of plurality is not the only approach in Indian dialogue circles, as there are different interpretations of plurality of religions.[54] Against the idea that pluralism helps to construct a universal theology of religion, Raimon Panikkar has developed his radical pluralism (or radical interpretation of pluralism), where he criticizes any attempt to bring all religions into one single unified system.[55] According to him, pluralism does not mean plurality of religions or a reduction of them to unity.[56] Preferring the terms plurality and pluralistic attitude, he says that 'the pluralistic attitude accepts the stance that reality may be of such a nature that nobody, no single human group to be sure, can coherently claim to exhaust the universal range of human experience'.[57] He believes that such an understanding helps the adherents of religions to come together in what he calls a 'dialogical dialogue' in their search for understanding that reality.[58] His understanding of pluralism is identified as 'post-pluralism'.[59]

Another contemporary Indian proponent of dialogue, K. P. Aleaz, after evaluating exclusivism, criticized it for its superior attitudes and chauvinism, inclusivism which is nothing but a 'disguised exclusivism' and pluralism which considers religions as 'self-contained compartments', proposes what he calls pluralistic inclusivism.[60] This principle calls for a 'relational convergence of religions', which emphasizes commitment and conversion both to Jesus as well as to the religio-cultural context of India.[61]

Fourthly, pluralism also has faced a number of criticisms, especially by evangelical Christians in India as well as all over the world, for its relativizing of religions.[62] Responding to the criticisms, Russell Chandran says that in the pluralist model 'there is no attempt to integrate the religions into one particular religion. The integrity of the separate religions is respected, while recognizing the possibility of mutual learning from one another, mutual correction and reinterpretation.'[63] Commenting on the fear of relativism in pluralism, Michael Amaladoss, says that 'if we look at pluralism not in the abstract or in the material terms but in personal terms of freedom and relationship, then we will see its richness on the one hand and on the other the need to affirm and witness to one's own identity'.[64]

My intention here is not to assess the merits and demerits of pluralism arguments but rather to indicate that the evolving dialogical approach to other religions has given rise to many theological formulations concerning plurality of religions, as well as theologies opposing them. But what is overlooked by dialogists, among many others, is that how the very notion of religious plurality first of all came into existence is uncritically maintained in the dialogue circles. The fundamental problem with dialogue is not primarily found in its commitment to *plurality* that is inherent in human nature and life, but the emphasis on the plurality of *religions*, which completely misses the power structures underlying the creation of religion, religions and fixed religious identities as well as obscures the complex nature of human relations. This will be dealt with in Chapters 3 and 4.

(c) Dialogue and Christian Mission

While there was a progression in the construction of various theologies of religions and dialogue in India during the 1970s, there were also issues emerging from perspectives opposing dialogue – crucially the question of dialogue's relationship to Christian mission.[65] This is significant to dialogue in the context of criticisms posed by evangelical Christians and by non-Christians that has led dialogue promoters to spend much energy in defending dialogue from such criticisms. As a result, new perspectives on dialogue continued to emerge.

First, as I have noted earlier, positive Christian approaches to other religions within the ecumenical movements and elsewhere have often been resisted by evangelical Christians, as was the case in India as the dialogical approach was being developed. The accusations of the evangelicals were that dialogue leads to 'syncretism' and the dilution of Christian mission. The basic question here is that if all religions are valid, what happens to the Christian mission and proclamation which invites people of other religions to the Ultimate Truth that is only revealed by Jesus Christ? Arguing that dialogical approach betrays Christian mission, evangelicals in India are generally of the opinion that dialogue attempts to incarcerate mission. Summarizing the general evangelical stand, not only in India but throughout the world, Timothy C. Tennent says that among evangelical Christians,

> Dialogue is discouraged because non-Christian religions are dismissed out-of-hand as examples of human blindness and the fruit of unbelief. Sometimes non-Christian religions are regarded as the direct work of Satan. The result has been to avoid any serious dialogue lest Christians unwittingly place the gospel on equal footing with other religions.[66]

If the primary concern in mission is to bring the non-Christians to Christian truth, anything other than that is the dilution of the gospel. On the other hand, precisely these attitudes have been critiqued in dialogue. Criticizing Christian missionary activities which focus on conversion and the supremacy of Christianity from the perspectives of dialogue, Samartha says that

> the 'missiology of conquest' that leads to the statistical expansion of the Christian community and the diminishing of other communities should be given up. The political implications of horizontal conversations should be recognized and only vertical conversions to God accepted as legitimate.[67]

Analysing the exchanges between the evangelicals and the dialogue promoters, Israel Selvanayagam discusses the contradictions, connections, clarifications and corrections necessary for both the groups, and proposes a combination of them all.[68] Paulose Mar Gregorios (also Paul Verghese), a theologian from the Orthodox Church in India involved with WCC programmes, also maintains that there is a relationship between dialogue and evangelization.[69] In addition to these, there are a number of works where deconstruction and reconstruction of evangelism and mission is suited to a pluralist context. Arguing that verbal proclamation alone cannot be part of evangelism, Thomas Thangaraj says that 'our exclusive claims about our tradition are an expression of violence and a way of violating the other'.[70] He proposes evangelism without proselytism.[71]

   The second perspective is the criticism coming from non-Christians, especially Hindus, who were afraid of dialogue initiatives by Christians, lest it be another way of converting non-Christians. Murray Rogers makes public a letter written to him by his Hindu friend Sivendra Prakash which contains the fear of conversion and criticism for dialogue.[72] Prakash asks Rogers,

> Have you already forgotten that what you call the 'inter-faith dialogue' is quite a new feature in your understanding and practising of Christianity? … To allure us to dialogue you keep telling us that we have to learn from each other. … The main obstacles to real dialogue are on the one hand the feeling of superiority and on the other the fear of losing one's own identity. We may even say that the former is generally the result of the latter.[73]

Regarding this issue of using dialogue as a method to change others' religion, Samartha has criticized those who have attempted to use dialogue to convert non-Christians.[74] Warning against any such understanding, Gregorios says that

> whatever theological or other reasons we as Christians may have for engaging in dialogue with the people of other faiths, we should be explicit and honest about them. If we are engaging in dialogue with the secret intention of converting them, as many religious people in Islam, Judaism, Buddhism and Hinduism suspect, then our partner is bound to be wary and our dialogue inauthentic.[75]

Such issues and criticisms continue to be part of theological thinking in India. However, from my observation, what is significant here is that such criticisms and resistance by evangelical Christianity, Hindus and others have led the dialogists mostly to work within the framework of religious plurality or theology of religions based on conventional understanding of world religions, rather than going beyond it, in the process of responding to the criticisms.

(d) The Bible, Non-Christian Scriptures and Hermeneutics in Dialogue

Another major trend in dialogue in India deals with the place of the Bible in dialogue. The context where this issue becomes crucial is twofold: one factor is the context of the plurality of religions with scriptures of different religions; the second is the context where much criticism against dialogue is centred on the Bible – arguing that dialogue is not biblical.

The major question with regard to the context of the plurality of scriptures is this: If the Bible is important for the salvation of even non-Christians, what is the place of other scriptures? Given the many scriptures used by different religious followers, can anyone insist on the supremacy of one scripture? How should Christians treat the scriptures of other religions? The dialogue promoters have attempted to reflect on these issues. First, in dialogue, there is an affirmation of the plurality of scriptures.[76] Commenting on the importance of other religious scriptures for Christians, Samartha says that

> the presence of scriptures of other faiths creates a situation for Christians in Asia that is fundamentally different from that of Christians in the West. Surely, the hermeneutical tools necessary in a multi-religious situation cannot be the same as those developed in a mono-scriptural context. Further, in a multi-religious society the criteria derived on the basis of one particular scripture cannot be used to pass negative judgements on other scriptures regarded as equally authoritative by other faiths.[77]

Amalorpavadoss, a Roman Catholic thinker from India who has worked on inculturation and dialogue, has attempted to establish the importance of the non-biblical scriptures. As the founder-director of the National Biblical Catechetical and Liturgical Centre (NBCLC) in Bangalore, he got people of different religions to study scriptures together.[78] His contention was that in the context of multiple scriptures, the task of Christianity is to contribute to the non-biblical scriptures, rather than making negative judgements against them.[79] Arguing that Christians who are engaged in liberation struggles in Asia/India 'are discovering that the Word of God is found in scriptures and traditions of other religions as well as their own,'[80] Amalorpavadoss says that Christians in India

> benefit from the Indian scriptures for a deeper understanding of the biblical word and the Hindus benefit by the biblical word to re-interpret their scriptures and to discover the unknown riches and facets.[81]

Paulose Mar Gregorios also has made similar points. Maintaining that 'the Bible is an important element in the operation of the Spirit', he invites Christians in India to be open to the spirit of God in their attitudes to Scriptures in the multireligious context.[82]

In addition to the plurality of written scriptures, the importance of speaking the text in the Indian context is also highlighted in dialogue.[83] Commenting on this Samartha says that 'in cultures such as the Hindu and the Buddhist, even though scriptures were written very early, it was the recital and hearing of the Scriptures that operated as authority among people'.[84] But most often the scriptures (or recitations of them) that are referred to in these perspectives are that of dominant sections of people the fact which dialogue normally plays down. In spite of such indifferences, one can still see that dialogists repeatedly emphasize that a biblical hermeneutics in Asia/India must always take into consideration the presence of other religious scriptures and exhibit respect for them.

Secondly, against the question that dialogue is not biblical, dialogue promoters make painstaking efforts to establish that the Bible has a lot to offer dialogue,[85] as shown by the dialogue between Israelites and the rest of the people in the Old Testament, between Jesus and others in the New Testament and the pluralistic context in which biblical Christianity was evolving. On the other hand, generally considered conservative texts such as John 14 and similar passages from the Bible are interpreted and reflected in such a way that they become relevant for the pluralistic context.[86] One consequence of this has been that almost every dialogue meeting in India in the past few decades has witnessed the use of multiple scriptures for meditation and discussion. Not only are participants of dialogue asked to learn from each other's scriptures, but reading from different scriptures is a significant element in formal interreligious gatherings and worship.[87] Even this, however, is a problematic aspect of dialogue, as I will elaborate in Chapter 7.

(e) Dialogical Attitudes to Secularism

Regarding the relationship between dialogue and secularism or secularization in the Indian context, there are fundamentally two perspectives. First, while there are positive views appreciating secularism in the Indian context, in which all religions are to be respected, there is generally a negative attitude to secularization which aims to annihilate religions as in the Western context, a point made in Jerusalem in 1928 by William Hocking.[88] Even though this perspective is often challenged in the Indian context, where secularism is interpreted not as anti-religious but as multireligious, there is a general trend in dialogue circles to talk about the 'role of religions in the secular society'.[89] In this context, the importance of religions is affirmed, and how it functions within a secular context is discussed.

Second, there are also proposals for cooperation between religions and secular ideologies within dialogue circles. M. M. Thomas advocated this approach, and he invited Christians to participate in the 'struggles of secularism and secular men for an authentic understanding of man as he is confronted with the radical demand for meaningful personal human existence'.[90] In such a context, he maintained that the church should enter into dialogue with secular people and ideologies.[91] In this regard, Wilfred says that Christians in India need a politically based dialogue, where religions actively take part in secular affairs rather than keeping themselves away from them.[92] While the intention of the dialogists is to encourage Christians who are generally believed to be oblivious to social and political realities, the problem nevertheless is the reckless distinction that dialogists often make between religion and secularism.

Discussing 'religious dialogue with secularism', Paul Verghese says that while 'the dialogue really needed is between Christians and non-Christians about our common task in the world', maintaining that 'dialogue between two separate organized entities called the Church on the one side and the world on the other is not what is needed', for 'Christians are just as much part of the world as non-Christians'.[93] In other words, for him keeping Christians or religionists on the one side and the remainder on the other side does not work well. Nevertheless, there are ambiguities that are generally found in the dialogical attitudes regarding religious-secular dynamics which will be elaborated in Chapters 3 and 4.

To conclude this section on the various developments of dialogue since the 1970s, we can see that the significance of dialogue has been taken to different levels in India, by offering new ways to approach other religions, replacing exclusive models. However one of the limitations with most of these developments was the obvious fact that these discussions were mostly confined to elites and targeted elites in religious spheres, and this has contributed towards a strict formalization of dialogue. The elite assumptions and aspects involved in these developments of dialogue will be critically analysed in Chapter 7. Now I shall discuss the challenges brought to dialogue from liberation theologies especially in relation to the dominant Hindu traditions in India, which has provided yet another platform for it to be sharpened and contextualized in the Indian society.

4 Interreligious Dialogue and Liberation Theologies in India: Sanskritization of Theology versus Dialogue for The Welfare of Poor and Downtrodden

I have already noted that the religio-cultural climate of India/Asia is frequently emphasized in dialogue over against the Western situation. While this attitude continues to be one of the overarching themes in dialogue, gradually the socio-economic context of Asia/India for dialogue also has been conceptualized. According to this perspective, 'In a pluralistic and multi-religious society, the religions need to enter into dialogue for providing a common moral foundation to the political and social life.'[94] Pointing out that poverty and religiosity are two realities of Asia/India, K. C. Abraham, a contemporary Indian Christian thinker involved in dialogue, says,

> The national situation is complex, but the problem of poverty, amounting to destitution and misery for millions and the communal and/or religious conflict that threatens national unity are particularly urgent and deserve special emphasis when we consider the question of dialogue.[95]

His suggestion is that when all the spiritual sources from different religious traditions which lead towards human wholeness are brought together in dialogue, these evils can be done away with.[96] Francis Vineeth also holds similar perspectives:

> India is a land of great world-religions, cultural wealth, and at the same time a country of miserable poverty. Hence our dialogue must be with all the three aspects of our being. Dialogue with our cultural traditions takes us to the reality of inculturation. Dialogue with the other living religions is what we now call inter-religious dialogue. ... Dialogue with the poor of our country calls us for a theology of liberation. Evangelization is now to be understood in the form of this three-fold dialogue.[97]

Moreover, since the 1980s, dialogue, particularly Hindu–Christian, has come under criticism from liberation theologies in India. The challenges liberation theologies brought were to dialogue twofold. First, they attacked the Sanskritization of Indian Christian theology, including theologies of dialogue linked to the dominant Hindu traditions. Secondly, liberation theologies have also offered liberation themes to be incorporated in dialogue, and accordingly, there have been efforts to talk about a liberation theology of dialogue.[98]

A student of Indian Christian theology knows well that traditional Indian theology interpreted Christianity in India largely through the dominant Hindu brahmanical traditions involving Vedas, Vedanta and Upanishads.[99] Many of the Indian Christian theologians being converts from high-caste Hindu traditions, this was understandable. While such theologies had their advantages in the nineteenth century and in the early part of the twentieth century, this was unacceptable by the later part of the twentieth century, one reason being the increasing awareness of Sanskritization popularized by the Indian sociologist M. N. Srinivas. The original definition offered by him for Sanskritization was that it 'is the process by which a "low" Hindu caste, or tribal or other group, changes its customs, ritual ideology and way of life in the direction of a high ... caste'.[100] Generally this refers to the process by which anything adapts to the Sanskritic principles. In the theological circles in India, Sanskritization of theology meant adapting to the dominant Hindu brahmanical ways of life. Arguing that Sanskritized Indian Christian theology has neglected the millions of Dalits and their experiences, Dalit theology insisted on new ways of theologizing where the experiences of the oppressed people became the subject of theologizing rather than the theories and concepts drawn from the Hindu traditions. Criticizing the Sanskritization of the Indian Christian theology and pointing out the fact that Indian Christian theology has failed to take note of what was happening on the Dalit front,[101] Arvind P. Nirmal, one of the pioneers of Dalit theology, says that a Dalit theology represents

> a radical discontinuity with the classical Indian Christian Theology of the Brahmanic tradition. The Brahminic tradition in the classical Indian Christian Theology needs to be challenged by the emerging Dalit Theology. This also means that a Christian Dalit Theology will be a counter theology.[102]

In its criticisms of the Sanskritization of theology in India, Dalit theology has been supported by the growing Dalit movements in India,[103] especially the influence of B. R. Ambedkar,[104] who worked on Dalit development in India, and liberation theologies that were originally popular in Latin America and then moved worldwide. And, not only Dalits but other subaltern people such as Tribals and Adivasis, as well as women, are also critical of Sanskritized theology and dialogue.

Showing how Dalit theology needs to be critical of theology of religious dialogue in India, A. M. Abraham Ayrookuzhiel, an Indian Christian thinker, has reflected on Dalit religion in the context of dialogue.[105] Critically studying the Hindu–Christian dialogue activities, he maintains that 'it does not make much sense to think of Hindu-Christian dialogue in terms of classical Hindu philosophical systems as far as the general popular religious experience is concerned', which involves the experience of Dalits and other oppressed.[106] Franklyn Balasundaram,[107] James Massey[108] and Sathianathan Clarke[109] broadly share this view.

Secondly, building on the above criticisms, liberation theologies have also posed the challenge to dialogue of dealing with the socio-economic and political realities that are responsible for the livelihood of millions of poor and downtrodden in India. As a result, even though dialogue had begun to acknowledge socio-economic factors and common welfare, as discussed earlier, it now had to radically redefine itself. This led some theologians in India to work for a liberative theology of religions or liberative theology of dialogue in India.[110] S. Arokiasamy, a Roman Catholic theologian in India working on a liberation theology of religion, says,

> In a situation of poverty largely imposed and a pluralism of religions and humanistic ideologies which need to be critically understood, engagement in and commitment to liberation will be an inter-human and inter-religious project.[111]

For Amaladoss, 'Interreligious dialogue must descend from the level of experts to that of the ordinary people, the poor, who are struggling together for liberation and fulfilment. It will be shown more in symbols and gestures and common activity rather than in abstract discussions. It will be the dialogue of life and struggles.'[112] In the same vein, Wilfred holds that 'we cannot today meaningfully enter into a discourse of praxis of liberating dialogue without taking into serious account the colossal fact of the ideological critique of Indian religious traditions, especially Hinduism, on the part of the marginalized, especially the Dalits.'[113] Samuel Rayan, another Roman Catholic theologian in India, has also challenged what he calls 'socially neutral' dialogue. According to him, 'Dialogue is not authentic unless it leads to reinterpretation or rejection of all oppressive aspects of the religious heritage of both partners.'[114]

Emphasizing the relationship between liberation theology and dialogue, Dominic Veliath proposes that theology of religions should learn from theology of liberation concerning the primacy of orthopraxis over orthodoxy.[115] Ignatius Puthiadam also shares a similar view. He says that

> a genuine theology of religions will arise in any religion only if the religious community earnestly enters into the religious experience of other religious communities and at the same time in all earnestness immerse itself into the poverty and the culture of the people through dialogical and liberative activity.[116]

Thus liberation theologies in India, by challenging the Sanskritization involved in dialogue, have forced dialogue to rethink and redefine its boundaries and enlarge its horizons to include liberation themes in dialogue. As a result, themes and concepts such as 'preferential option for the poor in dialogue' have become popular, and they indicate that dialogue cannot be strictly between religions based on merely religious experiences of the adherents, and rather socio-economic realities such as the plight of the most disadvantaged should get a way into actual dialogue. In this context it should be also noted that some Indian Christian thinkers focusing on Dalits have developed dialogue with religions such as Buddhism and Sikhism which are also critical of dominant Hindu brahmanical traditions.[117] Even in such a radical redefinition of dialogue, one should note, the poor and marginalized (and their concerns) still remain passive subjects of dialogical discussions. This will be discussed and critiqued in detail in Chapter 7.

5 Dialogue in the Contemporary Context in India

In contemporary India, especially over the last two decades, dialogue has become significant due to an increase in what it claims to be 'religious conflicts'. This has resulted in thinking about and carrying dialogue activities for peace and reconciliation. Similar ideas existed earlier especially in the context of religious fanaticism and fundamentalism, but only rose to prominence after India witnessed what is generally described as Hindu–Muslim violence in the 1990s due to the demolition of the Babri Masjid in Ayodhya, after the somewhat earlier 'Hindu-Sikh violence'. More major violent events have occurred since the 1990s. 'Hindu-Christian violence' in 1998 and 'Hindu-Muslim violence' in 2002, both in Gujarat, and 'Hindu-Christian violence' in Kandhamal in Orissa in 2008 are some of the major violent events. In addition to these, in the global context, the terrorist attack on the World Trade Center in the United States in September 2001 also has become one of the often-cited contexts for the urgent need of dialogue in order to do away with religious violence.

In responding to the context of conflicts and violence, dialogue works generally in two ways. The first is to encourage more and more people to engage in dialogue for peace and reconciliation to help solve the problems between them. Communal harmony is emphasized as one of the most important necessities of the time. The underlying idea is that religions or misunderstandings among religious adherents play a major role in today's communal violence in Indian society, necessitating a proper understanding of religion. In such contexts, one of the foremost objectives of dialogue is to contain the conflicts and violence among people, dialogue and cooperation between people of different religions becoming necessary for peace-making. Commenting on the importance of conflict resolution in dialogue, Michael Amaladoss says that a

> real conflict resolution will have to be done in three phases: a restoration of justice and reconciliation, a solution to the problems that gave rise to the conflict and healing of memories. The efforts at conflict resolution will have to be supported by continuing efforts to promote community through dialogue.[118]

Thus, in the context of conflicts, tensions and violence, dialogue is posed as a necessary tool to work for peace-building among communities and as a conflict resolution principle. Andreas D'Souza, a former director of the HMI in the city of Hyderabad in South India, started in 1930 for the purpose of training Christian missionaries to work among Muslims and since the 1980s promoting dialogue, has worked on a 'theology of relationship' which insists on the necessity of dialogue to create peace and reconciliation among people who are divided in the name of religious conflicts.[119] He says,

> In order to promote interfaith dialogue what we need is not convergence, that is, unity in beliefs and practices but an openness to building relationships, restoring kinships or bonds with all people no matter who they are and to what particular religion they belong.[120]

While institutions such as HMI and CISRS continue their dialogue activities in this direction, increasingly there are also proposals to take dialogue to the grassroots where the violence and its consequences are more felt.[121]

The other perspective in dialogue is to challenge the religious fundamentalism and political tactics which underlie religious conflicts.[122] While the fundamentalism of each religion is critiqued, Hindu nationalism, linked not only to the majority religious community but also to the strong political representation by the BJP, gets more treatment in the Indian context.[123] There is basically a differentiation between Hindu and Hindutva, and while dialogue is encouraged with Hinduism, Hindutva is denounced. Warning against the temptation to identify Hindutva with Hindu tradition, Wilfred says that one should 'distinguish between *Hindutva as an ideology* and *Hinduism as practiced and lived by the overwhelmingly majority of the people*'.[124] Moreover, M. T. Cherian, who has recently done research on this theme, proposes a public dialogue in order to combat communal violence. For him, dialogue does not need to depend only on religion. He writes, 'It is possible to establish a peaceful society through dialogue not necessarily on the basis of religion but on the basis of the day-to-day living situation of the common public in society.'[125] Despite these rare voices, dialogue continues to work on the basis of religion as the central factor in violence as well as the solution for it.

The influence of the dialogical approach in the current context can be noted from the fact that there is increasing interest in religious plurality in various quarters including Pentecostals in India, generally dubbed exclusivists. Studying the works of Samartha, Rayan and Ariarajah, Geomon K. George, an Indian Pentecostal Christian, argues that Indian Pentecostals should not shy away from the question of religious pluralism, unlike in the past, and he invites them rather to face the question squarely. Terming his model 'pneumatological inclusivism', the basis for a Pentecostal approach to religious plurality and dialogue in the spirit, he says,

> Pneumatological inclusivism recognises the Spirit and logos outside the Church creating, renewing, and sustaining the activity of God in the world. Thus the question is not whether the Spirit is present among the people of other faiths, but how one discerns the Spirit of God in the religious traditions of other people.[126]

This is but one example for how dialogue has pushed towards an awareness of religious plurality in contemporary Indian Christian thought, even where it was not accepted until very recently, yet ignoring the fundamental problems associated with religious plurality itself and the notion of world religions.

This chapter has offered only a bird's-eye view of some major trends of dialogue in India over the last seven decades. I have shown the multiple trends and perspectives in dialogue and, against the differing contexts in India, indicated how dialogue has evolved to become one of the dominant approaches today encouraging Christians to have positive attitudes to other religions. The purpose of briefly outlining these trends is to offer a background for my discussion of the limitations of dialogue in Part II. Before doing so, I shall discuss the dialogue activities in Kanyakumari district, along with the background of the district, to show how the above trends in dialogue have been put into practice in a particular context.

Notes

1 Jose Kuttianimattathil, a Roman Catholic scholar in India, has researched dialogue in India and gives an account of theologies of dialogue in his lengthy volume, *Practice and Theology of Interreligious Dialogue* (Bangalore: Kristy Jyoti College, 1998), 78–107, 173–230.

2 There are many such dialogue thinkers and activists, hence it may not be possible to give all the details about them and their writing here; I will discuss them in the text wherever necessary.

3 There are numerous writings available in this regard, which include Coward, ed., *Hindu-Christian Dialogue*; Paul Knitter, *One Earth Many Religions: Multifaith Dialogue and Global Responsibility* (Maryknoll, New York: Orbis Books, 1996); John Parry, *The Word of God is Not Bound: The Encounter of Sikhs and Christians in India and the United Kingdom* (Bangalore: Centre for Contemporary Christianity, 2009); Leonard Swidler, *After the Absolute: The Dialogical Future of Religious Reflection* (Minneapolis: Augsburg Fortress Publishers, 1990).

4 I shall just mention only their names here and discuss their writings and contributions later in this chapter. Their biographical details and contributions are found in John C. England et al., eds, *Asian Christian Theologies: A Research Guide to Authors, Movements and Sources, Vol. 1: Asian Region, South Asia, Austral Asia* (Maryknoll, New York: Orbis Books, 2002).

5 Raimon (sometimes Raimundo or Raymond) Panikkar has a dual national identity as he was born of Indian and Spanish parentage and has lived in India working on Hinduism and dialogue.

6 Numerous works – books, articles and reports of interreligious meetings – related to dialogue have been published through CISRS since 1957 and are mentioned in its recent catalogue. CISRS, *A Catalogue of CISRS Publications: A Complete Listing of CISRS Publications 1953-2006* (Bangalore: CISRS, 2007). Works of Devanandan and Thomas are discussed later; other early publications of CISRS include Herbert Jai Singh, *My Neighbours*, 1964; *Interreligious Dialogue*, 1967; and Raymond Panikkar, *Trinity and World Religions*, 1970. See also Kaaj Baago, *Pioneers of Indigenous Christianity* (Bangalore: CISRS & Madras: CLS, 1969).

7 Some of the other major thinkers include J. Russell Chandran, who was the Principal of UTC, located adjacent to CISRS; M. M. Thomas, who led CISRS after the death of Devanandan; and Samartha. The CISRS catalogue cites all relevant names.

8 This journal, currently a quarterly, was launched in 1953, and numerous articles have been published in it since then.

9 Most of Devanandan's writings and reflections have been published by CISRS in three volumes, two posthumously. *Christian Concern in Hinduism*, 1961; S. J. Samartha and Nalini Devanandan, eds, *I Will Lift Mine Eyes unto the Hills*, 1963; Nalini Devanandan and Thomas, eds, *Preparation for Dialogue*, 1964. Later another volume was published: Herbert Jai Singh, *Inter-Religious Dialogue*, in which the first article was by M. M. Thomas entitled 'The Significance of the Thought of Paul D. Devanandan for a Theology of Dialogue,' 1–37. In the 1980s, UTC published selected writings of Devanandan in two volumes. Joachim Wietzke, *Paul D. Devanandan*, vols I and II (Madras, Bangalore: CLS/UTC, 1983 and 1987).

10 Devanandan, *Christian Concern*, v.

11 In this assembly, Devanandan delivered a speech on the theme 'Called to Witness,' *Ecumenical Review* 14, no. 22 (1962): 154–63.

12 Some of Thomas's writings on dialogue and related themes published by CISRS include *The Acknowledged Christ of Hindu Renaissance*, 1970; *Salvation and Humanisation*, 1971; *Man and the Universe of Faiths*, 1975; *The Secular Ideologies of India and the Secular Meaning of Christ*, 1976; *Some Theological Dialogues*, 1977; also *Risking Christ for Christ's Sake* (Geneva: WCC, 1999). Besides, there are also several postgraduate theses written on Thomas both in Indian and in foreign universities.

13 Devanandan, *Christian Concern*, 83.

14 Ibid., 85.

15 Devanandan and Thomas, ed., *Problems of Indian Democracy* (Bangalore: CISRS, 1962), especially the epilogue: 'The Sources of Christian Political Concern' (195–211); *Cultural Foundations of Indian Democracy* (Bangalore: Literature on Social Concerns, 1955); *Human Person, Society and State* (Bangalore: Literature on Social Concerns, 1957). See also Devanandan's earlier works, *Christian Issues in Southern Asia* (Bangalore: CISRS, 1959) and Thomas's compiled work, *Christian Participation in Nation-building*.

16 Devanandan and Thomas, *Problems of Indian Democracy*, 210.

17 Thomas, *Christian Participation*, 303.

18 Samartha and Devanandan, *I Will Lift Mine Eyes*, 126; Thomas, *Man and the Universe*, 146.

19 Thomas, *The Secular Ideologies*, 198.

20 Thomas Thangaraj, *Christian Witness in the Multi-religious Context* (Bangalore: CISRS, 2011). See also his other writings related to dialogue, *Relating to People of Other Religions: What Every Christian Needs to Know* (Nashville: Abingdon Press, 1997); *The Common Task: A Theology of Christian Mission* (Nashville: Abingdon Press, 1999).

21 Thomas Thangaraj, 'Hindu Universalism and Christian Catholicity,' in *Influence of Hinduism on Christianity*, ed. Gnana Robinson (Madurai: TTS, 1980), 13; see also his book, *The Crucified Guru* (Nashville: Abingdon Press, 1994), in which he attempts to construct a dialogue between Christianity and the *Saiva Siddhantha* tradition in South India.

22 K. C. Abraham, 'Dialogue in the Context of Indian Life,' in *Christian Concern for Dialogue in India*, ed. C. D. Jathanna (Bangalore: The Gubbi Mission Press, 1987), 48–63.

23 Michael Amaladoss, 'Liberation as an Interreligious Project,' in *Leave the Temple*, ed. Felix Wilfred (Maryknoll, New York: Orbis Books, 1992), 158–74.

24 Felix Wilfred, 'Inter-religious Dialogue as a Political Question,' in *Christian Witness in Society*, ed. K. C. Abraham (Bangalore: Board of Theological Education of the Senate of Serampore College, 1998), 187–202.

25 For instance, see M. T. Cherian, 'Public Dialogue and Dialogical Theology,' in *Jesus Christ: The Light of the World*, ed. Solomon Rongpi and Wati Longchar (Nagpur: NCCI, 2011), 133–44.

26 See Sara Grant, 'The Contemporary Relevance of Christian Ashrams: Reflections in the Light of Ecumenical Experience,' in *Culture, Religion and Society*, ed. S. K. Chatterji and Hunter P. Mabry (Bangalore: CISRS, 1996), 111–13; also Helen Royston, *Christian Ashrams* (Lewiston: Edwin Mellen Press, 1987).

27 Kuttianimattathil, *Practice and Theology of Interreligious Dialogue*, 54.

28 Harry Oldmeadow, A Christian Pilgrim in India: The Spiritual Journey of Swami Abhishiktananda *(Henri Le Saux)* (Bloomington: World Wisdom Inc., 2008), 7–8.

29 Thomas Matus, *Jules Monchanin (1895–1957) as Seen from East and West*, 2 vols (Delhi: ISPCK, 2001).

30 Abhishiktananda, 'The Way of Dialogue,' in *Interreligious Dialogue*, ed. Herbert Jai Singh (Bangalore: CISRS, 1967), 83.

31 Abhishiktananda, 'The Way of Dialogue,' 85.

32 Abhishiktananda, *Saccidananda: A Christian Experience of Advaita* (London: SPCK, 1974), xiii.

33 Abhishiktananda, *Hindu-Christian Meeting Point*, rev. edn (Delhi: ISPCK, 1976), 6.

34 Abhishiktananda, *Hindu-Christian Meeting Point*, 6.

35 J. A. Cuttat, *The Encounter of Religions* (New York: Desclee Company, 1960); *The Spiritual Dialogue of East and West* (New Delhi: Max Muller Bhavan, 1961).

36 Cuttat, *Spiritual Dialogue of East and West*, 45.

37 Murray Rogers, 'Hindu and Christian – a Moment Breaks,' in *Interreligious Dialogue*, ed. Herbert Jai Singh (Bangalore: CISRS, 1967), 104–17.

38 Bede Griffiths, *Christ in India: Essays towards a Hindu-Christian Dialogue* (Bangalore: ATC, 1986).

39 Bede Griffiths, *Christian Ashram* (London: Darton, Longman & Todd, 1966), 17.

40 Klaus K. Klostermaier, 'Hindu-Christian Dialogue,' in *Dialogue Between Men of Living Faiths: Papers Presented at a Consultation Held at Ajaltoun, Lebanon, March 1970*, ed. S. J. Samartha (Geneva: WCC, 1971), 11.

41 Klostermaier, 'Hindu-Christian Dialogue,' 11; see also his book, *Indian Theology in Dialogue* (Madras: CLS, 1986).

42 Klostermaier, 'Hindu-Christian Dialogue,' 12.

43 Some of Stanley Samartha's contributions to dialogue are found in *The Hindu Response to the Unbound Christ* (Bangalore: CISRS, 1974); *Living Faiths and the Ecumenical Movement* (Geneva: WCC, 1971); *Living Faiths and Ultimate Goals: A Continuing Dialogue* (Geneva: WCC, 1973); *Towards World Community: The Colombo Papers* (Geneva: WCC, 1975); *Faith in the Midst of Faiths: Reflections on Dialogue in Community* (Geneva: WCC, 1977); *Courage For Dialogue: Ecumenical Issues in Inter-religious Relationships* (Geneva: WCC, 1981); and *Dialogue between Men of Living Faith* and *One Christ – Many Religions*, which have been already mentioned.

44 Alan Race discusses these typologies in detail in his book Christians and Religious Pluralism (Maryknoll, New York: Orbis Books, 1983).

45 This attitude can be found in almost all Indian/Asian thinkers on dialogue. Samartha, *One Christ – Many Religions*; Dayanandan Francis and Franklyn Balasundaram, ed., *Asian Expressions of Christian Commitment* (Madras: CLS, 1992); Micahel Amaladoss, 'Another Asia is Possible,' available online http://latinoamericana.org/2004/textos/castellano/AmaladossOriginalEnglish.htm.

46 Felix Wilfred, 'Our Neighbours and Our Christian Mission: Deconstructing Mission without Destroying the Gospel,' in *The People of God among All God's People*, ed. Philip L. Wickeri (Hong Kong: Christian Conference of Asia, 2000), 97; see also Peter C. Phan, *Being Religious Interreligiously* (Maryknoll, New York: Orbis Books), 2004.

47 Wilfred, 'Our Neighbours,' 95.

48 Felix Wilfred, 'Dialogue Gasping for Breath? Towards New Frontiers in Interreligious Dialogue,' in *Living and Working with Sisters and Brothers of Other Faiths* (Hong Kong: Christian Conference of Asia, 1989), 68–86.

49 Wilfred, 'Dialogue Gasping for Breath?,' 69.

50 Ibid.

51 Ibid., 70. See also the articles in a book ed. Wilfred, *Leave the Temple: Indian Paths to Human Liberation* (Maryknoll, New York: Orbis Books, 1992), which talk about the importance of these aspects within theology of religions in the context of Asia.

52 In the Christian theology of religions, inclusivism is often placed between exclusivism and pluralism and associated with the idea of fulfilment. According to this perspective, there is truth in other religions but ultimately they fulfil only Christianity. Several missionary theologians in India such as T. E. Slater, *The Higher Hinduism in Relation to Christianity: Certain Aspects of Hindu Thought from the Christian Standpoint* (London: Elliot Stock, 1902); A. G. Hogg, *Christian Message to the Hindu* (London: SCM Press, 1947); *Karma and Redemption: An Essay toward the Interpretation of Hinduism and the Restatement of Christianity* (Madras: CLS, 1970); and J. N. Farquhar, *The Crown of Hinduism* (London: Oxford University Press, 1913) followed this perspective. See also Eric J. Sharpe, *Not to Destroy but to Fulfil: The Contribution of J. N. Farquhar to Protestant Missionary Thought in India before 1914* (Uppsala: Gleerup, 1965); and James L. Cox, 'Faith and Faiths: The Significance of A. G. Hogg's Missionary Thought for a Theology of Dialogue,' *Scottish Journal of Theology* 32, no. 3 (1982): 241–56; R. Panikkar, *The Unknown Christ of Hinduism: Towards an Ecumenical Christophany* (London: Darton, Longman & Todd, 1964).

53 Samartha, *Courage for Dialogue*, 97.

54 There are many works redefining pluralism in the Western context as well. For example, Mark Heim, questioning the theo-centric or christo-centric pluralism,

The Problem with Interreligious Dialogue

argues for a pluralism in terms not of ultimate reality but of ultimate ends such as salvation. Mark Heim, *Salvations* (Maryknoll, New York: Oribs Books, 1995). He identifies such a stance as post-pluralist.

55 Raimon Panikkar, 'A Self-Critical Dialogue', in *The Intercultural challenge of Raimon Panikkar*, ed. Joseph Prabhu (Maryknoll, New York: Orbis Books, 1996), 247–63.
56 Panikkar, 'A Self-Critical Dialogue', 250.
57 Ibid., 250–1.
58 Raimundo Panikkar, 'The Invisible Harmony: A Universal Theory or a Cosmic Confidence?', in *Toward a Universal Theology of Religion*, ed. Leonard Swidler (Maryknoll, New York: Orbis Books, 1987), 138, 141.
59 Jyri Komulainen, *An Emerging Cosmotheandric Religion? Raimon Panikkar's Pluralistic Theology of Religions* (Helsinki: University of Helsinki, 2003), 11.
60 K. P. Aleaz, *Dimensions of Indian Religion* (Calcutta: Punthi Pustak, 1995), 261–2.
61 K. P. Aleaz, 'Pluralistic Inclusivism – Viable Indian Theology of Religions', *Asian Journal of Theology* 12, no. 2 (1998): 283.
62 These criticisms are found in numerous works written from evangelical perspectives, some of which I have already mentioned. See also O. V. Jathanna's critical study of pluralism in India: 'Religious Pluralism: A Theological Critique', *Bangalore Theological Forum* XXXI, no. 2 (1999): 1–18. In the Western context Gavin D'Costa and his circle has made a responsive study in the book, *Christian Uniqueness Reconsidered* (Maryknoll, New York: Orbis Books, 1990), to John Hick and Paul Knitter, eds, *The Myth of Christian Uniqueness* (Maryknoll, New York: Orbis Books, 1987); see also Newbigin, *The Gospel in a Pluralist Society.*
63 J. Russell Chandran, 'The Significance of the Study of Other Religions for Christian Theology', in *The Multi-faith Context of India*, ed. Israel Selvanayagam (Bangalore: The Board for Theological Text Books Program of South Asia, 1993), 20.
64 Michael Amaladoss, 'The Pluralism of Religions and the Significance of Christ', in *Asian Faces of Jesus*, ed. R. S. Sugirtharajah (London: SCM Press, 1993), 100–01.
65 For a discussion on this, see Paul Mojzes, ed., *Christian Mission and Interreligious Dialogue* (New York: Edwin Mellen Publishers, 1991).
66 Timothy C. Tennent, *Christianity at the Religious Roundtable* (Grand Rapids, MI: Baker Academic, 2002), 11.
67 S. J. Samartha, 'The Temper of Crusades and the Spirit of Dialogue', *NCC Review* 104, no. 9 (1984): 477.
68 Israel Selvanayagam, *Evangelism and Inter-faith Dialogue* (Tiruvalla: CSS, 1993). See also his other writings in this regard, *Evangelical and Dialogical: Healthy Balance in a Multi-faith Context* (Delhi: ISPCK, 2012).
69 Paulose Mar Gregorios, *Religion and Dialogue* (Delhi: ISPCK, 2000), 162.
70 Thangaraj, *Christian Witness*, 11.
71 Ibid., 10.
72 Murray Rogers, 'Hindu-Christian Dialogue Postponed', in *Dialogue between Men of Different Faiths*, ed. Stanley J. Samartha (Geneva: WCC, 1971), 21–31.
73 Rogers, 'Hindu-Christian Dialogue Postponed', 22–6.
74 S. J. Samartha, 'Christian Concern for Dialogue in India', in *Christian Concern for Dialogue in India*, ed. C. D. Jathanna (Madras: The Theological Commission of the Synod of the Church of South India, 1987), 2.
75 Gregorios, *Religion and Dialogue*, 156.
76 Selvanayagam, *A Second Call*, 172–88.
77 S. J. Samartha, *The Search for New Hermeneutics in Asian Christian Theology* (Bangalore: Board of Theological Education of the Senate of Serampore College, 1987), iii, 49.

78 D. S. Amalorpavadoss, ed., *Research Seminar on Non-Biblical Scriptures* (Bangalore: NBCLC, 1975).

79 Amalorpavadoss, *Research Seminar*, 8.

80 D. S. Amalorpavadoss, 'The Bible in Self-renewal and Church-renewal for Service in Society,' in *Voices from the Margin: Interpreting the Bible in the Third World*, ed. R. S. Sugirtharajah (Maryknoll, New York: Orbis Books, 1991), 316.

81 Amalorpavadoss, 'Bible in Self-renewal,' 328.

82 Paulose Mar Gregorios, 'Hermeneutical Discussion in India Today,' *Indian Journal of Theology* 31, no. 314 (1982): 155.

83 Samartha, *One Christ – Many Religions*, 73–5.

84 Ibid., 74.

85 Israel Selvanayagam, ed., *Biblical Insights on Inter-faith Dialogue* (Bangalore: Board of Theological Education of the Senate of Serampore College, 1995); *Relating to People of Other Faiths* (Tiruvalla: CSS, 2004); see also Wesley Ariarajah, *The Bible and People of Other Faiths* (Geneva: WCC, 1985).

86 R. S. Sugirtharajah, 'Inter-faith Hermeneutics: An Example and some Implications,' in *Voices from the Margin: Interpreting the Bible in the Third World* (Maryknoll, New York: Orbis Books, 1991), 352–63; J. Russell Chandran, 'The Importance of Interreligious Dialogue Today: A Theological and Ethical Perspective,' in *Dialogue in India: Multi-religious Perspective and Practice*, ed. K. P. Aleaz (Calcutta: Bishop's College, 1991), 56; Matthew P. John, 'The Biblical Bases of Dialogue,' in *Interreligious Dialogue*, ed. Herbert Jai Singh (Bangalore: CISRS, 1967), 65–77.

87 I observed this personally in a number of dialogue meetings during my involvement with dialogue. The reports published about various meetings also include information on using multiple scriptures.

88 International Missionary Council (IMC), *The Christian Life and Message in Relation to Non-Christian Systems: Report of the Jerusalem Meeting of the International Missionary Council, March 24th–April 8th, 1928* (London: Oxford University Press, 1928).

89 S. J. Samartha, 'Inter-Religious Relationships in the Secular State,' in *Asian Expressions of Christian Commitment*, ed. Dayanandan Francis and Franklyn Balasundaram (Madras: CLS, 1992), 128–36.

90 Thomas, *Salvation*, 45.

91 Ibid.

92 Wilfred, 'Inter-religious Dialogue as a Political Question,' 187–202.

93 Paul Verghese, 'Dialogue with Secularism,' in *Interreligious Dialogue*, ed. Herbert Jai Singh (Bangalore: CISRS, 1967), 232–3.

94 Wilfred, 'Dialogue Gasping for Breath?,' 72.

95 Abraham, 'Dialogue in the Context,' 48; also his essay 'Inter-faith Dialogue for Humanization,' *Religion and Society* 46, no. 1/2 (1999): 65–76.

96 Abraham, 'Dialogue in the Context,' 63.

97 Francis Vineeth, 'Theology of Religions from the Perspective of Inter-religious Dialogue,' in *Religious Pluralism: an Indian Christian Perspective*, ed. Kuncheria Pathil (Delhi: ISPCK, 1999), 248–9.

98 In the Western context Paul Knitter has worked this perspective. 'Toward a Liberation Theology of Religions,' in *The Myth of Christian Uniqueness*, 178–218; 'Cosmic Confidence or Preferential Option?' in *The Intercultural Challenge of Raimon Panikkar*, 177–91; Paul F. Knitter, 'Responsibilities for the Future: Toward and Interfaith Ethic,' in *Pluralism and the Religions: The Theological and Political Dimensions*, ed. John D'Archy May (London: Cassell, 1998), 75–99.

In the wider Asian context, the Sri Lankan theologian, Aloysius Pieris has worked on linking liberation and religious plurality. Aloysius Pieris, *An Asian Theology of Liberation* (Edinburgh: T&T Clark, 1988).

99   Robin Boyd, in his book *An Introduction to Indian Christian Theology*, rev. edn (Delhi: ISPCK, 1975), which is one of the earliest introductions to Indian Christian thought, offers detailed discussions of such theologies and theologians.

100   M. N. Srinivas, *Social Change in Modern India* (New Delhi: Orient Longman, 1995), 6.

101   Arvind P. Nirmal, *Heuristic Explorations* (Madras: CLS, 1990), 142.

102   Nirmal, *Heuristic Explorations*, 144; see also Walter Fernandes, 'A Socio-Historical Perspective for Liberation Theology in India,' in *Leave the Temple: Indian Paths to Human Liberation*, ed. Felix Wilfred (Maryknoll, New York: Orbis Books, 1992), 9–34.

103   There are several works coming up in the field of Dalit movements in India. For instance, see M. C. Raj, *Dalitology* (Tumkur: Ambedkar Resource Centre, 2001); Gail Omvedt, *Dalit Visions: The Anti-Caste Movement and the Construction of an Indian Identity*, rev. ed. (New Delhi: Orient Blackswann, 2006); Eva-Maria Hardtmann, *The Dalit Movement in India: Local Practices, Global Connections* (New Delhi: Oxford University Press, 2011); D. R. Nagaraj, *The Flaming Feet and Other Essays: The Dalit Movement in India* (New Delhi: Permanent Black, 2013); Eleanor Zelliot, *Ambedkar's World: The Making of Babasaheb and the Dalit Movement* (New Delhi: Navayana Publications, 2013).

104   For the primary writings of Ambedkar, see Valerian Rodrigues, *The Essential Writings of B. R. Ambedkar* (New Delhi: Oxford University Press, 2002).

105   Abraham Ayrookuzhiel, 'The Religious Factor in Dalit Liberation: Some Reflections,' in *Culture, Religion and Society*, ed. S. K. Chatterji and Hunter P. Mabry (Bangalore: CISRS, 1996), 212–26; *Essays on Dalits, Religion and Liberation* (Bangalore: CISRS, 2006), especially chapter 7: 'The Dalits, Religions and Inter-faith Dialogue.'

106   A. M. Ayrookuzhiel, 'The Living Hindu Popular Religious Consciousness and Some Reflections on it in the Context of Hindu-Christian Dialogue,' *Religion and Society* XXVI, no. 1 (1979): 21.

107   Franklyn J. Balasundaram, 'Dalit Theologies and Other Theologies,' in *Frontiers of Dalit Theology*, ed. V. Devasahayam (Delhi and Madras: ISPCK and Gurukul, 1997), 251–69.

108   James Massey, *Indigenous People: Dalits* (Delhi: ISPCK, 1994); *Downtrodden* (Geneva: WCC, 1997).

109   Sathianathan Clarke, *Dalits and Christianity* (New Delhi: Oxford University Press, 1998).

110   Xavier Irudhayaraj, ed., *Liberation and Dialogue* (Bangalore: Claretian Publications, 1989); Anthoniraj Thumma, *Breaking Barriers: Liberation of Dialogue and Dialogue of Liberation* (Delhi: ISPCK, 2000). I have already mentioned that theologians such as Paul Knitter and Aloysius Pieris have been working similar perspectives of dialogue outside the Indian context.

111   S. Arokiasamy, 'Theology of Religions from Liberation Perspective,' in *Religious Pluralism: An Indian Christian Perspective*, ed. Kuncheria Pathil (New Delhi: ISPCK, 1999), 301.

112   Amaladoss, 'Liberation as an Interreligious Project,' 166.

113   Wilfred Cited in Knitter, *One Earth Many Religions*, 163.

114   Samuel Rayan, 'Spirituality for Inter-faith Social Action,' in *Liberation and Dialogue*, ed. Xavier Irudayaraj (Bangalore: Claretian Publications, 1989), 70.

115 Dominic Veliath, 'Jesus Christ and the Theology of Religions: A Conspectus of Models,' in *Religious Pluralism: An Indian Christian Perspective*, ed. Kuncheria Pathil (New Delhi: ISPCK, 1999), 176.

116 Ignatius Puthiadam, 'Theology of Religions in the Indian Context,' in *Religious Pluralism: An Indian Christian Perspective*, ed. Kuncheria Pathil (New Delhi: ISPCK, 1999), 213.

117 For example, see James Massey's article, 'Guru Nanak Devji's Teachings in the Context of Inter-faith Dialogue,' in *From Truth to Truth* (Delhi: Centre for Dalit Studies, 2008), 106–12; Godwin R. Singh, 'Inter-religious Dialogue between Sikhism and Christianity,' in *Fundamentalism and Secularism*, ed. Andreas Nehring (Madras: Gurukul, 1994), 298–309.

118 Michael Amaladoss, *Making Harmony* (Delhi: ISPCK, 2003), 159.

119 Andreas D'Souza, 'Reconciliation in Practice: The Indian Experience,' *Journal of the Henry Martyn Institute* 21, no. 2 (2002): 94–6. For a study of HMI, see Diane D'Souza, *Evangelism, Dialogue, Reconciliation: The Transformative Journey of the Henry Martyn Institute* (Hyderabad: Henry Martyn Institute, 1998).

120 Andreas D'Souza, 'Theology of Relationship,' *The Forum In-Focus* 14 (2002–3): 5.

121 Dayanandan Francis, *Reflections on Inter-faith Themes* (Delhi: ISPCK, 2007), especially chapter 5: 'Dialogue with the Hindus at the Grassroot Level.' Also, A. Pushparajan, *From Conversion to Fellowship: The Hindu-Christian Encounter in the Gandhian Perspective* (Allahabad: St Paul Press, 1990).

122 Gnana Robinson, 'Why is Fundamentalism a Problem Today?', in *Fundamentalism and Secularism*, ed. Andreas Nehring (Madras: Gurukul, 1994), 9–15.

123 Wilfred, 'Our Neighbours,' 81.

124 Ibid.

125 Cherian, 'Public Dialogue and Dialogical Theology,' 142.

126 Geomon K. George, *Religious Pluralism: Challenges for Pentecostalism in India* (Bangalore: Centre for Contemporary Christianity, 2006), 233.

Chapter 2

The Practice of Dialogue: A Case from Kanyakumari District

In the light of the discussion in the last chapter on the theoretical and theological trends in dialogue in the Indian context, this chapter looks at how those trends have manifested in practical activities of dialogue. While the very nature of the practice of dialogue may differ from context to context, I selected for my study Kanyakumari district in Tamil Nadu, South India, where dialogue activities are undertaken among people from more than one religion, especially Hindus, Christians and Muslims. As mentioned earlier, I conducted the fieldwork there in 2007 and in 2008. My fieldwork was primarily to study the dialogue activities in the district for the past four or five decades. This chapter provides a brief outline of the dialogue activities in the district, after discussing the general background of the district, based on my field study and my experience of living there for more than thirty years and my involvement with dialogue activities for more than a decade.

1 Kanyakumari District: Its People and Background

(a) Geographical Location

Kanyakumari district, which is one of the thirty-two districts in Tamil Nadu, is the southernmost district in India. It is also called 'Kanniyakumari', which is the proper transliteration of the term in Tamil. The district is 1,672 square kilometres and occupies 1.29 per cent of the area of Tamil Nadu. The district is bounded by three oceans – the Bay of Bengal to the East, the Indian Ocean to the South and the Arabian Sea to the West – with Kerala State to the West and Tirunelveli district to the North. The district has four taluks[1]: Agasteeswaram (also Agasteeswarem), Thovalai, Kalkulam and Vilavancode. The capital of the district is Nagercoil (also Nagerkovil), which is in the taluk of Agasteeswaram.

Kanyakumari also refers to a particular place in Kanyakumari district. This is a small town, and in terms of administrative subdivisions, it is a *panchayat* town.[2] It is a tourist spot as well as a place of pilgrimage, particularly since waves from the Indian Ocean, Arabian Sea and Bay of Bengal come together at one point, echoing the merging Ganga, Jamuna and mythical Saraswati rivers in North India at the town of Prayag near Allahabad. The sunrise and sunset can be seen from here, and the water from this place, as in Prayag, is considered to be holy by the Hindus, who come from all over India to Kanyakumari for pilgrimage. There is a memorial to Vivekananda[3] on a rock in the sea, reached by ferry; a memorial to Gandhi (Gandhi Mandabam); a 133-foot statue of Tiruvalluvar, a famous Tamil poet; and a memorial to K. Kamaraj, the former chief minister of Tamil Nadu. Kanyakumari is also known as Cape Comorin.

(b) Historical Background

Discussing the overall background of Kanyakumari district is a critical task as there are differing views, usually determined by the caste or religious identity of the historian.[4] But understanding Kanyakumari's past is crucial for understanding and analysing the conflicts within which local dialogue activities take place. What is now Kanyakumari district and the southern part of Kerala were together known as the State of Travancore from the eighteenth century to the mid-twentieth century.[5] Travancore was ruled by kings even after the independence of India in 1947, when generally most of the small kingdoms were unified into the Indian state. When it joined the Indian Union in 1949,[6] Travancore was merged with Cochin, which was the northern part of today's Kerala, and became the State of Travancore-Cochin. However, people in the southern part of Travancore, today's Kanyakumari, wanted to join Tamil Nadu, since the majority were Tamil-speaking. But the State of Travancore-Cochin objected, in part because it depended on this region for rice.[7] Agitation began among Tamils in the region,[8] and finally, on the recommendation of the State Reorganisation Act, 1956 (Act XXXVII of 1956), this region joined Tamil Nadu on 1 November 1956, and became a separate district.[9]

(c) People, Society and Social Life: Caste Structure

How slavery and the caste system first entered South India is still a contested area of research. There is no evidence for caste in early Tamil literature.[10] The roots of caste and slavery in South India are traced to 'the conquest of southern India by the Aryans and the consequent fusion between them and the inhabitants of the land', which caused 'the birth of the Caste System and the institution of slavery which is closely allied with the former'.[11] The initial evidence for caste appeared during the South Indian rule of Chola dynasty in the twelfth century, and it has survived until today,[12] albeit weakened, it is claimed, due to modernization and its consequences. This argument is also extended to Kanyakumari district. It is said that

> the caste system in the society has weakened to a great extent especially after independence because of growth of education and improvements in transport and communication. The rigid social divisions in terms of caste noticed and dwelt on at length by the British historians are no longer as significant as they were in those days.[13]

Nevertheless, this argument with regard to society in India in general and in the Kanyakumari district in particular is disputed, and attempts are made by historians, sociologists and anthropologists to show that caste is a continuing reality.[14] Moreover, day-to-day realities among people are also evidence that caste remains an inevitable feature in government policies, particularly for education and employment[15]: belief in the irrelevance of caste is held by Hindu nationalists who stress religious divisions.[16]

Table 1 shows the population in Kanyakumari district by caste communities as of the 2001 census.[17]

Scheduled Castes include castes like Pariahs (also Parayas), Pallars and Sambavas (also Sambavars) who are spread throughout the district.[18] Another Scheduled Caste community, the Paravas, live in the coastal area and are involved in fishing and pearl-diving.[19] Kanis are the main Tribal group in the district in the Western Ghats.[20] Most Backward Communities such as Mukkuvas live along the coast and are involved in fishing: almost all are Roman Catholic.[21] Among Backward Communities, Nadars are the majority community in the region, in terms of number, and they follow established religions like Hinduism and Christianity.[22] Other Communities include castes such as Vellalas; Nairs; Krishnavagaiyars, who are also called Kuruppu; Kerala Mudalis and Brahmins. These are 'people with caste', and most are caste Hindus.[23]

(d) Education, Employment and Economic Background

In Tamil Nadu, Kanyakumari district had the highest level of literacy (88.11 per cent) as per the 2001 census.[24] Primarily a domain of the high castes, education became common for all irrespective of caste only after the London Missionary Society (LMS) came to this region and to Travancore in the nineteenth century.[25] In 1836, Malayalam became the mandatory language in the schools in Travancore.[26] Today many schools and colleges in the district belong to Christian institutions such as Roman Catholic and CSI churches; there are also many government schools and colleges. Tamil is the primary language, Malayalam being spoken in the western parts of the district bordering Kerala.

Table 1 Population in Kanyakumari district by caste

Caste community	Percentage	Number
Scheduled Castes	8	134,083
Scheduled Tribes	0.4	6,704
Most Backward Communities	3.4	56,985
Backward Communities	70.2	1,176,576
Other Communities (Forward Communities)	18	301,686
Total Numbers	100	1,676,034

Source: State Planning Commission, *District Human Development Report: Kanyakumari District* (Madurai: Dhan Foundation, 2011).

Agriculture is the primary activity in the district, producing coconut, paddy, rubber, pepper, banana and many other fruits, tapioca and cashew. Among these, paddy and rubber are the primary cash crops. There are also various agricultural research stations and laboratories. The many educational institutions in the district provide a source of employment for people. And, since many schools and colleges which receive government aid are in the hands of either churches or caste Hindus, each employs people from the respective communities. One of my Hindu interviewees in Gramam said this generated ill feelings among Hindus from Nadar and other Scheduled Castes who were neither Christian nor caste Hindu, and is a source of tension.[27]

(e) Religions and Cults in Kanyakumari District

Table 2 shows the population by religious affiliation as per the 2001 census.[28]

As shown in the table, Hinduism, Christianity and Islam are the three major religions professed in Kanyakumari district. Hindus follow Saivite and Vaishnavite traditions and many other folk traditions. This district has had a strong Vaishnavite influence from early times, as many kings showed interest in it.[29] This political inclination supported the growth of Vaishnavism, expressed in many oral traditions and Vaishnavite temples.[30] The district was also influenced by Saivite traditions, after the incursion of Cholas to southern Travancore in the early period, with many Jain temples becoming Saivite under the later Chola kings.[31] Early attempts to convert the upper-caste people to Christianity in the southernmost parts of India during the sixteenth century were challenged by some rulers such as Naikkars,[32] who extended the awareness of Saivism among the common people with eight *maths* (temples) for Lord Siva, two in today's Kanyakumari district.[33] In spite of their affinity to Vaishnavite traditions, the Travancore kings maintained good relations with Siva temples.[34] There are sixty-four popular Siva temples found in the district,[35] and twelve Sivalayams (temples of Siva), with special worship on

Table 2 Population in Kanyakumari district by religion

Religion	Percentage	Number
Hindus	51.2703	859,307
Christians	44.4744	745,406
Muslims	4.1980	70,360
Jains	0.0046	77
Sikhs	0.0018	31
Buddhists	0.0016	26
Others	0.0067	113
No Religion	0.0426	714
Total Numbers	100	1,676,034

Source: State Planning Commission, *District Human Development Report: Kanyakumari District* (Madurai: Dhan Foundation, 2011).

the day of Sivarathri.[36] There are also temples for Muruga, son of Siva, mostly in the hills and mountains.

Folk deities are associated with Saivite traditions, the male folk deity, Sudalaimadan, being the image of Siva.[37] There are also many temples for goddesses, goddess worship being an important aspect of religious life here.[38] Goddess worship tradition is generally known as *Amman Vazhi* (way of the mother). Muttharamman, a popular female folk deity, is seen as Parvathi, Siva's wife, and is believed to have received *varam* (boon) from Siva enabling her to be worshipped by people. The images of weapons and *thiruneeru* (a flour-based material distributed to devotees during *pooja* and applied on the body and on the forehead during worship) in the folk temples are associated with Saivite traditions.[39] Moreover, the very name of the district – Kanyakumari – is the name of a female deity: Kanyakumari literally means 'virgin daughter' or 'virgin girl'. The Kanyakumari Amman temple located in Kanyakumari, close to the sea, represents Parvathi, Siva's wife.[40] The Mandaikadu temple, located in the area where the 1982 clashes started, was built to worship a female seer who worshipped there and was the first national temple of the Travancore monarch in 1805.[41] There are many other mother goddesses who are worshipped in the district, but Mutharamman, usually called the 'village deity', is the most popular. It is said that when the Hindu Nadars converted to Protestantism in the nineteenth century, they made a vow in Mutharamman temples that they would not return to their mother religion.[42] There is a special *Kodai* (festival) in these temples once a year or every three years.[43]

The *Ayya Vazhi* (the way of the father) movement is another tradition in the district which is often associated with Hinduism. This cult is a tradition which began in a small village Swamithoppu (near Gramam) in the southern part of the Kanyakumari district during the mid-nineteenth century, and spread to other districts in Tamil Nadu and to some parts of Kerala and other states. This cult was founded by a man named Muthukutti, now called by his followers Ayya Vaikundar, who claimed to be an avatara of Vishnu[44] and born in 1809 in Travancore in the oppressed Nadar caste. In the nineteenth century this tradition was believed to have influenced the lower-caste struggles against the upper castes in Travancore. Muthukutti became a leader of the people, challenging the caste hierarchy as well as teaching people spiritual principles. Those who follow him today are called Ayya Vazhi Bhakthas, and the temples of this cult are called '*pathi*'.[45] The central *pathi* is in Swamithoppu, where Muthukutti was buried. This cult is very popular among Nadar castes, and other people irrespective of caste also participate in it. Even though non-Ayya Vazhi people identify them as Hindus, most Ayya Vazhi people prefer to be known by their own name, rather than as Hindus.[46]

European Christianity came to Travancore during the fifteenth and sixteenth centuries, Syrian or Thomas Christians having lived in southern Travancore since the second century. The Portuguese arrived in South India at the end of the fifteenth century, and some attempted to convert the Syrian Christians in Kerala into Roman Catholics. When that failed they turned their attention to the Mukkuvas who were living in the coastal areas from Cochin to today's Kanyakumari district.

Their conversion to Christianity, however, was not good news to Syrian Christians, who considered themselves superior.[47] At this time, there was another fishing community, Paravas, living in the eastern and western coasts of today's Tamil Nadu and Kerala, who also wanted to become Christians and gain Portuguese protection from troublesome Muslims.[48] Eighty-five Parava leaders went to Cochin and were baptized, thus beginning Roman Catholic Christianity in Kanyakumari.[49] The Roman Catholic missionary Francis Xavier then came to Travancore, leading to mass conversions among the coastal Mukkuvas, virtually all of whom are Roman Catholic. Later, inland people converted to Roman Catholic Christianity, including castes such as Nadars and Vellalas. Thus until the beginning of the nineteenth century, Roman Catholic Christianity was the only Christianity which functioned in this region, other than the Orthodox Church for the small group of Keralite elites in the area.[50] The Roman Catholic Churches in the district came under Kottar Diocese (Kottar is a semi-urban centre which has been the headquarters of the Roman Catholic missionaries since Francis Xavier) from 1930, when the diocese split off from Kollam (now in Kerala) Diocese. There are about 500,000 members in this diocese as of the year 2000.[51]

In south Travancore, Protestant Christianity was introduced among an outcaste community called Sambavas. The first Protestant convert in Travancore was Vethamanikkam,[52] who invited William Tobias Ringeltaube, an LMS missionary working in the northern parts of Tamil Nadu, to come to Travancore[53]; as the area was controlled by the East India Company, Ringeltaube had to seek permission from Colonel Macaulay, which was granted.[54] Ringeltaube then established the first Protestant churches in the region. In the light of this incident, Agur, a local, twentieth-century church historian, says that but for brave interference of that one Company man, no missionary could have come to Travancore.[55] Ringeltaube started his work in a village called Mylaudy, which is in east Kanyakumari. He gave equal importance to church-building and educating the local people. LMS missionaries Charles Mead, Charles Malt and James Russell continued Taube's work in Travancore.[56] Even though initially the Sambavas were the focus of the missionary work of LMS missionaries, later Nadars, also at the bottom of society, converted to Christianity in large numbers due to oppression and suffering they were facing from the 'high-caste' people.[57] Slowly the Sambavas and other castes felt that they were sidelined within the church, and so when the Salvation Army came to the region, the Sambavas and other outcastes embraced it.[58] Currently there are about 300 Salvation Army churches in the district, with 50,000 members. Later American Lutheran Church missionaries also worked among the Sambavas.[59] There are now a few Lutheran churches, and their seminary – Concordia Theological Seminary – in the district.[60]

Churches established by the LMS missionaries were known as LMS churches, becoming part of the CSI when it was formed in 1947 as 'CSI South Travancore Diocese'.[61] After Kanyakumari district was formed in 1956, the CSI South Travancore Diocese split into CSI South Kerala Diocese and CSI Kanyakumari Diocese in 1959. Today there are about 500 churches and 300,000 members in the CSI Kanyakumari Diocese.[62] In addition, there are many Pentecostal Christians living in the district,[63] belonging to different Pentecostal groups such as the Indian Pentecostal Church, Assemblies of God, Ceylon Pentecostal Church and many independent churches. Commonly Pentecostals are often termed 'fringe groups' by the members of the mainline churches because they are seen as representing somewhat the extreme fundamentalist side of Christianity with no interest in dialogue, holding exclusivist views towards other religions and insisting on the superiority of Christianity.[64]

The arrival and growth of Islam in Travancore is a less researched field, but there are many oral traditions existing today regarding Islam in Travancore, which arrived long ago. According to Samuel Mateer, a missionary historian during colonial times, 62,639 Muslims lived in Travancore in 1861.[65] Arabs came to the coastal area of today's Kerala as merchants from about AD 712,[66] Shi'as and Sunnis settling and propagating their faith in Travancore some hundred years later.[67] The Muslims in this region are called *Mappillai*, *Tulukkan* and *Matthen*. The term Mappillai has emerged due to Arabs marrying women from Kerala, Tullukkan refers to those who have come from Turkey and Matthen refers to a male from Mecca.[68] Colachel, Kottar and Thengapatanam are a few villages in today's Kanyakumari district where Muslims are believed to be living since the eighth century,[69] forming many *mohallas* (neighbourhood).[70] Some of the mosques in the district are more than 700 years old and witness to Islam's contribution to Indian arts and culture.[71] Currently, there are two Muslim colleges offering education to people. Muslims are involved in trading activities, and are the third major religious community in the district.

It is believed that Buddhism came to Kanyakumari in the time following emperor Ashoka,[72] one of the Ai dynasty kings who ruled this region, and Vikramadhithya Varagunan (AD 885–925) possibly being a Buddhist, while also favouring Jainism.[73] There are Buddhist elements in the Mandaikadu Bhagavathi Amman temple. The Bhakthas who come to Mandaikadu from Kerala used to chant *Amma Saranam*, *Devi Saranam*, which is similar to the *Sangam Saranam*, *Dharmam Saranam* of Buddhism. One deity in the temple is believed to be Buddha; the folk deity 'Sastha' is assumed by local people to be an image of Buddha.[74]

Jains came to South India over two millennia ago, their traditions being popular until the end of the Venad kings.[75] From the fourth to the tenth century, Jains came to pilgrimage sites in the region.[76] The Nagaraja temple in Nagercoil was a Jain temple until the sixteenth century, although it and many others became Saivite during the Chola period.[77] Archaeological works undertaken by the Tamil Nadu government have unearthed the significance of Jainism in early South India, especially in Kanyakumari district, leading to renewed interest in Jainism among dialogue activists in the region.[78]

In today's context, even though Buddhism and Jainism have almost disappeared in the district, as Table 2 shows, Hinduism, Christianity and Islam are vibrant. As Kanyakumari district is very small, daily interactions between members are inevitable. Because of this multireligious nature of the district, this district is often stated as a model district for others, yet the absence of and need for dialogue is pointed out by dialogists from time to time.[79] I will return to discuss this anomaly in Chapters 6 and 7, where I will discuss the ambiguities found in dialogue circles regarding the relationship between people in the district.

(f) Political Background

Kanyakumari district has seven state constituencies: Kanyakumari, Nagercoil, Colachel, Padmanabhapuram, Thiruvattar, Vilavancode and Killiyoor.[80] While six of these seven constituencies constitute the parliamentary constituency called Nagercoil, the Kanyakumari state constituency was under Tiruchendoor constituency, until the 2004 parliamentary elections.[81] Since 2009, the Kanyakumari Lok Sabha constituency represents all state constituencies.[82] The Indian National Congress has won the Nagercoil seat, fourteen out of fifteen times between 1957 and 2009,[83] the BJP winning in 1999.[84] In the recent election of 2014, the BJP won again. The Tiruchendoor Lok Sabha seat usually goes to the Congress party,[85] and in 2009, it went to the United Progressive Alliance (UPA) led by the Indian National Congress. In the Tamil Nadu state assembly elections Dravida Munnetra Kazhagam (DMK) and Anna Dravida Munnetra Kazhagam (ADMK) are the two major political parties, others including the Indian National Congress, Communist Party of India, Communist Party of India (Marxist), Marumalarchi Dravida Munnetra Kazhagam (MDMK), Desia Murpokku Dravida Kazhagam (DMDK) and BJP. Kanyakumari district is one of the few areas contested by the BJP since its inception, and the first seat won by BJP in 1996 was Padmanabhapuram in Kanyakumari district.[86] In the most recent elections conducted in six legislative assembly constituencies in the district, in 2011, ADMK won two seats, the UPA (DMK and INC being allies) winning four.[87]

As the religious identities of people are almost equally divided between Hindu and Christian in the district, political parties have been attempting to make use of those identities in their electoral competition. In this context, BJP's arrival, with its focus on Hindutva ideologies, has aggravated the tensions between political parties in the district.[88] It is generally observed that Muslims, Christians and communists join to vote against BJP.[89] However, the local voting pattern does not just follow religious identities; various other issues such as caste, region and other issues play a role.[90] Nevertheless, religious identities are used in campaigns, especially by the BJP, whether they work out in the end or not — a process thought to aggravate tensions between people of different religions.[91] In short, Kanyakumari district has long been a region of many different faith traditions and different caste communities, and there is and perhaps has always been the potential for certain groups, including political parties such as BJP, to explicitly manipulate religious identity for political ends.

2 A Brief Outline of the Practice of Dialogue in Kanyakumari District

My purpose in this section is to show the development of dialogue in the district and the agencies, organizations and major activists involved, and to outline the programmes undertaken to further dialogue in order to discuss later how they are promoting elitist dialogue. In order to study and understand the dialogue organizations, activists and programmes, I make use of published works such as books, articles, brochures, information and notices about dialogue programmes, unpublished materials such as theses and reports, interviews with dialogue activists during my fieldwork and my observations from my experience of participating in dialogue for many years.

(a) The Context of Dialogue in the District

There are different opinions found among dialogue activists on the origin of dialogue in the district, and in my interviews they were particularly emphasizing the beginning of dialogue. For some, especially Roman Catholics, dialogue has been part of the community here since the 1950s for developing common spirituality and mutual understanding.[92] For others it is attributed to the influence of international ecumenical efforts through Vatican II and WCC, which provided encouragement for initiating dialogue activities. Roman Catholics hold that Vatican II was instrumental in the progress of dialogue activities in the district[93]; Protestants cite the influence of the work of CISRS, Bangalore, WCC and the activities of the Tamil Nadu Theological Seminary (TTS), Madurai, which is around 200 kilometres from Kanyakumari. All these laid the ground for Christian involvement in local dialogue since the 1970s.[94]

The predominant view on the emergence of dialogue in the district is related to the occurrence of the 'Mandaikadu religious conflicts' between Hindus and Christians in 1982. For instance, Abdul Salaam, a Muslim dialogue activist, said that

> Mandaikadu[95] was the real context in which the absence of dialogue and relationship between religious communities was seriously felt and efforts were needed to heal the wounds inflicted by the clashes. Generally, the people in the district were relating to each other as brothers and sisters, but Mandaikadu was a black mark because it broke all those relationships. Mutual suspicion started to grow among people, and all of a sudden everyone started to look at each other with mistrust and hate.[96]

Many dialogists hold a similar view that dialogue activities in the district are fundamentally linked to the conflicts. P. Nagalingam, a dialogue activist from the Hindu community, a retired principal in a local college, said that after the clashes, 'dialogue and communal harmony have become the existential necessity for the people belonging to different religions living in the district.'[97] Even those who hold the view that dialogue was functioning even before Mandaikadu affirm that with Mandaikadu the objectives of dialogue changed. Tobias says,

> Dialogue in Kanyakumari district in the pre-Mandaikadu period was concentrating much on the themes of common spirituality and meditation.

However, after the occurrence of Mandaikadu conflicts in 1982, the main objectives in dialogue are to work for peace and reconciliation between conflicting religious communities. It does not mean that the earlier themes of spirituality and contemplation have been given up, rather they serve as one of the means in dialogue for working for peace and reconciliation.[98]

This presentation of dialogue as a new entrant into the district – even though the particulars of its arrival may vary – is one of the popular discourses in dialogue that allows little space for the ongoing everyday relations among people. It has almost become the reality in the dialogue circles in the district that one cannot speak about dialogue without reference to the Mandaikadu religious conflicts.

(b) Organizations and Activists Involved in Dialogue

The emergence of various dialogue organizations and activists is always set against such a context of religious conflicts. The Roman Catholic Church in Kanyakumari has its Dialogue Commission – even though it was set up in 1975, dialogue activists associated with it claim that it became active after the Mandaikadu clashes.[99] CSI Kanyakumari Diocese, the major Protestant denomination in the region, worked through its programme called Multi-Religious Education by Extension in Tamil (MEET) for a while in the 1970s and 1980s and revived it in the last few years.[100]

Among Muslims in the district there are various organizations involved in social and dialogue activities based on Islam. Two such organizations are Islamiya Kalachara Kazhagam (Islamic Cultural Organization) based in Nagercoil, and Rahmaniya Sangam (Rahmaniya Society).[101] They mainly organize the celebration of different religious festivals and national days such as Independence Day and Republic Day and conduct seminars, consultations and public meetings on communal harmony and related themes.

The NGO CIRSJA, started as the CPJ in 1985, has been involved in interreligious activities for the last twenty-five years. Started in the aftermath of Mandaikadu conflicts, it promotes dialogue activities based on the assumption that religious misunderstanding among people is the cause of religious clashes, and that educating the people to understand different religions through dialogue is the only way to overcome these conflicts.[102] But, claiming that Kanyakumari district is a 'model district' for communal harmony, it has been involved in dialogue programmes at the national level in different states, called 'State-wide Conventions on Communal Harmony'.[103]

Thiruvarutperavai (literally meaning 'the Council of Revered Grace'), another NGO, was founded immediately after the Mandaikadu riots in 1982. The idea was inspired by the visit of Kundrakudi Adigal, a highly revered Hindu Sadhu in Tamil Nadu who was the Acharya of the Kundrakudi Ashram in Ramanathapuram near Madurai and well known for his ideas on religious harmony during the aftermath of the conflicts.[104] Its primary programmes include conducting occasional dialogue meetings and celebrating religious festivals. Dialogue activists from different religions have given leadership to this organization.[105]

In addition, there are a number of other NGOs in the district which, although their primary work is not on dialogue and communal harmony, are occasionally involved in such programmes. Moreover, government officials such as the district collector, superintendent of police, district court judges and other local administrative and police officials also encourage interreligious programmes by addressing participants on communal harmony. This is done mostly in public meetings on themes related to communal harmony, and not in actual dialogue meetings. Ministers in both state and central government and MLAs and MPs also participate in such programmes and speak about communal harmony.[106] One of the obvious reasons for such encouragement from the government is for maintaining law and order in the district, and from that perspective they speak high dialogue.[107]

This plethora of dialogue organizations in a relatively small district is an example for how dialogue has been central to many of the educated elites there. There is often a pride in multireligious groups giving leadership to these organizations or their programme committees. Such multireligious leadership and the occasional coming together of different religious people, rather than the everyday life situations of people with all the attendant limitations, is projected as an example of the ideal living situation in a multireligious context. For instance, at another level, one of the dialogists in the district in an informal discussion said that how during the late 2000s India had a Sikh prime minister, a Christian at the head of the party that formed the government, a Hindu president and a Muslim vice-president. This is a perfect example of dialogical situation according to him. This kind of essentialism has posed serious problems for dialogue.

(c) Dialogue Programmes

Due to their assumption of the lack of dialogue among common people, these organizations are rushing to conduct interreligious programmes at various levels: continuing, short-term and occasional programmes. Continuing programmes are the raison d'être of interreligious organizations, and short-term programmes are run for a limited period to promote dialogue. In addition, occasional dialogue programmes are arranged in connection with festivals or other celebrations. In terms of their execution, both long-term and short-term programmes are of two types: bringing people into a central place or going out to them. Programmes of the former type are held usually in the capital of the district, Nagercoil, or semi-urban places such as Kanyakumari, which is some 20 kilometres from Nagercoil or Marthandam, which is around 35 kilometres from Nagercoil.[108] Many interreligious organizations are also located in one of these places. For instance, the head offices of both the CSI and the Roman Catholic Church – and so their respective departments for dialogue – are located in Nagercoil, CIRSJA in Kanyakumari, and PWDS in Marthandam. The second type of execution programme is to go and visit villages and arrange awareness programmes, training people and celebrating festivals. I shall discuss some of the dialogue programmes below.

(i) Dialogue Meetings Actual dialogue meetings are arranged regularly, perhaps once or twice a month, which target the interested people who are obviously elites. An attitude of openness to other religions is firmly expected from the participants. Tobias said that they 'invite people who are open-minded about other religions. It is a necessary criterion for dialogue, so dialogue is just meant for them.'[109] For Panivanban Vincent,

> the participants should be willing to learn from other religions, and should not come with the attitude of superiority of their religion attitude. And they should appreciate the multi-religious context and be willing to work for peace and harmony in the context of religious conflicts.[110]

This shows how the attitude of openness is formalized in dialogue circles. Those who attend these meetings are mostly males over the age of forty, with few women and youth.[111] When asked about the participation of women and youth, Panivanban Vincent said that 'the absence of youth and women is often felt, but the development is not satisfactory'.[112] Even though education is not a primary criterion, most of the dialogue participants are educated people such as pastors, teachers, lecturers – some retired – and some working in government and private sectors.[113]

In the dialogue meetings, the participants are expected to talk about their respective religions and to actively participate in discussions.[114] Often in these meetings common themes are approached from different religious viewpoints[115] by the respective religious adherents, who would have done some research and reflection on the theme, followed by discussions.[116] Some of the themes discussed in the dialogue meetings are communal harmony, spirituality, common community, salvation, revelation of God, justice, peace, nation-building, religion and women, religion and poverty, science and religion, scriptures, non-violence, unity, humanism in religion, and religion and politics. The participants of dialogue believe that these kinds of meetings are essential for keeping communal harmony in society.[117] The elite nature of the dialogue programmes also can be understood in the light of the places where dialogue meetings are regularly arranged: Concordia Theological Seminary, Scott Christian College, Sethu Lakshmi Bai School, Pon Jesley School Roman Catholic Bishop's House, all in Nagercoil Nesamony Memorial Christian College in Marthandam College; and Anmeega Thottam, Thozhamai Illam, CIRSJA and the Young Men's Christian Association Campus in Kanyakumari.[118] Auditoriums and halls are also hired for this purpose.[119]

Occasional dialogue meetings are also arranged, which may conclude with public meetings on the theme of communal harmony. Such meetings are usually attended by people from other districts and even other states.[120] Nationally and internationally recognized scholars are invited to talk about the themes related to dialogue and peace, followed by discussion. Unlike the regular dialogue meetings, occasional dialogue meetings last for from one day to three days. Interreligious worship is given emphasis, and it is experimented during these rather 'residential' dialogue programmes.[121]

(ii) Awareness Programmes for Dialogue The dialogists in the district also heavily insist on the awareness programmes about dialogue arranged for various groups of people. First, awareness programmes for school students and college youth are prominent, with meetings arranged in schools and colleges.[122] Interested teachers are consulted, and through them arrangements are made. The teachings of different religions on themes such as peace, justice, unity and harmony are brought out for students. At college level, students are encouraged to think about how their respective disciplines (mainly in humanities and social sciences) can help the cause of communal harmony and unity among people.[123] Some other forms of awareness programmes include inviting students to participate in competitions such as essay, slogan and poetry writing, and creating music and songs related to the communal harmony theme.[124]

Secondly, awareness meetings are arranged for people in villages, and for this self-help groups in rural places are made use of.[125] Workers in the dialogue organizations go to different villages usually in the evening from 4.00 pm to 6.00 pm; some meetings have half-day or one-day programmes. The common point emphasized in these meetings is that for a harmonious life in the district people should have deep faith in their own religions, should learn to respect other religions and should not consider their religions to be superior to other religions. Interested and efficient people who would further popularize the ideal of dialogue are identified and invited to regular dialogue meetings.[126] Local-level youth groups are also then formed to continue awareness activities in the area.[127]

Thirdly, awareness programmes are arranged aiming at the wider public audience in the district. These are primarily communal harmony processions and peace rallies on foot or bicycle,[128] attended by the workers and members of interreligious organizations. Sometimes local school and college students are also involved in such processions and rallies.[129] Communal harmony slogans are prepared and recited as the rally moves.[130] These processions end in public meetings where the wider audience is addressed by dialogue activists and other political and government dignitaries regarding the importance of peace and harmony in society.[131] Games and sports are also used to create awareness, and various athletics including marathon races are conducted, especially before public meetings on this theme.[132] As I observed in the Introduction, common people often view these programmes as one-time events conducted like a public meeting involving political authorities in the district.

(iii) Training Programmes for Dialogue In addition to awareness programmes, dialogue organizations and activists in the district are also involved in training programmes to further their task of overcoming conflicts. Conferences and seminars or workshops are conducted for people interested in dialogue for two to three days. Such events are a little different from regular dialogue meetings, as scholars of religion and dialogue come and give talks or read papers, which the participants then discuss. Here the focus is more on how to dialogue, and on the objectives and nature of dialogue. Hence unlike the actual dialogue meetings they serve more to train participants. However, they also serve as actual dialogue

programmes, because people from different religions attend.[133] Tobias said that he has been involved in organizing many training programmes, and he felt that residential programmes are more productive in leading to dialogue than the regular dialogue meetings because participants experience 'living together'.[134] Moreover, in these programmes interreligious worship is arranged for the participants, demonstrating the importance of dialogue.[135]

Moreover, reflective assignments are given to the participants in these meetings, and they are asked to go to nearby villages to talk to people from other religions and make a report when they come back. On the basis of their experience further suggestions are offered by the organizers about how the participants should approach people of other religions dialogically.[136] The feedback session is intended to help all participants. Tobias said participants find the exercise very helpful in improving their dialogical skills.[137] Training for pastors is also arranged. These illustrate how a kind of 'living together' and a multireligious situatedness is somewhat 'created' during these programmes, ignoring how people live with multiple identities in their ordinary situations.

(iv) Multireligious Celebration of Festivals Celebrating different religious festivals as a multireligious group is considered to be an important aspect of dialogue programmes in Kanyakumari district,[138] executed in various ways depending upon the scope and interest of each organization. Diwali, primarily celebrated by Hindus, Ramzan celebrated by Muslims and Christmas by Christians are some festivals of interest to local dialogue activists. Sometimes each festival is celebrated individually, and sometimes they are celebrated together as most fall between October and January.[139] They take place in urban and rural centres. Festivals in Nagercoil tend to be rather elitist, dialogue organizers being invited as well as government officials and political personalities. Three people representing Hinduism, Christianity and Islam talk about the respective festivals, sometimes approaching all festivals from one religious perspective. Sometimes these celebrations are followed by a shared dinner.[140]

The celebrations of festivals as multireligious groups also are conducted in villages, usually sponsored by local dialogue organizations. A village in the district is selected – sometimes this is called 'adopted' – by the interreligious groups for this event.[141] Mixed-faith sites are preferred, and the interreligious groups, with the help of the local village leaders, do the preparations[142] and invite local politicians and district administration officials. The main part of the programme contains speeches on festivals and communal harmony; although in villages discussions do not follow speeches.[143] The multireligious celebration of festivals is seen as one of the most fruitful ways of making grassroots people aware of dialogue. One of my interviewees, Kasthoori Chokkalingam, a Hindu dialogue activist, opined that 'this is the only effective way through which we can take dialogue to the "ordinary" people at the grassroots'.[144]

In the previous chapter I offered a theoretical background for my discussions. In this chapter I discussed how many of the features noted in theologies of dialogue are practically executed in Kanyakumari district. This discussion illustrates how even in a relatively rural district dialogue remains elitist, aiming to thrust its own understanding of religious plurality and identity, ignoring living experiences of common people. Based on these, Part II will critically discuss how ideas on religion(s), world religions and religious-secular distinctions have been developed and incorporated in dialogical activities in India and specifically in Kanyakumari district; how the notion of 'religious' conflicts is uncritically accepted and posed as the context of dialogue; and how elite dialogue has neglected the actual everyday intercommunity relations among people at the grassroots.

Notes

1 A taluk is a subdivision of a district.

2 A panchayat refers to a rural or urban local government administrative body.

3 Swami Vivekananda is one of the Hindu revivalists of the nineteenth century. He is believed to have visited Kanyakumari and prayed on a rock (at a particular point inside the sea) on which this memorial has been erected.

4 For example, C. M. Agur, from Sambava caste community, which is a Scheduled Caste community, was one of the first locals to write the church history of the area, *Church History of Travancore* ([1903] New Delhi: Asian Educational Services, 1990). He traced the origin of Christianity in Travancore to one Vethamanikkam from his community. This was not questioned for almost 100 years, but recent writings show the author was related to Vethamanikkam and perhaps biased in claiming the local origin of Christianity to his community; K. Sukumaran, *Kristhuvukku Mutharkani? [The First Fruit for Christ?]* (Nagercoil: Santhini Publishers, 2004). Other recent local history takes the lens of caste conflicts especially between Nadars and Nairs (also called Pillai). Ivee Peter and D. Peter, *Malayali Aathikkamum Thamizhar Viduathalayum [The Domination of Malayalis and the Liberation of Tamils]* (Nagercoil: Kanyakumari Institute of Development Studies, 2002); K. Sukumaran, *Cherar Varalaarum Makkal Vaazhviyalum [The History and Life of Cheras]* (Nagercoil: Santhini Publishers, 2005). Hindutva-influenced history divides the district on the basis of religion and not caste, which they insist is disappearing from the district. For instance, see M. Gopalakrishnan, ed., *Gazatteers of India, Tamil Nadu State: Kanyakumari District* (Madras: Government of Tamil Nadu, 1995), 117.

5 Peter and Peter, *Malayali Aathikkamum*, 1.

6 Ibid., 132.

7 Ibid., 35–6.

8 These agitations and the subsequent violence by the state to control the protests by the Tamils in the region are important for this study, as these tensions are also linked to the current religious violence as shown by some of the social scientists working in the region. These will be elaborated in Chapter 6, where the case study of religious conflicts in the district is undertaken.

9 C. Thangamani, ed., *Kanyakumari Maavattam: Arasiyal-Samuga Varalaru [Kanyakumari District: Political-Social History]* (Chennai: Kanyakumari District Historical Council, 2005).

10 A. L. Basham, *The Wonder that was India*, Fontana Ancient History, 3rd impression (Delhi: Rupa & Co., 1975), 151; S. Manickam, *Slavery in the Tamil Country: A Historical Overview* (Madras: CLS, 1982).

11 Manickam, *Slavery in the Tamil Country*, 15.

12 Basham, *Wonder that was India*, 151.

13 Gopalakrishnan, *Gazetteers*, 117.

14 Contemporary local writing shows that both historical and contemporary life is based on caste differences. Writing on the social, cultural and historical contexts of the district, Ivee Peter, D. Peter and Sukumaran challenge the no-caste notion in the district. Peter and Peter, *Malayali Aathikkamum*, xiii−xvii, see past and present tensions between Tamils in Kanyakumari and Malayalis (people living in Kerala) as caste conflicts between Nairs and Nadars in the region; this will be discussed in Chapter 6. See also Sukumaran, *Kumari Sirpi Nesamonyum Thenkumari Thamizh Makkalum* [*Kanyakumari Maker Nesamony and the Tamil People of South Kanyakumari*] (Nagercoil: Sandini Publishers, 2004); *Cherar Varalaarum; Kumariyai Meeton Marshan Nesamony* [*Marshal Nesamony, the Saviour of Kanyakumari*] (Nagercoil: Shanthini Publishers, 2007). The prevalence of caste as a basis of discord is commonly held by those opposed to Hindu nationalists: C. Chokkalingam, *Matham, Panbaadu: Sila Maruthedalhal* [*Religion and Culture: Some Re-searches*] (Nagercoil: Thinnai Publishers, 2000).

15 For instance, governments in India still ask for caste details for education and employment.

16 GoTN, *Venugopal Commission*, 20−1; for a critique of Hindutva's position on this, see Satish Deshpande, *Contemporary India: A Sociological View* (New Delhi: Penguin, 2003).

17 State Planning Commission, *District Human Development Report: Kanyakumari District* (Madurai: Dhan Foundation, 2011), 5.

18 Gopalakrishnan, *Gazetteers*, 118.

19 Ibid., 117.

20 Ibid., 120−1.

21 Ibid., 117; see also S. R. Narcheesan, *Kumari Kristhavargalin Payana Paathai* [*The Journey of Christians in Kanyakumari*] (Nagercoil: Nanjil Publishers, 2000), 113−16.

22 Gopalakrishnan, *Gazetteers*, 117. For a general study of Tamil Nadu which also includes information about Nadars in Kanyakumari region, see Robert Hardgrave, *The Nadars of Tamil Nadu* (Berkeley: University of California Press, 1969).

23 Gopalakrishnan, *Gazetteers*, 117−18.

24 http://www.tn.gov.in/schooleducation/statistics/table7and8.htm.

25 Ivee Peter and D. Peter, *Samaya Thondargalum Samudhaaya Marumalarchiyum* [*Religious Leaders and Social Reformation*] (Nagercoil: Kanyakumari Institute of Development Studies, 1999), 75−92. Dick Kooiman, 'Who is to Benefit from Missionary Education? Travancore in the 1930s,' in *Missionary Encounters: Sources and Issues*, ed. Robert A. Bickers and Rosemary Seton (Surrey: Curzon Press, 1996), 153−73.

26 A. K. Perumal, *Thenkumariyin Kathai* [*The Story of Kanyakumari*] (Chennai: United Writers Publishers, 2003), 290.

27 Vishnu, Interview, Gramam, 2 June 2008.

28 State Planning Commission, *District Human Development Report*, 5.

29 Perumal, *Thenkumariyin Kathai*, 194.

30 S. Padmanabhan, *The Contribution of Kanyakumari to the Tamil World* (Nagercoil: Kumaran Pathippagam, 1981), 18−19.

31 Perumal, *Thenkumariyin Kathai*, 201.

32 Narcheesan, *Kumari Kristhavargalin*, 44−5.

33 Perumal, *Thenkumariyin Kathai*, 202−6.

34 Ibid., 202.

35 S. Padmanabhan, *Temples in Kanyakumari District* (Nagercoil: Kumaran Pathippagam, 1980).

36 Perumal, *Thenkumariyin Kathai*, 206. Sivarathiri means the great night of Siva.

37 Gopalakrishnan, *Gazetteers*, 118−20.

38 Vikraman Thambi and Shenbaga Perumal, *Varalatril Mandaikadu* [*Mandaikadu in History*] (Kanyakumari: Triveni Publishers, 1988); see also Perumal, *Thenkumariyin Kathai*, 213−19.

39 Perumal, *Thenkumariyin Kathai*, 213.

40 M. Immanuel, *Kanniyakumari: Aspects and Architects* (Nagercoil: Historical Research & Publications Trust, 2007), 2.

41 Perumal, *Thenkumariyin Kathai*, 213.

42 Ibid., 216.

43 Ibid., 217.

44 Some studies on this movement are found in Peter, *Samaya Thondargalum*; G. Patrick, *Religion and Subaltern Agency: A Case Study of Ayya Vali* (Chennai: Department of Christian Studies, University of Madras, 2003); V. Yesudhason and R. Isaac Jayadhas, *History of Tamil Society and Culture since 1336* (Kanyakumari: MCL Roy Publications, 2002), 33−6; R. Ponnu, *Thenkodiyil Oru Samuthaya Puratchi* [*A Social Revolution in Southern End*] (Nagercoil: Thenkumari Publishers), 1987.

45 Perumal, *Thenkumariyin Kathai*, 220.

46 Parvathi, Interview, Gramam, 23 June 2008. Parvathi is a resident of Gramam and a follower of the Ayya Vazhi.

47 Narcheesan, *Kumari Kristhavargalin*, 30.

48 Perumal, *Thenkumariyin Kathai*, 252.

49 Narcheesan, *Kumari Kristhavargalin*, 30. By the seventeenth century, it is believed, there were about 80,000 Catholics living in fifty different places in South Travancore.

50 Gopalakrishnan, *Gazetteers*, 121.

51 Narcheesan, *Kumari Kristhavargalin*, 9.

52 Joy Gnanadason, *Oru Marakkappatta Varalaru* [*A Forgotten History*] (Madurai: Indian Kalvi Kazhagam, 1998), 50. But as I have mentioned earlier there are now disputes about this.

53 Narcheesan, *Kumari Kristhavargalin*, 97.

54 Peter, *Samaya Thondargalum*, 81.

55 Agur, *Church History*. For a study of relationship between missionaries as colonial administrators in the wider missionary context, see Andrew Porter, *Religion versus Empire? British Protestant Missionaries and Overseas Expansion, 1700−1914* (Manchester: Manchester University Press), 2004.

56 Peter, *Samaya Thondargalum*, 75−127.

57 J. W. Gladstone, *Protestant Christianity and People's Movements in Kerala 1850−1936* (Trivandrum: Seminary Publications, 1984). Also, M. Immanuel, *The Dravidian Lineages − A Socio-Historical Study: The Nadars through the Ages* (Nagercoil: Historical Research & Publications Trust), 2002.

58 Narcheesan, *Kumari Kristhavargalin*, 118−19.

59 D. Christudas, *Impact of Lutheran Mission among Sambavars in South Travancore from 1907 to 1956* (New Delhi: ISPCK, 2008), 31−71.

60 In the initial days of dialogue in this district, this seminary has provided space for conducting dialogue meetings. Rajamony, Interview.

61 Narcheesan, *Kumari Kristhavargalin*, 135.

62 http://www.csi-kanyakumari.org/About.htm.

63 Narcheesan, *Kumari Kristhavargalin*, 186.

64 I have seen this common practice in the district. In my interviews, Samuel Dhasan, a Christian layman involved in dialogue, was critical of Pentecostal attitudes to dialogue. For him, because Pentecostals affirm the superiority of Christianity and continue their conversion activities, the other religious communities view all Christians in the district with suspicion. Dhasan, Interview, Kottaram, 26 June 2008. He discusses similar concerns in his book *Samaya Amaippukkalum Samuthaya Pracchnaikalum* [*Religious organizations and social problems*] (Kanyakumari: Centre for Peace and Justice, n.d).

65 Samuel Mateer, *The Land of Charity* (London: John Snow & Co., 1871); Perumal, *Thenkumariyin Kathai*, 273.

66 Gopalakrishnan, *Gazetteers*, 123.

67 Perumal, *Thenkumariyin Kathai*, 274.

68 Ibid., 273.

69 Abu Hashima, *Pettagam: Kumari Mavatta Muslimkalin Varalaattru Pokkisham* [*Box: The Historical Treasure of the Muslims of Kanyakumari District*] (Nagercoil: Rahmaniya Society, 2001), 157.

70 Hashima, *Pettagam*, 195.

71 Perumal, *Thenkumariyin Kathai*, 278.

72 Ibid., 239.

73 Ibid., 240.

74 Thambi, *Varalatril*, 9.

75 Perumal, *Thenkumariyin Kathai*, 242.

76 Ibid., 242−3.

77 Padmanabhan, *The Contribution of Kanyakumari*, 31−2.

78 Sitaram Gurumoorthy, *Kanyakumari Mavatta Tholliyal*; *Kanyakumari Mavatta Kalvettukal* [*Kanyakumari District Inscriptions*] (Chennai: GoTN Archaeology Department, 2008). Also Rajamony, Interview.

79 This is common in the district, and often mentioned by dialogue activists and government official or political elites in big public meetings on communal harmony: almost every informant referred to it, as does writing on dialogue focusing Kanyakumari district. For example, see Jegat Kaspar, *Intha Mann Mathaveriyai Vellum* [*This Land will Do Away with Religious Extremism*] (Kanyakumari: Naalai Publication, 1995), 31. In this text the author wonders how this district, known for communal harmony, has become a place for religious clashes, and he is optimistic that the district will eliminate extremism. Also, Maria Vincent, *Urayadal Vazhi Uravai Valarppom* [*Let Us Improve Our Relationships through Dialogue*] (Nagercoil: Nanjil, 2000).

80 http://www.travelindia-guide.com/assembly-elections/tamil-nadu/kanniyakumari-constituencies/.

81 http://election.rediff.com/slide-show/2009/may/12/slide-show-1-constituency-profile-kanyakumari.htm.

82 Ibid.

83 Election Commission of India (ECI), *Statistical Report of General Elections*, 1957−2009. These are available in their ECI website.

84 ECI, *General Elections, 1999*, vol. 1, 230.

85 ECI, *General Elections, 1957−2009*.

86 ECI, *General Elections, 1996*, 376.

87 http://eci.nic.in/eci_main/CurrentElections/eci2011.html.
88 Ponneelan, Interview, Nagercoil, 5 July 2008. Ponneelan is a popular Novelist who has won the Sahitya Akademi award.
89 One of my interviewees from the BJP political sphere mentioned this to me in his accusations against Christians and Muslims. Velan, Interview.
90 Recently there was an interesting article criticizing the claim that people vote only according to religious affinities. Shahid Siddiqui, 'Believe Me, Muslims are Not a Herd,' *The Hindu*, 5 February 2012.
91 Kaspar, *Intha Mann*, 43–5.
92 Tobias, Interview; Panivanban Vincent, Interview, Kanyakumari, 24 June 2008. Vincent is a Catholic priest who is involved in dialogue activities.
93 Jayaraj, Interview, Kanyakumari, 6 June 2008. Jayaraj is a Roman Catholic priest and the secretary of the Dialogue Commission in the district.
94 Rajamony, Interview. He has detailed several dialogical activities in the district in an article published by CISRS. 'Dialogue in Kanyakumari in the Context of Mission.' *Religion and Society* XXVI, no. 1 (1979): 78–87. J. Solomon, Interview, London, 6 October 2007. J. Solomon is a presbyter of the CSI Kanyakumari Diocese, associated with CISRS and dialogue organizations in Kanyakumari district, and is now working in the United Kingdom for promoting dialogue in schools. Israel Selvanayagam, noted in Chapter 1, also hails from this district and has been actively engaged in dialogue in the district, in TTS, in the general Indian context and international circles: interviewed in Birmingham, 5 October 2007.
95 Sometimes in the context of dialogue, 'Mandaikadu religious conflicts' are referred to as just 'Mandaikadu.'
96 Salaam, Interview.
97 P. Nagalingam, Interview, Nagercoil, 12 July 2008. Nagalingam is a Hindu dialogue activist, retired principal of a local college.
98 Tobias, Interview.
99 To my question that if Mandaikadu conflicts were a turning point why was there a dialogue commission before the conflicts, their response was that the changed approach of Vatican II to other religions as well as the specifically multireligious nature of the district were the reasons for such initiatives being taken even before the clashes happened.
100 C. Rajamony, *Samaya Panmayum Suthanthiramum* [*Freedom of Religion and Pluralism*] (Nagercoil: Pushba Publishers, 1993), 45–8.
101 M. Ahmad Khan, Interview, 3 July 2008.
102 Gnana Robinson, 'From Apartheid to Dialogical Living in India: The Need of the Hour,' *Religion and Society* 46, no. 1/2 (1999): 82–96.
103 CIRSJA, *Annual Report*, 2002.
104 Khan, Interview.
105 Maria Vincent, Interview, Thuckalay, 9 July 2008.
106 While I was working with CIRSJA, I often observed this trend. Peace Trust, *A Report on Inter-religious Celebration of Deepavali* [*Diwali*] *Festival on October 20, 1998 at Surankudi Village*, Kanyakumari, 1998; CIRSJA, *A Report of Multi-religious Celebration of Diwali, Ramzan and Christmas in the S.L.B. Hr. Secondary School, School, January, 5, 2002*, Kanyakumari, 2002.
107 I have personally witnessed such acknowledgement many times from government officials such as district collector, and politicians and ministers.

108 Almost all my interviewees involved in dialogue mentioned these places as the location of their regular dialogue programs.

109 Tobias, Interview.

110 Panivanban Vincent, Interview.

111 Nagalingam, Interview.

112 Panivanban Vincent, Interview.

113 Dhasan, Interview.

114 Rajamony, Interview.

115 S. Shenbaga Perumal, Interview, Mandaikadu, 13 July 2008. Perumal is a Hindu lay person involved in dialogue, working as a teacher in a school, hails from a village near Mandaikadu.

116 Tobias, Interview.

117 Ibid.

118 Rajamony; Tobias; Jayaraj; Interviews; Arthur J. Harris, Interview, Marthandam, 10 July 2008.

119 Auditoriums and halls in lodges are also hired for dialogue meetings, sometimes freely given by the owners as this involves community welfare work; Dhasan, Interview.

120 Dhasan, Interview. CIRSJA has arranged some such meetings. CIRSJA, *Annual Report*, 2000, 2001, 2002.

121 Tobias, Interview.

122 Harris, Interview.

123 Dhasan, Interview. Dhasan said that while as a professor, he arranged such programs in Scott Christian College, Nagercoil and Nesamony Memorial Christian College, Marthandam.

124 Nagalingam, Interview.

125 Self-help groups are increasingly popular in India, helping rural women to gather regularly and also to manage their finances by saving, and extending loans for small business. Such gatherings are made use of for creating awareness about dialogue and harmony.

126 Tobias, Interview.

127 Rajamony, Interview.

128 CIRSJA, Thiruvarutperavai and the Dialogue Commission in the district arrange such programs from time to time in which political personalities such as central and state ministers and MLS and MPs have participated. Many of these programs are centred on Nagercoil.

129 Dhasan, Interview.

130 CIRSJA has prepared a list of slogans for this purpose and circulated it among interreligious organizations in the district.

131 Nagalingam, Interview.

132 Salaam, Interview.

133 Tobias, Interview.

134 Ibid.

135 Panivanban Vincent, Interview.

136 Tobias, Interview.

137 Ibid.

138 I discuss this topic only briefly here, elaborating the elite nature of dialogue in Chapter 7.

139 CIRSJA has initially celebrated these festivals individually with other multireligious groups, but in recent times it celebrates all three together in December or January. Dhasan, Interview.
140 Nagalingam, Interview.
141 Robinson, 'From Apartheid,' 92.
142 Dhasan, Interview.
143 Rajamony, Interview.
144 Kasthoori Chokkalingam, Interview, Nagercoil, 4 July 2008.

Part II

LIMITATIONS OF RELIGIOUS PLURALITY,
CONFLICT AND ELITISM

Chapter 3

'RELIGION' AND 'WORLD RELIGIONS':
SOME CONTEMPORARY APPROACHES

Any discussion of dialogue or activity to promote it starts with the assumption that the context in which dialogue has to take place is a religiously pluralistic context. Many times it is also said, in the dialogue circles, that the world is 'increasingly becoming multireligious' due to globalization, internationalism or other reasons, so dialogue is urgent. The underlying notion, which is very obvious, is that religious pluralism or plurality of religions is the necessary condition for dialogue. The emphasis on religious plurality is made also to challenge the exclusivist attitudes of a particular religion to other religions, in which the former normally expects a removal of the latter. This is the main reason that pluralistic approach to religions is presented as advantageous within the field of theology of religions leading to the promotion of dialogue. Not only at the theological level but also at the pragmatic level, the notion of religious plurality or multireligious situatedness simply exists. The emphasis on plurality in dialogue may encourage religious followers to be open to diversity, and appreciate the people of other religions, yet there are serious problems with the notion of plurality of *religions* which are simply ignored.[1] For, a whole lot of assumptions about religion are found underneath this notion of plurality of religions. The aspects that are ignored include the very idea of religion and its plural religions, the idea of world religions, religious-secular distinctions, the maintenance of fixed religious identities for people and similar factors.[2] Further, dialogue proposes to solve the problems arising out of people living in religiously pluralistic contexts. But on the contrary, the notion of religious plurality makes dialogue only more problematic. It is problematic because in dialogue there is uncritical acceptance of several factors that come with assumptions of religious plurality.

Important in this discussion are the questions regarding where and how the contemporary ideas on 'religion' and its plural 'religions' as well as religion as an entity distinct from secularity (or politics, economics, society, etc.) have been constructed. One area that is identified is the whole sphere of the colonial experience of the past few centuries. The idea of religion and its supposed opposite, 'secularism', the use of 'world religions' category and the identification of people in the colonies primarily through their religious affiliation have been shown to be the products of Western colonialism. There has been a rigid distinction in the West between the true religion of Christianity and the false non-Christian religions for most of its history, construction of religious-secular distinctions during the European Enlightenment period and interpretation of the lives of people in their colonies in this manner. Local elites in colonies such as India have further appropriated these notions uncritically and have heavily used them in their writings and activities.[3] In the recent scholarship in the field of religious studies, investigations into these notions have become noteworthy. While this chapter discusses some of these approaches that critique the notion of religion and its plural religions or world religions and the religion-secularism distinctions in order to set the stage for the subsequent discussion, the next chapter critiques how dialogue in contemporary India has uncritically accepted these Western and elite constructions and appropriated them in their discourses and practices of dialogue.

1 Western Colonial Constructions of Religion and Religions

(a) Postcolonial Framework

Postcolonialism or postcolonial theory offers a theoretical framework to study the societies which have been colonized in the past. Primarily built on the work of Edward Said's *Orientalism*, the postcolonial framework is not one-dimensional, and there are different viewpoints within it. Those who are using it are broadly divided between two groups: one places post-colonialism as the period after colonialism, and the other argues that postcolonialism 'is best used to designate the totality of practices, in all their rich diversity, which characterise the societies of the post-colonial world from the moment of colonization to the present day, since colonialism does not cease with the mere fact of political independence and continues in a neo-colonial mode to be active in many societies'.[4] I use postcolonialism in the latter sense, arguing that colonialism and colonial forms of knowledge continue to impact the people in once-colonized countries although 'official' colonialism has ended and that postcolonialism is useful in critiquing the ongoing influence of Western colonial forms of life and activities on former colonies and working on ways to overcome them. As Robert Young says, postcolonialism is primarily involved in shifting 'the dominant ways in which the relations between Western and non-Western people and their worlds are viewed'.[5]

Accordingly, the materials under consideration in postcolonialism are those produced both in the West and in the colonized countries during the time of colonialism and those produced even today which carry the influence of colonialism. The anthropological theories, used to legitimize colonialism and imperialism and portray 'the peoples of the colonized world as inferior, childlike, or feminine, incapable of looking after themselves (despite having done so perfectly well for millennia) and requiring the paternal rule of the West for their own best interests',[6] are a significant subject of postcolonial criticism. A common focus is thus how colonial administrators, Oriental scholars and Western Christian missionaries viewed the people and their life in the colonized territories, constructing theories and producing images about them for home consumption in the West.

Two important aspects of colonialism that concern the postcolonial framework are knowledge and power, which were foundational for imperial authority over people in colonies.[7] Knowing the 'other' was crucial for imperial domination, as it became a mode by which the colonized people 'were increasingly persuaded to know themselves: that is, as subordinate to Europe'.[8] This knowledge which was produced by Westerners about the colonized territories is the primary factor that is being evaluated and critiqued in postcolonialism, because of its association with power and imperialism. Therefore postcolonialism 'involves a conceptual reorientation towards the perspectives of knowledge, as well as needs, developed outside the west'.[9] Moreover, it

> seeks to intervene, to force its alternative knowledges into the power structures of the west as well as the non-west. It seeks to change the way people think, the way they behave, to produce a more just and equitable relation between the different peoples of the world.[10]

In this way, postcolonialism not only critiques the continuing Western forms of knowledge and power, but also proposes alternatives to them.

There are two contentious areas when considering how imperial knowledge production in the colonial context in India aided imperial domination. The first is the agencies involved in perceiving, defining and interpreting people in India, and the other is the lenses through which these agencies interpreted them. While the former is about Western colonialists, Orientalists and European missionaries involved in framing the lives of colonized people and their cultures through producing several kinds of theories, the latter is about looking at the bases of those theories in the West. One such lens used in understanding and interpreting people in India was the notion of religion developed in the Christian West, shaped by the European Enlightenment and passed on to India through colonialism. A postcolonial framework helps to identify the trends and nuances involved in this process and to discuss this aspect and deconstruct the notion of religion(s) and fixed religious identities in order to construct how the realities are and have been among common people in India. While the postcolonial framework primarily critiques the West for its constructions of religion, for the past few decades it also has incorporated subaltern approaches which critique not only the colonial elites but also the elites in the colonies who have contributed to the forms of power and control of people in India.

(b) Christian West and the Creation of Religion

In critically studying the notions of religion(s) and religions as now understood, there are two important dimensions. The first is that what is understood to be religion in the modern context in relation to 'major world religions' is rooted in the Christian West which was developed in the Hellenistic context. In other words, what is referred to as 'religion' when one speaks about, say, Hinduism is basically a Western Christian idea of 'religion'. The second aspect is to do with the construction of religion as a separate system or unit in society. This notion primarily came into being during the European Enlightenment when 'religion' was separated from other categories such as 'politics'. That this notion of religion is a modern myth created during the European Enlightenment in the seventeenth and eighteenth centuries is one of the arguments of the scholars who are investigating the power relations associated with this phenomenon. They have shown that the idea of religion as a distinct entity, as understood in the post-Enlightenment period, was not found in the 'pre-modern' era.[11]

As the modern conception of religion(s) is different from the understanding of religion in the pre-modern era, many are engaged in finding out how it prevailed at that time. Richard King, S. N. Balagangadhara and others show how religion and religions were understood in the times of the Romans. Balagangadhara contrasts 'religion' as understood in the pre-Christian era with the Christian understanding of it. He quotes from Cicero, the Roman philosopher of two millennia ago, who defines religion in that context:

> For religion has been distinguished from superstition not only by philosophers but by our own ancestors. Persons who spent whole days in prayer and sacrifice ... were termed 'superstitious'. ... Those on the other hand *who carefully reviewed and so to speak retraced all the lore of the ritual* were called 'religious' from *relegere* (to re-trace or re-read), like 'elegant' from *eligere* (to select), 'diligent' from *diligere* (to care for), 'intelligent' from *intellegere* (to understand); for all these words contain the same sense of 'picking out' (*legere*) that is present in 'religions'.[12]

Thus religion as interpreted by Cicero in the pre-Christian context refers to the condition that one should follow the rituals of one's ancestors. On the contrary, staying with prayer and sacrifice were considered to be superstitious or irreligious. Commenting on the definition of religion offered by Cicero, King says,

> This understanding of the term seems to have gained provenance in the 'pagan' Roman empire and *religio* virtually synonymous with *traditio*. As such it represented the teachings of one's ancestors and was essentially not open to question. Primarily *religio* involved performing ancient ritual practices and paying homage to the gods. ... If *religio* is primarily about continuing the tradition of one's ancestors, the term clearly denotes an inherently pluralistic context. There can never be one *religio* since there are a variety of different social and ethnic groups with traditions and histories of their own.[13]

The idea that religion meant worshipping a supernatural power or God or that it was occupied with the questions of truth and falsity was unknown to Romans, according to the definition provided by Cicero. However, this understanding of *religio* came under attack within the early Christian context. In order to distinguish the Christian 'truth' from the false pagan traditions, Lactantius, an early Christian theologian who lived in the third century, attempted to offer a different meaning for *religio*. Balagangadhara quotes from him:

> We are fastened and bound to God by this bond of piety, whence religion itself takes its name. The word is not as Cicero interpreted it from 'rereading', or 'choosing again' *(relegendo)*. ... For if superstition and religion are engaged in worshipping the same gods, there is slight or rather no difference ... because religion is a worship of the true; superstition of the false. And it is important, really, why you worship, not how you worship, or what you pray for. ... We have said that *the name of religion is taken from the bond of piety, because God has bound and fastened man to Himself by piety. ... They are superstitious who worship many and false gods; but we, who supplicate the one true God, are religious.*[14]

Thus the meaning of religion changed from following one's ancestors' traditions or rituals to worshipping the 'true' God in the early Christian context. It has now come to denote the relationship between God and human. This change in definition was necessary for Christianity to gain a dominant place in relation to other Roman 'pagan' traditions. As King argues, 'The Christian transformation of *religio* functioned not only to capture authority for Christians in Roman society but also to exclude certain groups from equal consideration. Those who did not bow down to the Almighty and Supreme Deity, worshipping other gods, were now "alterized" as pagan (*paganus*: village idiot) and superstitious.'[15] This notion became strengthened as Christianity received state recognition during the period of Emperor Constantine in the early fourth century. Moreover, 'The redefining of *religio* also served to establish the monotheistic exclusivism of Christianity as the normative paradigm for understanding what a religion is.'[16]

There is no doubt that this understanding of religion, primarily based on Christian theology in the West, is predominant in modern times when referring to 'religion' in general and to many of the 'world religions' in particular. This Christianized version of religion 'strongly emphasizes *theistic belief* ... exclusivity and a fundamental dualism between the human world and the transcendent world of the divine to which one "binds" (*religare*) oneself'.[17] Moreover, the Christianized model of religion also assumes that doctrine is the fundamental essence of religion and stresses the importance of the written scriptures and their correct interpretation.[18] The Roman idea of religion as following the customs or traditions of one's ancestors, or as ceremony, was replaced by the Christian insistence on attitude and belief based on doctrines. This has led to the condition where 'the emphasis on the significance of inner conviction was eventually matched, and even perhaps overshadowed, by a long process of objectification' in which 'the notion of religion as something expressed objectively in written creeds, doctrine, or stated belief'.[19]

This shows the continuity between religion as perceived and interpreted today and as has been done in early Christian developments in the West. In both the modern conceptions of religion and the Christian understanding of *religio*, 'a great deal of emphasis upon a faithful adherence to doctrine as indicative of religious allegiance, upon sacred texts as of central importance to religious communities and to questions of truth and falsity as of paramount importance to the religious adherent or "believer"' is found.[20] This model of religion developed in the Western Christian context has replaced the Roman idea of religion where the question of truth and falsity in religion was not a primary issue. But the tendency to interpret world religions along the lines of truth and falsity has largely been a result of the influence of Western Christianity through colonialism. But before discussing how the West applied this understanding of religion to interpret non-Western and non-Christian religions, another trend in the Western construction of religion should be noted: the construction of religious-secular distinctions during the Enlightenment.

(c) Religious-Secular in European Enlightenment

While 'religion', defined in the Western Christian context, came to mean worshipping the true God of Christianity as against the remaining traditions which were superstitious, in the European Enlightenment context, interest in religion concerned its location in human life. Thus, Timothy Fitzgerald argues,

> Even some historians seem comfortable with the idea that religion somehow can always be identified in ancient, medieval or modern history, in any society speaking any language. ... But this sits awkwardly with the observation that, for much of the period leading up to the eighteenth-century Enlightenment, and arguably for long after, the English term 'religion' stood for Christian Truth, usually Protestant Truth, as revealed in the Bible. And during much of the same period, 'politics' was not conceived as an independent domain separated from religion, and therefore in that modern sense was not articulated.[21]

This also shows that in developing the concept of religion as a distinct entity, it is not only theologians and religious leaders but also academic scholars in various fields and the 'secular intellectuals' of the Enlightenment who have played a major role by taking for granted that religion as now understood has existed for a long period. True, religion and religious systems did exist as inner convictions and expressions of those convictions in the ancient period, but not as a category separated from other walks of life. Commenting on this, Peter Harrison says thus:

> That there exist in the world such entities such as 'the religions' is an uncontroversial claim. ... However ... the concepts 'religion' and 'the religions', as we presently understand them, emerged quite late in Western thought, during the Enlightenment. Between them, these two notions provided a new framework for classifying particular aspects of human life. ... Whereas in the Middle Ages the concern of the Christian West had been with faith – a 'dynamic of the heart' – in the seventeenth century attention shifted to the impersonal and objective 'religion'. Increasingly this term came to be an outsider's description of a dubious

theological enterprise. Along with 'religion' came the plural 'religions' – 'the Protestant Religion,' 'the Catholic Religion,' 'Mahometanism,' 'heathen Religion' and so on.[22]

This illustrates that understanding religion as separated from 'secularism' or 'politics' is a new trend that came into existence since the Enlightenment. Similarly, that religion is *a part* of society is a very recent and modern concept, the basic nature of society being equated with its secular nature while religion is merely one unit, often a private one, in *secular* society. It is seldom understood that this European Enlightenment distinction between religion and secularism remains a fundamental cause for stereotyping many communities and nations.

Analysing the works of seventeenth- and eighteenth-century European philosophers such as John Locke and William Penn, Fitzgerald shows that ideas of religious-secular appeared only in this context when empirical science became dominant in society. He argues that there have been fundamentally two dominant perceptions of religion through the last few centuries:

> One is of encompassing religion, where nothing properly exists outside religion since it represents Truth, which is all-embracing. In this model, 'politics' and 'economics' are embedded, and all 'facts' are subordinated to Christian redemptive values that give them meaning. This model of religion is hierarchical, and all things that exist have their proper place and function within the teleological whole. Individual persons exist in so far as they find their proper subordinate place in this context of hierarchical relationships. That which opposes it is pagan superstition and belongs in Hell.[23]

This model of religion existed in pre-modern Europe where Christianity was equated with religion. Certainly Christianity was hierarchical in that first, it contrasted the true religion in Christianity with the false religion of superstitions and heresies, and second, as Fitzgerald observes, it infused every aspect in society with Christian values. But with the emergence of Enlightenment and the popularization of its ideals, religion became a separate category. Fitzgerald notes:

> The second concept of religion, which ... is hegemonic today, cuts across the first, or stands it on its head. The idea of religion as a private soteriological belief essentially separated from politics, or the idea of religious societies having essentially different purposes and characteristics from political societies, has become institutionalized in Western liberal democracies and exported through the processes of colonization to many societies where no such distinction was conceivable in the local language. This idea of religion was powerfully articulated ... in the seventeenth century, and was developed and transformed into a conception of secular, rational, political 'man,' especially through the American constitutional process, which produced the most powerful charter for representing this political essence. At the same time, and as an integral part of this discourse, a notion of the secular as the non-religious, the natural, the

rational, was generated as the superior ground from which to observe and order the world.[24]

In this way, a distinction between sacred and secular was created in order to acquire a higher place for the secular and to push religion to the margins. Nevertheless, even though the 'secular' intellectuals of the European Enlightenment are responsible for this distinction, one cannot deny the role played by 'religionists' also. On the one hand, some of them pointed out how religions were taken seriously by people *in spite of* secularism or secularization. One does not need to cite detailed evidence for this, for it has been a clear pattern over the past few centuries. On the other hand, there are 'religionists' claiming a higher ground of authority when they speak from a secular position. Here the secular nature is viewed as superior to the religious. For instance, studying the attitudes to religion and secular among the Roman Catholics in west Mexico, Trevor Stack points out that secular knowledge is considered as a higher ground for even talking about religious devotion.[25] He argues that influenced by the hegemony of the secular, 'people in west Mexico had become used to the idea that there was a secular "outside" to religion.'[26] He further says that 'those educated in church seminary schools were in a strong position to produce and gain authority from secular knowledge. ... Secular knowledge was something that clerics (and those with clerical education) could do well and benefit from.'[27] When these clerics became narrators in their church, they 'were able to claim a special kind of "higher ground," one that lay "outside" the world of their narrative subjects, and from which they could look in on their narrative subjects.'[28]

In the Indian context, it is quite normal among Christians (and Muslims) that they would appeal to the secular nature of India and the secular constitution of India when it comes to responding to the attacks on religious minorities, while the same in other contexts would emphasize 'religions against secularism and secularization', or at least 'religions in the context of secular ideologies.'[29] In the first, secularism is considered to be a higher ground that should protect all irrespective of their religious affiliations, and in the second there is somewhat an inferior place for secularism compared to religion. While I am not critical of the religious minorities' right to appeal to the constitution during the times of majority violence, nevertheless, such patterns indicate the ambiguities found between challenging secularism and appealing to the secular constitution, and revitalizing religious-secular distinctions. In my opinion, the issue at stake both in the secular claim of superiority over religion and in the religious claim of superiority over the secular, or claiming a higher ground for secular in both, is that the religion-secularism distinction is simply accepted without question.

(d) Colonialism and the Creation of Religion and Religions for the Colonies

How did Western and Western Christian assumptions behind religion and religions become such powerful categories in the non-European world? It is here that European colonialism and the forms of knowledge it generated in its colonies became significant. The major medium through which the modern myth of religion became popular lies in the Western colonial efforts to understand and interpret or 'know' the colonized people and their lives. For understanding this, discussing how the colonial administrators, Western Orientalists, missionaries, travellers and settlers understood the lives and practices of colonized people, and interpreted them to the West, becomes important.

Western Orientalists are a major group of people involved in perceiving and interpreting the lives of people in India along the lines of religion. Those who critique Orientalism have conducted remarkable studies, revisiting and critiquing the vast number of materials produced by the Orientalist scholars during colonial rule. What is pointed out in these studies is that often what the Orientalists were doing was applying Western frameworks, which they thought were superior to the available cultural forms of the colonized, to interpret the colonized. One such factor was religion. The religion framework, already constructed in the West, helped them to apply their notions of religion to the cultures and traditions in colonies. Richard King investigates how the Western Christian notions of religion were applied to 'religions' in India.[30] It is also well discussed by Edward Said in his classic work *Orientalism*. Said mainly looks at the Middle Eastern context, but other scholars such as Wilhelm Halbfass[31] and Ronald Inden[32] have critiqued how Orientalists and Indologists were instrumental in promoting Western analytical frameworks to interpret people in the colonized Indian subcontinent.

One of the major aspects in the Orientalist discourse is that it presents its knowledge of Orientals as not only different from but also superior to the knowledge Orientals have of themselves. While the Orientalist knowledge of the Orientals was claimed to be rational, scientific and objective, 'Oriental' knowledge was considered to be irrational, unscientific and subjective – therefore inferior to that of the Orientalist. As Inden notes, Orientalist knowledge is

> privileged in relation to that of the Orientals and it invariably places itself in a relationship of intellectual dominance over that of the easterners. It has appropriated the power to represent the Oriental, to translate and explain his (and her) thoughts and acts not only to Europeans and Americans but also to the Orientals themselves. But that is not all. Once his special knowledge enabled the Orientalist and his countrymen to gain trade concessions, conquer, colonize, rule, and punish in the East. ... In many respects the intellectual activities of the orientalist have even produced in India the very Orient which it constructed in its discourse.[33]

Thus what is predominant in Orientalism is not just knowledge about Orientals, but the power relations within which that knowledge is expressed and used.

The other group involved in promoting the Western conception of religion to the colonies are the Western Christian missionaries. In their efforts to propagate Christian gospel to 'non-Christians', they viewed those traditions through Christian lenses.[34] Regarding the role of Christian missionaries in the Empire, there are broadly two perspectives. First, Christian missionaries worked together with other colonialists such as colonial administrators and Orientalists supporting colonialism. Second, missionaries and colonialists had different agendas in that while the former were involved in saving souls, the latter were involved in establishing imperial dominance over colonies. Works such as *Orientalism* by Edward Said are critiqued for failing to make the distinction between the purposes of colonialists and missionaries.[35] Nevertheless, it is true that the imperial ethos and rule did influence the missionaries in their activities. The influence of Orientalist scholars and colonialists can be found in much missionary interpretation of the colonized people and their 'religions'. For example, Oddie argues about how far Christian missionaries in India during the colonial period viewed and interpreted Hinduism through the lens set up by Orientalists, European travellers and colonial administrators.[36]

Another agency which played a crucial role in constructing religion and religious identities for people in colonies is comparative religion, developed in the West in the nineteenth century.[37] The 'comparative study of religion' is considered as one of the formative factors of dialogue. But a critical look at it within a post-colonial framework shows that this has been one of the most active agencies in constructing religion and religions. While the Western Orientalists, travellers and settlers, missionaries and colonial administrators were generating their knowledge through perceiving and interpreting the people in India and their life and traditions, the comparative religionists in Europe made efforts to organize them in order to provide a platform for the comparative study of religion. The latter constructed each religion as a *single entity* comprising many traditions coalesced into a *religious whole* identified with one label. This helped them to place each religion against the other before comparing them. While critically studying how the imperial comparative religionists helped to imagine religion for people in colonial southern Africa, David Chidester observes that

> theorists of an imperial comparative religion, in developing a 'secular' science of religion, were engaged in distinguishing between the real and the imagined, distinguishing between the 'reality' of empire and the 'imaginary' world of people subjected to the military force, economic exploitation and social dislocation of colonization. ... In the process, imperial theorists defined their imaginary world under the rubric 'religion' as a 'disease of language', as 'primordial stupidity' or as 'primitive survivals' from human prehistory that should have long ago disappeared in the advance of modernity.[38]

The works of comparative religionists in India based on similar attitudes to these also saw the people in India through the lens of religion and interpreted them as 'pre-modern' and 'child-like'. They had no problem in presenting the lives of people in India in terms of pre-modern yet clearly separated religious systems in order to be compared and contrasted with the modernized and secularized Christianity.

(e) Construction of Hinduism in India

The above discussion has shown that Orientalists in the colonized countries, Christian missionaries and comparative religionists in Europe were all involved in promoting the Western idea of religion in the other parts of the globe. With regard to India, they were involved in constructing Hinduism which they perceived and interpreted as *the* religion of people of India. It is important to clarify how this was done, as it impacted on the colonial construction of all religions in India and thus on current dialogue.[39]

Broadly speaking, two major aspects were involved in constructing Hinduism. One was applying the Christian idea of 'religion' to perceive and interpret Hinduism. The other aspect is that only a few traditions from India were taken to be 'Hinduism', and these selected traditions came to represent the whole of traditions in India. These were brahmanical traditions which attracted the incomers. As a result, what happened was not only that just a few brahmanical traditions were interpreted as Hinduism but also that *this* Hinduism came to refer to the traditions of most of the people in India, feeding the idea that 'Hinduism' is the default tradition. Thus, Richard King says that 'the notion of a Hindu religion … was initially invented by Western Orientalists basing their observations upon a Judaeo-Christian understanding of religion. The specific nature of this "Hinduism," however, was the product of an interaction between the Western Orientalist and the Brahmanical Pundit.'[40]

Many scholars who have argued for the invention of Hinduism have shown that the use of the term 'Hinduism' to refer to a religion or 'Hindu' to refer to a religious identity is a recent phenomenon which was absent in the pre-colonial era. Of course the term 'Hindu' was found, but that referred to people in that geographical area. It has been often shown that 'the term "Hindoo" is the Persian variant of the Sanskrit *sindhu*, referring to the Indus river, and as such was used by the Persians to denote the people of that region.'[41] The term Hindu thus had nothing to do with religion. The indigenous use of this term by Hindus themselves could be found in the fifteenth and sixteenth centuries, but this 'usage was derivative of Persian Muslim influences and did not represent anything more than a distinction between "indigenous" or "native" and foreign (*mleccha*).'[42] It did not have specifically religious connotations until Western Orientalists and comparative religionists developed this trend in the colonial period. King notes that

'Hindu' in fact only came into provenance amongst Westerners in the 18th century. Previously the predominant Christian perspective amongst the Europeans classified Indian religion under the all-inclusive rubric of Heathenism. On this view there were four major religious groups, Jews, Christians, Mahometans (i.e. Muslims) and heathens. Members of the last category were widely considered to be children of the Devil, and the Indian Heathens were but one particular sect alongside the Africans and the Americans (who even today are referred to as American 'Indians' in an attempt to draw a parallel between the indigenous populations of India and the pre-colonial populations of the Americas) … as

Western knowledge and interest in India increased, the term 'Hindu' eventually gained greater prominence as a culturally and geographically more specific term.[43]

Initially referred to as pagans or heathens, the people in India soon became 'Hindus' – and their *religion*, Hinduism – as the Western Orientalists, missionaries and comparative religionists continued to apply the Western notion of religion to 'religions' in India. As a result, Hinduism in its current meaning emerged in the colonial context. King thus says,

> The term 'Hinduism' seems first to have made an appearance in the early nineteenth century, and gradually gained provenance in the decades thereafter. ... However, it is not until the nineteenth century proper that the term 'Hinduism' became used as a signifier of a unified, all-embracing and independent religious entity in both Western and Indian circles. The *Oxford English Dictionary* traces 'Hindooism' to an 1829 reference in the *Bengalee* (volume 45), and also refers to an 1858 usage by the German Indologist Max Muller.[44]

Another feature that is significant in interpreting religion in India and constructing Hinduism in terms of the Western conception of religion was bias towards scriptural traditions — textualization. Western literary bias, a significant feature of the European Enlightenment, also played its role in constructing Hinduism. Western presuppositions about the role of sacred texts in 'religion' predisposed Orientalists to focus on such texts as the essential foundation for understanding the Hindu people as a whole.[45]

> Protestant emphasis upon the text as the locus of religion placed a particular emphasis upon the literary aspects of Indian culture in the work of Orientalists. ... Many of the early European translators of Indian texts were also Christian missionaries, who, in their translations and critical editions of Indian works, effectively constructed uniform texts and a homogenized written canon through the imposition of Western philological standards and presuppositions onto Indian materials. Thus the oral and 'popular' aspect of Indian religious tradition was either ignored or decried as evidence of the degradation of contemporary Hindu religion into superstitious practices that bore little or no relation to 'their own' texts.[46]

The colonial construction of Hinduism along the lines of Western categories has given rise to many consequences in the present context. Clearly the current political affairs and the efforts of Hindu nationalists show how this category has created dangers for people in formerly colonized countries. Talal Asad is right when he says in relation to his Islamic context that 'while religion is integral to modern Western history, there are dangers in employing such a normalizing concept when translating Islamic traditions'.[47] The Western colonial construction of Hinduism has indeed raised many problems in the political power structures in India, and it is important to note how this concept continues to influence dialogue.

(f) Colonialism and Religious Identities

Western colonial construction of religion is not simply a construct of concept or theory; it is also political. We already noted that a self-awareness of identity was raised among people in India in terms of 'Hinduism' and 'Hindu' identity. Thus, the notion of religion helped to construct identities based on religion for people in the colonies. In constructing religious identities, another factor played a crucial role: the colonial administration of the British government in India. Supported by the findings of the Western Orientalists (some of whom were also administrators), the colonial administration was involved in producing religious identities for people in India. This was mostly done in the process of recording events in India and in conducting the census. As Friedhelm Hardy says, 'It would appear that there is an intrinsic connection between the "Hinduism" that is being constructed in the political arena and the "Hinduism" of academic study.'[48]

It should be noted that not only the Orientalists and Indologists were involved in constructing the categories of religions. They did it conceptually and mostly within academic fields. However, the colonial administrators strongly influenced the making of fixed identities for the people they governed, and it should be remembered that all permanent members of the Indian civil service had to learn regional languages and traditions, which would in many areas weigh their understanding heavily in the direction of elite Hindu ideas. The census taken during the colonial period is important in this regard. British government introduced census-taking in India in the 1870s, and since then 'religion' has been a predominant factor along with caste to refer to people's identity. All British censuses compartmentalized Hindus, Christians and Muslims into three separate homogenous communities. In this regard, Peter Gottschalk observes, 'The British used religion as a primary criterion for the categorization not only of time but also of society. The decadal Census of India, initiated in 1872, sought to delineate South Asian societies principally via categories of caste and religion.'[49]

Thus in various ways the colonial administrators in India were categorizing people along the lines of their religious identities. Religions were created and presented to the public, identities being constructed within each frame. It has often been said by historians in India that the colonial census-taking and categorization of people in terms of religion is responsible for many of the Hindu–Muslim conflicts in Indian society. In fact the record of events by the British colonial government also illustrates how the notion of 'religious conflict' or communalism was invented by colonialists in India. Gyanendra Pandey, a subaltern historian, has done a significant study showing how communalism was constructed in North India. Studying the colonial construction of communalism, Pandey observes,

> By the end of the nineteenth century, the dominant strand in colonialist historiography was representing religious bigotry and conflict between people

of different religious persuasions as one of the more distinctive features of Indian society, past and present – a mark of the Indian section of the 'Orient.' This particular reading of Indian history was distinguished not only by its periodization in terms of the European experience ('ancient,' 'medieval,' 'modern'), nor simply by its use of communal – more specifically, religious – categories to differentiate these periods of Indian history. ... The historical reconstruction was characterized also by an emptying out of all history ... from the political experience of the people, and the identification of religion, or the religious community, as the moving force of all Indian politics.[50]

He maintains that by 1920s the British government in India 'drew up elaborate lists of Hindu-Muslim riots that had occurred in the country in the recent past. ... The record of Hindu-Muslim strife was also extended further back, to the beginnings of colonial rule.'[51] Focusing on colonial interpretations of 'Hindu–Muslim' riots in Banaras, Pandey quotes from the District Gazetteer of Banaras about an incident in 1809:

> The only disturbance of the public peace [in Banaras during the first half of the nineteenth century] occurred in 1809 and the following year, when the city experienced one of those convulsions which had so frequently occurred in the past owing to the religious antagonism of the Hindu and Mussalman sections of population.[52]

Pandey observes that this particular reference to Banaras became the yardstick for the whole of India when in the 1920s and 1930s an assessment of its constitutional and political condition was undertaken. History books reiterated the theme. A memorandum was prepared for submission to the Indian Statutory Commission of 1928, and it referred to the 'grave Banares riots' of 1809 as evidence of the usual state of Hindu–Muslim coexistence, describing them as 'one of those convulsions which had frequently occurred in the past owing to the religious antagonism of the Hindu and Muslim sections of the population.'[53] Commenting on this, Pandey says,

> This particular description is of course lifted straight from the account contained in the Banares Gazetteer of 1907, quoted above. Notice that scarcely a word is altered in the text: and yet the change of contexts completely transforms the statement. What applied to a *particular* city – the experience of 'convulsions' in the past and the 'religious antagonism' of the local Hindus and Muslims – now applies to the country as a whole. Banares becomes the essence of India, the history of Banares the history of India.[54]

Thus we can note that categorizing people in India in terms of their religious belonging has been a relatively new phenomenon associated with Western colonialism in India, leading to what has become 'religious conflicts' in India. This continues to have a powerful effect among Indians. Whether 'religious conflict' has anything to do with the understanding or misunderstanding of religions or not, talking up religious identity to maintain political power and dominance has been a hallmark of politics in India – colonial or contemporary. The issue of religious conflict is significant for dialogue as well, and I will discuss in Chapter 6 how 'religious conflicts' in general and the 'political use of religion in conflicts' in particular are dealt with in dialogue in India.

2 The Role of Indian Elites in Constructing Religion and Religious Identities in India

While studying Western colonial constructions of religion in India, one aspect that is important but often neglected in scholarship is the role played by elites in India in appropriating colonial notions in their thought and deliberations to their advantage. Sometimes an overemphasis on the role played by the West leads to the neglect of the Indian role in creating religion and fixing religious identity in India. In other words, the role of Indian elites is played down as part of overemphasizing the Western role. Writers who favour this view blame the West as the sole reason for constructing religion and fixed religious identity for people in India, totally ignoring any local contribution. This is the case for the construction of religion and related categories, but can also be applied to most of the Western forms of knowledge and systems that were exercised in perceiving and interpreting the situation in India.

Some scholars and researchers who focus on the Indian context argue that while Western constructions of religious identities based on Western Enlightenment ideals cannot be ignored, nevertheless they alone cannot be held responsible for all the constructions of religion and religious identities in India. Such scholars argue that an emphasis on religion, religious performance and religious identities did exist in pre-colonial or pre-modern India, and was usefully exploited by the Western colonialists.[55] Challenging the notion that 'self-identification, exclusion, and tensions among religious groups on the Subcontinent derived solely from the colonial encounter', Gottschalk observes that these arguments, 'ignore evidence from a variety of sources that demonstrates that Western imperialism only aggravated and gave modern shape to religious discrimination that existed long before'.[56] Thus the pre-colonial situation with regard to the existence and construction of religion and religious identities in India remains a contested area. But one should not, however, play down the role played by Indian elites during the colonial period. While the Western Orientalists, missionaries, travellers and settlers and colonial administrators were doubtless involved in creating fixed religious identities for people in India, the elites in India accepted and appropriated the argument in order to work out strategies for their own ends. Below I discuss two such elite groups: first the 'Hindu elites' and then Indian Christian theologians.

(a) Hindu Elites

Hindu elites, or those who are generally termed as Hindu reformers, appropriated the colonial construction of religion – Hinduism in the Indian context – for many reasons.[57] Basically it provided them with a Hindu identity which they mostly accepted enthusiastically, for it helped them in the process of their self-identification in the context of their struggle against outsiders – the Western colonialists. Further, reformers and revivalists such as Ram Mohan Roy, Vivekananda and, later, Radhakrishnan were involved in comparative study of religions – usually comparing Hinduism with Christianity and sometimes with Islam. The use of Hinduism and Hindu identity in their deliberations helped them mainly on two accounts. First, it consolidated Indians under one identity, and secondly, it linked Hinduism with the struggle for Indian independence against the British rule. While the former aspect helped them to encourage non-Christians and non-Muslims in India to come under one Hindu identity, the latter provided them with a Hindu nationalist framework in their fight against the British. One can see both of these elements in the writings and activities of the elites mentioned earlier and organizations such as Brahma Samaj, Arya Samaj and Deobandi with which they were associated. Commenting on the activities of people like Vivekananda and M. K. Gandhi, Richard King observes,

> Orientalist notions of India as 'other worldly' and 'mystical' were embraced and praised as India's special gift to humankind. Thus the very discourse that succeeded in alienating, subordinating and controlling India was used by Vivekananda as a religious clarion call for the Indian people to unite under the banner of a universalistic and all-embracing Hinduism.[58]

One can note, looking back from the present context, how these trends have helped the Hindu extremists to work for a homogenized Hindu identity in which they attempt to include Dalits and Tribals as well as work on a Hindu national identity which excludes those who do not share the parameters set by the exponents of Hindutva: 'one nation', 'one religion', 'one culture' and 'one language'.

More importantly, the role played by the Hindu elites in constructing religions and religious identities has to be looked at in terms of the nature of Hinduism they advocated and represented. It has been often pointed out that one of the reasons for the selection of brahmanical traditions by the Western Orientalists was the influence exerted on them by the elite Brahmins in India. Thus King says of the elite Brahmins who influenced the Western Orientalists,

> The high social, economic and, to some degree, political status of the *brahmana* castes has, no doubt, contributed to the elision between brahmanical forms of religion and 'Hinduism'. This is most notable, for instance, in the tendency to emphasize Vedic and brahmanical texts and beliefs as central and foundational to the 'essence' of Hinduism, and in the modern association of 'Hindu doctrine' with various brahmanical schools of the Vedanta.[59]

Further, quoting C. A. Bayly, King notes the fact that 'the administrative and academic demand for the literary and ritual expertise of the Brahmins placed them in a position of direct contact and involvement with their imperial rulers, a factor that should not go unnoticed in attempting to explain why Western Orientalists tended to associate brahmanical literature and ideology with Hindu religion *in toto*'.[60]

This is a crucial point, because while there were a number of traditions, known as religious, among people in India, only a few of them were selected to be 'the Hindu religious system'. It included mostly the traditions deriving from Vedas, Vedantas and Upanishads to which the upper-caste people such as Brahmins belonged. Among them, one may note, the *advaita* tradition was more prominent than others. We can see this mainly in the expositions of people such as Vivekananda and Radhakrishnan. Not only were these dominant traditions selected to *represent* Hinduism, but also they were posed as the *whole* of Hinduism under which all other traditions in India are to take shelter. These are some of the ways through which Western colonialism and Orientalism helped the Hindu elites to appropriate the notions of religions and religious identities. By appropriating these, the elites in India on the one hand attempted to create one Hindu identity incorporating all Indians and on the other worked out a Hinduism based solely on dominant traditions, completely ignoring and downplaying all other traditions and resources.

(b) The Role of Indian Christian Elites

The other group that uncritically accepted and appropriated the Western constructions of religion, world religions category and religious identities for people in India are some of the upper-caste Christians who are now termed the pioneers of Indian Christian thinking or indigenous Christianity.[61] They talked about Christianity in relation to brahmanic Hinduism and took for granted that Hinduism (or the only version they accepted) was one single and uniform entity. They were mostly concerned with the Christian missionaries' attack on Hinduism, in response to which they emphasized what they claimed to be the positive aspects of Hinduism, with no critical approach whatsoever to the notion of Hinduism as the religion of India. In responding to the criticism made against Hinduism by Christian missionaries, Indian Christian theologians, like their Hindu counterparts, affirmed an Indian/Asian religious superiority over Western Christianity, and this process did not allow them to see the problems with the 'creation' of religions in India.

In looking for ways to relate Hinduism and Christianity, Indian Christian thinkers (as well as some missionaries) emphasized indigenization, attempting to relate Christianity to India through inculturation and the Indianization of Christianity. Like the Hindu elites, they also undertook comparative study of Hinduism and Christianity. The initial efforts in this direction are found in the works of the early Jesuit missionaries, among whom Roberto de Nobili (1577–1656) is considered to be the pioneer for contextualization and for adopting Hindu religious (brahmanic) symbols and traditions.[62] Later thinkers such as K. C. Sen,[63] Krishna Mohan Banerjee,[64] Brahmabandhab Upadyaya,[65] A. S. Appasamy[66] and Sadhu Sundar Singh[67] also made various efforts along the same lines.

The *Bengal Christian Herald* (which was later called *The Indian Christian Herald*), started by Kali Charan Banerjee of Bengal and a few others, in its first issue in 1870 insisted: 'In having become Christians, we have not ceased to be Hindus. We are Hindu Christian, as thoroughly Hindu as Christian. We have embraced Christianity, but we have not discarded our nationality.'[68] *The Hindu Church of the Lord Jesus* founded in southern Tamil Nadu, *The Calcutta Christo Samaj* founded by Krishna Mohan Banarjee and the *National Church of Madras* founded by S. Parani Andi are a few early attempts for indigenous Christianity in India.[69] The very names of these movements indicate how these Indian Christians conceived of indigenous Christianity. It simply meant a 'Hinduized' Christianity.

One of the central features in the writings of the Indian Christian thinkers who made efforts to indigenize Christianity is that they related Christianity to Hinduism in its Vedic and Vedantic traditions in order to find parallels between the two faiths. The *Arian Witness*,[70] by Krishna Mohan Banerjee, attempted to show the parallels between the Old Testament and the Vedas, with Christianity a logical conclusion of Hinduism. Another thinker, Parani Andi, did the same in his lecture 'Are Not Hindus Christians?' in Madras in 1849.[71]

Brahamabandhab Upadyaya, another notable Indian Christian thinker, wrote in the same mode. Sensing the difficulties of Western Christianity in appealing to the people in India, Upadyaya argued for an Indianized Christianity which should take Hinduism.[72] Though a baptized Christian, he called himself Hindu-Christian or Hindu-Catholic.[73] He incorporated the *avatara* concept in Indian Christianity as well as the worship of gods and goddesses.[74] He allowed worship of Sarasvathi, a Hindu goddess, as a symbol of wisdom in Christian institutions and encouraged Christianity to assimilate these traditions and transform them.[75] Sadhu Sundar Singh also made efforts to indigenize Christianity – his theology is identified as 'the water of life in an Indian cup'.[76]

In the first half of the twentieth century, the Madras Rethinking Group[77] was involved in working for indigenous Christianity in India, thinkers such as P. Chenchiah and Vengal Chakkarai, who were part of the group, emphasizing the importance of Hinduism for Indian Christians. Chenchiah as a convert from Hinduism was always proud of his Hindu heritage. His conviction was that his Hindu heritage would deepen his understanding of Christian faith, and this inspired his whole work.[78] For him the converts in the past days hated Hinduism and surrendered themselves wholeheartedly to Christianity. But, he said, converts now have to regard Hinduism as their spiritual mother and discover the supreme value of Christ, 'not in spite of Hinduism, but because Hinduism has taught them to discern spiritual greatness'.[79] For him, loyalty to Christ and a reverential attitude towards the Hindu heritage need not confront each other.[80]

We may note that these earlier Indian Christian efforts for indigenization and inculturation are loosely related to the later development of dialogue.[81] However, what is important here is the fact that many of these Indian Christians who strove for indigenization and inculturation were high-caste Hindu converts who were relating Christianity to the dominant forms of religion in India, appropriating it to their own elite discourse. Even though the terms suggested that they were attempting to relate Christianity to India or to interpret and embed Christianity in Indian traditions, what they were actually doing was a *Hinduization* of Christianity – a Hinduism based on dominant upper-caste traditions. In this regard, as was the case among the Hindu revivalists, *Advaita* was a major tradition used by many of the Indian Christian thinkers as well to play a significant role in interpreting Christianity to India.[82]

The idea of discrete religion and religions and religious identities was constructed during the colonial period, imported to India by various Europeans, and appropriated uncritically and heavily used by Indian elites during the same period. This chapter has surveyed some of the currently available approaches to look at the problem of constructing religion as a distinct entity separated from other realms of life, the location for the construction of religion(s) and religious identities – with their negative connotations, which also has led to the fixation of religious identities for people living in the colonies such as India, as well as the participation of local elites in such processes. The influence of the Western constructions of religions and religious identities and the continuing Indian appropriation of them are still evident today, different constituencies in India using these categories uncritically or at least pragmatically. One such constituency is found in the dialogue movement in contemporary India. How have the dialogue promoters in India, when they are concerned with dialogue activities in the context of the plurality of religions, uncritically appropriated and used these categories in their works is discussed and interrogated in the next chapter.

Notes

1 Recently the idea of religious pluralism has been scrutinized in some works which call for moving beyond this framework to interpret and understand religions. For example, see criticisms of religious plurality in general. See Courtney Bender and Pamela E. Klassen, eds, *After Pluralism: Reimagining Religious Engagement* (New York: Columbia University Press, 2010). The twelve essays in this book along with an introduction by the editors (titled 'Habits of Pluralism') vividly discuss the limitations of religious pluralism and various issues connected with that. See also Giuseppe Giordan and Enzo Pace, eds, *Religious Pluralism: Framing Religious Diversity in the Contemporary World* (Heidelberg: Springer International Publishing, 2014).

2 In the light of the trends in dialogue in India outlined in Chapter 1, my observation is that what is lacking in dialogue is a postcolonial approach to religion and plurality of religions, which can help to unearth the Western constructions of today's world religions between which dialogue is necessary. Of course, the West is often critiqued in dialogue in India, but not for constructing the category of world religions. It is critiqued rather in the context of the 'age-long' Asian plurality of religions which is set against the secular West, which, in my view, reiterates the notion of the Western construction of world religions and religious-secular distinctions.

3	See Peter Gottschalk, *Beyond Hindu and Muslim: Multiple Identity in Narratives from Village India* (New Delhi: Oxford University Press, 2001), 13.

4	Bill Ashcroft et al., 'Preface,' in *The Post-Colonial Studies Reader*, ed. Bill Ashcroft et al. (London and New York: Routledge, 1995), xv.

5	Robert J. C. Young, *Postcolonialism: A Very Short Introduction* (New Delhi: Oxford University Press, 2003), 2.

6	Young, *Postcolonialism*, 2.

7	Edward Said talks about this in his book, referring to Arthur James Balfour's speech on Britain's presence in Egypt in the House of Commons, on 13 June 1910. Edward Said, *Orientalism* (New York: Pantheon, 1978), 32.

8	Bill Ashcroft et al., 'General Introduction,' in *The Post-Colonial Studies Reader*, ed. Bill Ashcroft et al. (London, New York: Routledge, 1995), 1.

9	Young, *Postcolonialism*, 6.

10	Ibid., 7.

11	Some of the recent prominent works include: Peter Harrison, *Religion and the Religions in the English Enlightenment* (Cambridge: Cambridge University Press, 1990); King, *Orientalism and Religion*; S. N. Balagangadhara, *'The Heathen in His Blindness': Asia, the West and the Dynamic of Religion* (Leiden: E. J. Brill, 1994); Timothy Fitzgerald, *The Ideology of Religious Studies* (New York: Oxford University Press, 2000); 'Encompassing Religion, Privatized Religions and the Invention of Modern Politics,' in *Religion and the Secular: Historical and Colonial Formations*, ed. Timothy Fitzgerald (London and Oakville: Equinox Publishing Ltd., 2007), 211–40; *Discourse on Civility and Barbarity* (New York: Oxford University Press, 2007); Tomoko Masuzawa, *The Invention of World Religions* (Chicago: The University of Chicago Press, 2005); Brent Nongbri, *Before Religion: A History of Modern Concept* (New Haven: Yale University, 2013). See also W. C. Smith, *The Meaning and End of Religion: A Revolutionary Approach to the Great Religious Traditions* (London: SPCK, 1978); Jonathan Z. Smith, *Imagining Religion: From Babylon to Jonestown* (Chicago: University of Chicago Press, 1982); Russell McCutcheon, *Manufacturing Religion: The Discourse on Sui Generis Religion and the Politics of Nostalgia* (New York: Oxford University Press, 1997).

12	Cicero, De Natura Deorum, II.72, cited in Balagangadhara, *Heathen in His Blindness*, 241.

13	King, *Orientalism and Religion*, 35–6.

14	Lactantius, *Institutiones Divinae*, IV.28. Translated by Sister McDonald, 1964, 318–20, quoted in Balagangadhara, *Heathen in His Blindness*, 242.

15	King, *Orientalism and Religion*, 36–7.

16	Ibid.

17	Ibid., 37.

18	Ibid., 38.

19	Oddie, *Imagined Hinduism*, 13.

20	King, *Orientalism and Religion*, 38–9.

21	Fitzgerald, 'Encompassing Religion,' 214.

22	Harrison, *Religion*, 1.

23	Fitzgerald, 'Encompassing Religion,' 234–5.

24	Ibid., 235.

25	Trevor Stack, 'A Higher Ground: The Secular Knowledge of Objects of Religious Devotion,' in *Religion and the Secular: Historical and Colonial Formations*, ed. Timothy Fitzgerald (London and Oakville: Equinox Publishing Ltd., 2007), 47–69.

26   Stack, 'A Higher Ground,' 57.

27   Ibid., 59.

28   Ibid.

29   This will be elaborated in Chapter 4.

30   King, *Orientalism and Religion*, Chapters 4–6.

31   Wilhelm Halbfass, *India and Europe: An Essay in Understanding* (Albany: State University of New York Press, 1988).

32   Ronald Inden, *Imagining India* (Bloomington: Indiana University Press, 1990); also 'Orientalist Constructions of India,' *Modern Asian Studies* 20, no. 3 (1986): 401–46.

33   Inden, *Imagining India*, 38.

34   See Oddie, *Imagined Hinduism*.

35   Oddie, '"Orientalism" and British Protestant Missionary Constructions of India in the 19th Century,' *South Asia* 17, no. 2 (1994): 27–42.

36   Oddie, *Imagined Hinduism*, 22–4.

37   F. Max Muller, *Introduction to the Science of Religion* (London: Longmans, Green, 1873).

38   David Chidester, 'Real and Imagined: Imperial Inventions of Religion in Colonial Southern Africa,' in *Religion and the Secular: Historical and Colonial Formations*, ed. Timothy Fitzgerald (London and Oakville: Equinox Publishing Ltd., 2007), 155; also see his book *Savage Systems: Colonialism and Comparative Religion in Southern Africa* (Charlottesville: University of Virginia Press, 1996).

39   I have already mentioned in the Introduction of this book some recent literature discussing the invention or construction of Hinduism in India during the colonial period.

40   King, *Orientalism and Religion*, 90.

41   Ibid., 98.

42   Ibid., 99.

43   Ibid., 99–100.

44   Ibid., 100.

45   Ibid., 101.

46   Ibid.

47   Talal Asad, *Genealogies of Religion: Disciplines and Reasons of Power in Christianity and Islam* (London: John Hopkins University Press, 1993), 1.

48   Friedhelm Hardy, 'A Radical Reassessment of Vedic Heritage: The *Acaryahrdayam* and Its Wider Implications,' in *Representing Hinduism: The Constructions of Religious Traditions and National Identity*, ed. Vasudha Dalima and H. Von Stietencron (New Delhi: Sage Publications, 1995), 48.

49   Gottschalk, *Beyond Hindu and Muslim*, 27.

50   Gyanendra Pandey, *The Construction of Communalism in Colonial North India*, 2nd ed. (New Delhi: Oxford University Press, 2006), 23–4.

51   Pandey, *Construction of Communalism*, 24.

52   Ibid., 27.

53   Ibid., 28.

54   Ibid.

55   Some of the authors who have a similar perspective include C. A. Bayly, 'The Pre-History of "Communalism?"', *Modern Asian Studies* 19, no. 2 (1985): 177–203; *Indian Society and the Making of the British Empire* (Cambridge: Cambridge University Press, 1988); Marc Gaborieau, 'From Al-Beruni to Jinnah: Idiom, Ritual and Ideology of the Hindu-Muslim Confrontation in South Asia,' *Anthropology Today* 1, no. 3

(1985): 7–14; Peter Van der Veer, *Gods on Earth: The Management of Religious Experience and Identity in a North Indian Pilgrimage Centre* (London: Athlone, 1988); *Religious Nationalism: Hindus and Muslims in India* (Berkeley: University of California Press, 1994). Also see Gottschalk, *Beyond Hindu and Muslim*.

56   Gottschalk, *Beyond Hindu*, 19.

57   There is a large amount of literature available discussing how these Hindu elites were involved in reviving or reforming Hindu culture, Hindu ethos, Hindu tradition, etc. Especially in the context of Hindu nationalism, several critical studies have looked into the various influences on these thinkers and the different shapes their ideas and activities took. For instance, see B. R. Purohit, *Hindu Revivalism and Indian Nationalism* (Sagar: Sathi Prakashan, 1965); David Ludden, *Making India Hindu: Religion, Community, and the Politics of Democracy in India* (New Delhi: Oxford University Press, 1996); Vasudha Dalmia, *The Nationalization of Hindu Traditions* (New Delhi: Oxford University Press, 1997); Partha S. Ghosh, *BJP and the Evolution of the Hindu Nationalism: From Periphery to Centre* (New Delhi: Manohar, 2000); Chetan Bhatt, *Hindu Nationalism: Origins, Ideologies and Modern Myths* (New York and Oxford: Berg 2001); Shamita Basu, *Religious Revivalism as a Nationalist Discourse: Swami Vivekananda and New Hinduism in Nineteenth Century Bengal* (New Delhi: Oxford University Press, 2002). See also Richard Fox Young, *Resistant Hinduism: Sanskrit Sources on Anti-Christian Apologetics in Early Nineteenth-Century India* (Vienna: Institüt für Indologie der Universität Wien, 1981).

58   King, *Orientalism and Religion*, 93; see also Brian K. Pennington, *Was Hinduism Invented?: Britons, Indians, and the Colonial Construction of Religion* (New York: Oxford University Press, 2007).

59   King, *Orientalism and Religion*, 102.

60   Ibid., 103; also, C. A. Bayly, *Indian Society and the Making of the British Empire* (Cambridge: Cambridge University Press, 1988).

61   Some of the noted among them are Keshab Chander Sen, Brahmabandhab Upadayay and the Madras Rethinking Group, in which theologians like P. Chenchia and Vengal Chakkarai played a prominent role.

62   Vincent Cronin, *A Pearl To India: The Life Of Roberto de Nobili* (London: Rupert Hart-Davis, 1959).

63   David C. Scott, *Keshub Chunder Sen* (Bangalore: CLS/UTC, 1979); Manilal C. Parekh, *Brahmarshi Keshub Chunder Sen* (Bombay: Vaibhav Press, 1926); *The Brahma Samaj: A Short Story* (Rajkot: The Oriental Christ House, 1979); P. C. Mozoomdar, *The Life and Teachings of Keshub Cunder Sen* (Calcutta: Baptist Mission Press, 1887).

64   K. P. Aleaz, *From Exclusivism to Inclusivism: The Theological Writings of Krishna Mohun Banerjea*, vols 1–2 (Delhi: ISPCK, 1998); K. M. Banerjea, *Dialogues on the Hindu Philosophy* (Madras: CLS, 1903); Robert Caldwell et al., *Christianity Explained to a Hindu, Or, Hinduism and Christianity Compared* (Madras: CLS, 1893).

65   Julius Lipner and George Gispert-Sauch, *The Writings of Brahmabandhab Upadhyay*, vols I–II (Bangalore: UTC, 2002). Gregory Blake Spendlove, *A Critical Study of the Life and Thought of Brahmabandhab Upadhyay* (Deerfield: Trinity International University, 2005); Sebastian Painadath and Jacob Parappally, eds, *A Hindu-Catholic: Brahmabandhab Upadhyay's Significance for Indian Christian Theology* (Bangalore: ATC, 2008).

66   H. A. Popley, *A. S. Appasamy* (Madras: CLS, 1933); A. J. Appasamy, *An Indian Interpretation of Christianity* (Madras: CLS, 1924).

67   B. H. Streeter, *The Message of Sadhu Sundar Singh* (New York: Macmillan, 1921); Friedrich Heiler, *The Gospel of Sadhu Sundar Singh* (London: George Allen & Unwin, 1927); Sundar Singh, *Sadhu Sundar Singh: Essential Writings*, 2nd ed. (Maryknoll, New York: Orbis Books, 2005).

68   Cited in Kaaj Baago, *Pioneers of Indigenous Christianity* (Bangalore: CISRS & Madras: CLS, 1969), 3.

69   Baago, *Pioneers of Indigenous Christianity*, 17.

70   Krishna Mohun Banerjea, *The Arian Witness: Or Testimony of Arian Scriptures in Corroboration of Biblical History and the Rudiments of Christian Doctrine, including Dissertations on the Original Home and Early adventures of Indo-Arians* (Calcutta: Thacker, Spink & Co., 1875).

71   Baago, *Pioneers of Indigenous Christianity*, 17.

72   Lipner, *Writings of Brahmabandhab*.

73   Timothy C. Tennent, *Building Christianity on Indian Foundations: The Legacy of Brahmabhandhav Upadhyay* (Delhi: ISPCK, 2000), 19–22.

74   Tennent, *Building Christianity*, 323–7.

75   Baago, *Pioneers of Indigenous Christianity*, 46.

76   Boyd, *An Introduction*, 92–109.

77   See O. V. Jathanna, 'The Madras Rethinking Group and Its Contributions to the Development of Indian Christian theology,' *Religion and Society* 44, no. 3 (1997): 74–97.

78   Boyd, *An Introduction*, 163–4.

79   P. Chenchiah, 'Jesus and Non-Christian Faiths,' in *Rethinking Christianity in India*, ed. A. N. Sudarisanam (Madras: A. N. Sudarisanam, 1938), 49.

80   Chenchiah, 'Jesus and Non-Christian Faiths,' 49.

81   For instance, see Griffiths, *Christ in India*. Also, Raimundo Panikkar, 'Indic Theology of Religious Pluralism from the Perspective of Interculturation,' in *Religious Pluralism: an Indian Christian Perspective*, ed. Kuncheria Pathil (Delhi: ISPCK, 1999), 252–99.

82   For a discussion on this, see K. P. Aleaz, *Christian Thought through Advaita Vedanta* (Delhi: ISPCK, 1996).

Chapter 4

Religious Plurality and Dialogue

In the previous chapter I discussed how the ideas of religion, world religions and religious identities were created in the Enlightenment period in Europe and transferred to colonial India. These constructions are still appropriated and used in the discourses of those who study India, particularly the religious identities of, and religious (or communal) conflicts among, Indians. Commenting on the Indian appropriation of the Western colonial constructions of religion and religious identities, Peter Gottschalk observes that 'unfortunately, professional scholars of South Asian civilization, the very sources who should most challenge such impressions, often reinforce them through their work'.[1]

In this chapter, I explore further the notion that theologians and religious leaders engaged in dialogue with the affirmation of plurality of religions are one such group, uncritically working with colonial inventions of religions and religious identity in their deliberations. There are various aspects in dialogue related to the Western and elite constructions of religion that need a critical look, but in this chapter I discuss three of them: first, the invitation to either cooperation between religions against secularism and secularization or dialogue with secular ideologies – both of which maintain the religious-secular distinctions; second, the notion of world religions category; and, leading on from that, the third aspect: identifying people or fixing identities for them primarily in terms of religion.

1 Religion, Religions, Religious Identities and Dialogue

(a) Dialogue and Religious-Secular Distinctions

Generally, there are two basic trends in maintaining religious-secular distinctions in contemporary society: either secularists make religion into something inferior and irrational, by which what they intend is to privatize religion beyond the public domain, or religionists maintain a firm distinction between religion and secularism (or secularization) in their discourses, considering secularism to be a threat to religion, against which religion should be defended. Some religionists consider secularism as an ideology different from religion – religion is more about having the faith element, whereas secularism is more about ideology, but *both* of these can work for the common humanity or welfare, hence a dialogue between them is also possible. While dialogists will be opposed to the hard-core interpretations of the self-proclaimed secularists that religion is irrational, they can be put in either of the religionist camps mentioned above – considering secular as materialistic and hence inferior, or proposing that religion and secularism (precisely secular ideologies) can cooperate and come together occasionally. 'Taking religions seriously', 'affirming religious importance' and 'bringing together different religions in dialogue in order to save their future' are some frequently heard slogans in the dialogue discourse.

Broadly speaking there are three major perspectives in dialogue with regard to secularism which lead dialogists to maintain distinctions between religion and secularism: the idea that secularism is *anti-religion* in that it is an enemy of religion; the idea that secularism or secular ideology is *another kind* of religion; and the idea that secularism or a secular framework offers a *higher ground of authority* in the dealings of human beings. These three attitudes are not neatly maintained, since there are also ambiguities involved: the same dialogist may exhibit different attitudes depending on the context, as I will show later in this chapter. However, my primary purpose is to show that these three perspectives of dialogists all fundamentally maintain the religious-secular distinction: the basic assumption that 'religion or secularism' is a valid dichotomy is not challenged.

While Christian attitudes to secularization are a centuries-old problem after the European Enlightenment consolidated such a distinction, the attitudes to secularism within the 'religiously pluralistic context' may be traced back to the World Parliament of Religions (WPR) in Chicago in 1893 and the second World Missionary Conference in Jerusalem in 1928. In the Jerusalem conference, W. E. Hocking[2] suggested all religions unite against this common enemy. Even though uniting religions or religions coming together against secularism was not supported, nevertheless the view that secularism was the common enemy of all religions was accepted in the conference. Such a religions-against-secularism or secularism-against-religions idea was also present in the WPR, which is seen by many as foundational for contemporary dialogue.[3] The WPR stressed repeatedly that religion is a separate entity, especially in relation to the secular world or secular society. Its fifth objective was 'to indicate the impregnable foundations of Theism, and the reasons for man's faith in Immortality, and thus to unite and strengthen the forces which are adverse to a materialistic philosophy of the universe'; or consider the sixth objective, which was

> to secure from leading scholars, representing the Brahman, Buddhist, Confucian, Parsee, Mohammedan, Jewish and other Faiths, and from representatives of various Churches of Christendom, full and accurate statements of the spiritual and other effects of the Religions which they hold upon the Literature, Art, Commerce, Government, Domestics, and Social life of the peoples among whom these Faiths have prevailed.[4]

In all these, 'religion' has been taken as a separate unit or system in life. Even though the term 'secular' is absent, one can nevertheless conclude that religion is put forth as a separate entity distinct from secularism, which is 'a materialistic philosophy of the universe'. In fact this separation runs through the deliberations in the parliament; and indeed Barrows, in his preface to the proceedings, says that 'religion is the greatest fact of History'.[5]

One can find similar attitudes in dialogue in India today. The ideas that religion is an alternative to secularism, that religion is superior to secularism and that religion is more enduring than secularism are reiterated in Indian dialogue circles. The general premise is that religions have something to contribute to the well-being of society despite the common assumption that they are obstacles to human development in society. Talking about the role of religions and dialogue in secular society in the late 1960s, Herbert Jai Singh says that religions are

> claiming universality of relevance, scientific rationality and personal and social salvific qualities for daily living. They claim to bring peace and love to a world perpetually living under the shadow of thermo-nuclear war. They promise mental peace to modern man whose nerves are perpetually on edge. In every faith there is a growing interest in the life of this world ... under the influence of religious aspiration, there has been a new heightening of social consciousness.[6]

Singh says that it is this context which sets the stage for dialogue.[7] In fact this idea of the role of religions in secular society, or a 'secular society', is important for dialogue. The basic assumption is that religion and society are seen as separate entities, and while society is characterized by its secular nature, religion is just a tiny but influential part of that society.

Against the often strident claim of secular ideologies that religions have no positive role to play, the dialogue promoters stress, equally stridently, the importance of religion for human beings. Thus Samartha holds that 'since religions have endured in history for a much longer period than any secular ideology, the possibility that religions might still offer resources to recover the sense of wholeness of life should at least be explored seriously instead of being rudely rejected as of no consequence'.[8] The necessity of dialogue becomes important in such a context in order to protect religion(s) from secular assault, the future of religions being hopefully protected if different religions come together in the service of humanity. Similarly, K. L. Seshagiri Rao, a Hindu dialogue activist, says that 'the future usefulness of any religious tradition ... depends on its ability to cooperate with other traditions'.[9] Raimundo Panikkar also expresses a similar attitude when he talks about Hindu–Christian dialogue: 'In such dialogue lies the future of religions.'[10] In this regard the *religious* nature of peace, with the emphasis that religions working in dialogue have a great peace potential for peace, is a common theme.

Talking about the future of dialogue in the context of secularism, Samartha maintains that

> secularism ... banishes the sacred from all life, and therefore rejects inter-religious dialogue as a hindrance to human progress. One of the contributions of inter-religious dialogue is critically to recover the religious dimension of human

life at a time when there is a retreat of the secular and a return of the sacred into the arena of history.[11]

He articulates the importance and urgency of dialogue, claiming that 'while it is true that organized religions have often failed to provide answers to the problems of justice, the same judgement is true in the case of contemporary secular ideologies as well' and that 'there is today a growing uneasiness about the adequacy of the secular way of life and an increasing sensitivity to the transcendent dimension of life'.[12] However, Samartha also talks about the aspirations of people to live together, setting aside religion and the secular: 'The separation of life into the sacred and secular is being questioned today by many people. They are deeply aware of the wholeness of life. Religious insights, particularly those that hold together humanity, nature and God in a cosmic unity may be important here'.[13] Nevertheless he still demands that religion be considered along with secularism to make people whole, rather than questioning the separation itself.[14]

The second aspect with regard to the attitudes towards secularism in dialogue is the talk about dialogue between religions and secular ideologies. In this sense, secularism or secular ideologies are seen to play as positive a role for humans as religion. Devanandan and M. M. Thomas were two Indian Christian thinkers who linked dialogue with secularism. Devanandan was critical of the general Christian attitudes to secularism and secularization in the West. Challenging the Jerusalem 1928 report on secularism, Devanandan held that this should not be the situation in an independent India. He maintained that 'the position seems to have shifted since Jerusalem (1928), when missionary thinking was inclined to hold secularism was the common enemy of all religion. Today the antithesis between what is described as religious and what is regarded as secular has no longer the same validity'.[15] He was convinced that in the Indian context, secularism could be a corrective when religion becomes other-worldly and pietistic. This he related both to Christianity and Hinduism – inviting Christians to work with other religious and secular traditions for the sake of common humanity and inviting Hindus to 'effect a synthesis between the traditional worldview and contemporary secularism'.[16] In similar vein, M. M. Thomas also said that

> Christianity, renascent religions, and secular faiths, are all involved in the struggle of man for the true meaning of his personal social existence. ... The relation between Christian faith and other living religions and secular faiths is passing to a new stage, because they not only co-exist in the same society but also cooperate to build a secular society and culture. It is within such co-existence and cooperation that we can best enter into dialogue at the deepest level on the nature and destiny of man and on the nature of ultimate truth.[17]

Many Indian Christians have developed their ideas of dialogue in relation to secularism from the pioneer works of Devanandan and Thomas. Thus while some consider secularism as anti-religious, others interpret it as another ideology or quasi-religion with which world religions should dialogue for the common good.

Thirdly, sometimes, there is also a higher place attributed to secularism among the dialogue promoters in India.[18] In the previous chapter I noted Trevor Stack's study of such a trend in west Mexico.[19] In the Indian context, M. M. Thomas, even though he does not perceive that religion and secularism are antagonistic,[20] nevertheless talks about the dialogue between religions and secular ideologies while appealing to the secular constitution of India when attacks were carried out on Christians.[21] The secular democratic framework on which Indian polity is based is often put forward as a solution to religious extremism, based on Nehru's vision of a secular India in which secularism is not anti-religion, but rather respects all religions equally.[22]

Studying the use of secularism in dialogue, it is clear that there are ambiguities in the way it is maintained: as anti-religion, as another kind of religion and as a higher ground of authority. Of course it depends upon the context: the invitation to religions to come together is extended to insist that they are the key aspect in society in the context of secularization; the necessity of the dialogue of religions with secular ideologies is emphasized in the context of working for the welfare of human beings; the appeal to the secular nature of the society/nation is made in the context of the domination of religious majorities against the religious minorities. Nevertheless, in all three perspectives the notions of religious-secular distinctions are maintained. Thus the topic of secularism, secularization or secular ideologies in dialogue shows dialogue constructing religion(s) on the one hand and maintaining religious-secular distinctions on the other hand. In doing so, it continues to exercise the Western Enlightenment constructions of religion, and fails to critique the power structures within which these distinctions were created and maintained.

(b) Dialogue and World Religions Category

The existence of dialogue presupposes many world religions between which it takes place, such as 'Hindu-Christian dialogue', 'Christian-Muslim dialogue', 'Buddhist-Christian dialogue', 'Jewish-Christian dialogue' and so on. In all these, the religions involved are considered to be single homogenized systems which are differentiated from each other. Seldom does dialogue question this notion of 'world religions'. Faith and beliefs are distinguished,[23] and 'unorganized and organized' religions are differentiated,[24] faith seen as inherent in all human beings with beliefs or religions as established systems. For instance, Panikkar defines faith as 'the connection with the beyond' however one chooses to envision it, which

> may lend itself more or less to ideation, but no set of words, no expression, can
> ever exhaust it. And yet it needs to be embodied in ideas and formulas – so much
> so that faith incapable of expressing itself at all would not be human faith. Such
> expressions we have called beliefs, in accordance with what tradition has always
> felt.[25]

Thus the distinction between faith and beliefs is understood in terms of inner convictions and outer expressions of those convictions, a view maintained by

Panikkar and others. Religion and religions may also be distinguished in terms of one governing essence (religion) and many formulations of that essence (religions). In this regard, it should be noted that Hindu thinkers such as Vivekananda and Radhakrishnan have attempted to construct a universal religion – religion behind religions. On the other hand, comparative religion which underlies the construction of world religions category is considered to be both an antecedent of dialogue in the colonial period and the basic platform on which dialogue between religions can take place. An interest in religious beliefs, doctrines and performance is seen as the crucial element for fruitful dialogue.

Moreover, because dialogue primarily deals with Hinduism, Buddhism, Sikhism, Christianity, Judaism and Islam as world religions, it seldom acknowledges on the one hand, the different traditions within each world religion and on the other hand, traditions that ignore such apparent boundaries. There are usually internal differences in beliefs, doctrines and attitudes within each world religion, for each has its cultures, sects and denominations, with unique traditions and beliefs which do not always conform to generic or elite orthodoxy. Moreover, syntheses of religious traditions are attempted or unconsciously practised by religious adherents, but these are ignored because dialogue is based on world religions category. 'Popular religions' or traditions among marginalized people such as Dalit or Tribal which criss-cross the artificial categories of dialogue are usually ignored – a reason that these traditions have challenged dialogue, as discussed in Chapter 2.

(c) Hinduism in Dialogue in India

I concentrate on Hinduism in the discourse of dialogue because Hinduism has been represented as *the* religion of India, and Christian attempts to relate to Hinduism in the Indian context are more frequent than to any other religions. This is also, as discussed in the previous chapter, because modern discourse uses this 'religion of India' constructed by Western colonial elites and Indian elites in the colonial period. First, dialogue takes the dominant traditions within Hinduism to be the Hindu religion – the religion of all Indians except Christians, Muslims and Jews – and any dialogue with Hinduism is with high-caste or brahmanical traditions, a mode much challenged by liberation theologies in India, particularly Dalit. The dialogue promoters themselves realize the problem,[26] but they continue because these traditions are believed to be 'classical' and authoritative, indeed synonymous with 'Hinduism': the masses are ignored. This is exactly what Western Orientalists did during the colonial period – not only inventing and creating Hinduism, but constructing it both in terms of their own European biases and with a focus on the available 'high texts'. These attitudes are found in the works of Abhishiktananda,[27] Samartha,[28] Panikkar[29] and many others, who take the Vedas and Vedantas, especially Advaita Vedanta, as the most authoritative tradition in Hinduism, and therefore the basis for dialogue.

Secondly, dialogue consciously or unconsciously treats Hinduism as a single religion. Of course many traditions within Hinduism are talked about – multiple deities and various kinds of rituals and worship – but when it comes to *interreligious dialogue,* Hindu–Christian or Hindu–Muslim dialogue is between two clearly defined essentialized entities. Consider Klostermaier on Hinduism:

> Hinduism is organizing itself; it is articulating its own essentials, it is modernizing and it is carried by a great many people with strong faith. It would not be surprising to find Hinduism the dominant religion of the 21st century. It would be a religion that doctrinally is less clear-cut than mainstream Christianity, politically less determined than Islam, ethically less heroic than Buddhism … it would address people at a level that has not been plumbed for a long time by other religions or prevailing ideologies. … Hinduism by virtue of its lack of ideology and its reliance on institution, will appear to be much more plausible than those religions whose doctrinal positions petrified a thousand years ago or whose social structures remain governed by tribal mores.[30]

Hinduism is interpreted as *a religion,* similar definitions and interpretations of Hinduism being the norm in dialogue. The problem is not only for Hinduism but for all religions presented as one homogenous and generalized unit in discussion with another. Moreover, treating Hinduism as one religion embracing everything other than foreign religious elements in India has enabled Hindu nationalists or Hindutva ideologues to homogenize the identities of marginalized people such as Dalits and Tribals and exercise power over them. In my opinion, dialogue unwittingly contributes to Hindutva because it does not critique the notion of 'one Hinduism' – the Hinduism that is essential for dialogue to be carried out.

Thirdly, what is called the 'Hindu renaissance' has also played a key role in dialogue. Devanandan[31] emphasized this again and again, arguing that resurgent Hinduism is important for dialogue. But what is this resurgent Hinduism? It appears little more than the use of Western colonial constructs of Hinduism which helped elites in India to self-identify and Hindus to consolidate. Uncritical of the factors behind and the context of the power structures involved in the 'Hindu reformation', dialogue has interpreted renascent Hinduism as the crucial valued partner in dialogue with other religions, as Devanandan has done, and it continues similar directions even today.

Fourthly, with regard to Hinduism, Hindu tolerance is often cited as a principle to be emulated against aggressive Islam or Christianity. The notion of Hindu tolerance has been popularized by elites such as Vivekananda, and Christian dialogue accepted it. However, the endorsement of ideas such as 'Hinduism is known for its tolerance' or 'Hinduism accommodates everything' has many problems. The idea that Hinduism is known for its tolerance or *ahimsa* and non-violence is now challenged.[32] Romila Thapar observes that '*ahimsa* as an absolute value is characteristic of certain Sramanic sects and less so of Brahmanism',[33] on which today's Hinduism has been constructed. She further says that this 'notion appears in the *Upanisads,* but it was the Buddhists and Jains who first made it foundational to their teaching'.[34]

Finally, there are also ambiguities for dialogue activists regarding Hinduism in the context of Hindutva. Some would say that they are different – the first being the partner in dialogue, the latter an extremist deviation in Hinduism.[35] While Hinduism is accommodated in dialogue, Hindutva in India is critiqued within the framework of the secular polity of India often referred to by dialogists, as discussed earlier. Of course Hindutva ideologists may not accept the division – but dialogue holds this ambiguity, as was clear in Kanyakumari district. The dialogue promoters in Kanyakumari are associated with the Vivekananda Kendra in Kanyakumari district, which popularizes Vivekananda's ideals such as religious harmony, while they are also aware that these 'ideals' are exploited for the rise of Hindutva ideology in the contemporary period. One of my interviewees, a Roman Catholic priest in Kanyakumari, said, 'The religious tensions in Kanyakumari district have begun to rise after Vivekananda Kendra was founded in the district.'[36] Nevertheless he said that he is invited occasionally (more often earlier) to Vivekananda Kendra to teach Christianity, citing this as Hindu–Christian dialogue. This illustrates the ambiguities prevalent among dialogue activists.

My purpose in this section is not to criticize those who follow many traditions which are identified as 'Hindu' but to critique how 'Hinduism' has been appropriated uncritically in the discourse of dialogue, and how this can be an oppressing reality, given that the power of colonialism, Orientalism and Indian dominant traditions is involved in imagining such a category. Moreover, as noted above, this issue is not confined to Hinduism, for other world religions such as Christianity and Islam have also been constructed in similar ways.

(d) Dialogue and Religious Identities

Another problem is the fixed identities constructed for people assuming an identity between the tradition and actual belief. Believing and belonging are two basic aspects of religious identity, yet normally dialogue assumes congruence between religious identity and religious belief, often using the phrase 'believing community' or 'community of believers', based on a supposed shared set of beliefs and doctrines. Herbert Jai Singh, for example, assigns a clear religious identity to his neighbours in his book *My Neighbours* (Men of Different Faiths). He speaks of them as Hindu, Muslim, Sikh, Buddhist, Jain, Parsi, Christian, discussing the doctrines and beliefs of their religions.[37] Similarly, Wesley Ariarajah speaks of his neighbours in terms primarily of religious identity.[38] Commenting on defining Christian identity in a multireligious world, Samartha says that

> the intra-Christian and inter-religious debates need to be constantly related to each other for the sake of mutual criticism and mutual enrichment. While the former is very necessary in order for Christians to sharpen their profile and define their identity in a religiously plural world, the distinctiveness of a religious community cannot be truly defined without reference to other communities of faith.[39]

Indeed almost all dialogue promoters who talk about the primacy of religious identities of people actually interact, chat and cooperate with many other people who have different kinds of identities. Yet when it comes to the discourse of dialogue, they switch primarily to religious identity.

One of the issues that has to be looked at with regard to the primacy given to religious identity in dialogue is that because of it, dialogue in India has attempted to construct an Indian or Asian identity based on religions which had their ancient origin in that continent, as opposed to Christianity which, it is claimed, was developed in Western culture. I have discussed this issue in Chapter 1. In this regard Samartha says that 'Asia is the birthplace and home of many religions and cultures, some of which originated earlier than Christianity.'[40] This construction of Indian religious identity or Asian religious identity as against 'Western religion' or indeed irreligion is evidence of Indian dialogue activists appropriating the Western Orientalist construction of India (and Asia).

This naming of people along fixed religious identities leads to several consequences. Three of them are worth mentioning here. First, talking about and using fixed religious identities of people in dialogue often downplays the intra-religious identities of people. Second, the identities that cross religious boundaries among ordinary people are ignored. Third, the ability of individuals to construct multiple identities for themselves and to use them consistently in their dealings with other individuals is underestimated. While dialogue has failed to affirm these aspects with regard to religious identity, people at the grassroots consistently maintain a bundle of identities which move beyond religious identities, which is but one of several options, as I shall discuss later.

2 Beyond Religious Identity

How do ordinary people negotiate fixed religious identities based on world religions category? Do they challenge Western colonial as well as Indian elite constructions of religions and religious identities in general and their appropriation by dialogue in India in particular? One of the significant features with regard to religious identity among people at the grassroots – mostly in village India – is that they cross religious boundaries in constructing their own as well as others' identities. In spite of the informal evidence available that common people do not relate with each other primarily in terms of religious identity, those who talk *about* them conclude that they *are* divided by religions. Ethnographic studies treating the negotiation of religious identity are either lacking or ignored by dialogue. Even the Subaltern Studies Collective that has worked on several aspects of non-elite contributions for nationalism have rarely questioned the world religions category or identities based on those categories for people in India. In this regard Peter Gottschalk, whom I have discussed already, has done a remarkable study on how people in village India relate (and negotiate) with each other beyond religious identity which are sustained by multiple identity narratives. He has proposed multiple group identities among Hindus and Muslims in India by focusing on multiple identity narratives in a village, Arampur, in Bihar, and challenges those who continue to define and interpret the identities of Indians primarily in terms of religion.[41]

(a) A Multiple Identity Approach

Gottschalk talks about four perspectives that are currently found with regard to the scholarly study of religious identity in India[42]: the singular identity approach by which the scholars imagine 'discrete and singular realms of religious life detached from broader patterns of social, economic, or ritual interrelation' and describe 'the ritual lives of Hindus and Muslims ... as neatly contained within exclusive spheres of temple and mosque'[43]; the conflict approach that studies religious identities in the context of communal conflicts; the historical approach that looks at the historical constructions religious identity; and the composite identity approach where 'some scholars consider religious identity as one element among others within a particular group's larger sense of identity.'[44] Critiquing these approaches, Gottschalk argues for a case of multiple group identities. He maintains that

> those who do focus on a specific group and explore the various facets of their identity often say little about the possibility of multiple identities among individual members, some of which may not be shared by all in the group. ... The narratives that they relate about their homeland, their families, and themselves reflect the variety of group identities that form their personal identity like the atoms of a molecule. Like molecules, individuals adapt to changing environments by changing their internal arrangement, allowing them to bond with one set of molecules at one moment and another set at another moment without ever losing their internal consistency.[45]

Thus ordinary and common people live with multiple group identities that help them to relate with each other in various contexts. Commenting on the academic and elite downplaying of multiple identities in favour of discrete units, Gottschalk says,

> Perceiving the importance of religion in Indian society, many scholars erroneously conclude that this society can be described solely in terms of religious identity. Attempting to do so, these scholars overlook the nature of any individual as a conglomerate of various identities and fail to see the interests around which these identities form. By emphasizing only religious identity, scholars rarefy religions, removing them from the social milieu in which they develop. ... A study of group identity in India demonstrates how religious interests inform and are informed by other concerns in Indian constructions of society, and how narratives told by Indians can reflect these interests.[46]

In the Indian context today, a critical study of how people construct religious identities is especially important, because conflicts between 'Hindus' and 'Muslims' are often associated with their religious identities that divide them. Gottschalk continues:

> This pattern reveals a weakness in the notion of communal identity because the term implies that Hindus and Muslims identify only with a community of

other Hindus and Muslims. Although some Indians may embrace and propagate such an identity, few Indians live with such a singular self-understanding. Overreliance on the communal notion is akin to examining identity with a very narrow view – recognizing the importance of one aspect of an individual's identity but ignoring many other possible social bonds. … However … many Hindus and Muslims do not live within discrete and distinct religious worlds but practice faith lives that obscure clear identity boundaries.[47]

Against these perspectives that make religious identity the primary marker of the identities of people in India, Gottschalk invites scholars to study the multiple identities that are prevalent among people, without disregarding the role of religious identity. He concludes that despite the maintenance of religious identities among people, they 'have interacted and continue to interrelate in private and public arenas – even those identified as "religious" by participants – sharing identities beyond their religious ones'.[48] Gottschalk identifies this as a multiple identity approach. Commenting on multiple identities, he says,

Scholars who rely on a singular identity model commonly describe groups and individuals by Hindu or Muslim affiliations first, by regional location or caste second, and then by other qualifications. Thus, they ignore the identities that Hindus and Muslims may share despite their differing religious identities, such as those based on living in a shared neighbourhood, village, state, or nation. And, they also miss the possibility of shared religious identities, such as those that result from the melange of devotional traditions, including Sufism and *bhakti*, that have influenced one another in north India at various times.[49]

A multiple identity approach to how people maintain identities when they relate with each other can bring home many insights challenging the dominance of religious identity. First, the intra-religious identities constructed and maintained among people who do not always accept identities based on world religions category and rather formulate identities in terms of particular local or personal traditions within a religion system. Second, the maintenance of multiple identities where religious identity is one of several identities and maintenance of multiple identities in terms of caste, language, region, occupation and so on. I shall discuss how these aspects are found in Kanyakumari district later, but I shall now briefly note the long history of multiple identities in the pre-colonial and colonial period, despite elite constructions to the contrary.

(b) Religion and Identity in the Everyday Life During the Pre-Colonial and Colonial Period

Attempting to set out multiple identities – intra-religious identities, and group identities beyond religious identities – among the common people in earlier times is difficult, because the sources predominantly represent elite perspectives on religion and religious identity. Commenting on this, Gottschalk observes that

> the history of South Asian religious identities and community interrelations suffers for lack of historiographic sources for the period preceding European imperialism. The sources available generally describe large, elite institutions rather than local, popular expressions. For this reason, most scholars attempting to explore pre-colonial and early colonial religiosity commonly turn to the records of governments ... or organizations ... and attempt the difficult task of discerning broader religious sentiments.[50]

This observation can be extended to religion and religious identity of people in the colonial context. However a deconstruction of these sources by critically studying them as well as studying the oral traditions and narratives found among people in India can be used to reconstruct how ordinary people in India may have used these identities.[51]

Jews and Christians have lived in India since just before and just after the beginning of the Common Era, and appear to have coexisted with Hindus.[52] There are some attempts to study this in dialogue, even though the primary purpose is to show that dialogue has a long history.[53] Nevertheless those studies provide some insights on the life of people. The fact that the Synod of Diamper in 1599 forbade many of the customs and practices of Syrian Christians and that it considered those customs as pagan indicates that Christians interacted with their neighbours and used many of their traditions. Commenting on this, A. M. Mundadan says that 'these prohibitions and restrictions imposed by the Synod are a witness to the communal harmony and cordial relations that existed between Christians and Hindus'.[54] Some of the customs the Syrian Christians followed included building churches after the fashion of the local Hindu temples; using royal umbrellas (*muthukuda*), musical instruments and torches in their processions, which were also used in Hindu possession; imitating the Hindu *prasad* in the offerings of edibles, money, fowls and sweets; and following the Hindu marriage custom of tying a *thali* (chain or yellow thread) around the neck of the bride by the bridegroom and administrating the temple properties by a *yogam* (assembly).[55] These suggest that Christians and their neighbours related to and learnt from each other.

Even though colonial and post-colonial (after independence) historiography reads fixed religious identities into the pre-colonial period, contemporary scholars have argued that there is evidence of people who lived beyond religious identities. Poet Kabir, born into a Muslim weaver's family in Varanasi in the sixteenth century, is cited as one example. In the context of conflicts between Turks and Hindus, it is believed, he attempted to provide a nameless devotionalism through his Bhakti poetry which moved beyond Hindu and Islamic beliefs, attracting both Hindu and Muslim followers. Gottschalk observes that 'among the numerous precolonial religious institutions in South Asia, the Kabir Panth and other *nirgun bhakti* groups were more likely to foster inclusive devotional practices through their imageless devotions'.[56] Another example is Guru Nanak (1469–1539), the first guru of Sikhism, who is, according to Gottschalk, 'assumed to have favoured a synthesis of Islam and Hinduism … and, like Kabir, promoted a devotional identity that transcended those of Muslim and Hindu'.[57] Of course these ideas are not without criticisms,[58] but in the context of current Hindu–Muslim violence in India, these studies become significant. They affirm that people living in the pre-colonial period are believed to have related to local practices rather than supra-local labels, readily incorporating more than one religious identity in a 'nameless devotionalism', as the followers of Kabir did, or a nameless practice.

Similar attitudes with regard to religious identities are found among Bauls, a group of mystic minstrels living in Bengal. Jeanne Openshaw, who has done work on these people,[59] says that 'Bauls define themselves in opposition to those they judge to be "orthodox," Hindu or Muslim'.[60] This group of people, who are known for their music and enigmatic songs, wish to identify themselves as being in *bartaman*, which is opposed to *anuman*. While *bartaman* refers to 'an ideal of self-dependence based on one's own knowledge', *anuman* refers to 'others' knowledge or conjecture' and 'is epitomised by Hindu or Muslim "orthopraxy" or "orthodoxy," which is in turn legitimised by scripture and religious authorities'.[61] Against the state of being in *anuman*, Bauls adopt an approach of 'rejection and equalising, rejecting all paths classified as *anuman*, and equalizing all persons in terms of their humanity, that is, as human beings (*manus*)'.[62] For them, 'all conventional distinctions drawn between person and person are denied validity', and they 'favour an ideology of non-discrimination, or of non-dualism (*advaita*), a term apparently appropriated and substantially transformed from its more idealist, orthodox sense'.[63] Like the followers of Kabir, Bauls also bring challenges to the notion of fixed religious identities such as 'Hindu' and 'Muslim' for people in India.

There is also clear evidence of multiple intra-religious identity, constructed and used in terms of specific religious traditions within Hinduism, evidence which challenges the Hindutva idea of one Hinduism. Arguing against the notion that Hinduism is a single religion, Romila Thapar, a historian on ancient India, says the indigenous view of religion in India holds that there were two religious groups, 'Brahmanism and Sramanism with clear distinction between them. They are organizationally separate, had different sets of beliefs and rituals, and often disagreed on social norms'.[64] While Brahmanism was the dominant tradition followed by upper castes, Sramanism was popular among marginalized people. She also points out that there have been internal differences, with some conflict, between different religious traditions such as Saivism and Jainism, Saivism and Buddhism and Saivism and Vaishnavism, where Saivism was a dominant tradition that persecuted others.[65] Commenting on this she says that 'what is significant about this persecution is that it involved not all the Saivas but particular segments of sects among them. The persecution was not a *jehad* or a holy war or a crusade in which all Hindu sects saw it as their duty to support the attack or to wage war against the Buddhists or Jains'.[66] Arguing for a multiple identities in pre-colonial India, Thapar says that 'identities were, in contrast to the modern nation-sate, segmented identities. The notion of community was not absent but there were multiple communities identified by locality, language, caste, occupation and sect. What appears to have been absent was the notion of a uniform, religious community readily identified as Hindu.'[67] She concludes that 'if the history of religions in India is seen as the articulation not only of ideas and rituals but also the perceptions and motivations of social groups, the perspectives which would follow might be different from those with which we are familiar.'[68]

In spite of all the power structures involved in the notion of religion(s) and religious identity as noted in the last chapter, little has been done in dialogue to critique the notions of religions and other related categories. On the contrary these notions are generously popularized to promote dialogue instead of challenging and critiquing the myth of these categories and the associated Western rational bias. Moreover, dialogue follows the same principle regarding religious identities. On the one hand homogenized religious identities are endorsed – such as Hindus, Muslims and Christians – as if there are no internal, denominational or sect-based differences between them. When placed in dialogue, the illusion created is that each religion is a single entity, and the question of intra-religious dialogue is seldom raised. In the Hindu case, there are many people classed as Hindus who reject that label. What does dialogue with Hindus mean, or with Christians where certain groups exclude themselves and are so excluded by their 'brethren'? These are complex issues which are avoided in dialogue. Instead of understanding the grassroots experience with regard to religion, world religions category and religious identities, dialogue continues to engage in uncritically accepting these notions. Not only does dialogue fail to critique these modern colonial myths, but it popularizes them through elite dialogue discourses by constructing elaborate theologies, models and methods of dialogue which are all influenced by the notions of religion and religions and religious identity. How this has affected the notion of 'religious conflicts' prevalent in contemporary dialogue discourse in India is discussed in the next chapter.

Notes

1   Gottschalk, *Beyond Hindu and Muslim*, 13. There is another similar work that also challenges the Hindu and Muslim divide. See David Gilmartin and Bruce B. Lawrence, *Beyond Turk and Hindu Rethinking Religious Identities in Islamicate South Asia* (Gainesville: University of Florida Press, 2000).

2   *Report of the Jerusalem Meeting*, 369. Also see William Ernest Hocking, *Rethinking Missions: A Laymen's Inquiry after One Hundred Years* (New York and London: Harpers & Brothers Publishers, 1932).

3   John Henry Barrows, ed., *The World's Parliament of Religions: An Illustrated and Popular Story of the World's First Parliament of Religions, Held in Chicago in Connection with the Columbian Exposition of 1893*, vols I and II (London: 'Review of Reviews' Office, 1893). However, the perspective that WPR was organized for anything like dialogue or unity of religions is challenged in the contemporary scholarship by some like Eric J. Ziolkowski, who argue that the idea of Western and Christian supremacy was still dominant in the parliament. See Eric J. Ziolkowski, ed., *A Museum of Faiths: Histories and Legacies of the 1893 World's Parliament of Religion* (Atlanta, Georgia: Scholars Press, 1993).

4   Barrows, *WPR*, vol. I, 18.

5 Barrows, *WPR*, vol. I, vii.
6 Herbert Jai Singh, 'Preparation for Dialogue,' in *Inter-Religious Dialogue*, ed. Herbert Jai Singh (Bangalore: CISRS, 1967), 42–3.
7 Singh, 'Preparation for Dialogue,' 43.
8 Samartha, *One Christ – Many Religions*, 42.
9 K. L. Seshagiri Rao, 'Human Community and Religious Pluralism: A Hindu Perspective,' in *Dialogue in Community*, ed. C. D. Jathanna (Mangalore: The Karnataka Theological Research Institute, 1982), 162.
10 Panikkar, Raimundo, 'Foreword: The Ongoing Dialogue,' in *Hindu-Christian Dialogue: Perspectives and Encounters*, ed. Harold Coward (Maryknoll, New York: Orbis Books, 1989), ix.
11 Stanley J. Samartha, *Between Two Cultures* (Bangalore: Asian Trading Corporation, 1997), 168.
12 Samartha, *One Christ – Many Religions*, 42.
13 Ibid., 43.
14 Ibid.
15 P. D. Devanandan, *The Gospel and the Hindu Intellectual* (Bangalore: CISRS, 1958), 22–3.
16 Devanandan, *Gospel and the Hindu Intellectual*, 23.
17 M. M. Thomas, 'The World in which we Preach Christ,' in Witness in *Six Continents: Records of the Meeting of the Commission on World Mission and Evangelism of the World Council of Churches, held in Mexico City, December 8th to 19th, 1963*, ed. Ronald K. Orchard (London: Edinburgh House Press, 1964), 18.
18 For example, see M. M. Thomas, *The Secular Ideologies of India and the Secular Meaning of Christ* (Madras: The Christian Literature Society, 1976); and *Man and the Universe of Faiths* (Bangalore: CISRS, 1975).
19 Stack, 'A Higher Ground,' 47–69.
20 Thomas, *Christian Participation*, 303.
21 See M. M. Thomas, 'Inter-religious Conversion,' in *Religion, State & Communalism*, ed. J. John and Jesudhas Athyal (Madras: The Academy of Ecumenical Indian Theology and Church Administrations, 1994), 95–131.
22 Thomas, *Salvation*, 45.
23 Raimundo Panikkar, *The Intrareligious Dialogue* (New York: Paulist Press, 1978), 1–23.
24 Samartha, *One Christ – Many Religions*, 42.
25 Panikkar, *Intrareligious Dialogue*, 18.
26 Samartha, *Between Two Cultures*, 168.
27 Abhishiktananda, *Hindu-Christian Meeting Point*.
28 Samartha, *Hindu Response*.
29 Panikkar, *Trinity and World Religions*.
30 Klaus Klostermaier, *A Survey of Hinduism* (New York: State University of New York Press, 1989).
31 Devanandan, *Christian Concern*.
32 William R. Pinch, *Warrior Ascetics and Indian Empires* (Cambridge: Cambridge University Press, 2006). Also see the section on saffron warriors in Edna Fernandes, *Holy Warriors: A Journey into the Heart of Indian Fundamentalism*, revised and updated ed. (New Delhi: Penguin Books, 2006).
33 Thapar, 'Imagined Religious Identities?: Ancient History and the Modern Search for a Hindu Community,' in *Religious Movements in South Asia 600–1800*, ed. David N. Lorenzen (New Delhi: Oxford University Press, 2004), 344.
34 Thapar, 'Imagined Religious,' 344.

35 Wilfred, 'Our Neighbours,' 81.
36 Interview, Panivanban Vincent, Kanyakumari, 24 July 2008.
37 Singh, *My Neighbours*.
38 Wesley Ariarajah, *Not without my Neighbour: Issues in Interfaith Relations* (Geneva: WCC, 1999).
39 Samartha, *Between Two Cultures*, 145.
40 Ibid., 174.
41 Gottschalk, *Beyond Hindu and Muslim*.
42 Ibid., 35-8.
43 Ibid., 35.
44 Ibid.
45 Ibid., 39.
46 Ibid., 4.
47 Ibid., 39.
48 Ibid., 33-4.
49 Ibid., 36-7.
50 Ibid., 18.
51 In this regard, how ordinary people in the Tamil region used religious identity for emancipation in the context of Buddhist challenges to orthodox religion during the colonial period is discussed in G. Aloysius, *Religion as Emancipatory Identity: A Buddhist Movement among the Tamils under Colonialism* (Bangalore: CISRS, 1998).
52 Anand Amaladass, 'Dialogue between Hindus and the St. Thomas Christians,' in *Hindu-Christian Dialogue: Perspectives and Encounters*, ed. Harold Coward (Maryknoll, New York: Orbis Books, 1989), 13-27.
53 Amaladass, 'Dialogue between Hindus,' 16.
54 Mundadan, *History of Christianity in India*, vol. 1 (Bangalore: TPI, 1984), 27.
55 Thekkedath, *History of Christianity in India*, vol. 2 (Bangalore: TPI, 1982), 139-40.
56 Gottschalk, *Beyond Hindu and Muslim*, 22; also David N. Lorenzen, *Kabir Legends and Ananta-das's Kabir Parachai* (Albany, New York: State University of New York Press, 1991).
57 Gottschalk, *Beyond Hindu and Muslim*, 22; also W. H. McLeod, *Guru Nanak and the Sikh Religion* (Delhi: Oxford University Press, 1968), 158-61.
58 Linda Hess and Shukdeo Singh, *The Bijak of Kabir* (New York: Oxford University Press, 2002), 5.
59 Jeanne Openshaw, 'The Web of Deceit: Challenges to Hindu and Muslim "Orthodoxies" by "Bauls" of Bengal,' *Religion* 27, no. 4 (1997): 297-309; *Seeking Bauls of Bengal* (Cambridge: Cambridge University Press, 2004); also, *Writing the Self: The Life and Philosophy of a Dissenting Bengali Baul Guru* (New Delhi: Oxford University Press, 2009).
60 Openshaw, 'The Web of Deceit,' 298.
61 Ibid., 297.
62 Ibid., 303.
63 Ibid., 304.
64 Thapar, 'Imagined Religious,' 336.
65 Ibid., 344.
66 Ibid., 345.
67 Ibid., 347.
68 Ibid., 356.

Chapter 5

Are Religions in Conflict?

In the last two chapters I discussed issues that need critical attention for dialogue in the context of the plurality of religions – namely the religion-secularism distinctions, world religions category and fixed religious identities – and noted that dialogue has serious problems due its uncritical acceptance of the plurality of religions as well as its failure to critique the power structures associated with the construction of religion and its plural religions. I now move to deal with another issue – religious conflicts – in the context of which dialogue is carried out to ease tensions and conflicts between people. My contention is that while there are a number of issues and roles involved in actual conflicts between people, stressing a conflict's religious nature can feed overall anger, which does not achieve better relationships, contrary to the objectives of dialogue.

In relation to the Indian context, some clarifications are necessary about the terms 'religious' and 'communal' conflicts: the other terms used for conflicts in these contexts are violence, clashes, riots and the milder 'tensions'. Communal conflict is generally defined as conflict between communities, based on religion, caste, ethnicity or language. Although communal conflict in India literally refers to conflict between such communities, religious conflict and communal conflict are often used synonymously, implying that religious conflicts are or express communal conflicts in India and South Asia. Also, broadly speaking, though it may not be the case always, while the term communal conflicts has been generally used in the fields of sociology, anthropology and history, the term religious conflicts is used in the field of theological and religious studies. Of course, nowadays the term 'religious violence' is increasingly used as if it is common.

In this chapter I look critically at two aspects regarding religious conflicts. First, the general assumption that many, if not all, conflicts in the world today are religious conflicts in that religion in one way or the other is the *cause* of the conflicts, either religion as a belief system or religion as an identity. Either or both, in this view, can start or stoke an erupting conflict, or conflicts between adherents of different religions occur due to their particular religious identities.[1] The second assumption is the claim more common in dialogue that religion is an *instrumental* rather than a causative factor in religious conflicts. The dialogue activists who belong to this camp believe that it is the use and misuse of religion in the hands of powerful elites that leads to conflicts between masses belonging to different religions.[2] Politicians aspiring for political power and control are singled out as major culprits in manipulating religion to create conflicts among people. While this political explanation of religious conflicts helps to understand the complex power structures involved in religious conflicts, it has limitations because it categorizes religion and politics as separate systems. It may well be true that the political class in general and individual politicians, in their search for power and control over the masses and to mobilize the public to strengthen their vote bank, try to exploit all the available opportunities. However, whether their activities can be called *religious* conflicts or not, and whether the conflicts created or produced are *between* people with fixed religious identities, are important questions to be raised. Moreover, why should one always use a 'religious' framework to understand and explain multidimensional conflicts which are commonly performances of aspiring for and expressing power of different kinds? Here my argument is that it is not strictly the political or other *uses of religion* but the very *naming* and *interpreting* of any conflict as religious which needs attention.

1 Religion as the Cause of Conflicts

The notion that religions are the cause of conflicts is based on at least two basic assumptions. First, it is assumed that religions are fundamentally prone to violence, and thus they create conflicts among people. Those who hold this view believe that religions encourage their adherents to kill each other.[3] The idea here is that religions, particularly religious texts, incite followers to engage in violence.[4] Building on this notion, dialogue promoters generally think that conflicts between religions seem to be generated because of some religious texts, especially when they are misinterpreted. For example, if biblical texts such as John 14.6 and Acts 4.12 (salvation comes only through Jesus Christ) are taken literally, they imply the superiority of one religion over the other and thus lead to tensions between religious adherents.[5] This is also the same case with the concept of *jihad* in Islam. Second, dialogue may claim that while religion and religions contain 'good' things, the lack of proper understanding of these teachings by the rioting followers causes conflicts.[6] In other words, it is not religion as such but the misunderstanding of religions which is behind causing religious conflicts. Such misunderstanding can apparently be corrected by teaching as part of dialogue. I shall discuss these two aspects below.

(a) 'Religions Prone to Violence'

The 'religions-prone-to-violence' mantra is normally proclaimed by secularists, who assert that secular ideologies based on reason and rationality do not kill people or, if so, that such violence or killing is justifiable. Yet while rejecting part of that secularist argument, and pointing out secular violence, religionists nevertheless accept the notion that religions are prone to violence. For instance,

Samartha differentiates established religions from 'religions' and maintains that established religions have the nature to divide people. He maintains that

> established religions have often divided people and nations and given rise to tensions and conflicts. They have held scientific progress, resisted social change, and have often added religious fuel to military conflagrations making reconciliation more difficult. Of all the wounds human beings inflict on each other, religious wounds are the most difficult to heal.[7]

According to him, the term 'religions' here refers not to 'the established institutions of religion or systems of belief or boundaried social groups with their sense of separation from others, but the spiritual resources within religions'.[8] It is the established religions (or world religions) that create barriers, preventing better relationships between people. Hence Samartha concludes that 'established religions with their conflicting claims' are 'barriers to community rather than bearers of peace'.[9]

This perspective is also maintained among the dialogue activists in Kanyakumari district. Many of the dialogists I interviewed maintained that religions have both potentials to instigate violence between religious followers as well as resources for working out peace and harmony among people. The conclusion is that it is up to the followers to choose. Abdul Salaam, a Muslim dialogue activist in Kanyakumari, felt that religion has divided the people in a district which was otherwise peaceful,[10] referring to the Mandaikadu religious conflicts. In such observations the fundamentalist and exclusivist people in both Christianity and Hinduism were accused of instigating their adherents to fight each other.[11]

The notion that religions are prone to violence does have its critics, who see it as a modern myth invented especially by the West in the context of its relationship with the East, particularly the Middle East and Islam. This has been effectively argued by William Cavanaugh, who has analysed recent religious violence discourses prominent in the West.[12] Criticizing the notion that religions are prone to violence, Cavanaugh argues that religious violence is a myth exercised by the 'secular' West against the 'religious' Middle East. Scrutinizing the works of scholars like Mark Juergensmeyer[13] and Charles Kimball,[14] who have argued that religions make their adherents become violent and murderous, Cavanaugh argues that religious violence is a discourse of the secular West intended to divide bad 'terrorising Islamic violence' from good secular Western violence (the war on terror) working for peace. Cavanaugh's conclusion is that 'religious violence' is used by the West to dominate the East.[15]

Violence in South Asia is argued not on the basis of secularist versus religionist, but supposedly rather between different religious adherents. Nevertheless, Cavanaugh's analysis is useful, because the point he makes strongly is that religious violence exists only in the discourse of those who want to exercise power and domination over others: it is a myth, not a reality. This is true in the Indian context and in Kanyakumari district, where those who maintain the religious violence myth are people with vested interests who want to exercise power and domination over others at many levels. Moreover many complex socio-economic factors involved in conflicts between people are easily played down when one uncritically accepts the notion that religions are prone to violence.

Another way of reflecting on 'religious violence' is based on identity. People belonging to different religions fight with each other because the identity of the 'other' is considered to be a threat to one's own. Thus when identities are constructed on the basis of religion and then opposed to each other, some see religious conflicts arise. Talking about the Indian context, for example, Michael Amaladoss maintains that 'communalism based on religion has been a problem from the beginning. ... Hindu-Muslim riots have become a recurrent feature in some areas in India.'[16] And, for Samartha,

> throughout history the diversities of ... religion have led to serious conflicts between people. There are indeed 'demonic' possibilities within the structures of plurality. Different religious communities within particular countries in the world have clashes with each other resulting in immense human suffering. ... The Hindu-Buddhist-Jain conflicts during the earlier period in India's history, later on, the Hindu-Muslim clashes which unfortunately recur even at present, and now the Hindu-Sikh tensions are examples.[17]

Thus one often talks about the problem in Kashmir between India and Pakistan as Hindu–Muslim conflicts; the Sri Lankan–Tamil ethnic conflicts as Buddhist–Hindu–Muslim–Christian conflicts; the American occupation of Iraq and the West's dealings in the Middle East as a Christian–Muslim conflict; and the Israeli–Palestine problems as a Jewish–Muslim conflict.

All these accounts ignore not only the different and mostly complex power structures that are responsible for conflicts between human beings in the particular regions and elsewhere, but also the many identities of the people involved in these conflicts. The issue at stake again is the question of fixed religious identities which are believed to be behind religious conflicts. The question of how people in India have been ascribed fixed religious identities during the colonial period has been discussed in previous chapters. The notion that the conflicts are between religious communities or between people with fixed religious identities is one of the fundamental reasons behind attempts for dialogue to work for better relationships between these religious communities. In other words, the existing context is perceived as religiously divided, which then allows dialogue between religions as the solution to overcome these religious divisions. Precisely it is here that a serious limitation of dialogue becomes evident.

(b) Misunderstanding of Religions as the Cause of Religious Conflicts

One of the causes of religious conflicts, according to some dialogue promoters, is the misunderstanding prevalent among religious adherents about their own as well as their neighbours' religions. The assumption here is that all religions are different ways to one God, teaching their adherents to be in peace and harmony with others, and that when people fail to understand these basic truths of religions, religious clashes occur between them. In such situations, it is believed, dialogue can bring together people of different religions to work for a better understanding of religions among people, minimizing conflict and creating peace. Such an approach sees religions as normally or inherently good, so where they are (or are thought to be) a source of or adjunct to violence, the reason must lie in the failure of followers to understand. Gnana Robinson, who is promoting dialogue activities through CIRSJA, an organization involved in interreligious activities in Kanyakumari district, believes that misunderstanding between people of religious adherents leads to religious conflicts and propose that proper understanding should be created through dialogue.[18] He says,

> It is a sad fact that in India, as well as in several other parts of the world, 'Religion' has become the ground for hostilities and divisions ... any religion which contributes to hostility and destruction among people is not worthy to be called religion. ... Many of those who subscribe to hate campaigns on the basis of religion, either do not understand their own faiths as well as the faiths of their neighbours or they use religion just for the sake of personal and political ends, having no faith commitment to that religion.[19]

Religious misunderstanding is then often related to religious exclusivism and fundamentalism. The misunderstanding that religions cause conflicts is based on the following assumptions: religions can engender better relationships between people, but misinterpretation of these resources can lead to the emergence of religious conflicts; religious conflicts occur because of claiming one's religious superiority over other religions; ridiculing and criticizing the religious beliefs, symbols, rituals and practices of other religions due to the lack of proper understanding of religions by adherents.[20] These are just some misunderstandings between religions which interreligious workers believe cause conflicts.

This attitude can be found among dialogue promoters in Kanyakumari also. Claiming that the causes for conflicts lie not in religion, but in followers who fail to understand the existence and purpose of religion, Tobias said, 'Religion can only unite people. It cannot divide. If it divides, then it cannot be religion'[21]:

> Religions help people to unite and struggle for common life issues. Humanism (the exact translation of the Tamil term is 'caring for humans') is the basic philosophy of all religions. Therefore, if all religions do the same job – making human – then there is the only possibility that religions have to cooperate with each other. There is no possibility that they should conflict with each other.[22]

Thus religion cannot damage relationships between religious people. But the problem occurs 'when this basic aim of religions to unite human beings is forgotten and distorted, giving rise to religious conflicts'.[23] Thus, for Tobias, 'When Hindus understand Christianity and Christians understand Hinduism and both understand Islam, then the resulting fact will be that humans are equal.'[24] But on the contrary, if conflicts continue and humanity does not become one, it will perish. Hence for future survival, a proper relationship between religions is necessary and should be effected through dialogue.[25]

With regard to these ideas of dialogue on religious conflicts, it is my contention that religious misunderstanding as the cause of religious conflicts represents a very narrow understanding of conflicts between people. On the one hand it limits the problem to belief systems in religions, an elite view often held by ritual practitioners, and on the other it fails to understand different issues related to conflicts between people. It simply accepts the notion of religions prone to violence with a slight modification that misunderstanding causes it. Socio-economic factors, other forms of domination and inequality in society and the beneficiaries of the clashes between people, their tactics, methods and purposes in dividing people in the name of religion, are seldom paid attention to in this perspective of religious conflicts.

Against the conventional understanding in dialogue that religions cause or are used in conflicts among people, many anthropological and sociological studies in India as well as in the global context have brought out complex issues in understanding religious conflicts. One of the prominent explanations of these studies is that the power interests based on socio-economic factors lead to religious conflicts. For instance, a group of scholars have undertaken a study of the communal riots in post-independence India and have come to the conclusion that behind many of the conflicts which are termed religious are socio-economic factors and political power issues. Asghar Ali Engineer, one of the leading scholars of Islam in India and a dialogue activist, has undertaken a number of case studies of communal or religious clashes in India which are generally considered and projected as Hindu–Muslim riots. His primary finding is that while religion plays a role in these conflicts, mostly the socio-economic growth of people is behind their occurrence.[26] The same is true with Kanyakumari district, and some of the socio-economic and political factors involved in these religious conflicts are discussed in the next chapter in my case study of the 1982 clashes.

Such tracing out and arguing for the importance of socio-economic factors is a useful perspective for understanding religious conflicts. Dialogue is increasingly incorporating these perspectives,[27] yet it still holds to the notion of religion-and-violence and to divisions based on religious identities. But why should socio-economic factors lead to or be seen as 'religious' instead of 'socio-economic' conflicts? Why should only the religious identity of people be labelled and the many other factors, interests and identities be ignored? Who is involved in the process, or who is orchestrating it? Before discussing these questions, let me pick up on the idea of the political preference for religion as a source of conflict.

2 Religion as an Instrument in Religious Conflicts: *The Political use of Religion*

As I mentioned earlier, while some dialogue activists maintain that misunderstanding of 'religions causes conflicts between people', others emphasize the instrumental nature of religious conflicts. For the latter, misunderstanding by followers can readily be exploited by power-seeking elites in society. Here the instrumental nature of religion in religious conflicts is emphasized. Commenting on religious conflicts, Amaladoss maintains that

> in the multi-religious context of today, religious fundamentalists are not that violent. They may be aggressive proselyters in the field of religion. But they do not normally indulge in violence. Violent behaviour results when religious emotions are used to promote economic and political goals. Religion then becomes communalistic. Leaders of communal movements may themselves be non-believers or at least non-practising. But they (ab)use the religious emotions of the masses in a coldly calculating, rational manner.[28]

This suggests that religious fundamentalism (or misunderstanding of religions) is less a cause of 'religious' conflicts than is the political manipulation of religions, a view opposed by some dialogue activists and many secularists.

Moreover, the emphasis on the instrumental nature of religion in religious conflicts is often set against those (mainly 'secularists') who accuse religions of breeding communalism in India. In such contexts, Samartha says that

> one must be careful not to blame religions alone for these troubles. Studies by sociologists, political scientists, economists and theologians bring out the fact that to single out 'religions' as the only cause of these conflicts is to over-simplify a highly complex matter. It is pointed out that all too often these are secular riots in which religions are cunningly used for political or economic purposes.[29]

Commenting on the instrumental nature of religions in religious conflicts, Samartha maintains that

> studies on recent communal clashes ... have brought out the point that religions are 'not the *causative* factor but the *instrumental* factor in such clashes. ... It is made to appear as the *causative* factor.' Economic and political factors, and the question of power relations between different groups and political parties, play a large role in these riots. Therefore to call them *religious* or *communal* riots is quite wrong.[30]

Vested political interests predominate in India where religion is instrumentalized, for power-seeking politicians use, misuse, exploit and manipulate religions to attain and maintain power. For dialogue activists, 'The increasing politicization of religions is a disturbing feature of contemporary Indian life. ... [It] threatens the secular character of the State, hinders the process of national integration, gives rise to anxiety, fear, tension, and conflicts in society, and has global implications as well.'[31] In India, political parties associated with the ideologies of Hindutva or Hindu nationalism who try to mobilize 'Hindus' for gaining and maintaining political power in the state and central governments are especially likely to use this strategy.

The political use of religion is primarily understood to mean politicians who mobilize people, *creating* or producing conflicts between people of different religions and inciting different religious communities to fight each other. Politicians' use of 'religious' symbols and 'religious' emotions of people are often cited as examples of their manipulation of religion. Hindutva organizations who misuse religious symbols such as Ram and temples for Ram, Ganesa and cow slaughter are referred to here.

In such a context, a dialogue activist maintains that 'at a time when because of historical reasons, because of economic and political power politics, religion is used as a means to obtain and hold on to power and money, patient dialogue is the way open to us to break down communalism, fanaticism and violence'.[32] This patient dialogue is to be built on the peace potentialities that are available within religions for maintaining peace, harmony and reconciliation, which are 'seldom brought out ... except *after* the event. It is because of the recurrence of these riots, which fly out as sparks from within a volcano, that inter-religious dialogues are even more important in our country to reduce tensions, resolve conflicts and tame political passions *before* conflagrations set in.'[33] For a dialogue activist in Kanyakumari, 'Religion and politics join together to create religious conflicts. This has become the order of the day. Of course, all social institutions are politicized. But due to emotional and sentimental reasons, religion stands at the top.'[34] Of course, comment on the political use of religion for religious conflicts is not an issue confined to dialogue alone. Many social scientists and others also share this view. Before critiquing some of the limitations of the political use of religion for religious conflicts, I shall offer perspectives by scholars other than the dialogue promoters.

Paul Brass, in his classic work, *The Production of Hindu-Muslim Violence in Contemporary India*, argues against the general notion that communal riots are spontaneous furies of mobs. 'The whole political order in post-Independence north India and many, if not most of its leading as well as local actors ... have become implicated in the persistence of Hindu-Muslim riots. These riots have had concrete benefits for particular political organizations as well as larger political users.'[35] The primary beneficiaries of these riots, for Brass, are the organizations under the umbrella *Sangh Parivar* which exercises the ideology of Hindu nationalism, and are involved in the task of mobilizing people for politics within their Hindu religious identity. Several analysts of communal violence in India have taken this approach, insisting that the political establishment, particularly the Hindu nationalist organizations, is responsible for the recent conflicts in India. This has helped them to contextualize particular communal violence incidents both within the wider context in India and in the local context where the communal violence has occurred.

Steven Wilkinson offers another perspective to study communal violence including religious violence. Studying Hindu–Muslim violence in India, he argues that electoral competition is the factor which decides whether communal violence should occur or not. He says that

at the local level ... individuals have many ethnic and nonethnic identities with which they might identify politically. The challenge for politicians is to try to ensure that the identity that favours their party is the one that is most salient in the minds of a majority of voters. ... Parties that represents elites within ethnic groups will often – especially in the most competitive seats – use polarizing antiminority events in an effort to encourage members of their wider ethnic category to identify with their party and the 'majority' identity. ... These antiminority events ... are designed to spark a minority countermobilization (preferably a violent countermobilization that can be portrayed as threatening to the majority) that will polarize the majority ethnic group behind the political party that has the strongest antiminority identity. When mobilised ethnic groups confront each other, each convinced that the other is threatening, ethnic violence is probable outcome.[36]

In addition to the point that the politicians exploit the identity that favours their vote bank, Wilkinson also raises an important question as to why violence breaks out in some cities and towns and not in others. This helps to understand 'the variation in patterns of violence within states'.[37] His argument is that it is the political elites who decide whether there should be a communal clash in a particular place and in a particular time, depending on their political calculations. They produce it only when it helps consolidate their vote bank.

However, the idea of the political and other use of religion held in dialogue has limitations in understanding and interpreting Indian 'religious' conflicts. First, the phrase 'political use (or misuse or manipulation or exploitation) of religion' is very ambiguous and does not explain specifically the process through which political use of religion is taking place. Often what dialogue means by 'use of religion' is not clear, or not differentiated from what a social scientist might mean. Secondly, 'using religion to fight' is a questionable phrase, for it assumes that religion is one of two separate categories, and the other is politics, and that both influence each other. In arguing for political manipulation of religions, dialogue not only accepts boundaries between religion and politics but evades accusations that religions breed communalism and conflicts by insisting religion plays only an instrumental and not a causative role. My point here is not to argue that religions *also* cause conflicts, but rather to say that the boundaries between these systems are not as clear as often portrayed by many people including those who are engaged in dialogue.

Thirdly, the political explanations for communal conflict or religious conflict indicate that the actual conflict that happens is *between* two communities which the politicians wish to see fighting for their own tactical purpose. It indicates that the political elites and their supporters just instigate conflict between people using religion, and that they *stay away* during the ensuing conflict between what could be seen as their victims or puppets. Yet one of the groups involved in fighting does support the organizing political party and thus has agency. It is a conflict *between* a mob which is involved in the mobilization of people identifying with the majority religious identity and the people of the 'other' religious identity, or it is an attack *by* the former *on* the latter. For example, in what is called Hindu–Muslim conflict where religious mobilization for politics is undertaken by the Hindutva forces, the conflict is either between the mob that supports the Hindutva parties and the Muslims who retaliate to their conflict, or simply, it is the violence exercised by the former on the latter. Hence the conflict is not between two communities with equally powerful identities, whether religious or otherwise. The attacks on Sikhs following the assassination of Indira Gandhi in 1984, the attacks on Christians in Dangs in Gujarat in 1998 and on Muslims in Gujarat in 2002 (Gujarat pogrom) and the attacks on Christians in Kandhamal, Orissa, in 2008 are some examples of this. But in the studies of communal conflicts by dialogue activists and others, phrases such as the endurance of 'Hindu-Muslim conflict' and 'Hindu-Christian conflict' are used uncritically to give the impression that actually conflict has happened *between* people of these communities and that the communities are equally resourced in political and legal terms.

Some of the recent studies on religious conflicts in India critique the notion that conflicts occur *between* two religious communities, suggesting they are also within groups. One of the frameworks within which this is critiqued is the majority versus minority conflicts. In this perspective, communal conflict in India is understood as anti-minority violence. Many scholars who study communal conflicts in India take this perspective. Ravinder Kaur, critiquing the notion that the communities involved in communal violence in India are 'evenly matched groups partaking in a ritualised outbreak of violence that tends to threaten the otherwise "peaceful co-existence" of different religious communities in India', argues that 'the episodes of violence in the last two decades ... challenge this widespread notion of two inimical religious groups engaged in reciprocal violence'.[38] For her, violence is mostly anti-minority. She finds two problems with a collective approach to communal violence which ignores internal division.

> *One*, communal conflict is presented as an action-reaction phenomenon where each community fuels the conflict further. The eruption of violence is somehow always linked to a kind of provocation from other side. Thus, Muslims and Hindus, somehow, become equal partners in the instigation of violence or at least in the creation of a potentially inflammable situation. ... *Two*, the term 'communal' seems to have acquired a meaning that has far outgrown its literal one, that is, something shared by a community. Its noun-based derivative 'communalism' now denotes hatred for the 'other' community in an almost ahistorical and decontextualised mode. The role of state institutions, political organisations and media, in instances of conflict, remains unreflected and detached from the idea of two inimical communities opposed to each other. The very concept of community itself within 'communal' seems to have a fixed, timeless and an unchallenged characteristic to it. It implies the existence of a pre-fabricated entity of community that is essential to actualise the inter-community violence. The mobilisation aspect, or the role of the organisations in constructing a community around popularly recognised symbols, is thus completely overlooked.[39]

Thus the identities of the communities involved in conflicts are not equal, according to Kaur. In such a context where the politically motivated group or the politically constructed community attacks a community with a discernible and different 'religious identity', the events that result are not conflicts *between* religious communities. However, the political manipulation which leads groups to fight and the political will to ignore economic and equity division overlooks and simplifies this reality.

Fourthly, the idea of the political use of religion often indicates that conflicts actually exist between *religious* communities because of the negative use of religion in the hands of politicians. Here the question that has to be raised in relation to the idea of the political use of religion is whether politicians actually produce any *religious* conflicts, when an actual incident of violence takes place between groups of people. It is true that politicians may produce and aspire to produce violence and conflicts among people in order to mobilize a section or a few sections of people who would be expected to support them for power, but they may not actually produce *religious* conflicts between two communities with different religious identities fighting each other. In other words, when it is said that politicians instigate conflicts between people and as a result conflicts occur, the fundamental question is whether the conflict is between people acting on the basis of their different *religious* identities, or whether many other identities of people such as region, caste, ethnicity, family and others are also involved. Even though people aspiring for political power try to interpret these conflicts as religious, as I will argue in the next chapter in the case study of the 1982 clashes in the Kanyakumari district, in an actual conflict many identities of people are involved, and many socio-economic and even personal issues are behind the melée. One needs to move beyond the notion 'political use of religion' which is ambiguous, which is somewhat an escapist statement to put the entire blame on what is taken to be the political sphere, which views politics and religion as entirely two separate entities and which holds that what finally occurs is a *religious* conflict. What is to be understood clearly is how any conflict can be named as religious (whether the religious identities are realized or not realized in those conflicts), for capturing and maintaining power *not only* in political domains, but also in various aspects of life.

3 *Naming and Interpreting of Conflicts as Religious*

As I have noted, religious conflicts that politicians or others try to create are neither *religious* conflicts nor conflicts *between* religious communities, despite claims by the dialogue promoters and others who support the view that political manipulation of religions leads to conflicts between people with different religious identities. If religious misunderstanding does not lead to religious conflicts, and if the political manipulation of religions does not lead to the actual conflicts between people with different religious identities, then where do the origins of religious conflict lie? Of course conflicts happen between people with many identities self-constructed as well as imposed. But how do they *become* religious conflicts, or become named as such, and for whose benefit might this be?

My argument is that religious conflicts exist primarily in the discourses of political elites (i.e. those who are in political power) as well as others who need such a discourse for maintaining power at different levels. In the context of political power aspirations, *naming* conflicts as religious helps religious mobilization for strengthening voter support. Similar processes are also found at different levels including personal problems between people where religious identities are added to strengthen one's cause. As we will see in Chapter 8, where the grassroots relationships between people are discussed, such naming and interpreting of conflicts as religious is possible not only among elites, but also among ordinary people.

This leads to the issue of the importance of *naming, interpreting* and *projecting* conflicts as religious for certain power interests. This aspect is seldom discussed in studies on communal conflicts or religious conflicts in contemporary India. Scrutinizing the act and process of naming any conflicts as religious conflicts is important, because it is this discourse that helps those who seek to strengthen and extend their power over others. Here the very naming of a particular incident of violence between people on one aspect of multiple identities serves to further the tension between people and maintain the namers' power. My argument is that it is not the misunderstanding of religion or the political use of religion that are solely responsible for religious conflicts. Rather, it is *naming conflicts* among individuals and groups, who live with multiple identities, *as religious* for vested interests that is crucial. The dialogue promoters seldom recognize this when talking about either religions causing conflicts or religious people being instruments in the hands of politicians in creating conflicts.

Some scholars studying communal conflicts have noted this aspect of the discourse. Paul Brass discusses naming and interpreting communal violence within the framework of blame displacement after the actual communal violence incident has taken place. He sees three phases in the process of communal riots: preparation or rehearsal, activation or enactment and explanation or interpretation. The third phase is to do with the communal discourse, in which the incident of communal violence is named to control its meaning. Brass identifies this mainly with 'blame displacement', and says that in addition to politicians, many other elites in society are also implicated. For me, however, naming and controlling the meaning of violence does not just concern blame displacement, but is a much more calculating act. Naming an incident of violence – violence between one political mob and a distinctly 'other' or the political mob's attack on the latter – as violence between communities with assumedly parallel community identities is intentional and carefully planned. In political circles the resulting discourses help politicians much more than the actual conflicts. Therefore it may not be correct to say that the political use of religion create conflicts, but rather that in maintaining the discourse of religious conflicts in the present context, politicians, among many power mongers, play a major role. Especially in the Indian context, the Hindutva forces and their political allies who spend much of their efforts in mobilizing Hindus for their vote bank maintain this discourse. How and why conflicts are named as religious is discussed below.

First, it is true that politicians are involved in conflicts, and they produce conflicts with the support of the mob (or politically constructed community) that favours them. But these are not religious conflicts, because, as I have already discussed, the conflicts are not between two inimical groups with parallel identities each representing one coherent and cohesive religious identity; it is in their naming and interpreting of these conflicts as religious that actually 'religious' conflicts exist. Thus religious conflict is not a reality, but it is an illusion, a myth within a carefully constructed discourse.

Second, politicians aiming for more political power can interpret any conflict between groups of people in society as religious. When two or more people fight for different reasons they have multiple identities and different reasons. There are conflicts between friends, conflicts in family, in occupation, in a village and so on. But building on the already available religious conflicts discourse, politicians can pick up the religious identities of the people involved in conflicts, a process which helps maintain their powers. There are many examples in India, and Kanyakumari is no exception. In fact, as I have noted earlier, in the very discourse of 'Mandaikadu religious conflicts', Hindutva politicians play a major and continuing role in such naming.

During the time when I was undertaking my field research there were some tensions in Kanyakumari district. There were efforts by the district administration to pipe drinking water from an inland village called Vellimalai to a nearby fisherfolk village called Kadiapattanam, which is on the coast. While the Hindu Nadars and other high-caste Hindus are the major group of people in Vellimalai, the Roman Catholic fisherfolk Christians live in Kadiapattanam. The people in Vellimalai agitated, fearing that they may run short of drinking water in the future. But within hours of protest by the people in Vellimalai, BJP and other Hindutva politicians in the district gathered in the village to insist that the district administration was favouring Christians against the Hindus who will lose their resources.[40] Similarly in June 2008 there was a land dispute between a CSI church in a village called Pillayarpuram and people who happened to be Hindus in the village. The problem became serious when Hindus wanted to use the church land as a pathway. When the church stopped it, immediately BJP and other Hindutva politicians from that and adjacent districts gathered, ending in a clash between them and police. But in the discourse of the BJP politicians in the following days, the land dispute was sidelined, and the incident interpreted as a conflict between Hindus and Christians as representatives of their 'religions'.[41] Such a pattern is common, multiple reasons for conflict being interpreted as religious for Hindutva reasons.

Third, even when there are no conflicts between people with different religious identities, politicians (among others) can maintain the discourse that there are such conflicts, which exist purely in their discourses. People may live together irrespective of their differences, but still the power mongers insist they live in conflict. Yet as will be discussed in Chapter 8, people live together despite various conflicts. But the crucial point to note here is that dialogists seldom make any efforts to question such discourses prevalent among politicians and other elites aspiring for power, often limiting their criticisms to the politicians' use of *religion* for/in an actual conflict.

Fourth, it is not only politicians who maintain this discourse but many other groups with vested interests. The idea of political manipulation often implies that only politicians are involved in such activities or that they are the primary culprits. But this is not the case always. Confining the situation to politicians using religions leaves out or ignores the role played by many other groups in society who also for their vested interests with power, control and domination over others at various levels in society (not entirely in the political arena) name conflicts as religious. But interestingly, to interpret or project a particular conflict, even in a local village context, one does not need to be a politician. Even ordinary people with vested interests can name and project personal conflicts as religious in order to appeal for more support. Thus the myth of religious conflicts is used for formal political power and equally for localized political power, however limited that may seem, to control others. So it is not the *use* of religion in conflicts which is in question but the *utility* of naming a conflict as religious, enabling power accumulation and controlling others.

Similarly, the dialogue promoters, by overemphasizing the role played by politicians, seldom talk about the role played by established religious leaders such as bishops, gurus, imams and so forth. At times, these groups are also involved in mobilizing people in terms of their religious identities for various reasons. This is true with the 1982 conflicts in the district – both with Hindu and Christian leaders – where religious leaders attempted to mobilize people along religious identity lines, which gave religious colour to the conflicts.[42] In these conflicts, one of my interviewees said that a wall poster from some of the Hindu religious leaders used terms such as Hindu and Christian, and a bishop organizing a funeral procession for the Christians who were killed in a police shooting appealed for firm religious identity.[43] Dialogue activists simplify or ignore this reality and mostly blame politicians.

However, grassroots people accuse not only politicians but also religious elites of maintaining religious conflicts, with some villagers insisting that both politicians and religious leaders attempt to interpret conflicts as religious for selfish reasons.[44] This dimension is missing in elite perceptions of religious conflicts as they rarely criticize how the religious leaders and others name conflicts as religious for their vested interests. Moreover, while the phrase 'religious conflicts' is popular among dialogue activists to talk about the necessity of dialogue, the people at the grassroots quickly interpret the conflicts in terms of their multiple dimensions. The trend among them is that there are several reasons for conflicts, and it is mostly personal conflicts that *become* religious conflicts.[45]

Fifth, dialogue activists talk about the political use of religion as a reason for conflicts and miss out other factors beneficial to politicians such as caste, region, language and even personal conflicts, depending upon the context. Dialogue activists seldom talk about these other spheres, attributing great importance to the 'political use of religion'. However, people at the grassroots are more aware of the abilities of politicians to use any available possibilities,[46] and this seems a crucial difference between dialogue activists and grassroots people. Thus what is called religious conflict is mostly a clash between political mobs and their 'others', or a political mob's attacks on the latter, or politicians (and also religious leaders) naming and interpreting existing as well as non-existing tensions between people as religious clashes. Therefore, whether religious conflict happens or not, whether any conflicts that happen between people in society are religious conflicts or not, politicians among other power elites *need* the 'religious conflict discourse' for political ends. In other words, my argument is that those scholars and analysts of religious conflicts who rightly point out the fact that political power aspirations are behind religious conflicts in the 'political use of religion' often fail to understand that religious conflicts can be a myth existing only in the *discourse* of political and other elites who continue to score points by maintaining and exercising it.

Political elites think that such interpretation will keep the situation tense based on the simple divide-and-rule policy. However even when the Hindutva organizations such as Rashtriya Swayamsevak Sangh (RSS) try to maintain their discourse on religious conflicts, interpret it as religious and use it for mobilizing people, one can find that socio-economic issues and identities, and not primarily religious identities, are kept to the fore even among its members. The following narrative illustrates this. One of my interviewees was sharing an interesting experience he had regarding how RSS, which works for the religious mobilization of Hindus, is viewed by its members. He is a school teacher, two of whose colleagues from different parts of the district were RSS members. He explained:

> These two colleagues have different caste identities – one from a Pillai [Pillai is a high caste community in Kanyakumari and people in this caste community are referred to as Other Communities (OC) or Forward Class/Community according to the Indian government regulations] and the other from Nadar community [Nadar community is referred to as Backward Class]. I met them separately and asked them why they have joined an organisation which is known for extremism and dividing people on the basis of religion. The colleague from Pillai community said to me that their community in the past owned good amount of lands in the district, but now most of them have been bought by people from Nadar community and they are slowly dominating them. In order to check their domination he needed an organisation to stand and hence he had joined the RSS. The colleague from Nadar community said that people from Pillai community used to oppress them in the past, not allowing them to freely move, and gave them a lot of troubles. Now the Nadar community has grown up in socio-economic status, but still the people from Pillai community try to look down upon them and to dominate them. To challenge their domination he needed a platform and hence he had joined the RSS.[47]

This illustrates that even when a political organization tries to mobilize Hindus against other religious communities, it maintains the notion that people are divided on the basis of religious identities and interprets conflict between people as religious, nevertheless the struggles between its own members are more socio-economic and not primarily of religion. Yet the platform on which they have chosen to fight each other is provided by a system which propagates religious distinctions. Thus even though socio-economic issues on the one hand and religious identity on the other hand are interlinked in the above case, nevertheless, the primary reason for involvement is socio-economic, even though that of the organization, in public discourse, is religious difference. The simple acceptance of the political use of religion in creating religious conflicts seldom brings out these perspectives.

My idea in arguing that there is no religious conflict is not to protect 'religion' or 'world religions' from being the causes of conflicts. In fact, as discussed in the previous chapter, I question their very separation and categorization. Neither do I argue that every conflict is non-religious, as if religious identity does not play any role at all in conflicts – partition violence in India, the 2002 violence in Gujarat and the 2008 violence in Kandhamal are some examples where religious identities did play a role. Rather, my argument is that conflicts where multiple factors and identities are involved cannot be reduced to religious conflicts. More importantly, in the Indian context, I argue that the continuing discourse on religious conflict – whether it creates religious conflicts or not – gives the political elites as well as others seeking power the chance to attribute created conflict to religion. Rather than understanding these conflicts merely through religious identity, or for that matter any other single identity of human life such as caste, region, ethnicity and so on, one must see them linked not only to political power but also to power in each area of life where elites try to control non-elites.

The dialogue promoters believe that religions, or misunderstanding of religions, and the political use of religion are responsible for the occurrence of religious conflicts today. This perspective has ignored various factors which are involved in the clashes between people as communities. In this chapter, I have been primarily concerned with the various factors found in what are considered to be religious conflicts: not misunderstanding of religions but rather various socio-economic factors, and not political use of religion but rather the naming of conflicts as religious by political elites as well as others who have vested interests of power. Thus we have not religious *conflicts* but religious conflict *discourses* and a constructed mythology of conflict. By continuously propagating this myth and thinking that they are bridging warring religious communities and making peace and harmony between adherents of different religions, the dialogue promoters are, in fact, furthering the existence of this myth, exploited by people for their own power ambitions. The same trend is found among the dialogue activists in Kanyakumari district who have uncritically accepted the naming of conflicts between people in the district in 1982 as religious by the political elites. How different factors are involved in those conflicts, and how they became 'religious' conflicts, are discussed in the next chapter by undertaking a case study of the dialogical discourse of the religious conflict.

Notes

1 Many of my interviewees from dialogue circles in Kanyakumari fall into this camp for whom conflicts between religions in the district is the necessary context for dialogue between religions.

2 For some discussions on religious conflicts from this perspective, see Michael Amaladoss, 'Dialogue as Conflict Resolution,' available online at http://sedosmission. org/old/eng/amaladoss1.html; Samartha, *One Christ – Many Religions*, 51–65; 'Inter Religious Relationships in the Secular State,' 131–2; and Puthiadam, 'Theology of Religions,' 194–6.

3 See Mark Juergensmeyer, *Terror in the Mind of God: The Global Rise of Religious Violence* (New Delhi: Oxford University Press, 2000); Charles Kimball, *When Religion Becomes Evil* (San Francisco, CA: HarperSanFrancisco, 2002).

4 Juergensmeyer, *Terror in the Mind of God*, 81.

5 In such a context, dialogue promoters are involved in offering different interpretations of such exclusivist texts.

6 Robinson, 'From Apartheid,' 82–96.

7 Samartha, *One Christ – Many Religions*, 42.

8 Ibid.

9 Samartha, *Courage for Dialogue*, 121.

10 Salaam, Interview.

11 Dhasan, Interview.

12 William T. Cavanaugh, 'Colonialism and the Myth of Religious Violence,' in *Religion and the Secular: Historical and Colonial Formations*, ed. Timothy Fitzgerald (London and Oakville: Equinox Publishing Ltd., 2007), 241–62.

13 Some of the works of Mark Juergensmeyer in this regard include *The New Cold War?: Religious Nationalism Confronts the Secular State* (Berkeley, CA: University of California Press, 1993); and *Terror in the Mind of God*, which has been already mentioned.

14 Kimball, *When Religion Becomes Evil*.

15 Cavanaugh, 'Colonialism and the Myth of Religious Violence,' 241.

16 Amaladoss, 'Liberation as an Interreligious Project,' 158–9.

17 Samartha, *One Christ – Many Religions*, 7.

18 Robinson, 'From Apartheid,' 82–96.

19 Gnana Robinson, 'India, the Great Nation, Whose Pride is at Stake,' in *Unite to Serve*, ed. Gnana Robinson (Kanyakumari: Kanya Peace and Justice Publications), 6.

20 Dhasan, Interview.

21 Tobias, Interview.

22 Ibid.

23 Ibid.

24 Ibid.

25 Ibid.

26 Asghar Ali Engineer, ed., *Communal Riots in Post-Independence India* (Hyderabad: Sangam Books, 1991). In this book Engineer provides case studies of some major communal conflicts in India. Also, see Veena Das, ed., *Mirrors of Violence: Communities, Riots and Survivors in South Asia* (New Delhi: Oxford University Press, 1990).

27 I have discussed the incorporation of socio-economic issues in dialogue in Chapter 1.

28 Amaladoss, 'Dialogue as Conflict Resolution.'
29 Samartha, *One Christ – Many Religions*, 57.
30 Samartha, 'Inter-Religious Relationships,' 131–2.
31 Samartha, *One Christ – Many Religions*, 58–9.
32 Puthiadam, 'Theology of Religions,' 195.
33 Samartha, 'Inter-Religious Relationships,' 131–2.
34 Nagalingam, Interview.
35 Paul R. Brass, *The Production of Hindu-Muslim Violence in Contemporary India* (New Delhi: Oxford University Press, 2003), 6.
36 Steven I. Wilkinson, *Votes and Violence: Electoral Competition and Communal Riots in India* (Cambridge: Cambridge University Press, 2005), 4.
37 Wilkinson, *Votes and Violence*, 5.
38 Ravinder Kaur, 'Mythology of Communal Violence: An Introduction,' in *Religion, Violence and Political Mobilisation in South Asia*, ed. Ravinder Kaur (New Delhi: Sage, 2005), 23.
39 Kaur, 'Mythology of Communal Violence,' 25–6.
40 *Daily Thanthi* (a Tamil newspaper), 31 May 2008.
41 *Dinakaran* (a Tamil Newspaper), 10 June 2009.
42 Perumal, Interview.
43 Interview, confidentiality requested. The informant was a dialogue activist but did not want to affirm it openly.
44 Parvathi, Interview.
45 Ibid. I will elaborate the grassroots attitudes to conflicts in Chapter 8.
46 Focus-group Interview, Mohammed.
47 C. Chokkalingam, Interview, Nagercoil, 4 July 2008.

Chapter 6

DIALOGUE AND THE MYTH OF RELIGIOUS CONFLICTS: A CASE STUDY

In the last chapter I analysed two major claims in dialogue in India: that religions or misunderstanding of religions by religious adherents and the political use of religion are the primary reasons for religious conflicts. In evaluating these claims I made two points. First, various socio-economic factors – not just misunderstanding of religions – as well as multiple identities of people – not just their religious identities – are part of what are claimed to be religious conflicts. Secondly, the naming and interpreting of conflicts as religious by people with vested interests in society, especially people with vested interests for power, is a more significant element than the political use of religion, which basically indicates that politics and religion are two separate categories.

In this chapter I further develop these arguments by undertaking a case study of conflicts that took place in Kanyakumari district in 1982 which dialogue activists and many others generally term 'Mandaikadu religious conflicts' or 'Mandaikadu Hindu-Christian conflicts'. The dialogue activists in the district insist that these conflicts happened between Hindus and Christians in the district because of their misunderstanding of each other's religion. I argue that these conflicts were primarily between people with different caste identities, but from a week after these conflicts started on 1 March 1982 until now, they have been labelled religious conflicts. My argument is that they did not occur primarily due to misunderstanding of religions *nor were they between people with fixed religious identities*. On the contrary, the actual incidents of violence involved different identities of people and many sociopolitical issues, all of which have been consistently subsumed under the category of religious conflicts.

Of course, the conflicts I analyse in this chapter happened more than thirty years ago, and one may have reservations about the rationale of doing a case study of the incident today. Also it is true that some people in the district prefer to forget those 'bad times' or risk disturbing a fragile peace.[1] Moreover, from the field research perspective as well, doing a case study of conflicts between people that happened long ago is problematic, given the paucity of first-hand sources.[2] Nevertheless, doing a case study of these conflicts is necessary even after a long time, because they have not been forgotten and are revived almost daily by forces with vested interests. More importantly, it is the portrayal of these conflicts as religious that continues to serve the power interests of those who want the discourse to stay alive. Especially, portraying these conflicts as Hindu–Christian has been a systematic effort of those aspiring for political power, especially by the supporters of Hindu nationalist organizations to mobilize Hindus for political purposes. What I will be attempting in this case study is to show that dialogue activists, for various reasons, simply accept these clashes as religious in their dialogue activities, and that they seldom acknowledge the multiple issues behind these 'religious' clashes.[3]

1 Conflicts in Kanyakumari District in 1982: A Case Study

The case that I present here is not a complete coverage of Kanyakumari district in 1982. As with any dramatic event, different accounts of the incidents of 1982 are maintained by different people, whose viewpoints are mostly coloured with their own interests. What is presented first here is the story as it is generally narrated by those who believe that what happened in 1982 were 'religious conflicts'. One such group which provides this version of 1982 conflicts are dialogue activists. Others include politicians, the government officials and the Hindutva forces in the region. What the dialogue activists say about these clashes forms the subject of my case. In Chapter 8, where I discuss the grassroots perspectives on dialogue and relationships between people, I shall set out the same story from the perspective of those who did not see these conflicts as religious. Here I provide some of the basic details about the events before analysing them.

Mandaikadu is a small village in Kanyakumari district where people with Hindu and Christian identities live. The village is about 20 kilometres away from Nagercoil, the capital of the district. The village is on the coast, the sea forming the southern border of the village. Fisherfolk Christians, who are members of the Roman Catholic Church, live in the coastal area, and Hindus of different castes live in the northern part of the village. In the northern part, there is a temple belonging to Hindus which is known as *Mandaikadu Bagavathi Amman Temple*. The deity worshipped in the temple is Bagavathi Amman, a female deity. Every year in March, there is a festival in the temple which lasts for ten days. Devotees in the local village as well as nearby villages attend the festival, and it is also attended by many devotees from the nearby state of Kerala. Normally, it is claimed that the devotees who come to attend the festival go to bathe in the sea – for which they need to cross the fisherfolk area – as part of their worship in the temple. During the festival in 1982, there were quarrels between the fisherfolk Christians and Hindus, which ended in police killing six people from the fisherfolk community on 1 March 1982.[4] The tensions extended throughout the district, and two more people were killed from the fisherfolk community in another village, Manakudi, on 15 March 1982. The circumstances around these incidents are generally known as 'Mandaikadu religious conflicts' or 'Mandaikadu Hindu-Christian conflicts.'

(a) The Sources

The sources of this case are the people and documents that insist that the 1982 conflicts in Kanyakumari district were religious conflicts, meaning that those conflicts were caused by a misunderstanding or a manipulation of religions. These perspectives on the 1982 conflicts were gained during interviews with the dialogue promoters which I undertook during my field research in the district in 2007 and 2008. In addition to personal interviews, I have also utilized some texts written largely as part of the rationale for dialogue in the district.

There are also some other writings regarding the 1982 conflicts which I will be using in the case analysis section. These include the Venugopal Commission report, which was set up by the Tamil Nadu state government in order to probe the police killings during conflicts. This is the only publicly available official document about the conflicts, which also locates the 1982 conflicts in the 'religious conflicts' framework. As I already mentioned, the local politicians for their vote-bank ends continue to project the conflicts as religious conflicts, while some historians and social scientists in the district are critical of that projection, and I was able to conduct interviews with one local politician and a few social scientists in the district. A few writers have analysed these clashes in order to find the causes of conflicts,[5] and some critique the notion of the Mandaikadu conflicts as religious by analysing them within the framework of caste inequality.[6] I make use of all these sources and insights drawn from them in my case analysis.

(b) The Case: Dialogue Activists' Version of 'Mandaikadu religious conflicts'

The case that I present below is the version of the Mandaikadu conflicts that is prevalent among the dialogue activists in India, collected through my interviews and collated to make their view clear. After presenting the case I will analyse it – the dialogue activists' version of Mandaikadu conflicts – in the light of various factors in the overall context in the district.

(i) The 'pre-Mandaikadu' Situation in Kanyakumari District Dialogue promoters generally hold that Kanyakumari district was known for its peace and communal harmony until 1982 when conflicts broke out between Hindus and Christians in Mandaikadu. This they call the pre-Mandaikadu situation and, just as there are BC and AD, some respondents said there should be 'pre-Mandaikadu' and 'post-Mandaikadu' to mark the fact that the district was peaceful in the former period, while the situation deteriorated in the latter period due to the Mandaikadu conflicts.[7] Most of the dialogists see the earlier period as one of communal harmony when different religious people – mostly Hindus, Christians and Muslims – lived peacefully as neighbours.

(ii) The Role of Christian Conservatives and the Mandaikadu Religious Conflicts One of the major factors that led to Mandaikadu conflicts in the district, according to the Christian participants in dialogue activities, was the evangelical activities that were undertaken by the extremist or fundamentalist Christians in the district.[8] These Christians, some clergy and lay people from the mainstream churches in the region – the CSI, the Lutheran Church and the Roman Catholic Church – and many from the Pentecostal churches were hostile to their religious neighbours, particularly Hindus. Being convinced of the superiority of Christianity over other religions, these so-called 'fundamentalist' Christians ridiculed and condemned

the religious activities of local Hindus, abhorring their deities and preaching against other religions, their beliefs and practices.[9] Moreover they arranged for public conventions and continued to attack other religions, distributing tracts with messages such as 'Christianity is the true religion' and 'Jesus Christ is the only saviour'.[10] Not only did they distribute these tracts in public places, but they also went to the areas surrounding Hindu temples and other Hindu religious places to distribute tracts and preach against Hinduism.[11] They organized conventions in Mandaikadu during the festival in Mandaikadu Bagavathi Amman temple in March every year. The Travancore government stopped this in the 1940s, but this resulted in every church arranging an annual convention,[12] at which Hindus were referred to as 'heathens', 'devil worshippers' and 'children of the devil'. According to the Christian dialogue activists, the Christian conservatives did these things due to their misguided belief that Christianity was the only true religion.[13]

These exclusivist attitudes of evangelical Christians led to strong reactions from the Hindus in the district, with verbal or physical opposition in some places, especially by Hindus belonging to Hindu extremist organizations such as RSS and Hindu Front. There were some incidents where the extremist Christians and the extremist Hindus were fighting with each other.[14] This kept the situation in the district tense and ultimately led to the Mandaikadu conflicts.

(iii) Pre-1982 Situation in Mandaikadu Village In spite of the Christian fundamentalist attitudes to Hinduism and Hindu reactions to them in Mandaikadu, the situation in Mandaikadu village, according to some advocates of dialogue, was one of peace and harmony until the Mandaikadu religious conflicts. During the Mandaikadu temple festival, both Christians in Mandaikadu and the nearby villages, and Muslims living around, used to contribute money and other items for the festival. The Hindus in turn, during the festival, used to decorate the shrine near the temple which belonged to the Roman Catholic Christians, giving offerings there on their way to their sea-bath. Thus in Mandaikadu Christians and Hindus were living together and celebrating festivals together.[15]

(iv) The Mandaikadu Incident of 1982 But unlike earlier times, because of the religious tensions prevalent among Hindus and Christians in the district at this time in 1982,[16] Hindus and Christians were divided in Mandaikadu when the festival in the Mandaikadu Bagavathi Amman temple began in March. Because of the already existing religious tensions due to both groups' exclusivist attitudes, the Hindus and Christians in Mandaikadu were involved in fighting with each other. The Christians were not happy with the celebration during the festival, because for the first time, there were many outsiders at the temple festival belonging to Hindu extremist organizations such as Rashtriya Swayamsevak Sangh (RSS), Vishwa Hindu Parishad (VHP) and Hindu Front.[17] The already tense local situation led both parties to confront each other during the festival. The Hindus were using loudspeakers, some directed at the shrine. In retaliation, the Christians directed loudspeakers from the shrine towards the temple, increasing the tension.[18] The Hindu devotees, as in every year, came to take a bath in the sea, but were stopped by the Christians, further increasing tensions.[19] When it was reported that the

Christians attacked and molested the Hindu women who came to bathe in the sea, tensions were erupting, and the police were called; in order to stop the mob violence they fired, and as a result six Christians were killed in Mandaikadu.

(v) The Spread of Mandaikadu Religious Conflicts The news about the violence between Hindus and Christians in Mandaikadu spread to other parts of the district, furthering violence between Christians and Hindus. One dialogist mentioned that 'those Hindus and Muslims who had been living in peace and harmony for many years now suddenly started to fight each other'.[20] The 'religious' violence escalated, and many places where Christians were living were attacked by Hindus and vice versa. Two more Christians were killed in Manakudi, another village in the district, by police when they were gathering to attack Hindus. Thus the local religious conflicts persisted for months, according to the 'religion and violence' interpreters, and divided the 'whole district' on the basis of religion.[21]

(vi) The post-Mandaikadu Religious Conflicts Situation According to the dialogue promoters, some reputed religious leaders and lay people in society, interested in religious harmony and peace, tried to stop the conflicts between Hindus and Christians. They joined together and went to visit the people in the affected areas as an interreligious group, which impressed the Hindus and Christians who were involved in conflicts. When they talked to the people about the need for religious harmony, it made a great impact on the people.[22] However, religious tensions still persist in the district and the situation is still tense, with people afraid that religious conflicts such as 'Mandaikadu' can occur again.[23] This, say the dialogue activists, can be ameliorated or even resolved through dialogue teaching people to understand their religion properly and stop fighting in the name of religion.

(c) Case Analysis: Situating the Case in its Context

(i) Problems with the Dialogical Narrative In the light of materials and different perspectives available about the district, which I will elaborate below, I must start by saying that the narrative presented by the dialogue promoters about the Mandaikadu religious conflict and events related to it lacks many points and has contradictions. Moreover, the narrative does not contextualize what happened in Mandaikadu village, or it does so inappropriately or insufficiently. The only contextualization they offer is that of religious misunderstanding promoted by the evangelizing activities of the 'fundamentalist' Christians and their attack on Hinduism.

    One of the major contradictions in the narrative is the interreligious dialogue proponents' claim about the peaceful situation before the 1982 conflicts. The repeated claim is that Kanyakumari district was a 'peace park' before Mandaikadu religious conflicts.[24] Nevertheless, even while affirming that it was a 'peace park', Christian dialogue activists point to the efforts of Christian conservatives which shamed Hinduism and Hindus, and thus induced reactions from the Hindus even before 1982. It should be noted that, in the history of Christianity in India, the efforts for Christian proselytization of other religions' members by some

Christians, and the demeaning of other religions and their beliefs, go back to the arrival of Western colonial Christianity in India: these were not new developments of the 1980s. However, according to the promoters of dialogue, these efforts by Christians played a major role in instigating religious violence in the district. This view – that Christian conservatives are the root causes of Hindu–Christian violence – is said in the context of being self-critical by the Christian participants in dialogue who are termed 'Christian liberals'.[25] At the outset it seems that 'Christian liberals' took the blame for religious violence on themselves or people belonging to their religion. However, they blamed only the 'Christian fanatics'– the fanatic 'other' within Christianity, people who understand neither Christianity nor other religions properly, and whose misunderstanding of religions led to religious violence in the district. This is an act of de-contextualization of the situation by the people promoting dialogue who *want* to conclude that religious misunderstanding causes religious violence and can be rectified only by dialogue activities. What is ignored, in my opinion, is the fact that the call for conversion has existed among some Christians for centuries, and dialogue activists fail to ask why only at this time it has led to 'religious' conflicts between Hindus and Christians in the district, thus fail to properly contextualize the conflicts.

In the narrative of the dialogue promoters, Mandaikadu village is the central sparking point for the religious violence over the past thirty years. Nevertheless, in spite of this powerful projection of the Mandaikadu conflicts as the context of dialogue, little appears in the narrative about what happened in Mandaikadu, what were the local factors that led to conflicts between people in Mandaikadu and how it spread to other parts of the district. These questions are important because they shed light on the process of conflicts between people in 1982. In other words, while hurrying to conclude that what happened in Mandaikadu was a religious clash between Hindus and Christians, the dialogue promoters either play down the different identities that were involved in the conflicts or fail to note that, in what they call religious violence, there were identities of people involved which were other than religious identities.

Let me elaborate this. When I asked about the caste identities that were involved in these conflicts, there was a hesitation among the dialogue activists from the Nadar community to admit openly that Nadar Christians were also involved in attacking the fisherfolk Christians.[26] Such acknowledgement does not help in seeing the conflict as a Hindu–Christian conflict. On the other hand, asking for confidentiality, and in low voice, one dialogue activist from the fisherfolk community told me that 'there were some Nadar Christians also involved in attacking fisher-folk community in some parts of the district, however, it would not be advisable to talk about this as it would affect the relationships between Nadar Christians and fisher-folk Christians in the district'.[27] This indicates clearly that there is awareness, at least among some dialogue activists, about the caste identity in the conflicts, but it is not openly admitted because the issue then becomes intra-Christian conflicts where 'interreligious' dialogue may not have much of a role to play. This is a crucial limitation of dialogue not only in Kanyakumari district, but anywhere they talk about the occurrence of religious conflicts.

(ii) Caste Identities Involved in 'Mandaikadu religious conflicts' In Mandaikadu, people who were involved in conflicts had many identities, including predominantly caste and religious (Table 3). On the one side were fisherfolk, who were Roman Catholic Christians from a caste community called Mukkuva, and on the other side people with multiple caste and Hindu religious identities. According to the caste gradations, the fisherfolk people, mostly confined to the coastal area, come under Most Backward Caste (MBC). The non-fisherfolk in the Mandaikadu village include Nadars who belong to Backward Caste, and Nairs, Pillai and Krishnavagaiyar belonging to Forward Caste.[28] The latter among Hindus are also called caste Hindus. Nadars are the majority people in Mandaikadu, as they are in Kanyakumari district.

In Mandaikadu village what happened during the Hindu festival in 1982 was a clash between the fisher and non-fisher people. Of course the actual conflicts occurred in relation to the festival in the Hindu temple, but when they spread to the other parts of the district, they did so as tensions between fisher and non-fisher, coastal and inland people, specifically between Mukkuvas and Nadars (Table 4).[29] It did not spread even as conflicts between fisherfolk *Christians* and non-fisherfolk *Hindus*. There were many inland villages – where Hindus, Christians and Muslims of non-fisherfolk communities lived – which either attacked the coastal villages in retaliation, or were gathering together to protect the inland villages if the fisherfolk came to attack. The same was true for fisherfolk who were either attacking non-fisher villages or were protecting their villages from the attacks of non-fisherfolk. The rumours were primarily about fisherfolk attacking non-fisher people, or vice versa. Gramam village, where I did field research regarding the grassroots people living together in spite of religious differences, was one such village where Hindus, Muslims and Christians were preparing to face attacks from fisherfolk in the nearby village of Manakudi, as there were rumours of attack.[30] Moreover, an inland village called Samathanapuram, where most of the people were Christians belonging to CSI, was attacked by the inhabitants of Kovalam, a nearby coastal village, in which

Table 3 Identities of groups involved in conflict in Mandaikadu

Group 1	Group 2
Coastal	Inland
Fisherfolk	Non-fisherfolk
Roman Catholic (Denomination)*	Amman Vazhi (Sect)*
Christian*	Hindu*
Mukkuvas	Nadars
	Nairs
	Krishna Vagai
	Pillai (Vellalas)
	Chettiyar
Most Backward Class/Caste/ Community	Backward Class/Caste/Community Other Communities (also known as Forward Castes)

*indicates the identities that were not in conflict during the actual conflicts.

Table 4 Identities of groups involved in conflict Outside Mandaikadu

Group 1	Group 2
Coastal	Inland
Fisherfolk	Non-fisherfolk
Roman Catholic*	Roman Catholic, Protestant (CSI, LMS, Lutheran, Salvation Army, Pentecostal etc)*
Christian*	Hindu (Multiple sects within)*
	Muslim (Sunnis, Shias, Sufis)*
	Christian (Multiple denominations within)*
Mukkuvas	Nadars
	Nairs
	Krishna Vagai
	Pillai (Vellalas)
	Chettiyar
Most Backward Class/Caste/	Backward Class/Caste/Community
Community	Scheduled Castes
	Other Communities (also known as Forward Castes)

*indicates the identities that were not in conflict during the actual conflicts.

it is claimed three people were killed, two Christians and one Hindu.[31] These developments suggest that caste identities played a greater role in these conflicts than did religious identities. Dialogists simply fail to ask the basic question of why Christians from one area should come and kill two Christians in another area in 'Hindu–Christian' violence!

It is also significant that some participants in dialogue activities in the district admitted to me that 'some' of the non-fisherfolk Christians – mainly Nadar Christians belonging to the Protestant Church as well as to the Roman Catholic Church in which the fisherfolk Christians are also members – kept quiet when the inland villages attacked the coastal ones.[32] These problems continued for several days, and as a result the fisherfolk were prevented by the non-fishers from selling fish in the inland fish markets. One of the local political leaders from the BJP, for whom the Mandaikadu conflicts were Hindu–Christian religious conflicts, admitted that inland Christians and Hindus jointly attacked the fisherfolk, adding that these Christians later joined with coastal Christians to attack Hindus.[33]

Moreover, maintaining caste difference and caste inequality is stronger than religious divisions in many parts of India. The religious identities of people may be attacked, or people may be attacked for belonging to a particular religion, but such identity is usually seen as an 'extra' identity, caste identities always remaining crucial to the ordering of rank. This is still true in Kanyakumari district. The general stereotypes among some inland people about fisherfolk, which I often heard in my childhood, are that 'the fisherfolk lack the sixth sense', are 'illiterate', 'drunkards', 'always fighting with others' and 'not knowing how to be in peace with others'. Among people at the grassroots who do not have knowledge of dialogue, for example in Gramam, as I will show later, the 1982 conflicts were seen as an inland versus coastal problem that also involved occupational issues (selling and buying fish), and that is still the case.

Thus the Mandaikadu incident was initially between people who had fisherfolk Christian identity and non-fisherfolk people who had inland Hindu identity, and it spread to other parts of the district as a fisherfolk versus non-fisherfolk problem, irrespective of tradition. It did not spread as a Hindu–Christian problem. This goes against the narrative provided by the dialogue activists, and raises the question: What made these primarily caste-based conflicts into religious conflicts, or what made them spoken about as such? How did the turn occur? Who were the agents and beneficiaries in suggesting these conflicts were religious? How and why did this narrative come to dominate in the district for about twenty-five years? This leads to the wider political context in India as well as in Kanyakumari district, where the Hindu nationalist forces, with their political representation in the BJP, started emerging powerfully. One of their primary goals was to mobilize people with Hindu identity for political purposes. Before that another factor which plays a primary role in shaping this discourse must be discussed: the Venugopal Commission report.

(iii) Venugopal Commission Report and the Mandaikadu Religious Conflicts The Venugopal Commission was set up by the Tamil Nadu government to probe into the police killings of fisherfolk Christians during the 'Mandaikadu conflicts between Hindus and Christians'. But it started the enquiry with the outcome of religious tensions already in mind, setting out incidents of so-called religious tensions in the district during the previous years as indicative of the potential for religious violence between Hindus and Christians, and readily concluded that what happened in March 1982 were religious conflicts between Hindus and Christians. It blamed the conversion activities by the Christians and the extremist attitudes of the Hindu organizations such as RSS for claiming that they were guardians of Hinduism. It said nothing about the Hindutva forces' mobilization of religion for political ends, unlike the Liberhan Commission report, which concluded that religious mobilization for politics was one of the reasons for the demolition of the Babri Masjid in Ayodhya in 1992.[34] Despite providing detailed accounts of incidents where the 'Hindus' were even searching for 'fisherfolk' people to attack, it still maintains that the problem was one of religious clashes.[35] While this projection – that what happened were religious conflicts due to hostility to each other's religions – has benefited the Hindutva forces and their tactics in religious mobilization for politics, it has been uncritically accepted by the dialogue promoters who continuously propagate the notion that there is *religious* violence to show that dialogue is the solution for a context which is marked by religious misunderstanding, differences and hostilities.[36]

(iv) The Rise of Hindutva and the Religious Mobilization for Politics Electoral constituencies in India, where religious minorities such as Muslims and Christians can be a major force in deciding the victory of a political candidate, have been paid special attention by the Hindutva forces since their emergence. These have

successfully mobilized support for their political parties – in South India, it is BJP – by producing what they term religious violence. Kanyakumari district, with its many Christians, became a target of these Hindutva forces from the early 1980s.[37] BJP contested for the first time in Kanyakumari district in Nagercoil – one of the seven constituencies for Tamil Nadu state assembly – in the 1980 Tamil Nadu state assembly elections. It lost the elections, and within two years Kanyakumari district witnessed 'religious conflicts'.[38]

Some of the participants in dialogue talk about the role of the Hindu extremist organizations such as RSS and Hindu Front in the Mandaikadu conflicts.[39] However, these organizations and their members are mostly understood by the dialogue people as extremist Hindus who have failed to understand the core teaching of their religion, which is 'tolerance' towards other religions. Also, these organizations and their members are viewed in parallel to the Christian conservatives who are involved in denigrating other religions. Sometimes they are termed 'not-true-Hindus', just as the Christian conservatives are called 'not-true-Christians' on the assumption that they understand neither their own nor others' religions properly.[40] In all these, only the extremist 'religious' side of Hindutva is highlighted: how they have used the discourse of 'religious conflicts' for their advancement in the district is not brought out.[41]

In fact the Hindutva forces first entered the Kanyakumari district in the 1960s, when there were attempts to establish the Vivekananda Kendra in Kanyakumari. When it erected a memorial for Vivekananda in the Indian Ocean about 400 metres from the seashore, and started a ferry, it faced opposition from local fisherfolk people because their livelihood was affected.[42] Later these problems were retrospectively presented as Hindu–Christian problems, or Christian opposition to Hindu religious life.[43] However, local Hindutva forces tried to mobilize people from the 1980s, after which 'religious conflicts' started to occur. Employing almost all the tactics that Hindutva had used earlier against Muslims, particularly in northern and western parts of India, in Kanyakumari district the Hindutva forces were involved in constructing stereotypes of Christians and Muslims, portraying both as foreigners who are unpatriotic to India. They organized processions and public meetings in which Christians and Muslims were the constant targets of derogation and attack. The Hindutva groups also used the recently published 1981 census to argue that Christian numbers were growing, which would affect the Hindus.[44]

It is in such a context that the Mandaikadu conflicts occurred. The triggering incident for the conflicts occurred between fisherfolk Christians and Hindus. Nevertheless, in spite of the presence of Hindutva, and its use of 'religious conflicts' to yield fruits for its religious mobilization of Hindus for politics, the conflicts spread as *caste*-based conflicts rather than religious clashes. However, later the tactics of Hindutva forces took root when it published pamphlets which blamed 'Christians' for their attacks on 'Hindus'.[45] Since then caste identities have been underplayed in the projection, with religious identities highlighted as the cause of conflict. Even though this aspect of Hindutva is not critiqued in dialogue circles, there are others who have studied the conflicts from a social and political point of view irrespective of their religious affiliation.[46]

(v) The Usefulness of 'religious violence' Discourse for Political Benefits A critical look at the political history of the district in post-independence India, particularly the political developments of BJP and its supporting organizations in the district, helps us to understand how the discourse of 'Mandaikadu religious conflicts' has helped the BJP to gain political power. Just before these conflicts, the BJP contested elections in Nagercoil, the capital of the district and one of the seven state assembly constituencies in the district. The BJP candidate got 693 votes, which is less than 1 per cent of the total votes.[47] However, after the Mandaikadu conflicts in 1982, which strengthened religious mobilization efforts of BJP, it opted to move from Nagercoil to another constituency in the district, Colachel, for the 1984 state assembly elections. Mandaikadu area comes under this constituency, and the BJP's move explains what it expected from the 'Mandaikadu religious conflicts'. This time again, the candidate who contested in Nagercoil contested for BJP, and received 32,996 votes, 38.64 per cent of the total votes,[48] losing the election by just 0.69 per cent. In fact, as in the 1980 elections, BJP lost all the Tamil Nadu seats it contested in the 1984 elections, but its share of the vote in Kanyakumari district jumped from less than 1 per cent of votes in 1980 to 38.64 per cent, a greater increase than elsewhere in the state. It is a reasonable assumption that the discourse of the Mandaikadu 'religious conflicts' might have helped them. In the 1989 elections, it contested five constituencies in the district – Kanyakumari, Nagercoil, Padmanabhapuram, Vilavancode and Killiyoor. And although again unsuccessful,[49] it secured a good number of votes. In the 1991 elections, it contested all seven constituencies in the district and finished in third place.[50] The 1996 state assembly elections was a milestone in the history of BJP in Tamil Nadu and in Kanyakumari district as it won a seat for the first time in Tamil Nadu in the Padmanabhapuram constituency after contesting in all seven constituencies in the district. Similarly the Lok Sabha elections also indicate the gradual growth of BJP and other Hindutva parties in the district. It first contested in the district (in the Nagercoil constituency, which comprises all state assembly constituencies in the district, except the Kanyakumari constituency, which comes under the nearby Tiruchendoor Lok Sabha constituency)[51] in 1989 and secured 7.12 per cent of votes; it won 18.82 per cent in 1991, 30.25 per cent in 1996 and 45.08 per cent in 1998. It secured 50.21 per cent of votes in 1999 and won the seat for the first time in Kanyakumari district.[52]

Of course, BJP did not make this progress only because of the situation in the district. Rather the wider national context of Hindu nationalist propaganda for one Hindu nation, one Hindu religion and one Hindu culture, and the many tactics used by BJP for religious mobilization for politics at the national level, helped the progress of BJP. Its stereotypes against religious minorities, especially Muslims, at the national level at that time helped the BJP in the district to stereotype the Christians along the same lines. Nevertheless, the projection of the Mandaikadu conflicts discourse has been a significant aspect in the BJP's political campaign since 1982, and a factor which contributed to the BJP's growth in the district.[53] In their campaigns, these religious conflicts are projected to their Hindu voters as the efforts of Christians (as well as Muslims) in the district to dominate the Hindus, destroy Hinduism and deprive Hindus of all their rights. Thus the BJP and its supporters have continued to hang onto this myth until today in their politics and propaganda.

(vi) Approaching Mandaikadu Conflicts from the Perspective of the Problems Related to the Formation of Kanyakumari District in 1956 Even though the Hindu nationalist forces in the district continue to propagate the 'reality' of Mandaikadu religious conflicts, and the dialogue proponents in the district have also accepted the notion, a caste-based analysis has been used in looking at Mandaikadu conflicts[54] by some local social scientists and historians. They acknowledge that what happened in 1982 was seen as religious conflicts, and maintain that the conflicts occurred primarily because of the Hindutva forces in the district. However, pointing out the fact that most of the people associated with Hindu nationalism in the region are Hindus from high castes such as Nair, Pillai and Krishnavagaiyar, these analysts locate the conflicts in the wider historical context of the formation of the Kanyakumari district. When the states were reorganized in independent India, people in the southeast parts of southern Travancore (now Kanyakumari), who were mostly Tamil-speaking people, opted to join Tamil Nadu, rather than Kerala where Malayalam is the main language. Struggles started between the Tamil- and the Malayalam-speaking people. However it was not just a linguistic problem, as the majority of the Tamil-speaking people who opted to join Tamil Nadu were Nadars (Backward Caste), and the majority of the Keralites who opposed this move were from Nair caste (Forward/high caste). Nair–Nadar problems have a long history, as the Nair domination over Nadars and the reactions from Nadars have existed in the region for centuries. Thus the issue of joining Tamil Nadu became yet another struggle between Nadars and Nairs, and it was also political. Nadars held together irrespective of religions (almost half of the Nadars have converted to Christianity in the district, and the rest remain Hindu) and so the Nairs tried divide-and-rule tactics to split up the Nadars into their different religious identities.[55] This was not successful, and the Kanyakumari district was formed for Tamil-speaking people. However the tensions between Nairs and Nadars continued even after the formation of Kanyakumari district.

Those who argue for this background locate the Mandaikadu conflicts within this context. Their idea is that even though religious conflicts were organized and expected by the Hindutva forces in the district in which most are caste Hindus, especially Nairs, they expected conflicts to happen between Hindu Nadars and Christian Nadars, because the Nairs wanted Nadars to be divided religiously.[56] But because of the circumstances, the conflicts occurred between fisherfolk Christians and Hindus. Nevertheless, within a short time this fact had disappeared, and the 'real' tension was ascribed to Hindu and Christian Nadars. The problem with this approach to 'Mandaikadu conflicts' is that in spite of pointing out the fact of caste domination rather than the religious differences of people, still these analysts identify the 1982 conflicts as religious conflicts. The organizational aspects, and the political tactics of the Hindutva forces, are not paid proper attention.

2 Mandaikadu Conflicts and Interreligious Dialogue

In my view, dialogue is not responsible for the 1982 conflicts in the Kanyakumari district. It may also not be responsible for inventing the notion of religious conflicts in the district. However, as the above study has shown, it is responsible for keeping the discourse of religious conflicts alive because it has uncritically accepted the myth of religious conflicts which is used by Hindutva forces, among others, in the region, and continues to construct and propagate this myth. In other words, the dialogue activists who should critique the notion of religious conflicts and fixed religious identities of people in order to create peace and harmony in society instead uncritically accept and appropriate the discourse and concretize it through their writings and activities.[57] This might further damage relationships rather than create peace and harmony.

My argument in this and the previous chapter is that the idea of religious violence is a myth existing only in the discourse of people who play off the religious identities of people to fulfil their vested interests for power. But people fight with each other not always because they misunderstood religions, nor because their opponents believe in or belong to other religions. It is true what we call religious elements are present here, but basically there are complex factors such as aspirations for political and other forms of power and different kinds of mobilizations for it, socio-economic factors including caste inequalities and even personal factors. But all these factors are made to culminate in conflicts mainly to benefit those elites who can use discourses of religious conflicts for their vested interests. On the contrary, the sharing of common religious space, as mentioned by Susan Bayly, who nevertheless places the conflicts in 1982 within the framework of 'religious fundamentalism', is still present among most of the ordinary people in the district.[58] The naming and projecting of conflicts between people as religious conflicts benefits those who attempt to maintain power, especially in the political arena.

While conflicts between different groups including religious groups have a long history across the world, the notion that most of the conflicts in the world are religious conflicts is a discourse which is developed to achieve certain purposes for many people, yielding fruits for those who hold to it. Interreligious proponents and other scholars often submit the evidence of religious fundamentalism for these 'religious conflicts'. Religious fundamentalism, which is claimed to underscore a belief in one's religious superiority over other religions, and attacking other religions and their beliefs, are not new things, but nor do they inevitably produce 'religious' conflicts. For example, in modern India, religious fundamentalism began especially when colonial Christianity came and attacked the religions and traditions of the local people, who retaliated. However, what we witness as religious conflicts are new developments which are associated with nationalism, political power and other forms of power in India.

Perhaps one of the problems with the dialogue activists, in the light of the fact that most of them are Christians, is that religious differences, and therefore, religious conflicts and conflicts between people, enable them to articulate theologically about dialogue. In other words, in order to build up a theological rationale for dialogue, religion is necessary. Religious differences (and leading on from them, religious conflicts) are emphasized in such discourses, to maintain the basis for religious dialogue. These theological articulations – their nature and methods – accept and uphold belief in 'religious violence'. One of the statements often heard in the context of what is perceived as religious violence is that one is fighting with other religious people to protect his or her religion. However, this statement has to be critically appraised, not only because what religion *is* still is a contested area, but also because the statement itself is ambiguous. How does one fight to protect his or her religion? Just because the names of the religions or religious symbols are used by a few people in attacking others, does it mean that they are fighting for their religion? A fighter may conceivably be fighting for his or her religion, but very clearly fights for himself or herself! And the most explicit and implicit aspect involved here is actually power of many kinds. One fights in the name of religion to attain or maintain power: this cannot be identified or interpreted as 'religious violence'.

Moreover, while 'religious violence' is primarily executed and participated in by those who use religions for political reasons and other socio-economic reasons, the reminder that there have been religious conflicts or there is the possibility of religious conflicts creates tensions, fear and apprehension about other religions among ordinary people who otherwise may not fear the presence of others. In other words, it is the projection that there are religious conflicts or there has been religious violence in the past which creates fear and hate about others.

The emphasis on the discourse of religious conflicts or naming conflict as religious in this book is not to deny that people are targeted and attacked for belonging to a particular religion at all. Politically, as the BJP government at the centre in India today with a majority in Lok Sabha, there are a number of violent activities against religious minorities which are being witnessed day by day. The Ram Janma Bhoomi issue, the demolition of Babri Masjid and attacks on religious minorities in various parts of the country are some other examples for how people are attacked for belonging to particular religions. However, as I have argued in the previous chapter, these cannot be strictly called religious conflicts because political mobilization for consolidating vote banks runs behind many of these attacks, and because in the abovementioned cases one cannot say two inimical groups fight with each other – rather, mostly it is an attack by one politically motivated mob on the other. But buying into the notion of the political (and other) elites that there are actual religious conflicts can only help those vested interests to further their agenda. It is here that the problems in dialogical discourse of religious conflicts become very apparent.

While criticizing the discourse of religious conflicts in Kanyakumari district, and pointing out the caste and other factors involved, my intention is not to suggest that conflicts based on caste are justifiable whereas religions are not! Belonging to the Nadar community in the district, I am convinced that any conflict between the Nadar community and others is not going to be helpful to anyone, other than aggravating hate towards each other. But my point is that in the current climate in

India, and around the globe, the religious conflicts discourse yields more power to the power mongers at broader levels. The unfortunate development in the projection of religious conflict is that this myth has been uncritically accepted and propagated by the promoters of dialogue who try to put forth dialogue as a solution for such contexts. By doing this, whether they are successful in creating dialogue between 'hostile religious groups' or not, they certainly help the political and other power-mongering elites maintain this myth. The worst aspect is that even those dialogue promoters who rightly point out the existence of different factors in what are termed religious conflicts, nevertheless still continue to talk about the actual occurrence of 'religious' conflicts, as they do with the 'Mandaikadu religious conflicts', rather than critiquing the 'religious conflicts discourse' in the hands of those who aspire for power at any cost.

Notes

1 One of my interviewees, a Hindu dialogue activist, said that he had produced a small booklet (mentioned earlier, *Varalaatril Mandaikadu*) on the history of Mandaikadu and its temple, but had avoided mentioning the conflicts lest it create tensions among people. Perumal, Interview.

2 I could still collect data for this research, but these were mainly from secondary sources.

3 All my twenty-nine interviewees from the dialogue group mentioned that dialogue activities in Kanyakumari have to be primarily understood in the context of the Mandaikadu conflicts.

4 The number of people who were killed varies as different groups claim different numbers. But the number provided here is as per the government record. GoTN, *Venugopal Commission*, 7. There are claims that many people went missing.

5 For example, Matthew, 'Hindu Christian Communalism', which has been already mentioned.

6 Sukumaran, *Kumari*, 174–82.

7 Salaam, Interview.

8 Dhasan, Interview.

9 Rajamony, Interview. Also Dhasan emphasized this point quite often. Dhasan, Interview.

10 Robinson, 'From Apartheid', 90–1.

11 Rajamony, Interview.

12 Ibid.

13 Robinson, 'From Apartheid', 90–1.

14 Tobias, Interview.

15 Ibid. Also Salaam, Interview.

16 There is no clarity or concrete information about why in this particular year tensions were prevalent among them, but dialogists always cite the general fundamentalist activities of Christians in the district and the increasing hostility resulting from the mobilization of RSS and other Hindutva forces in the region.

17 Dhasan, Interview.

18 Ibid.

19   Perumal, Interview.
20   Salaam, Interview.
21   Ibid.
22   Khan, Interview.
23   Many of my interviewees are of this opinion.
24   Salaam, Interview; also Nagalingam, Interview.
25   Dhasan, Interview.
26   Ibid.
27   As I have been using the real names of my interviewees from the dialogue group, I am
     not giving the name of the person here as confidentiality was asked for.
28   Rajamony, Interview.
29   The Venugopal Commission report contains many incidents violence between
     fisherfolk Christians and non-fisherfolk Hindus where the fisherfolk were targets as
     fisherfolk, and not as Christians. GoTN, *Venugopal Commission*, 83–140.
30   Mohammed, Interview.
31   Jacob, Interview.
32   Rajamony, Interview; also Tobias, Interview.
33   Velan, Interview.
34   Government of India, *Liberhan Commission Report*, 2009.
35   GoTN, *Venugopal Commission*, 103–105.
36   Robinson, 'From Apartheid,' 85–93; also many other dialogists think in this way.
37   ECI, *Statistical Report on General Election, 1980 to the Legislative Assembly of Tamil
     Nadu* (New Delhi: Elections Commission of India, n.d.).
38   C. Chokkalingam, Interview.
39   For instance Tobias, Dhasan, Harris and Panivanban Vincent mentioned this.
40   Jayaraj, Interview.
41   In my opinion, an acknowledgement that 'religious conflicts' are not real but
     primarily remain in the discourse of especially Hindutva forces may not help
     dialogue which invites people to live together in the context of 'religious' conflicts. I
     will elaborate how this discourse has helped Hindutva in the next section.
42   GoTN, *Venugopal Commission*, 3.
43   C. Chokkalingam, Interview.
44   GoTN, *Venugopal Commission*, 19–21.
45   Perumal, Interview.
46   One such study critiquing Hindutva is done by a school teacher, not primarily a
     dialogue activist, in the district. Chokkalingam, *Matham, Panbaadu*.
47   ECI, *General Election, 1980*, 280.
48   ECI, *General Election, 1984*, 291.
49   ECI, *General Election, 1989*, 321–3.
50   ECI, *General Election, 1991*, 319–21.
51   Since the 2009 Lok Sabha elections, all the seven state assembly constituencies in the
     district have been merged into the Kanyakumari Lok Sabha constituency.
52   ECI, *General Elections* (New Delhi: ECI, 1989–99).
53   C. Chokkalingam, Interview.
54   Sukumaran, *Kumari*, 174–82.
55   Peter and Peter, *Malayali Aathikkamum*. The whole book is concerned with this
     issue.
56   Sukumaran, *Kumari*, 175.

57   As mentioned earlier, all my twenty-nine interviewees from the dialogue circle
     emphasize that dialogue in the district is necessary in the context of 'religious'
     conflicts, which, in my opinion and as I have shown thus far, is a myth that exist only
     in the discourses for power.
58   Bayly, 'Christians and Competing Fundamentalisms,' 736–7.

Chapter 7

DIALOGUE AS ELITIST

In this chapter we turn to another problem in dialogue which is a rather common one and has been raised from time to time: the elite nature of dialogue. In the beginning of this book I discussed various theoretical and practical developments in dialogue in India over the last seven decades which have helped dialogue to become one of the significant aspects in religious life and theological reflection. I also noted that, in the process, the importance and inevitability of dialogue has been emphasized over and over again, and the nature, method and objectives of dialogue also have been set by the theologians involved in dialogue – which has led to more of formalization of dialogue.

Criticism of elitist dialogue is not a new issue, and dialogue has been repeatedly critiqued for this, including by those who are engaged in it. Anyone who wants to take a 'make dialogue better approach' often points out how it gets stuck among elites. Also, in dialogue circles one may quite often hear complaints about the complete hold of elites on dialogue and a lack of participation among people at the grassroots, or simply common people. But history shows that little has been done to address the elite problem effectively in dialogue, even though nowadays one can often hear about non-elitist dialogue or the participation of grassroots people in dialogue.[1]

However, in my observation, the criticisms aimed at elitist dialogue are done with the assumptions that dialogue *remains* elitist, and it has not *reached* the common people. In other words it is a participatory question where it is said that either grassroots people do not (or, are not encouraged to) participate in dialogue or there is simply no dialogue among them. Questions such as 'why do they need dialogue' or 'do they not have resources among them for maintaining their relationships' do not get any attention in dialogue: there is always a ready-made answer available which holds that lack of dialogue among common people leads to religious conflicts, so they need dialogue. The solutions for the absence-of-dialogue grassroots contexts are offered in terms of 'taking dialogue to the grassroots' or 'reaching the grassroots'. These notions clearly express the need for involving many grassroots people in dialogue. This is still an elite perspective, and it brings more problems than those with what is actually seen as elitist. This is because of the assumption that the lack of dialogue among people leads to conflicts in society, especially religious conflicts. In this sense, non-elitist dialogue, for a dialogist, is about promoting dialogue among non-elites. In other words, the simple question is how to liberate dialogue from elite holdings? The answer is, 'take' it to non-elites or make more non-elites participate in organized dialogue. It is very rarely concerned with learning from the non-elites about the ways they interact and relate and negotiate with their neighbours. This is exactly the problem of dialogue, because it is still the dialogue programmes that dominate even in what is proposed as non-elitist dialogue. The problem becomes more acute when the absence of dialogue is posed as a cause of the problems and violence among ordinary people. My problem generally is not so much to do with the lack of participation of non-elites in dialogue as to do with the dialogical elites' attitudes towards common people and their ordinary living experiences. The issue here is the failure of those engaged in dialogue to learn from ordinary people and ordinary life situations regarding how they live their everyday lives amid tensions, rather than teaching them how to dialogue.

This chapter therefore evaluates the elite nature of dialogue and its ignorance of people at the grassroots, who are all too often seen as passive listeners. I shall critique this against the everyday relationships among people in the next chapter. In so doing, I shall compare and contrast the elite nature of dialogue with the actual relationships among people at the grassroots with different religious identities, in the light of the insights received from Gramam, where Hindus, Muslims and Christians live. My primary argument is that while dialogue may work well in the theological field to construct better models to approach other religions, ordinary people's handling of conflicts, and their everyday relationships amid obvious tensions, contribute more than dialogue activities towards maintaining peace and harmony in society. By stating this I do not want to sound as if I am essentializing or idealizing the relationships among common people against the activities of the dialogists, but I am of the opinion that the relationships and negotiations among common people in ordinary life situations are more diverse and complex than what the elite dialogists think. More importantly, what is pressing is to understand them in all their complexity rather than treating them as common and inferior from an elite-centric point of view.

Let me define elite and non-elite in relation to my research. The elites are those religious leaders, pastors and theologians who are educated and belong to higher socio-economic rungs in society, and who tend to have a stronger influence on society; mostly men. These are the people who espouse formal dialogue programmes for peace and harmony in society, as these programmes offer them an opportunity to exert their eliteness over others. Non-elites are people who have a particular religious identity, and other identities; are not highly educated or ordained; are often female; are usually living in villages and have not participated in dialogue programmes. These are the people who are usually invited by dialogue promoters to come and *take part in* dialogue, with the objective of being taught. Such an invitation 'from on high' stems not so much from a negative attitude to their interreligious grasp as from an ignorance about their lived lives and potential contribution.

1 *The Subaltern Approach*

Elite descriptions of 'their' society and consequent bias have been critically appraised 'from below' for quite some time now.[2] The core subaltern view is that such elite approaches ignore, undermine or control lived realities among the non-elites, the ordinary people. Within the field of religion and theology in Christianity, this 'from below' approach has been applied in many ways. One of the important developments in the 1970s was the rise of liberation theologies in Latin America which spread to other parts of the world. This was a 'from below' approach to theologizing, which critiqued systematic theology preoccupied with philosophy and doctrines, and emphasized the importance of lay and often marginalized people's theologizing. In India, Dalit and Tribal peoples have critiqued the dominant traditions for ignoring them, Dalit theology (as noted in Chapter 1) opposing elite Indian Christian theology's preoccupation with the dominant modes of Hinduism.

One of the prominent 'from below' approaches in India has been the works of the Subaltern Studies Collective since the 1980s.[3] The subaltern studies method generally refers to the writings of a group of scholars, mostly from India, about South Asian society since the 1980s concerning Indian nationalism and historiography and the contributions of the submerged classes to that evolution. There were ten volumes under the title 'Subaltern Studies' between 1982 and 1998, and many more in similar vein. While there is no single method directing the writings of the scholars in the Subaltern Studies Collective, there is a core uniting all their writings: the rejection of any elite humanities writing which ignores subaltern realities.

Ranajit Guha, the editor of the first six volumes of 'Subaltern Studies', and one of the influential scholars who figured out the basic assumptions behind the subaltern studies, explicated the methodology in the first volume. The term 'subaltern' in Subaltern Studies means 'inferior rank', taken from Antonio Gramsci's writing on the working class. Guha and his colleagues use the term for 'the general attribute of subordination in South Asian society whether this is expressed in terms of class, caste, age, gender and office or in any other way'.[4] Clarifying the terms elite and subaltern, Guha explains that the term 'elite' has been used to 'signify *dominant* groups, foreign as well as indigenous'. And, 'the terms "people" and "subaltern classes" have been used as synonymous'.[5] He further says that 'the social groups and elements included in this category represent *the demographic difference between the total Indian population and all those who we have described as the "elite"*'.[6] Using a subaltern studies approach to study dialogue in India helps to identify and discuss some of the elite aspects of dialogue which have ignored the role that common people play in enriching the entire scheme of social relationships by exercising their multiple identities. It also helps to understand and appreciate the ways ordinary people construct and maintain multiple identities for themselves and others.

2 Elite Features in Dialogue: Dialogue as an Elite Work

(a) The Imperative of Dialogue

One of the aspects that differentiate formal dialogue from the informal grassroots that include interreligious relations is the imperious top-down element of formal dialogue. While there are interactions between people of different religions going on in their everyday lives at many levels, the assumption in invitations to dialogue is that people are divided along religious lines and that there are no effective or proper relationships among them: this totally ignores the existing everyday relations based on multiple identities. For many dialogue activists what is going on between people in everyday living is apparently not enough to create peace and harmony.[7] Herbert Jai Singh, a theologian in India actively involved in dialogue, has pointed to the fact that the modern world has provided fast accessibility between people, and says that in such a situation 'there can be little doubt that men and women are constantly conversing across national, cultural and religious boundaries'. However, for him, 'This by no means is dialogue, but it has given rise to a situation which favours and promotes dialogue'.[8] This is typical of the general negative attitudes of elite dialogists towards anything that is familiar or simple naturally leading to an unnecessary complexity being attached to what is otherwise ordinary.

For instance, Wesley Ariarajah cites some suggestions given by a regional formal dialogue meeting in India, which discussed 'how the future of Hindu-Christian relations could be built at local levels so that the dialogue would relate to daily life'.[9] The suggestions were (1) talking together, which he elaborates: 'We *need* to discuss with one another the problems we share in common in our communities'; (2) working together, which he interprets: 'One of the most profitable and powerful forms of dialogue is working together with our neighbours in concrete projects of social action. ... Such active and socially-conscious dialogue may especially serve to attract the energies and engage the commitments of young people who have drifted away from their religious traditions'; (3) living together – on which he says, 'We hear how Hindus and Christians live together in cities, towns and villages. ... However, living together *should* not be merely an accident of geography which places us in proximity to but not in relation to our neighbours. Our living together *should* be intentional – that we intend to create a community in which we all participate'; and (4) celebrating together – the fourth suggestion on which he comments thus:

> On national or regional holidays, Hindus and Christians might join together in their programs and celebrations. During appropriate religious festivals, Hindus and Christians might invite one another to visit, taking advantage of these occasions to become educated about and appreciative of the traditions of the other. On a more daily level, Hindus and Christians might arrange for mutual visits in temples, churches, ashrams, and homes. In all these cases, Christians and Hindus *should* prepare for such visits through programs of education and reflect on such visits in discussion.[10]

In all the four points, in one way or another, we see that somewhat directive language is associated with dialogue. Commenting on the above suggestions, Ariarajah maintains:

> Behind these suggestions lies the conviction ... that community, harmony, relationships, and so forth, do not happen automatically; that they cannot be taken for granted; that relationships *have to* be built, fostered, preserved and celebrated.[11]

These are the suggestions from Hindus and Christians involved in dialogue in different parts of India who were gathered under the auspices of the WCC in Rajpur, in the northern part of India.[12] Ariarajah has picked up from these suggestions provided by the participants to show that dialogue can be achieved primarily, if not only, through all people willingly participating in dialogue activities. While talking about the future of Hindu–Christian dialogue, Ariarajah suggests that it depends 'very much on persons who are willing actually to "work at it" by creating opportunities that become occasions of dialogue'.[13] It is towards this dialogue that all people are invited to take part in order to create peace and harmony in society. In this regard, the phrase 'dialogue at the grassroots' often refers to the efforts taken by dialogue activists *to take dialogue* to the grassroots, rather than to *learn from* the everyday living relationships among the people at the grassroots.[14] What are not paid attention to are the practical aspects that are found among people belonging to different religions who coexist in many parts of the world. In fact this directive and even supercilious language is typical of many contemporary dialogue activists in India.

(b) Formalization of Dialogue: Thinking about the Nature and Objectives of Dialogue

One of the most important aspects of thinking and writing on dialogue in India over the last three or four decades has been laying down the context, nature and objectives of dialogue. A lot of energy is spent on this by elite dialogists, and such a situation is not just limited to India. This is done to help those already participating in dialogue activities, and to encourage others to make dialogue work better and effectively. However, this is rather a problem of formalization of dialogue which is very much found in the elite dialogue circles. What happens in the process of formalization is that often the subtle, nuanced and messy issues involving non-elite people and ordinary situations are conveniently ignored. In other words, how understanding of religion and religious relations works in informal contexts is either ignored or undermined by the elite dialogists who are very much into formalizing and structuralizing dialogue with all the rules and codes.

(i) Stressing the Inevitability of Dialogue in a Multireligious Context One of the important features of dialogue in Indian Christianity, as well as globally, is to emphasize the inevitability of dialogue for Christians, spoken of from at least

two perspectives. First, the inevitable nature of a dialogical approach to other religions is emphasized against the context of religious plurality. Samartha holds that dialogue in the context of pluralism is inevitable, and it cannot be an optional activity.[15] He argues that people of faith who deliberately reject relationships and choose to remain isolated impoverish the community.[16] In such a context, dialogue is interpreted as inevitable and urgent,[17] and Christians are advised to be prepared to face it.[18]

The second drive for dialogue comes from affirming that dialoguing with neighbours of other religions is a basic Christian responsibility. The understanding here is that Christians are not isolated from their neighbours from different religions, and to be Christian means to be dialogical. This is one of the reasons the Christian understanding of the Trinity is often brought into focus when talking about dialogue.[19] Basing his understanding of dialogue on the Trinity, Panikkar says that 'the Trinity may be considered as a junction where the authentic spiritual dimensions of all religions meet'.[20] This means that for Christians the relationship within the Trinity points to the dialogue and relationship that they should have with their neighbours.[21] Not only the movement within the Trinity but also God's relationship to the world set the foundation for Christian dialogue with other religions. Paul Verghese (later Paulose Mar Gregorios) writes, 'The Christian understanding of creation as an act of grace and of God's love as extending to the whole of mankind is already an adequate basis on which to engage in dialogue with them, in love and openness without fear.'[22] For him, the motivation for dialogue comes from the love of Christ, who

> loves not only all men, but also all that is created. I am united to Christ in baptism and Chrismation. My mind is the mind of Christ. Therefore my love is non-exclusive and open to the whole creation. ... I as a member of that body have to express that love and compassion in faithfulness, integrity and openness with sympathetic understanding. This is sufficient and compelling reason for me to engage in dialogue with people of other faiths. It is love in Christ that sends me to dialogue.[23]

The insistence on the inevitability of dialogue in the Christian-initiated dialogue activities predominantly comes with the notion that there is no dialogue among people, or that dialogue is decreasing due to various conditions. The inevitability of relating is not stressed in terms of the natural conditions of plurality – which would help throw light on how people relate and negotiate with each other; rather what is attempted is a push for a dialogical responsibility in the name of its inevitability.

(ii) Presenting a Dialogical Approach to Other Religions as a Better Model within a Theology of Religions The dialogical approach to religions evolved to offer alternatives to the earlier approaches to other faiths, generally branded as exclusivism and inclusivism. Thus, even though there are differing opinions about the nature of plurality or the differences between religions or the common bases of dialogue such as God, Christ, the Trinity, salvation and similar themes, there

is basically an affirmation that the dialogue model is a better model to approach religions. Arguing that exclusive claims 'make it difficult, if not impossible, for persons belonging to different religious traditions to live together in harmony and to cooperate for common purposes in society',[24] Samartha says that

> dialogue stands for an attempt on the part of Christians in a post-colonial and pluralistic society to build up new relationships with their neighbours of other faiths. It gives them a call to discard the old, negative and triumphalistic attitude which has resulted in negative consequences. Essentially, dialogue is a mood, spirit and attitude in relationship.[25]

He further says that 'at a time when people of different cultures and religions are being drawn together for common purposes in the global community as never before, interreligious dialogue is an important means through which resources of religions can enhance the quality of life'.[26] Richard Taylor, formerly associated with the Christian Institute for the Study of Religion and Society (CISRS), argues that 'religious imperialism certainly must die for dialogue to live'.[27]

I have repeatedly noted that a dialogical approach based on a plurality has been much appreciated in the context of exclusive attitudes that harm social relationships. However, what dialogists fail to note is the fact that identities and interactions among people are not strictly based on religious identities. Nevertheless they continue to do so, which, directly or indirectly, only limits the plurality that they want to promote.

(iii) Projecting Dialogue as Creating Mutual Understanding of Religions One primary purpose of dialogue often talked about in dialogue circles is the necessity for the mutual understanding of religions both for their own existence and for the harmonious lives of their followers, one basic dialogical belief being that through dialogue a follower of religion not only understands the religion of his/her neighbours, but also understands his/her own religion. Thus, for Francis Vineeth, a Roman Catholic proponent of dialogue, 'A theology of religions which acknowledges other religions as valid sources of god-experience, as it transcends its own limitations, is also ready to perfect itself by the help of the other.'[28] This is generally identified as complementarity of religions, and is possible only through genuine dialogues between religions. For Klostermaier, dialogue is an attempt to understand people of religions not as opposed to each other or competing with each other; rather they are partners in a pilgrimage. Real dialogue, he says, challenges both partners.[29] Arguing against the notion that each religion is self-sufficient for its adherents, Gregorios says that 'experience has shown that when one sets out to learn deeply from other religions, one's understanding of one's own religion is transformed and deepened'. Panikkar identifies this process as mutual fecundation of religions though dialogue.[30]

The problem with all these perspectives is that the very idea of understanding or mutual understanding is rather monopolized, formalized and even imprisoned within the scope of dialogue. The projection that there is lack of understanding among people has problems, because it promotes a strictly elite perspective on what is 'understanding' itself. This leads to a situation in which most often 'mutual understanding' is the core area of dialogists, where 'learning' and 'knowing' are possible only through formal dialogue. This has serious limitations in the light of the way understanding and mutual understanding takes place among common people in the everyday, ordinary and familiar life situations which dialogue completely misses out.

(iv) Establishing Dialogue as the Best Model for Building Relationships Between Religious Adherents The mutual understanding of religions in dialogue is basically to build better relationships between people of different religions. A report from a dialogue meeting arranged by CISRS affirms that

> dialogue is based on the acceptance of our neighbour as a person, as our brother and God's Child. Even as it arises from this recognition of our common humanness, it contributes to the enrichment, on both sides, of our awareness of this common humanity. It deepens our sensitivity and promotes understanding and a sense of unity.[31]

Especially in the context of mutual mistrust and conflicts between different religious adherents, it is believed that dialogue will help create and maintain better relationships, and where this is vital for life, building relationships between adherents of different religions becomes more important. Moreover, dialogue is presented as giving 'the partners a greater knowledge of each other and of each other's religious traditions, and thus helps them to overcome prejudices, misinformation and negative attitudes. This in turn leads to a greater acceptance of each other with their religious traditions.'[32] But this also has problems. The main difficulty with this perspective is that dialogue seldom has space for relationships that are maintained but not always based strictly on dialogical models. The very claim that it remains the ultimate or best model for building relationships between different religious followers suppresses the enormous amount of resources, tools, activities and experiences found among common people which certainly serve better than formalized dialogue programmes.

(c) Prerequisites of Dialogue

Another feature of elite dialogue in contemporary India is that often there is an articulation of the 'prerequisites' of dialogue, which neatly excludes people who are actually living interreligiously or based on their other group identities. Dialogue is assigned a special status and not all people are considered qualified to undertake it. Thus Raimundo Panikkar maintains that 'dialogue is more than a casual or merely well-intentioned conversation .... [It] demands both a deep experience of one's own tradition and a sufficient knowledge of the other one.'[33] While referring to the authors who wrote about dialogue in the book *Hindu-Christian Dialogue*, he says that 'we cannot, and should not, engage in dialogue if we are not spiritually, intellectually, and humanly equipped for it'.[34] He further says,

> Dialogue ... has to be *duo-logue*. There have to be two *logoi*, two languages encountering each other, so as to overcome the danger of a double monologue. One has to know the language of the other, even if one has to learn it precisely from the other, and often in the very exercise of dialogue. Dialogue engages the intellect, the *logos*.[35]

This emphasis on the intellectual prerequisites for dialogue is one of the important elitist features of dialogue in India. As dialogue is believed to be an organized formal act rather than a voluntary and informal one, this emphasis is often made. Having a good knowledge of one's own religion and other religions, showing 'openness' of mind, being willing to learn from other religions, 'to feel one' with the dialogue partner and to change through dialogue are often cited as the important qualifications. Here one can see how the normal and ordinary activities of everyday life at the grassroots are set aside in favour of highly conceptualized and essentialized 'dialogue'. Visiting religious places of one's neighbours and entering their holy places are also expressed as qualifications for dialogue. For example, consider how Panikkar looks at himself as eligible for participating in dialogue:

> I have duly performed Hindu ceremonies (at Guruvayur, one of the most orthodox Hindu temples, for instance) and celebrated the Christian mysteries (in Shillong Cathedral, one of the most 'orthodox' Roman Catholic churches, for example). I have been dialoguing in Europe, America, and India; sitting in ashrams, gurukuls, universities, and bishops' houses; living in presbyteries and temples. Karma-*bhakti* and *jnana-yoga* are not unknown or foreign to me; the Vedas and the Bible are holy books for me and I have spent long years in practice, study, and meditation of both.[36]

The visiting of many places is one of the aspects believed to be important for genuine dialogue, despite such visiting being common practice in villages. For example, Klostermaier, who spent a few years in a Vrindaban, a Hindu holy place in North India, emphasizes the importance of being in India in order to participate in Hindu–Christian dialogue.[37] The list for the prerequisites for dialogue can go on, but what is important to note here is that how people at the grassroots, in spite of conflicts, relate with each other in their multireligious contexts, fulfilling a number of Ariarajah's points, discussed earlier, as they maintain at least a reasonable level of internal peace and harmony – perfection not being of this world.

(d) Interreligious Dialogue and Written Scriptures

The use of scriptures in dialogue is another feature that indicates the elite nature of dialogue. It should be mentioned that all the formal dialogues are in one way or another based on written texts, on which all the comparative studies which arise in discussions depend. The issue of the plurality of texts is discussed in dialogue, but these include only the written and formally accepted scriptures, excluding performed or oral texts. In other words, while there is a plurality of scriptural resources within each religious tradition, canonized scriptures which are usually the dominant ones within a given tradition are unquestioningly employed. This obviously reinforces elite authority usually built on strict orthodoxy (even while dialogue claims to challenge it) while excluding those at the margins.

Dialogue activists who talk about the role of scriptures also talk about the plurality of religious scriptures in a multireligious context,[38] or how the reading and exegesis of scriptures are different for different religious adherents.[39] One fundamental problem in these contexts is that what is considered to be knowledge of other religions is mostly the knowledge of the scriptures in other religions. This naturally leads to a subordination of the many non-scriptural aspects of religions. However, the more subtle problem here is that dialogue generally tends to accept the dominant readings and interpretations of these scriptures. It most often, in the process of juxtaposing religions, misses out on the rich heterodoxy as well as multiple interpretations of scriptures found within each particular 'religion'.[40] While dialogists may claim to be open to such multiple interpretations and heterodoxy, the very elite nature of dialogue precludes the usage of these.

Further in the contemporary dialogue, 'reading from multiple scriptures' has become a symbol of the routine dialogical relationship between the participants from different religions, often accompanied by interreligious worship using the various scriptures to indicate that dialogue activists accept the authority of multiple scriptures.[41] This also quite often remains at the superficial level because such worship is often limited to dialogue programmes and ignores the various ways of mutual sharing that takes place in practising rituals and thinking and speaking about God and religion in the everyday life situations of the common people.

(e) Discussion of Theological Concepts and Interreligious Dialogue

One of the central aspects of dialogue is theological and doctrinal issues – which is one important reason that such dialogue fails to appeal to people at the grassroots. What often happens is that educated lay and religious leaders participate in formal dialogue. One major theological issue that has dominated and still dominates most of the discussion in dialogue is the search for truth or the ultimate truth. As discussed in Chapter 2, defending plurality of religions and dialogue in the context of a mission against those who are opposed to pluralism, dialogue has produced theological reflections on many concepts such as God, Christ, the Trinity and salvation. However, this aspect of dialogue fails to represent the faith perspectives of the people at the grassroots levels for whom such issues are of little importance – as is indeed the case in many other religious groups. As already discussed, grassroots understanding of faith is more related to their daily life where they have to live with people of other religions, and to their culture, society and other aspects of life besides doctrines or beliefs. While studying the importance of lived religion against the religion informed by doctrines and creeds in Borneo and South Australia, Elizabeth Koepping says,

> Ritual specialists or teachers in particular tradition, represented ... by pastors and priests ... and imams and missionaries ... may regard enculturated non-doctrinal attributes as largely or totally irrelevant to the practice of a religion, the constructed doctrinal whole of which for them will ideally be expressed, in belief and action by individual adherents. Lay people. However, many consider the social identity and praxis aspects of 'religion' central to their lives, doctrines being not particularly important.[42]

For her, ordinary people 'identify themselves by the food they eat or reject, the friends they mix with and marry, and crucially the way they conduct, and conduct themselves at, funeral'.[43] Similar aspects may be found in different parts of the world with regard to lived religion.[44]

Moreover, in this connection, one should note that religious *experience* of a very specific kind is often emphasized in dialogue. This approach to dialogue is generally known as the 'contemplative approach', the proponents of which are often critical of the science of religion or comparative religion because it cannot deal with religious experience.[45] And in the Indian context, again, this kind of approach to dialogue concentrates on the Christian relationship to the dominant modes of Hinduism where mysticism is one of the vital religious experiences.[46] The emphasis on mystical or at least 'interior' religious experience illustrates that 'dialogue' is confined to those very few people who consider contemplation or meditation as crucial aspects of religious life.

(f) Interreligious Dialogue, Relativism and Syncretism

The question of syncretism and relativism is another issue that one can see quite often in the writings on dialogue. This question arises especially due to the challenges and criticisms put forth by conservative opponents of dialogue who fear that it compromises fundamental faith affirmations of their respective religions. This has led the dialogists to write extensively with an apologetic focus in order to ease these fears. It is in such a context that dialogue as 'commitment and openness' – meaning commitment to one's own faith and openness to other faiths – has been popularized.

Further, this issue also flares up in the actual dialogue process. Doctrinal discussions on topics cited earlier tend – certainly for Christians – to be controlled by anxiety lest those taking a clearly exclusivist position accuse dialogists of compromise which they would see as dangerous, even sinful. In such a context, the dialogue promoters spend much time in establishing theological and scriptural legitimacy for dialogue particularly to show that dialogue does not amount to syncretism. In spite of these efforts, in the context of the question of the relation between Christian mission and dialogue, the dialogical responses remain ambiguous.

While dialogue is much concerned with these issues, people within their ordinary life situations are seldom concerned about questions of relativism or syncretism which are primarily elite theological concerns. In fact socio-economic and political factors are of primary importance to people at the grassroots and influence their relations with people of other religions as they live them. Against this background the overstressed need for theological legitimacy leads to dialogue only between essentialized blocks.

(g) Common Platforms for Interreligious Dialogue

One of the issues with which dialogue activists are often involved is the question of the starting point for dialogue. There have been many efforts in this direction from the dialogue activists. 'Where should one start in dialogue with one's dialogue partner?' is the primary question. This obsession with common platforms and starting points for dialogue also has been typical of elitist dialogue in India. As mentioned, these range from commonalities of religions, theocentricism, christocentrism, soteriology, religious experience, religious potentials for social justice and peace to modernity, ethics, nation-building and communal harmony. Dialogue activists explicate much on common themes and platforms for dialogue but fail to look at the many common aspects in the everyday life of ordinary people which help to maintain relationships among them. Even the realities of common people have only become subjects of discussion, as dialogue talks about common platforms such as 'preferential options for the poor' and the like, but seldom are those who are engaged in dialogue willing to learn from these common and ordinary life experiences.

(h) Interreligious Dialogue and Reaching Grassroots

As I have mentioned earlier, one way the elite nature of dialogue becomes visible is through its emphasis on 'reaching grassroots' or 'taking dialogue to grassroots'. In this regard, celebrating religious festivals in villages is considered to be one fruitful way of reaching grassroots people with the purpose of giving them awareness about dialogue. Some of my dialogue interviewees expressed their opinion that this is the only way through which they can take dialogue to the 'ordinary' people. A village in the district is selected by the interreligious groups for this event. Mostly a village in which people belonging to all religions of the region – Hindus, Muslims and Christians – is selected, and the elite interreligious groups, with the help of the local village leaders, do the preparations.[47] As discussed in Chapter 3, scholars or religious leaders interested in dialogue are invited to speak about the meaning of the particular festival(s) from different religious viewpoints. They also invite local politicians and officials from the district administration who make speeches advocating dialogue for forging peace and harmony in the district. Because of the nature and participants of these programmes, the village people who come to attend these programmes seldom see them as interreligious programmes[48]; rather they regard them as political meetings.

An important issue about the dialogical celebration of festivals in villages is site selection. Multireligious villages are usually selected for such celebration of festivals because of the assumption that it is in these villages that there are more interreligious problems and that unity and solidarity need to be demonstrated there.[49] While villagers have to live together in reasonable multifaith amity, dissention is assumed by the organizing elite. In other words, the moment the multireligious nature of a village is considered, the assumption that there are tensions among the inhabitants because of such living experience becomes stronger. This is a crucial problem in dialogue and illustrates the ambiguities dialogists have about the multireligious context surrounding them.

In addition to reaching people through celebrations of religious festivals, the interreligious groups also endeavour to train villagers, gathering them together and addressing them about dialogue. The people at the grassroots are taught to have deep faith in their own religions, to respect other religions and not to consider their religions to be superior but rather believe that God's revelation is found in all religions. Interreligious training is aimed at students in schools and colleges as well. This indicates that there is a nature of dominance in dialogue, which completely ignores the non-elite relationships between people of different religions at the grassroots who use their multiple associations to interact and relate with each other.

Dialogue as practised today has many limitations when compared to the living experiences of grassroots people. It has an understanding of religions, religious identity and religious violence which have been influenced by colonial forms of knowledge. It has uncritically accepted these categories, which it has further popularized through its discourses. The actualities of interreligious relationships are conceptualized, essentialized and idealized, and in the process a lot of energy is spent on defining and defending dialogue. Defending dialogue becomes crucial and is associated with doctrinal issues, with anxieties about syncretism and relativism being directed against interreligious dialogue. It seeks for common platforms and starting points and delineates prerequisites for dialogue in a very meticulous way to include knowledge of religions, inner experience and spirituality. In its approach, discussion of theological, philosophical and ontological concepts and of doctrinal issues becomes the central activity. The use of religious scriptures in dialogue also sets limitations for a dialogue preoccupied with textualization.

In their articulation of religious conflicts, dialogue proponents often ignore the different socio-economic and political factors along with the power structures which underlie many conflicts, seeing conflicts between people through a religious lens held by elite power holders. Moreover, as this chapter has shown, dialogue activists often talk about grassroots dialogue meaning 'taking dialogue to the grassroots'. The patronizing assumption is that interreligious awareness is lacking among such people and that it is the responsibility of dialogue activists to educate 'these people' about it. What is ignored and subjugated in this process is the existence of various kinds of relationships based on multiple experiences and identities among people at the grassroots in their daily lives; to discuss them, we now turn to the next chapter.

Notes

1 See Rebecca Kratz Mays, ed., *Interfaith Dialogue at the Grassroots* (Philadelphia: Ecumenical Press, 2009).
   One of the authors in this volume put the core question about the non-elitist dialogue: 'How can interreligious dialogue move from the halls of academia to the grass roots where we contend it needs to be in the twenty-first century?' Hornung, 'Conclusion: Making Dialogue Real,' 97. However, in my opinion, even such works are limited because they talk about 'dialogue moving from elite to grassroots' rather than dialogue learning from grassroots people.

2 In the field of social sciences a critical study of power elites may be traced to C. Wright Mills's *Power Elite*, published in 1956 (a new edition was published by Oxford University Press in 2000 with a new afterword by Alan Wolfe). This text remains a classic study of the interlocking power systems of military, corporate and political elites in the North American context. In the theological field, liberation theologies since the 1970s have powerfully articulated theological perspectives and action against the elite (especially economic) domination and exploitation of the poor. In contemporary India, studies on the middle class bring similar perspectives. For instance see Pavan K. Varma, *The Great Indian Middle Class* (New Delhi: Penguin, 2007); Amita Baviskar and Rakay Ray, *Elite and Everyman: The Cultural Politics of the Indian Middle Classes* (New Delhi: Routledge, 2011).

3 Ranajit Guha, Partha Chatterjee, Gyanendra Pandey, David Arnold, David Hardiman, Sahid Amin, Dipesh Chakrabarty, Gautam Bhadra, Gyan Prakash and Susie Tharu, eds., *Subaltern Studies I-X: Writings on South Asian History and Society* (New Delhi: Oxford University, 1982–99); also Ranajit Guha, ed., *A Subaltern Studies Reader 1986-1995* (New Delhi: Oxford University Press, 1997).

4 Ranajit Guha, 'Preface,' in *Subaltern Studies I: Writings on South Asian History and Society* (New Delhi: Oxford University Press, 1982), vii.

5 Ranajit Guha, 'On Some Aspects of the Historiography of Colonial India,' in *Subaltern Studies I: Writings on South Asian History and Society* (New Delhi: Oxford University Press, 1982), 8.

6 Ibid.

7 Tobias, Interview.

8 Singh, 'Preparation for Dialogue,' 42.

9 World Council of Churches, *Religious Resources for a Just Society: A Hindu-Christian Dialogue*, Report of the Rajpur Meeting (Geneva: WCC, 1981), 17–18, Cited in Ariarajah, 'A World Council,' 254.

10 Ariarajah, 'A World Council,' 254–5. Emphasis added.

11 Ibid., 255. Emphasis added.

12 Ibid., 254.

13 Ibid., 255.

14 When I asked my dialogue interviewees what they think about dialogue in grassroots, none of them talked about learning from grassroots or about appreciating what is going on among common people, in spite of the everyday conflicts among them as well as their ability to solve many problems themselves. Rather the dialogists enthusiastically narrated about their dialogue programs *for* grassroots.

15 Samartha, *Courage for Dialogue*, 100.

16 Ibid.

17   Ariarajah, 'A World Council,' 254–5.

18   Panikkar, 'Foreword,' ix–xiii.

19   Panikkar, *Trinity and World Religions*.

20   Ibid., 42.

21   Ibid., 43.

22   Paul Verghese, 'Christ and All Men,' in *Living Faiths and the Ecumenical Movement*, ed. S. J. Samartha (Geneva: WCC, 1971), 162.

23   Gregorios, *Religion and Dialogue*, 157.

24   Stanley J. Samartha, 'The Cross and the Rainbow: Christ in a Multireligious Culture,' in *Asian Faces of Jesus*, ed. R. S. Sugirtharajah (London: SCM Press, 1993), 104.

25   Stanley J. Samartha, 'Dialogue in a Plural Society,' in *The Multi-faith Context of India*, ed. Israel Selvanayagam (Bangalore: The Board for Theological Text Books Programme of South Asia, 1993), 6.

26   Samartha, *Between Two Cultures*, 167.

27   Richard Taylor, 'The Meaning of Dialogue,' in *Interreligious Dialogue*, ed. Herbert Jai Singh (Bangalore: CISRS, 1967), 62.

28   Vineeth, 'Theology of Religions from the Perspective of Inter-religious Dialogue,' 248.

29   Klaus K. Klostermaier, 'Dialogue – the Work of God,' in *Interreligious Dialogue*, ed. Herbert Jai Singh (Bangalore: CISRS, 1967), 119.

30   Panikkar, *Trinity and World Religions*, 43.

31   Cited in Klostermaier, 'Hindu-Christian Dialogue,' 20.

32   Kuttianimattathil, *Practice and Theology of Interreligious Dialogue*, 589 (check the quote).

33   Panikkar, 'Foreword,' ix.

34   Ibid., xii.

35   Ibid., xiii.

36   Ibid., xi.

37   Klaus Klostermaier, 'The Future of Hindu-Christian Dialogue,' in *Hindu-Christian Dialogue: Perspectives and Encounters*, ed. Harold Coward (Maryknoll, New York: Orbis Books, 1989), 264. Also see *Hindu and Christian in Vrindaban* by the same author (London: SCM Press, 1969).

38   Samartha, *One Christ – Many Religions*, 66–86.

39   Harold Coward, 'The Experience of Scripture in Hinduism and Christianity,' in *Hindu-Christian Dialogue: Perspectives and Encounters*, ed. Harold Coward (Maryknoll, New York: Orbis Books, 1989), 230–50.

40   Each religion has plurality of scriptures and plurality of interpretation, even though canonization has led to the emphasis on 'oneness' of the scripture within each religion. A. K. Ramanujan's essay on *Three Hundred Ramayanas*, which has recently been removed from a university syllabus in India, is a classic example for the case of the plurality of interpretations of what is believed to be an authoritative scripture within Hinduism. Amartya Sen also talks of the significance of heterodoxy in Indian interpretations of scripture and tradition. Sen, *The Argumentative Indian: Writings on Indian History, Culture and Identity* (New York: Farrar, Straus and Giroux, 2005).

41   My observations during my personal involvement in dialogue; also during my interviews, many dialogists enthusiastically pointed out the importance of this aspect in dialogue.

42   Elizabeth Koepping, *Food, Friends and Funeral: On Lived Religion* (Berlin: LIT Verlag, 2008), 3–4.

43   Koepping, *Food, Friends and Funeral*, 4.

44   For a recent book on the importance of lived religion over doctrinal religion, see
     Graham Harvey, *Food, Sex and Strangers: Understanding Religion as Everyday Life*
     (Durham: Acumen, 2013).
45   Panikkar, *Trinity and World Religions*, 1–2.
46   For instance, Abhishiktananda bases Hindu–Christian dialogue on Advaita; *Hindu-
     Christian Meeting Point*.
47   My experience and observations.
48   This I could observe when I undertook follow-up programs in a village called
     Soorangudi in the district where multireligious celebration of festivals took place
     during 1998–9.
49   During my involvement in dialogue, I have witnessed such proposals in the planning
     meetings.

Part III

MULTIPLE IDENTITIES AS A CHALLENGER

Chapter 8

RELIGION, MULTIPLE IDENTITIES AND EVERYDAY RELATIONS
AMONG ORDINARY PEOPLE

One of the central arguments of this book is that contrary to the claim by dialogue proponents that the grassroots people need an awareness of dialogue to enable relatedness, people at the grassroots already relate (as well as negotiate, which includes conflicts among them) with one another. Without knowing what dialogue is, and without being influenced by elite forms of dialogue, the people at the grassroots exhibit knowledge of their religious neighbours, learn from each other, contribute to each other and live in solidarity. The various theological, doctrinal and procedural issues with which dialogists are involved mean very little for these people when it comes to relating with one another. This does not mean that they do not have any faith or faith traditions. They do have their understanding of religion and religious relations as well as in multifarious ways relating and negotiating with their neighbours every day. This chapter attempts to discuss how this is happening in one of the villages in South India based on the field research undertaken there for more than a year in two schedules. The purpose of this chapter is to record and show not only how the ordinary living experiences are different from elite forms of dialogue and elite observations of realities in ordinary life situations, but also how people discover their own ways of relating and negotiating in their everyday life. Everyday living and the complexities involved are often undermined in the process of neat theory-making or formalization of issues in elitist dialogues.

1 Gramam and its Background

As I mentioned in the Introduction, for my field research among the grassroots I selected a multireligious village, Gramam, in the eastern part of Kanyakumari district, midway between Kanyakumari and Nagercoil. The objective of fieldwork among the villagers was threefold: to study their understanding of religion(s) and religious identities and how they use their identities in relating to and negotiating with each other; to study and understand their attitudes to religious conflicts, and especially how they faced and responded to the Mandaikadu conflicts; and to study the ways in which they maintain relationships, including interreligious relationships. I visited other villages also, but Gramam was my central focus.

Gramam represents a typical village of the district, with Hindus, Christians and Muslims distributed among 130 families or 600 people.[1] It is surrounded by villages which are similarly multireligious, though with fewer Muslims.[2] One of its neighbouring villages is Swamithoppu (or Swamithope) which is the headquarters of a cult within Hinduism, Ayya Vazhi, discussed earlier.[3] The Ayya Vazhi temple is a pilgrimage site for South Indian followers, and almost all of Swamithoppu's inhabitants and members.[4]

Many Gramam Hindus also follow this tradition, going to Swamithoppu every Sunday morning and during the eleven-day festivals in January, June and September, and on the founder's birthday, 4 March.[5] Other Gramam Hindus follow *Amman Vazhi* (the way of the mother), focusing especially on the already discussed Mutharamman as well as other folk deities such as *Sudalai Madan*, one of the most worshipped and feared male deities.[6] Twice annually, a *Thiruvizha* (auspicious celebration) is observed in this temple – during May and November.[7] Most Gramam Hindus attend each other's festivals.[8] All the Gramam Christians are Protestants, most being CSI and some Pentecostal who go to the nearby village for worship.[9] There is also a mosque or *Palli* (literally meaning temple, school and rest). The distance between temple, mosque and church is hardly 200–300 metres.[10] Like many other villages in Kanyakumari district, Gramam is not segregated on the basis of religion or caste, houses being generally scattered so that most people have neighbours belonging to other religions. That said, immediate houses around each worship centre are predominantly the homes of adherents of the respective religions.[11]

Muslims are believed to have moved here about 150 years ago from other parts of the district, and from the nearby districts of Tirunelveli, Tuticorin and Madurai, for better employment opportunities, according to oral traditions prevailing among Muslims in Gramam.[12] Currently around 175 Muslims are living in this village, most with no formal education, and few educated beyond primary level.[13] All three tea shops found in this village are run by Muslims, and they are also involved in basket- and mat-making. Four Muslim men are currently working in Gulf countries as masons.[14]

About 200 Christians live in Gramam, more than 90 per cent of them being CSI attending the local CSI church.[15] They were converted in the mid-nineteenth century by the early London Missionary Society missionaries, and the church is believed to have been established in 1855.[16] Local oral traditions indicate that Gramam has had some associations with the first Protestant missionary in the region, William Tobias Ringeltaube, who worked in the surrounding villages and established churches.[17] The remaining 10 per cent attend the Pentecostal church in a nearby village. Some Christians in the village are educated; a few of them have worked as primary school teachers and as clerks in other departments of the government. The education level among Gramam Christians is higher than that of Hindus and Muslims.[18]

Except those linked to government work, mainly as primary teachers, most villagers are farmers and masons, with some carpenters. The traditional occupation for people in this village has been palmera-climbing, the job of Nadars.[19] Local youth are involved in more of automobile and mechanic works, and some who have a good education are in the process of getting into the engineering and computer field.[20] There is a fish and vegetable market everyday between 9.00 am and 11.00 am except on Sunday, fish being brought from nearby fishing villages. The market provides space, especially for women, for daily interaction and exchange of knowledge.[21]

2 Grassroots Relationships Among People with Different Religious Identities in Gramam

This section sets out Gramam villagers' views about interreligious and inter-group relationships, gleaned from visiting, observing and interviewing them, as described in the research methodology in the Introduction.

(a) Ordinary People's Knowledge of Interreligious Dialogue

Very few people in Gramam know what dialogue is. Some have heard about it, but there has been no formal interreligious programme in Gramam.[22] In fact none of my interviewees in Gramam knew the Tamil term for interreligious dialogue: 'Palsamaya Uraiyaadal', (literally meaning 'multireligious conversation'). People do speak to each other, converse with each other, but any concept such as dialogue is foreign to them. It is interesting to note that there was a CSI pastor working in the local CSI church who was one of the dialogue promoters. While he, as he said to me, was doing some interreligious work there, his flock did not quite see that. But some of the Hindus and Muslims said that they were very happy with this pastor, who was unlike the previous pastors of that church because he was very good with all people irrespective of religions and prayed for all people.[23] Nevertheless they did not see him as a dialogue man, perhaps because dialogue has not been a special thing for them.[24]

As I discussed in the beginning of this chapter, elitist dialogue often claims that knowledge of religions is important for the adherents of different religions and that dialogue, and only that, is a place where mutual understanding between people of different religions, the prerequisite of dialogue, is created. Yet this has little impact on people at the grassroots, because their experience seems to be different from the elite religious/interreligious experience. The use of language in dialogue is very selective; everyday terms are made into concepts. For example, 'multireligious friends' is a common term, but the same image in dialogue is used as 'partners in dialogue'. The common and ordinary terms and phrases are being conceptualized and essentialized in dialogue. This has no application for or influence on interreligious and other relationships among people at the grassroots.

(b) Intra-Religious Identities

People very often use intra-religious identities rather than religious identities based on world religions category. Against the agencies that try to put them into fixed religious identities – such as Hindus, Muslims and Christians – they consciously or unconsciously maintain a mixed palette of religious identities in constructing themselves. A specific identity, such as Christian or Hindu, comes to the fore only when they are in conflict for whatever reason whereby religious identity will be useful for one to challenge the other, or when the vested interests groups, usually religious leaders and politicians, dominate the masses as part of their power politics.

One way multiple identities can be observed is how people address each other in terms of their religious belonging. Usually one can note that, unlike identities strictly or primarily based on world religions, denominations in Christianity, cults and traditions in Hinduism and sects in Islam are given importance in constructing self-identity and the identities of others. The language that they use in this context is afforded significance. For example, in Kanyakumari district, when the CSI Christians address themselves or others refer to them, a Tamil word *CSI kaarargal* is used. The term *kaarargal* does not have a specific meaning when it stands alone, but linked to the term CSI it means 'CSI people' or people belonging to CSI, the word *Christian* being set aside: indeed in Kanyakumari district, particularly in Gramam, I never came across the use of CSI *Christians* (literally *Kristhavargal*), or Pentecostal *Christians* or Catholic *Christians* among people in Kanyakumari other than in formal contexts or by elites for a purpose. I could juxtapose my interactions with the people in villages with my interviews with dialogue activists who quite often used terms such as Hindus, Christians and Muslims.

This is also true with the Hindus in the district. There are Saivite, Vaishnavite, *Ayya Vazhi* (literally means 'the way of the father') and *Amman Vazhi* ('the way of the mother') people in the district. Even though some Christians and Muslims sometimes use the term Hindus to refer to them, most 'Hindus' in the area address themselves as *Ayya Vazhikaarargal* or *Amman Vazhikaarargal*. They do not normally construct their identities in terms of Hinduism. 'Some do identify us as Hindus but we prefer to be known as *Ayya Vazhi Makkal*,'[25] said one Ayya Vazhi follower: *Makkal* in Tamil means people (sometimes they use the term *Makkaal* which means children). In the same way, the term 'Muslim' is also not popular in villages in Kanyakumari district. They are often addressed as 'Thulukkans', believed to be a derivative of 'Turks', and referred to as people living close to the 'Palli', a common word in Tamil referring to 'school', to 'rest' and to the mosque.

During my fieldwork I was fascinated to note that even a district-level BJP leader from Kanyakumari district whom I interviewed, when talking about Hindus in the district and his own identity, used the terms such as Vaishnavite, Saivite, Ayya Vazhi people and Amman Vazhi people. He seldom used the term Hindu. He said, 'In the same house, I am a Siva Bhaktha and my sister is Vaishnavist, who follows Ayya Vazhi – but we are related.'[26] Here, he on the one hand identifies himself and his family members not primarily in terms of 'Hindu', and on the other hand suggests that his family identity stands above the religious identities. However, when I moved on to discuss the 'religious conflicts' in general and Mandaikadu conflicts in particular, suddenly he started to use terms such as Hindu, Christian and Muslim. Responding to my question about whether he thinks what happened in Mandaikadu in 1982 were conflicts between fisherfolk and Nadars (and thus a caste problem), he refuted it and said, 'What happened in Mandaikadu and subsequently in the district was a religious conflict. It was a Christian attack on Hindus in which many Hindus were affected.'[27] This suggests that even people with extremist religious ideologies, such as Hindutva, in their everyday life seldom utilize religious identity to refer to themselves or others (and this applies to people from other religions as well). But when it comes to power and ideology they switch codes, illustrating a core point in the constructions of religion as categories: the struggle for power.

The custom of posting wall posters in public places during religious festivals is common in Kanyakumari district, and this can indicate how religious identities function. This is a crucial factor, because when conflicts that are projected as religious appear in the district, wall posters by 'religious adherents' condemning each other are pasted up in public places in huge numbers. This was also true during the 'Mandaikadu conflicts' in 1982. One of my Hindu interviewees (a dialogue activist who requested confidentiality on several issues during the interview) informed me that within a week of the clash between fisherfolk and inland people (mostly Nadars) in Mandaikadu village, a poster was circulating in the district which contained names of six religious leaders, including the local RSS leader, and carried the message that 'we severely condemn the Christians who attacked Hindus in Mandaikadu'. He said that 'this wording was very unfortunate because it aimed to consolidate the Hindus in the district to fight against Christians following a clash which was not religious, and which ended in furthering of conflicts in the district for during the months followed'.[28]

However, this trend is not usually found in the everyday activities among people. It is important to note that during festivals in Amman temples or Ayya Vazhi temples, or in the conventions arranged by Christian churches, or in the celebrations among Muslims, one can rarely see terms such as Hindu, Christian and Muslim used in the wall posters. However, when religious mobilization is attempted following conflicts between two groups of people, these terms appear on wall posters. The agencies or individuals involved in these different contexts may be different, but the events indicate how and when religious identities based on world religions category appear.

Thus it is interesting to note that people's identities, in the religious sphere, as they express, are not based on strict Hindu–Muslim–Christian identities. They have denominational or cult-based or sect-based identities which are still religious. My intention in this section is not to show that ordinary people are always divided within each religion, nor to argue that they do not use religious identities at all, but rather to argue that most of the time, when referring to religion or religious identity, it is to a very specific sector within their 'religion', rather than a homogenized term: ordinary people construct their identities beyond world religions category and other group identities.

(c) Crossing Religious Boundaries and Multiple Group Identities

One of the features of identity construction among people at the grassroots is that they construct their self-identities based less, if at all, on believing, contrary to dialogue activists' assumptions, but on action, a flexible orthopraxy being more relevant than orthodoxy. Identities are constructed in terms of belonging to groups – groups of different kinds and not exclusively religious.[29] There are many people who, in various activities in their everyday lives, identify themselves as Hindus or Christians or Muslims not primarily in terms of doctrines – perhaps because some may know such ideas exist – but with a clear claim to a group identity. This does not mean that they never have religious belief or faith: they may do, but that is not the only factor in identity construction. The sense of belonging to a religious group, rather than believing deeply in the tenets of the religion, informs their identity, and belonging in terms of a variety of group identifiers is basic to this structuring of daily life.[30] I already noted above how the term *kaarargal* is used to refer to their identity which implies the meaning 'people' or 'belonging to'. Similarly, I could find three terms being used that distinguish between believing and belonging. The first one is *visuvasikkiren* or *nambugiren* (I believe), the second is *pinpattruguren* (I follow) and the third is *sertnthavar* (I belong to). While talking about their religious affiliation during the interviews, people in Gramam mostly used the term *sernthavar*, and sometimes, *pinpattrugiren*. Not once did they use the terms *visuvasikkiren* or *nambugiren* when talking about their religious identity.[31] Naturally these two terms are also part of their life, but only in relation to their respective worship places. My point is not to insist that believing in religion is entirely separated from belonging to it, but in maintaining identity in everyday lives, the latter becomes significant in the daily lives of people at the grassroots.

The construction of identity beyond a fixed religious label can be discerned through many of the oral traditions that exist among people. In Kanyakumari district, Hindus and Christians are present in almost in equal percentage, and there are oral traditions and narratives that help them to maintain identities that are beyond the religious identity. One narrative that is popular especially in Kanyakumari district, especially in coastal villages, is that the Virgin Mary and Amman are sisters. While the Virgin Mary represents the deity of the Roman Catholic Christians, Amman represents the popular female deity of Hindus in the district, especially among Nadars. This narrative maintains that because Mary and Amman are sisters their followers – sons and daughters – cannot be enemies, but only brothers and sisters. This narrative also has been appropriated in the Mandaikadu region, where it is said *Kadal Vazhi Vantha Kannalamma Malai Vazhi Vantha Madaikattu Amma* (Mary who came through the sea and Amman who came through the mountains). The message is – we are sons of sisters and why should we fight with each other. Even when the use of such oral traditions may indicate that religion has been a factor behind 'religious conflicts' in the district, they nevertheless help the people to construct their identities beyond religion. Similarly among ordinary people one can frequently hear the statements such as *emmathamum sammatham* (all religions are acceptable), God is one and all religions lead to one goal, and similar ideas about God and religion.

In a village about 2 kilometres away from Gramam, there is an Amman temple with many deities, one being *Vellaikarasamy* (literally, 'white god'). The tradition is that when one of the Christian missionaries was working among people here in the nineteenth century, there was a severe famine during which the missionary helped many people. While some people embraced Christianity, others revered him and worshipped him within their temple.[32] Telling and sharing these kinds of stories helps the people live together and have respect for each other. It also should be noted that, while on the one hand, such oral traditions are helping people to maintain their identities beyond religion, on the other hand, in the present context, the religious extremists, particularly the Hindutva forces, try to play down these stories, resisting any that cross-cut their insistence on a Hindu–Christian divide in the district.

The existence of multiple identities based on varied group interests can challenge the fixed religious identities constructed and appropriated in elite discourses. Caste, region, language, family status, occupation, gender, neighbour, friendship and many other factors play a role for people constructing group identities according to context and need. Moreover one should note that values play an important role when people construct and maintain multiple identities. One of my interviewees in Gramam observed, 'When a person comes before you nobody sees him/her in terms of religion. It also applies to you. As long as you are good, nobody bothers about your religion or any of your other identities. When there are good things, nobody looks at religious identity.'[33] Thus in the everyday living context, religious identities are less important than reputation, goodness, love and so on. Moreover, as I mentioned earlier, religious identities at the grassroots may have little to do with belief. One of my interviewees noted, 'The ordinary people ignore many issues, saying that god came to save all the people and worship any god. The problem only occurs when those who *know* about religion spoil the people. We do not *speak* about religion. When suffering comes we just look for any god to help us.'[34] Here it does not mean that people do not believe, but such beliefs are secondary when it comes to identity making. Another person observed, 'Personal conflicts arise first, only then comes the issue of religious difference and identity. This may be true with an affair or marriage or with any other matter. When their parents are positive, there are no problems. But when conflicts arise then the religious identity is used to separate the man and woman.'[35] Thus we can note that people do not assign a primary place for religious identities when it comes to day-to-day activities in life. 'No one will talk about religions and religious identity until problems come,' he commented.[36] This observation notes that problems between people are not created by religion or by having different religious identity, but these can be used by appealing to religious identity if necessary.

The interaction of multiple identities in a human being or among human beings is a common factor that has often been ignored at the cost of emphasizing religious identities, especially by those naming such identities for their own purposes. Dialogue activists may have many friends with whom they relate on the basis of many identities, but still they interpret other (and often lower-placed) individuals as functioning primarily within one religious identity. Among the people at the grassroots in Kanyakumari district the word 'neighbour' simply refers to people with whom they are in harmony irrespective of religion. One of my interviewees declared, 'When some problems occur for people whom I know, I go to help them, as a friend. My friends also do the same to me. Neither religious difference, nor any other differences, hinder such friendship.'[37]

During my fieldwork I observed that my interviewees in villages seldom used the term Muslim, Hindu, Christian when they responded to my questions. It was I who, given the research frame, used the terms such as 'Hindu', 'Christian' and 'Muslim' – despite being uncomfortable about using terms that they seldom used. They mostly used personal names even when referring to interpersonal conflicts. Indeed as I already mentioned, outsiders such as researchers or politicians with power interests are often criticized for escalating local conflicts to a larger level. A Hindu respondent (dialogue activist) challenged me by saying that it is those researchers and elite scholars who investigate religious conflicts who are responsible for them. He said,

> People live in peace. But mostly researchers like you come and ask questions about the past and that becomes a reviving of the wounds of the people. People seldom identify themselves as Hindus or Muslims or Christians, but when you reiterate these words, it leads towards tensions.[38]

He may be exaggerating, or even wrong, when he accuses researchers of being responsible for kindling religious conflicts among people, but he has a point regarding how people do not always understand themselves based on discrete religious identities. Yet he failed to be self-critical, not accepting that locally based dialogue activists popularize these terms more than does the occasional researcher. More importantly, as a dialogue activist he too used these terms and in my interview constantly referred to religious conflicts while placing dialogue as a solution to religious conflicts. Nevertheless, I observed that common people in the district seldom use these terms which refer to fixed religious identities. People used terms such as *way* and *marga*, rather than boundary-making discrete religion.

(d) Grassroots Perceptions of Religious Conflicts

People at the grassroots do not see that problems lie in religions, for conflict has many sources and dimensions which they are clear about. One woman respondent said that 'there is nothing called religious conflicts'.[39] She held that 'conflicts exist in different contexts in different ways. Even in a family two brothers are fighting, and families fight with their neighbours. One does not need religion at all to fight with another person.'[40] This is the way most of the people at the grassroots look at conflicts in society. As mentioned earlier, for people in Gramam, 'Conflict comes first, religion comes only after that.'[41] They are convinced that most of what are known as 'religious clashes' are personal problems related to socio-economic well-being, or problems due to selfishness or political manipulation or manipulation by people with vested interests for power. In order to aggravate the personal problems, religious or other identities are used. For example, a dialogue activist may say that religious superiority or a theological issue is a problem, but grassroots people source problems differently: selfishness,[42] jealousy,[43] politics,[44] economic issues and other factors.[45] One of my interviewees said, 'My idea is that selfishness is the reason. Conflicts between people occur basically due to selfishness and jealousy. These are personal problems between individuals. But these problems are often labelled and projected as religious in order to get wider support from others who share the same religious identity.'[46] While elite theorists including dialogists may find it difficult to conceptualize and understand these rather simple and familiar issues responsible for conflicts, and ignore the same when rushing to speak about the divisions in terms of neatly framed structures or fixed identities, the fact is that ordinary people are able to clearly perceive these factors behind conflicts in order to think about the solutions to mitigate them.

Another important fact is that the people at the grassroots are also aware of the process by which any small conflict can become a religious clash. They think that conflicts between individuals have to be stopped at the initial stage, lest it becomes a communal conflict, and mostly as a local community they make efforts to do so.[47] One of the elements that can covert a conflict between two or more individuals into a communal conflict is third-person involvement.[48] One woman interviewee said thus:

> The third person involvement can create conflicts between even mother and son. A third person will go and talk one thing to the son and the other thing to the mother, thus create problems. Until and unless there is an involvement of third person, even if you are enemies, you wouldn't come to fighting in the street.[49]

Among the major groups of people who are referred to as the 'third persons' in the context of religious conflicts are politicians, religious leaders and people with personal vested interests.[50] People believe that politicians misuse religions for vote bank politics which leads to tensions and conflicts among people. For one respondent,

> All people are good. But there are people to instigate. They are political and religious heads. They will kindle the 'feeling' of people to fight with each other. Few individuals will do this kindling act for their selfish reasons. Even the feelings of people who do not want to fight, are kindled by such activities.[51]

A prominent discussant on third-party involvement, already cited, explained further that

> when politicians and religious heads instigate, many people ignore what they say. But some, for many reasons, will follow these people: a group which is alcoholic, and has no work, go for making problems. People with families, works

to do, have and look for some prestige in society, and have the awareness that they should see the faces of the same people next day, will not go for conflicts. And the same politicians who have instigated these people to fight would come for solving it.[52]

The people in Gramam said that when problems occur between Hindus and Muslims or Hindus and Christians or Muslims and Christians in other parts of the district or elsewhere in India, they believe that the problems are happening somewhere for some personal reasons which have been religiously coloured.[53] One interviewee, responding to my question of the impact of 'religious' conflicts outside their village, said thus:

> During the problems after the demolition of the Babri Masjid, even though this raised concerns among Muslims in Gramam, we never thought of the nearby Hindus as enemies. It was considered as a clash that occurred somewhere between some Hindus and some Muslims. The same way here no Hindu supported the demolition of the Babri Masjid. When Godhra train burning took place and the clashes were going on in Gujarat, the Hindus here did not consider us as their enemies.[54]

Grassroots people's understanding of, and attitudes to, conflicts do not mean that there are no conflicts among them where religion is implicated. In fact there are some cases where religious identities of people are harnessed to maintain conflicts by those with vested interests. Two incidents can be mentioned here:

> A Christian poor couple was betrayed by a church-going rich Christian couple when the former's house collapsed in rain and he applied for government help. The Christian couple informed the government officials that he (the poor person) has a lot of wealth and saw that the poor person does not get help from government. When another person who happened to be Muslim saw this and asked the couple about this, he was told thus: 'It is between us Christians. You, Muslim, do not have anything to do with this.'[55]

This incident is very important, because religious belonging is used in a context of another problem, to aggravate it by adding one more platform for division or difference.

> There was a dispute between a Hindu man and a Muslim woman about a neem tree which was on the border of their lands. The dispute was about to whom it belongs, but in the course of dispute, it became a quarrel. Then the Hindu man threatened the woman saying that he would complain to the police that this woman belongs to 'Al-Umma Muslim terrorist group.'[56]

Like the above incident, this is also a problem which has nothing to do with religion or religious identity, but for personal reasons the difference in religious identity is misused. Of course appealing to religious identity (or any other identity depending upon the context) is normal during the conflicts, but such attitudes and actions are often undermined by those who research violence or attempt to offer solutions to it.

These are but two incidents which show that most of the time what is called a Hindu–Muslim or Hindu–Christian or Christian–Muslim problem is actually a personal problem which for strategic reasons has religious identity deliberately added. In order to activate the quarrel, there is a tendency to look for more weapons, and it is primarily religious difference or identity or belongingness which is used as a tool to negate a person, even though religious identity per se plays little role in conflicts. In other words, where a person is ostensibly attacked for not believing in a religion and for not belonging to a religion, the underlying reason is usually to do with economic well-being, social dignity or status, religion being used as an instrument to aggravate the conflict.[57]

Regarding the 1982 clashes in the district, many people in Gramam maintained that they never saw it as a religious problem at all, but one between coastal people and inland people.[58] This is contrary to what most of the dialogue promoters as well as politicians and religious figures in the district believe. One Muslim man from Gramam said, 'The fear was that the fisher-folk people may come against us and if they come we should escape, protect ourselves together. Protecting all the people in our village was a major thing, and all Hindus, Muslims and Christians were together.'[59] Thus, for Gramam people, the 1982 clashes were in no way religious clashes between Christians and Hindus, and they saw the incident and faced it through their 'village' identity. They continue to see it as a problem between fisherfolk who lived in the coastal area and people who lived inlands. Compare this with how dialogue projects these clashes to be religious!

(e) Naming and (Religious) Identity

I already discussed how people at the grassroots maintain multiple group identities and intra-religious identities as against the claim of dialogue activists that they are divided along the lines of fixed religious identities. The fixed religious terms based on world religions category such as Hindus, Muslims and Christians are seldom used by people in Gramam to refer to each other in the everyday context of their life. As I mentioned earlier, it was me who used these terms quite often for the sake of my questions in the interviews with them; they did not. During the interviews they used the names of people whom they were talking about (even in the context where I did not know who that person was) rather than mentioning their religious (or for that matter any other) identity. When they talked about the conflicts they had with others, they rarely referred to religious identity. Particularly when the Muslim woman was explaining to me about the conflict regarding the neem tree, I noticed that not even once did she mention the term 'Hindu' to refer to her opponent, using his name only.[60] Of course one can argue that one's religious identity can often be discerned through names, and this is true, yet the names of people with other religious identities rarely referred to their religious identities.

Elite dialogue activists tend to assume all villagers will be categorized by religious identity and base deliberations on that.

(f) Relativism: Experiential and not Theological

When people in Gramam talk about religions, they most often say that 'all religions are the same', and 'god is one'. They ignore many religious doctrinal issues, saying that god came to help all the people, and worship any god. They say, 'When suffering comes we just look for any god to help us.' One Hindu woman said, 'Our children used to go to functions in mosque and church, participate in them, eat whatever they give, and "worship their god remembering our god."'61 In the same way, Muslims and Christians also participate in many of the religious festivals of each other and of Hindus, without even learning about the festival. This kind of interaction and relativism at the grassroots is different from the so-called relativism at the elite level, Christian theologians of dialogue being particularly nervous of relativism, as is evident in many aspects of their writings. Grassroots relativism is neither doctrinal nor structured but social, seeing all religions as equally and almost interchangeably valid.

Yet dialogue discusses doctrines in institutional religions, and seems almost committed to doctrinization. This is because, of course, it mostly works within religious institutions, and hence the endorsement of religious authority is often sought for dialogue. Whenever religious conservatives object to dialogue, the proponents attempt both to defend dialogue and to reaffirm their own religious doctrines. As a result, much material is produced which can be termed 'dialogue on dialogue', further essentializing and formalizing what is already distant from people. But ordinary people exercise relativism in an easy manner, especially in the social planes, while still keeping their commitment and belongingness to their religious identity.

(g) Relationships at Grassroots as Spontaneous

Interreligious relationships, as well as other group relationships, among people in Gramam are spontaneous. They do not need any agency or a 'common platform' to relate with their neighbours from other religions, nor is prior knowledge of religions expected. Multiplicity is just part of everyday life. Their relationships are spontaneous simply because they coexist and relate with each other in a variety of informal ways.62 For them there is no such thing as starting points for dialogue or 'common platforms for building relationships'. Moreover the locations of interreligious relationships, unlike dialogue, are not selected beforehand. People meet in their houses, on their way, on roads, in tea shops and in many other such places.63 Thus their spontaneous interreligious relationships are bound to the unplanned location of their meeting. One of my interviewees said, 'We meet each other in our village every day. Irrespective of religions people help each other. Even for ordinary necessities we are dependent on each other.'64 They use terms such as *anna* (brother) and *akka* (sister) to address each other irrespective of religions. These are Tamil words used in the context of familial relationships.[65]

On the other hand, dialogue is mostly occupied with commonalities, starting points and common platforms. Theological concepts are often discussed and concepts such as theocentrism, christocentrism, uniqueness, commonalities and differences between religions dominate the agenda, in a carefully selected site. All this may not invalidate dialogue as an approach to religions in the context of exclusivist attitudes of certain religious followers, but it does make it of scant value as a 'teaching tool' for people using multiple identities at the grassroots to relate with each other.

(h) Solidarity with Each Other

For people at the grassroots, tension in the name of religions is one of many crises in which they help each other. They may not strictly differentiate one crisis from the other, but helping each other during the crisis is important for them, for in daily life they are dependent on each other. The people in Gramam narrated many incidents in which their neighbours irrespective of religions rushed to help. Once, there was fire in the mosque. Immediately the people who came to offer help were Hindus, who also helped and funded Muslims to rebuild it.[66] People support each other irrespective of religions during times of crisis. When Ayya Vazhi people needed a path to their temple, most Christians in Gramam offered their land for use.[67] If celebrations in religious worship places clash, there is a possibility of problems due to loudspeakers. This is commonly avoided by discussing programmes beforehand to avoid clashes.[68]

One Hindu man said that he regularly used to give a lift to the local pastor and imam. He believed that people from all religions see this and witness this, and this will increase confidence in them.[69] But in the dialogue circles people say that it is (just) the coming together of leaders and people from other faiths which will increase confidence among people belonging to different religions. However, dialogue mostly happens within four walls, but everyday life allows constant witness to these relationships.

(i) Celebrating Festivals Together: Not the Dialogical Way

While the promoters of dialogue think they have to go to villages to invite them to celebrate religious festivals together, villagers have long done that. The cooking of special food (meat and sweets) and making of a variety of sweets by all religious people is an important way of expressing solidarity with their religious neighbours celebrating a particular festival. In other words, when a particular religious festival is celebrated, village people mostly do not look at it merely as a festival of others, but for the community, and therefore make all the special foods and sweets and let off fireworks to share in the festivities. That their own children should not be deprived of these special items on those days when their neighbours celebrate festivals is one reason, but it is also seen as solidarity among people in terms of religious relationships.[70] This is normal and voluntary but is also seen as special. This poses a challenge to formal dialogue festival programmes arranged by elites, which in Kanyakumari is a very recent phenomenon, particularly after the 1982 clashes.

In addition to celebrating their religious neighbours' festivals, people also participate in the religious festivals and other celebrations of their neighbours. For church day in the CSI church (an annual celebration to remember the day the church was founded) in Gramam, all religious people gather in the church. When Muslims celebrate their twelve-day festival in their *palli* (mosque), Christians and Hindus from this village participate. When there is an eleven-day *Thiruvizha* (festival) thrice in a year and other celebrations in the Ayya Vazhi temple in Swamithoppu, the nearby village, most of the Christians and Muslims attend, participating in celebrations in the temple premises but not worship inside the temple.

(j) Use of Oral Traditions, Proverbs

The interreligious relationships of villagers are sustained through many oral traditions which include long stories or short proverbs about relationships between people, some of which I have already discussed. Of course, religious scriptures are used in worship, but may have little importance in everyday relationships including among religious adherents. People often recollect their memories of past relationships in Gramam between people belonging to different religions, which helps them resist the influence of people with personal vested interests who wish to change memories of the past to stress deep-seated religious conflicts.[71]

On the other hand, we noted that dialogue is obsessed with textualization. The use of religious scriptures in different ways dominates the elite dialogue. The importance of acquiring knowledge about other religions is often emphasized in dialogue. In such contexts what are mostly referred to are the scriptures of different religions. Dialogue proponents fail to note that the ordinary people are also 'learning' religious practices, concepts and beliefs as they live. There is also a lot of knowledge generated about people of other religions among the grassroots, which may not need the support of any canonized religious scripture. Another way the religious scriptures are used in dialogue is when different religious scriptures are placed side by side, and texts are read from different scriptures. It symbolizes the notion that the many scriptures exert authority on the participants of dialogue. But the realities among ordinary people in fact challenge every aspect of textualization that is prominent in elite dialogue.

(k) Solving Communal Tensions

Talking about ordinary, natural and familiar interreligious relationships among people in villages does not mean that there are no conflicts and tensions evoking religious identity: I have already referred to a few such tensions in Gramam. However, what is important is how people solve these tensions lest they become major incidents, and they do this by using simple everyday methods. One of the ways the problems between people with different religious identities get solved or are prevented from becoming a big 'religious' conflict is that the person who is responsible for the problem is rebuked by a person from the same religion.[72] This is common. For example, in the neem tree incident, mentioned earlier, it was another Hindu man who came and rebuked the man who abused and threatened the woman using her religious identity. In this way problems are defused before they become major religious conflicts.

I was fascinated to listen to an incident in Gramam in which a communal tension was solved before it became a conflict. A song was sung by an outside singer in a function among Muslims, who had arranged for an orchestra in connection with their celebrations. Christians and Hindus in the village had also contributed to it, and therefore gathered there with Muslims. During the orchestra, the singer sang a song in which the Muslim asks, 'Who said we are foreigners?' The singer sang this song twice. The next day it was alleged by the Hindu youth that Muslim youth gave extra money to the singer to sing that song for the second time. When there was about to be a confrontation, one of the Muslim men approached a Hindu man who was considered to be moderate and asked him to tell the Hindu youth that he (the Hindu man) liked that song sung by the Muslim singer so he had asked the singer to sing it again. When the Hindu man came and told this to the Hindu youth, the problem was solved and the Hindu youth who had gathered dispersed. Ethically, one may question this untruth, but the people were happy that the problem was solved![73]

This incident indicates that the people in villages continue to live in local communities where they try to resolve problems for themselves. However, a political elite or a person with vested interests for power in such a situation will try to protect his or her power, never taking the blame on himself or herself lest it jeopardize the loyalty of the wider group and make them vulnerable. In fact if political elites come across such a situation, they will all too often exploit the situation for their own purposes of accumulating and maintaining power. This shows the difference between political and other power aspiring elites and the local common people who solve the problems because they think that the loss ultimately has to be borne by them.

Talking about the conflicts between people and the ways by which people in traditional communities in India handled them, Madhu Kishwar says thus:

> What distinguishes ethnic hostilities in India from those of Europe is that, *left on their own*, our traditional communities have worked out eminently feasible norms for co-existence, including evolving common cultural symbols and spaces, and in sharing each other's rituals and festivities.[74]

However, it should be added, in my view, that the traditional communities did this in spite of the problems they had among themselves, for example, due to caste inequalities. She further says,

> Most traditional micro-societies ... worked out rules of co-existence through a consensual process. Decisions were made on the basis of customary practices

which kept evolving over time to meet with changing situations. Those who possessed the patience and skills to conciliate or manipulate local groups to elicit consensus among them about mutually agreed upon course of action were the most effective and sought-after leaders. The diverse communities inhabiting the Indian subcontinent were able to evolve fairly sophisticated and workable norms for co-existence because, unlike in Europe, there was no central religious authority mobilizing sections of the population under its umbrella against those professing different faith. Moreover, local communities remained largely independent of the political rulers at the top, just as the secular and the religious domains remained somewhat independent of one another. Therefore, local differences in almost all cases had to be settled locally without help or interference from outside political or religious authorities. The local people understood that failure to work out such ground rules leads directly to basic insecurity for all concerned. Hostilities and attacks on others at a local level have to be carried out at personal risk and expense.[75]

In my view, this is true even today in many village communities in India. The problems reach a different level when outsiders or power-mongering elites with intentions for power enter and exploit the circumstances. In the political culture today, outsiders enter in order to exploit the situation for their own purposes of attaining power, and this is an everyday activity of parties interested in dividing communities in order to attain and maintain political power. The practical intervention of dialogue activists in contexts of tension and their practical efforts to contain troubles may also contribute to the maintenance of elite power, *not* local empowerment. Yet dialogue activists meet together to *discuss* conflicts, and often claim that such coming together helps people who are taking part in conflicts. The situation is far more complex, and intrusion – however well-meaning – into a locally managed situation is easily detrimental.

3 The Limitations of the Elitist Dialogues

Thus we note that dialogue as practised today has many limitations when compared to the living experiences of grassroots people. It has an understanding of religions, religious identity and religious violence which has been influenced by colonial forms of knowledge. It has uncritically accepted these categories, which it has further popularized through its discourses. The actualities of interreligious relationships are conceptualized, essentialized and idealized, and in the process a lot of energy is spent on defining and defending dialogue. Defending dialogue becomes crucial and is associated with doctrinal issues, with anxieties about syncretism and relativism being directed against interreligious dialogue. It seeks for common platforms and starting points and also delineates prerequisites for dialogue in a very meticulous way to include knowledge of religions, inner experience and spirituality. In its approach, discussion of theological, philosophical and ontological concepts and doctrinal issues become the central activity. The use of religious scriptures in dialogue also sets limitations for a dialogue preoccupied with textualization.

In their articulation of religious conflicts, dialogue proponents often ignore the different socio-economic and political factors along with power structures which underlie many conflicts, seeing conflicts between people through a religious lens held by elite power holders. Moreover, dialogue activists often talk about grassroots dialogue meaning 'taking dialogue to the grassroots'. The patronizing assumption is that interreligious awareness is lacking among such people and that it is the responsibility of dialogue activists to educate 'these people' about it. What is ignored and subjugated in this process is the existence of various kinds of relationships among people at the grassroots in their daily lives.

In opposition to the claim by dialogue proponents that the grassroots people need an awareness of dialogue to enable relatedness, we have seen among people in Gramam that they already relate well with one another. Without knowing what dialogue is, and without being influenced by elite forms of dialogue, the people at the grassroots exhibit knowledge of their religious neighbours, learn from each other, contribute to each other and live in solidarity. The issues of syncretism and relativism do not affect them – but this does not mean that they do not have any faith traditions. Rather it indicates that people at the grassroots do not primarily understand their identity and their neighbours' identity in terms of exclusivist religion. They participate in and celebrate different festivals and interact with each other in their everyday life. Thus they maintain spontaneous living interreligious relationships in their everyday lives.

My purpose in this chapter is not to romanticize the experiences of the people at grassroots to argue that they live in perfect peace and harmony, or to idealize the village or rural life. Rather, I am aware that they do have everyday conflicts between them, but my point is that they also have resources to resolve them. One such resource is that they do not look at conflicts between them primarily in terms of religion. This is in fact a significant difference from how dialogue proponents look at and interpret 'religious conflicts'. These realities among people at the grassroots pose challenges to elite dialogue and point out its limitations. This means that it is not grassroots people who should learn from the dialogue activists, but rather dialogue activists who should learn from them about the nuanced, complex and subtle issues involved in the context of multiple group identities and about addressing conflicts in society effectively. Most importantly if a religious framework continues to be used to interpret most, if not all, of the conflicts in society, any attempts by dialogue to create better relationships may not bring the desired results: it will only make things worse. Precisely for this reason, there has to be an alternative to dialogue that can help understand the conflicts among people in a better way and that can lead to clearly articulate the issues of peace and harmony in society. In the next chapter I shall present a case for multiple identities based on the everyday living experiences of ordinary people and explore how it can serve as a challenger for interreligious dialogue.

Notes

1   Balan, Interview, Gramam, 5 June 2008. Balan was the Panchayat president during 2007–8.
2   Harun, Interview, Gramam, 8 July 2008. Harun, a Muslim in his fifties now, has been living here from his birth, and he is running a small business.
3   Patrick, *Religion and Subaltern Agency*.
4   Vishnu, Interview.
5   Murugan, Interview, Gramam, 15 June 2008.
6   Ishvara, Interview, Gramam, 2 June 2008.
7   Murugan, Interview.
8   Ibid.
9   Interview with Samuel, a retired primary school teacher, Gramam, 8 July 2008.
10 This is from my observation of Gramam.
11 My observations.
12 Harun, Interview.
13 Ibid.
14 Ibid.
15 Solomon, Interview, Gramam, 1 June 2008. Solomon, a member of the CSI church and a retired teacher, has worked on the history of this church.
16 Solomon, Interview.
17 Ibid.
18 My observation.
19 Palmera-climbing to collect palm juice, both for making jaggery – used for coffee, and in place of sugar – and for turning the juice into alcoholic toddy, is the traditional work of Nadars in Kanyakumari and surrounding districts. See Hardgrave, *Nadars of Tamilnad*.
20 Harun, Interview.
21 My observations.
22 Samuel, Focus-group Interview.
23 Murugan, Focus-group Interview.
24 Samuel, Focus-group Interview.
25 Parvathi, Interview.
26 Velan, Interview.
27 Ibid.
28 Confidentiality requested.
29 The relationship between believing and belonging are studied from different approaches in the contemporary context, especially in sociology of religion. Grace Davie, studying religion in Britain, has argued that while there was a strong sense of believing in religion among people, the sense of belonging was less since the formal observance of religious life was not impressive; *Religion in Britain since 1945: Believing without Belonging* (Oxford: Blackwell, 1994). Others have picked up the issue. While criticizing her definition for belonging as exclusive, Michael Winter and Christopher Short have argued that 'the commitment to a specific denomination may be even more striking than the level of religious belief but ... this is not necessarily translated into formal religious observance'. 'Believing and Belonging: Religion in Rural England, Review,' *The British Journal of Sociology* 44, no. 4 (1993): 638. David Voas and Alasdair Crockett have argued against believing without belonging and

shown that 'religious belief has declined at the same rate as religious affiliation and attendance, and is not even necessarily higher than belonging'; 'Religion in Britain: Neither Believing nor Belonging,' *Sociology* 39, no. 1 (2005): 13. Responding to the criticisms, Davie has worked on belonging without believing in Scandinavian countries; Grace Davie, 'Vicarious Religion: A Methodological Challenge,' in *Everyday Religion: Observing Modern Religious Lives*, ed. Nancey T. Ammerman (New York: Oxford University Press, 2006), 21–37.

30 I have observed that, in the ordinary living context, the 'belonging' is not strictly related to religious observance. It is more about their self-understanding of affiliation to a group and how they interpret their group identity. In this regard, Abby Day has done an interesting study among young people and has come up with the idea of 'believing in belonging', where belief is no longer confined to creeds and doctrines. Her finding is that young people shift 'the meaning of belief to describe affective relationships in which they feel they belong to. Such a shift necessitates a relocation of the transcendent to the everyday and social'; 'Believing in belonging: An ethnography of young people's constructions of belief,' *Culture and Religion* 10, no. 3 (2009): 263; also see her recent book *Believing in Belonging: Belief and Social Identity in the Modern World* (New York: Oxford University Press, 2011). Similar perspectives can be extended to understand people's identities at the grassroots.

31 My observations during a focus-group interview, as well as in my everyday life context in these rural contexts.

32 Brahma, Interview, Gramam, 29 June 2008.

33 Narayana, Interview, Gramam, 8 July 2008.

34 Vishnu, Interview. Emphasis is mine.

35 Narayana, Interview. This understanding was prevailing among many of my interviewees in Gramam. This became more evident when they spoke in the focus-group interviews I had arranged about how they responded to the Mandaikadu conflicts. They were talking between themselves about how they thought Mandaikadu conflicts were between fisherfolk people and inland people on the issue of teasing women; and how they stood together to protect 'their village' (the identity they had constructed for themselves in the context of the clashes), when news came that the nearby fisherfolk village people were planning to come and attack them on a night in early March 1982. This clearly indicates how identities are constructed differently even during conflicts.

36 Narayana, Interview.

37 Murugan, Interview.

38 Balarasu, Interview.

39 Parvathi, Focus-group Interview.

40 Ibid.

41 Mohammed, Focus-group Interview.

42 Samuel, Focus-group Interview.

43 Mohammed, Focus-group Interview.

44 Harun, Focus-group Interview.

45 Parvathi, Focus-group Interview.

46 Samuel, Focus-group Interview.

47 Mohammed, Focus-group Interview.

48 Parvathi, Focus-group Interview.

49 Ibid.

50 Ibid.

51 Harun, Focus-group Interview.
52 Parvathi, Focus-group Interview.
53 Mohammed, Focus-group Interview.
54 Ibid.
55 Harun, Focus-group Interview.
56 Fatima, Interview. Fatima who is in her fifties is a housewife from the Muslim community, and she narrated this incident that happened to one of her relatives in the village.
57 Mohammed, Focus-group Interview.
58 As I observed, all the focus-group interviewees looked at the conflict from this perspective.
59 Harun, Focus-group Interview. Note here that although the religious identities based on world religions are used, nevertheless they are subsumed within another identity – *our village*.
60 Fatima, Interview.
61 Parvathi, Focus-group Interview.
62 This was expressed and discussed by the interviewees in the focus-group when I asked them about their ways of relating.
63 Discussions in focus-group interviews.
64 Harun, Focus-group Interview.
65 Parvathi, Focus-group Interview.
66 Ibid.
67 Harun, Focus-group Interview.
68 Narayana, Focus-group Interview.
69 Ibid.
70 Saraswathi, Focus-group Interview.
71 Parvathi, Focus-group Interview.
72 Ibid.
73 Narayana, Interview.
74 Madhu Kishwar, *Religion at the Service of Nationalism* (New Delhi: Oxford University Press, 1998), XIII–XIV; emphasis added.
75 Kishwar, *Religion at the Service of Nationalism*, XV–XV.

Chapter 9

After Dialogue

This book began with the hypothesis that interreligious dialogue in India – which was primarily developed with the aim of broadening inclusive approaches among religions and encouraging harmonious relationships between different religious adherents – has problems because of its rootedness in the 'world religions' category and its uncritical acceptance of religion as a separate category distinct from other aspects of life. I identified three problems of dialogue. The first is the idea of religious plurality among dialogists that stems from the notion of the 'world religions' category and secular-religious distinctions. The second involves the notion that people are primarily divided in terms of religion and that religious conflicts occur due to this division, religion being the cause of or instrument in 'religious conflicts'. The third has to do with the elite nature of dialogue, which pays little attention to, or considers irrelevant, everyday relationships involving multiple identities among common people – even though dialogue activists continue to work on their wish 'to take dialogue to the grassroots', undermining the ways in which ordinary people perceive and practice religion and exercise multiple identities. I have discussed and critiqued these points by discussing current literature and the activity of dialogue promoters in India and by observing relations among followers of religions at the grassroots and interviewing them. In this chapter I pose three fundamental questions to dialogue pertaining to its usefulness, necessity and possibility as a way of summarizing the major arguments developed throughout this book, and I attempt to explore an alternative that can challenge both dialogue and all of the three notions that are questioned. This alternative may help to interpret the way common people perceive and practise religion and relate and negotiate with their neighbours, including religious neighbours, and challenge the fault lines of the 'world religions' category and the prejudices of dialogue that has its basis in world religions.

1 *Three Fundamental Questions to Dialogue*

(a) *The Myth of 'religions in conflict': Is* Inter*religious Dialogue Helpful?*

Let me start with the question of tensions and conflicts between religions which is the context of dialogue and which dialogue tries to do away with. Is *inter*religious dialogue helpful in the context of so-called religious conflicts which it attempts to overcome or solve? Does it mitigate or eliminate what are considered as religious conflicts or conflicts between religions? The emphasis here is on *inter*: Do conflicts occur *between* religions or between people with varied religion and other identities, and if it is the latter, does one need dialogue *between* religions? Is it helpful? With the notion that conflicts are taking place between religions, dialogists talk about dialogue between (or of) religions. Sometimes they also seem to imply that dialogue between religions can solve *any* (not just religious) conflicts in society. But what happens when the very notion of conflicts *between* religions is critiqued and proved to be a myth? What happens when the reality of many factors responsible for what is simplistically considered to be religious conflict is realized?

Of course, there is no harm in dealing with conflicts among individuals and groups if such action contains and reduces conflicts in the wider society and maintains better relationships. In fact it is necessary and indeed important in the midst of riots, war, bombing, killing, genocides and pogroms. But what happens when the very understanding of conflicts and the mode of dealing with them become dubious because there are multiple issues and identities involved rather than just religious concepts or religious identities? For, failing to understand the causes and complexities of conflicts also may lead to the furtherance of conflicts, and in this way, dialogue may contribute towards aggravating problems. If, then, such an approach generates myths and even exacerbates conflict, what benefit can it bring? Thus, while the intent to foster peace and harmony and to create better relationships among people may be appreciated and even endorsed, nevertheless the way dialogue sees conflicts primarily in terms of or through religion needs to be critiqued.

Since the notion that people have fixed religious identities based on world religions is accepted in dialogue, the idea that they are also divided (or relate with each other) primarily in terms of religions and religious identities is simply accepted as a baseline from which to overcome conflict. The understanding of religious conflict in dialogue is basically twofold, causal and instrumental: religions cause conflicts, and religions are used in conflicts. In the first, the lack of proper understanding of religions is said to lead people to conflict with each other. The presumption that religions are prone to violence – often propagated by those secularists who believe that religion is anti-secular – is accepted even in dialogue circles, perhaps because it suggests the solution. In the second, religion is assumed to be used by power-aspired elites for promoting conflicts among people. In explaining such instrumental causes of religious conflicts, dialogue in India normally holds that it is primarily politicians who use religion to create conflicts among people.

Yet, as pointed out in Chapter 5, both of these understandings have shortcomings. The idea that religions cause conflicts bypasses other issues – socio-economic and cultural – which may also be responsible. The idea of politicians using religions to invoke conflicts also has shortcomings due to the fact that political people are not the only ones to use religion for their power interests. A closer look at conflicts will show that *any* conflict can be interpreted as religious, not only by people aspiring for political power but for power of any kind, including 'religious', that can help them maintain domination and control over others. Further, the idea of the political use of religion in conflicts also indicates that two inimical groups of religious people are fighting through their own will or that of politicians. But in reality, during the occurrences of large-scale communal clashes, it is mostly one *politically* motivated mob with power interests that attacks the other, who, often, is at the receiving end. But in both understandings in dialogue about religious conflicts – causal and instrumental – the easier and less contentious notion that people are divided in terms of religion is uncritically accepted. Moreover, dialogue says little about how any people with power interests can make any conflict 'religious' by naming and interpreting it as such: it may be too hot a topic to handle. Dialogue activists focus on religion's place in healing conflict in part because that is their strength, and including clearly relevant issues in other areas may weaken their stance. Yet therein lies a potential problem, not only in ignoring the many other issues and reasons for conflicts among people, but in furthering the notion that people are primarily divided along religious lines that separate religion from other aspects.

In this regard one should be careful about talking about conflicts where only religious identities of people are used. Of course people with vested interests make use not only of religious identities, but also of identities based on caste, ethnicity, language and regions and many other collective identities which are presented in terms of communities. All these identities can help those who want to exploit the situation for their power aspirations. In fact caste identity may operate more powerfully, applying inferior and superior attitudes more effectively than religion. But generally conflicts cannot be confined even to caste as there are always multiple reasons including personal reasons for conflicts. However, in the present general Indian context, using religious identities has become quite popular and routine because it gives a broader world view in terms of the identities of people and avoids facing up to casteism.

Moreover, a crucial point dialogists often fail to understand is the power issues as well as power structures that are involved in conflicts between people. To legitimize and amass power, vested interests attempt to use these identities. Even while dialogists understand the reality that aspirants for political power may cause or use conflict, their understanding is only partial. This is because pointing the finger merely at politics and politicians is only part of the issue. But, in fact, power operates through many levels, even if overt political power can seem crucial. The reality is that anyone, including small people aspiring for political power or small people with vested interests in dominating and controlling others, can refer to religious identities not to *create* religious conflicts but to *name and interpret* any conflict or mild tensions among people as religious. As I mentioned earlier, personal problems and jealousy among people can in turn be named as religious conflicts.

The case study undertaken in Kanyakumari district on the three-decade-long dialogical discourse of the 'Mandaikadu religious clashes', discussed in Chapter 6, has shown that conflicts occur among people due to many reasons which are primarily involved with everyday life issues and not always specific identities. But when the power-interested elites enter into it and name and interpret them as religious, that can further tensions among people with different religious identities. Thus the issue of eve-teasing in Mandaikadu village and the consequent conflicts which had, in the immediate context, to do with caste *have become* religious conflicts between Hindus and Christians when the power-interested groups so named them. The Hindutva parties in the region are the prime perpetrators of this naming and interpreting process, expecting that will help them secure and consolidate the votes of Hindus – they have had some success in that, if not always, as I have shown through an analysis of election results in Kanyakumari district since 1982 – and at times Christian leaders also have attempted to use this discourse for their benefit. Unfortunately the dialogue activists in the region, who strip conflicts of individual meaning by putting them into the generic context of religious fundamentalism and misunderstanding, actually help these power-interested groups to perpetrate such naming, since socio-economic issues such as caste, economic and even personal issues behind these conflicts get little attention. Dialogue, in its claimed endeavour to create better relationships among people, often ends up in promoting the myth of conflicts between religions.

(b) *The Problem of the Elitist Dialogue: Is Interreligious* Dialogue *a Necessity?*

Is interreligious *dialogue* a necessity when actual relationships in everyday ordinary life situations are much more important and may further peace and harmony more effectively? The emphasis here is on the fact that relationships are primarily created and maintained in the context of everyday living experiences of people, and not in dialogue which is confined to a few interested elites. Therefore is *dialogue* a necessity? Dialogists talk a lot about the necessity, imperativeness and urgency of dialogue. But do we need it? Is it necessary for making better relationships among people? Is it necessary to create peace and harmony in society?

In fact the conceptualization of dialogue which is undertaken by elites undercuts the grassroots realities at least in two ways: first, the living experiences and relationships among people are ignored, differentiated from dialogue and described as ordinary, usual, simple, emotional and shallow; and second, dialogue is posed as a necessity or imperative for these people to follow. This ignorance of people's experiences and making dialogue a necessity is not a simple unconscious act but is preloaded with the notion that elites have the *power* to define and interpret how relationships are to be maintained among religious adherents, only through dialogue, and to promote it and make it a necessity.

This attitude naturally flows into what can be called dialogical hegemony or dialogical elitism. As discussed in Chapters 2 and 7, the location, process, method and content of dialogue are fundamentally concerned with elites who are interested in promoting dialogue. The nature of the interaction, such as the process of conceptualization and theologization of dialogue, demands participants have an elite education. Dialogue – which simply means conversation – is loaded with many essentialized characteristics. One of the reasons for such conceptualization and theologization has been to protect dialogue from those who insist that dialogue promotes syncretism and relativism and betrays the fundamentals of religions. This leads dialogue proponents to spell out prerequisites for participating in dialogue, the qualities necessary to be a 'partner in dialogue' and many such ideas. The emphasis on the teaching nature of dialogue, its urgency and necessity, are also often described, as are 'starting points and common platforms' for maintaining dialogue, such as theological concepts like christocentrism and theocentrism. True, sometimes the poor and marginalized are posed as a starting point in dialogue, yet only as *subjects* of discussion, not discussants. Questions such as the nature of actual relations between a Hindu landlord and a poor Christian or a rich Christian and a marginalized Muslim are neither a starting point nor a platform.

Not only are the people at the margins or the grassroots sometimes the subjects of discussion in dialogue, but they also become the targets for dialogue since the source of 'religious conflict events', that is, the misunderstanding of religion among followers, is usually sought among ordinary people. It is argued in dialogue circles, among many others, that religions easily affect such people, characterized in true colonial fashion as sentimental and emotional and therefore easily liable to 'indulge in' religious conflicts. The outcome of this attitude among dialogue activists is that 'these people' have to be educated about dialogue by professional dialogists through dialogue activities, awareness programmes, training for dialogue and the like. The need for dialogue to reach the grassroots is discussed, especially through celebrating religious festivals in villages, in order to educate the assumedly ignorant villagers and entice them to participate, even though already this is part of life among people who in their own ways relate and negotiate with each other. Such living relationships are usually ignored in dialogue, even though clear skills to mitigate or eliminate conflicts in the everyday lives are evidenced among the grassroots, which have been discussed in Chapter 8 based on the field research done in Gramam village.

Thus, both the ignorance of relationships among people and the invitation to consider dialogue as a necessity are basically an exercise of power on these people. In fact, the process should be the reverse. Instead of posing dialogue as a necessity, the elite dialogists should learn from the people about how they deal with conflicts and maintain relationships in their everyday life activities. Against this context, whether we need interreligious *dialogue* as practised to create and maintain better relationships among people becomes an important question.

(c) *The Limitations of Religious Plurality: Is Inter*religious *Dialogue Possible?*

The above two questions are related to the third question, which is the most important one: Is inter*religious* dialogue possible when the very category of religion as separate and the notion of world religions – each world religion as a unified whole which is different from or unrelated to other religion – is challenged? The emphasis here is on *religious*. The world religions have become a mere construction which has involved homogenization and categorization. When it comes to Hinduism in India in addition to the above aspects, selection and representation also become crucial. Can the notion of religion with such complexities and world religions created in a particular context to serve particular elites – colonial and native – help those who are concerned with creating peace, harmony and better relationships in society? Is it both possible and useful to have strict religious identities in terms of world religions?

The fundamental aspect that is crucial for the concept and practice of dialogue is the idea of plurality of religions. As is obvious, where dialogue occurs, it does so in a context of many religions, such as Hinduism, Christianity, Islam, Judaism, Sikhism, Buddhism and Jainism.[1] Questions such as the differences between religions are discussed both within as well as outside dialogue circles, but in what way, *if at all*, they are actually different on the ground is seldom paid attention to. This is primarily, I suggest, because each religion is presented as a unified whole, and the daily reality for those identified with a particular tradition is assumed to follow from such elite assumptions of difference. Yet even this begs the question of why and how religion is counted as a distinct entity separated from other 'systems' such as 'secularism' or 'politics' or 'science'. As discussed, the mere plurality of religions or the multireligious nature of the context is often overenthusiastically used as a starting point for undertaking dialogue activities.

But as argued in Chapter 3, recent scholarship shows that the idea of religion as a distinct entity and the consequent 'world religions' are recent constructions which took place since the European Enlightenment. Originally, associating the definition of religion directly with the idea of worshipping God became prominent during the time when Christianity started to attain state status in the West in the fourth century. This challenged the previous Roman idea that religion was just about following the customs and traditions of one's ancestors. This new idea of religion also differentiated true religion as worshipping the one true God and pagan or false religions as superstitious beliefs. While this categorization of true versus pagan religion was maintained in the West for many centuries, another dichotomy emerged during the European Enlightenment period when, with the advent of scientific reasoning and the experimental method, religion was separated from science, the latter being public and secular, and religion was pushed to the margins as irrational, superstitious and private. These categories were then exported to other parts of the world, where different understanding of religions and cultures were at work, through European colonialism. Colonial officials and writers saw much of the colonized world as religious (and therefore backward), while considering the colonizing empire as secular and superior.

This transportation of the idea of religion and religions worked itself out differently in different colonized contexts. For India, or Asia in general, the idea of East or Orient was invented and then identified with a religion, or religious practices, judged inferior. Colonial administrators, missionaries, travellers and settlers and Western Orientalists were involved in constructing these categories, and Indian elites simply accepted them rather uncritically. One of the major outcomes of this process was the colonialists' and the local elites' construction and then identification of Hinduism as *the* religion of India. Despite the fact that this colonially created Hinduism actually contained and represented only a few dominant traditions in India, this system has come to define the 'religion' of the vast section of people in India, with ascribed identities based on that construct.

This process has seldom been critiqued in dialogue in general, and certainly not in India, where the assumption of congruence between overall religious identity and the everyday life of the follower has been based on the masses' replication of the given system.

Moreover, as discussed in Chapter 4, there are ambiguities in dialogue regarding secularism and its relationship to religion. Dialogue oscillates between posing secularism, a secular nature and a secular constitution that respects all religions as the major characteristics of India, and placing religion as an important, if not the most important, aspect in the nation, outweighing secularism. As such, on the one hand there is an appeal to secularism to oppose attacks on 'religious' minorities, and the contribution of religion to secular society is stressed on the other hand. There is also a tendency, not only in dialogue circles, to distinguish Western secularism from Indian secularism, the former being irreligious and the latter multi- or plurally religious.[2] Yet what is overlooked is that this approach also maintains a religion – secularism distinction, without attempting to comprehend the nuances involved in the distinction, and lacking the will to understand how the distinction functions in the actual everyday life of people. Also, since dialogue accepts religion as a category, it readily accepts the world religions category, including the colonial view of Hinduism as one religion. Accordingly, much Christian-Hindu dialogue has concerned the intellectual and brahmanic traditions. Further, dialogue seldom pays attention to the multiple identities of people, overemphasizing their religious identities – dialogue is always between Hindus, Christians, Muslims, Sikhs, Buddhists, Jains and Jews and so on rather than between tailors, farmers and teachers who also happen to be Muslim or Christian. The multiple nature of an individual's identity and its impact on relationships with others' such identities is largely ignored. These realities illustrate that the dialogue that is based on religious plurality and world religions is seriously limited. Instead of offering solutions to the conflicts between religions it aims to address, it has only aggravated the problems by essentializing religious identities.

These issues have to be looked at primarily through the lens of power aspirations of elites, which dialogists often miss out, because ultimately the construction of categories such as religious and secular assisted the domination of one by the other. During the European Enlightenment, secularists referring to science and reason pushed religion to the margins, and since then religionists have challenged secularism. This ongoing struggle indicates that this distinction relates closely to the maintenance of power. Similarly, the construction of world religions and identities based on these categories also helped those in colonial power to rule and dominate people in the colonies. This continues even today, local elites making use of these separated categories and identities based on them to exercise their power. But the unthinking and uncritical (or maybe all too intentional) acceptance of religion, religions and world religions underpins dialogue with no discussion at all of the complex power issues involved. Is the ensuing interreligious dialogue not made dubious, even tainted, by association? Therefore, if religion and religions are dubious concepts, is inter*religious* dialogue really possible?

These questions indicate that in interreligious dialogue all these three elements – *inter* (between), *dialogue* and *religion* (or religious) are important, but if even one element is shown to be dubious, dialogue becomes problematic. Yet as this research has shown, there are problems and limitations with all three elements. Despite this, as we see today, interreligious dialogue has been posed as a successful system that helps to maintain better relationships in society, and hence inevitable and urgent.

2 After Dialogue: Exploring Multiple Identities as a Challenger to Dialogue and World Religions

The problems of dialogue which have been discussed in this book and summarized in the previous section indicate that dialogue, even though it claims to work for peace and harmony in society, on the contrary has essentialized the notions of religious plurality, conflict and elitism, and thus contributes to obstructing the understanding of how religion is perceived and practised in everyday life, and how ordinary people relate and negotiate with their neighbours. At times, a dialogical approach to religions may be believed to have offered an alternative to exclusivist models within theological discourses, since dialogue claims to work for better relationships between religious adherents and to help them overcome and resolve conflicts, but it may not be adequate for all situations. This book has argued that dialogue has, in fact, not understood how common people behave in terms of religion and identity simply because it has its roots in the faulty ground of world religions. Hence what is needed is not a dialogical model *for the people* but a better framework for understanding and interpreting *how people relate and negotiate*. By attempting to offer models, dialogue has only furthered the notions and myths of religion as a distinct category, and has ignored and undermined the complex identities functioning among people and their various everyday life issues. But what is needed instead is an acceptance of, based on learning from but not talking about, the lived realities of ordinary people, which dialogue fails to do. At present such people are at best theorized about from the point of view of dialogue activists, and that means usually elite people. Such theorizing in a rank-ordered society naturally replicates assumptions about 'their' childishness and lack of potential, of agency, of intelligence and so on. The very palpable fact that *all*, elite and villager, *live* with multiple identities does not enter the picture. Hence a crucial shift is necessary to understand that people do not always function as 'religious' people, but in that or any other identity which determines the way they live, relate and negotiate with their neighbours.

In such context, 'multiple identities of common people in the ordinariness of everyday life' can be explored as an alternative framework for understanding and interpreting common people's ways of relating and negotiating with their religious neighbours. Understanding and theorizing multiple identities has received serious attention in the fields of humanities and social sciences, and in the context of changes in contemporary society such as globalism, multiculturalism, diasporic life and groups competing for recognition, the importance of multiple identities is often stressed. In a recent work, *Identity Complex: Making the Case for Multiplicity*, Michael Hames-Garcia clearly sets the case for multiple identities in social life. Pointing out that social groups, as political actors or as demographic categories, normally 'tend toward a reductive homogeny of identities' even though personal identities are multifarious and complex, and emphasizing the 'interrelatedness of different forms of social identity', he argues for *multiplicity* in identities that can explain how social identities take shape through various processes by mutually constituting one another, pointing to the social interdependence of identities and deep relations of solidarity across differences.[3] Even though this study concentrates mainly on gender and racial identities in the American context, the theory of multiplicity can be applied to a context involving any identity.

Similarly, the everyday and ordinariness in identity formations is also highlighted by many theorists who have reflected on identity formation and processes. Referring to the fact that identity in the discourses is often complex and unclear, Sigrid Norris says that

> embedded in the group and the society but also in the psychology of the individual, identity appears to be impossible to bring together to truly make sense of and explain. Yet, when investigating real people in their everyday lives identity emerges; it becomes visible, explainable, and graspable. In the everyday actions that people perform, in the objects that people own, or the houses that people live in, identity becomes cogent when investigating people's families, friends, networks, and social groups that they belong to. When investigating identity in everyday life, identity suddenly appears loud and clear.[4]

This shows the importance of the ordinary life situations of the people for understanding how identities function among them which an elite theory/ discourse or theological doctrine/concept may not be able to clearly articulate. Commenting on the fact that what people do is closely related to their identities, Norris shows the importance of understanding such actions to comprehend the identity processes in everyday life. He says thus:

> People do things, and everything that people do is taking action. People eat, shop, work, bring up children, talk to friends, call relatives, build and furnish houses, listen to music, read magazines and newspapers, and do much more. When taking all of the communicative modes into consideration that people use in their everyday lives to *perform the actions* that they perform, suddenly the connections between actions and belongings, between individual and society, and between the hidden and the overt begin to make sense.[5]

In the light of these insights on identity and identity processes, what becomes clear is that multiple identities in everyday living situations can help to understand the way people relate with each other. In relation to the study of this book, the framework of multiple identities can also help to understand how people perceive and practise religion, keep religious identity as one of their identities and integrate their religious aspect of life with other aspects. It can challenge the notions dialogue has about religion and world religions, as well as about the religion and religious identity of the common people, and can open up new avenues to understand and interpret them.

For each of the three problems of dialogue discussed in this book, which show that dialogue has become ineffective because of its rootedness in the world religions category, multiple identities can offer better alternatives. Dialogue builds itself on religious plurality, yet in the process it reduces people's identities to fixed religious identities primarily based on world religions. On the contrary, multiple identities can help to explore the plurality of identities and relations. Dialogue tries to argue for its necessity in overcoming religious conflicts, but in the process believes religion either is associated with conflicts or can offer solutions to them. Multiple identities can help to understand and analyse the complex factors involved in causing conflicts, their consequences and the various players involved. Moreover, it can also help to understand and analyse how a conflict is named as or reduced to a 'religious conflict', and how ordinary people respond to conflicts with the help of resources available to them. Dialogue invites the common people to follow the models set by the elite dialogists. Multiple identities, on the contrary, can help to understand the ordinariness of everyday life experiences in which people relate and negotiate with each other. I shall discuss these three aspects and attempt to develop a case for multiple identities as a challenger to dialogue and world religions. I shall draw on the insights gained from the living experiences of ordinary villagers from the fieldwork data which I have discussed in detail in Chapter 8. I shall also utilize, where necessary, insights from similar or related issues researched, reflected and theorized in different contexts regarding how to understand and interpret the everyday living experiences of people.

(a) *Religious Plurality to Plurality of Relations and Identities*

I have repeatedly pointed out in this book that dialogue is emphasized in the context of a plurality of religions, or at least an awareness of the plurality, itself helped by dialogue. This approach may be justifiable in the context of theology of religions, and in my opinion, the claim of superiority of one religion over other religions – be it through exclusivism or inclusivism – needs a critique, and the critique has been offered, rightly, in the dialogical approach. I mentioned in the beginning of this book that, as an evolving student in the field of religious studies, I too have appreciated, the importance of the dialogical approach amid a plurality of religions to counteract people belonging to one religion who vociferously claim that only their religion holds the truth which all others must embrace, other paths being false and to be condemned.

However, looking at this from a wider context where religion or religious identity is only one aspect of life, what I appreciate primarily is *plurality*, and not just the plurality of *religions*. In other words, it is the *plurality* that is helpful when one perspective alone is ascertained as being insensitive to others. But the question of whether everything we call religion is actually that is a problem which I have analysed in this book. In this context, I propose that one needs to move from plurality of religions to plurality of *relations* and *identities*. In this regard, how people at the grassroots look at religion, religions and religious identities within their overall identities, which I have discussed in Chapter 4, can help.

'Why do you call us Hindus? We are not Hindus, we are *Ayya Vazhi makkaal*': this was the reaction I received from one of my interviewees, as I have discussed earlier, which reflected the attitude of many of my interviewees in Gramam, when I used the term 'Hindus' to address them in my interview with her.[6] For me, generally, this statement summarizes the whole understanding of identities prevalent among grassroots people. The direct challenge is that a self-understanding of a person or group of people may radically differ from how the non-members of the group view them. As a Christian resident in the district for over thirty years, I have most often witnessed Christians viewing the *Ayya Vazhi* (and also *Amman Vazhi*) people as Hindus, and I have also done that. But the field research for this book helped me to go to them and understand *their* sense of *their* identity. This means that when exposed to the expression of the self-understanding of the particular individual or group involved, in this case an *Ayya Vazhi* follower, the observer needs to understand how specific identities are constructed not in terms of where they fall short of the 'proper' world religion identity, but how this specific person (or persons) construct their particular identity at that time. At least four aspects seem to be involved in identity construction – how I view myself, how I view others, how others view me and how others view themselves in a specific time, place and context. Any construction of identities moves between at least these four aspects, and hence identities are not static and singular but fluid and multiple. This also indicates that the identities among common people in ordinary life situations do not need to be always based on world religions category or any one single category, and religious identities are only possible identities, all of which are formed and conditioned by several factors and concerns. The multiple identities I came across among grassroots people through my research cluster into three or more types.

First, the multiple identities among people can be viewed through intra-religious relations, or different identities within a religion. As I have pointed out regarding Kanyakumari district, people do not always use their religious identities to define the whole of their life and attitudes, and people belonging to each religion – Hinduism, Christianity and Islam – have different denominational, cult-based, sect-oriented identities within them. Accordingly, the specific and small denomination is usually cited as the identifier for Christians in Kanyakumari district such as CSI, Roman Catholic, Salvation Army, Lutheran, Pentecostal; and many of the Hindus would not prefer the term Hinduism in their daily context – using rather 'the way of the father', 'the way of the mother', Saivite, Vaishnaivite, etc.

Second, there are multiple religious identities or identities crossing a single religion. These are not dual or multiple membership to religions, but through their everyday life, people often cross fixed religious identities. Visiting, attending and eating in the worship places; using multiple scriptures (ignoring what others might call syncretism or relativism) and oral traditions along with other resources such as film songs, stories and the like – thus making their own hermeneutics – to refer to the welfare of human beings; being together in their work places; sharing a house with family members with different religious identities: all these are examples of the irrelevance or at least the continual crossing of so-called fixed religious identities.

The idea of multiple religious belonging and some of the issues related to it have been conceptualized in a book that appeared in the last decade: *Many Mansions? Multiple Religious Belonging and Christian Identity?*[7] Talking about the Western context, Catherine Cornille, the editor of this volume, says that

> individuals who no longer feel compelled to accept every single aspect of the tradition without question come to adopt a more piecemeal approach to doctrine, symbols, and practices governed by personal judgement and taste. From here, it is only a small step to the exploration and selective appropriation of elements of beliefs and practice of other religions.[8]

Cornille interprets multiple religious belonging in terms of three dimensions: 'focussing on the ultimate religious experience that lies at the base of all traditions'[9]; 'remaining faithful to the symbolic framework of one tradition while adopting the hermeneutical framework of another'[10]; and 'acknowledging the complementarity of religions'.[11] On the basis of these, the contributors to *Many Mansions*, some of whom are also dialogue proponents, discuss the reality of multiple religious belonging.

At the grassroots level also these dimensions may be found, but not at the level of theology or conceptualization, and it is indeed doubtful whether Cornille's 'remaining faithful to one tradition' exists as more than a pious hope in the wider context. People in Gramam construct their own hermeneutics of multiple religious belonging which may not be confined to single religions in terms of either symbol or framework. For example, when I visited Hindu homes, I could see deities of different religions in their worship rooms. A ten-day Muslim *Kodi Yettruthal* (flag hoisting) in the district has been taken from the *Ayya Vazhi* tradition which has such a ceremony.[12] Christians and Muslims offer rice or money to and accept the *namam* (or *thiruneeru*)[13] from Ayya Vazhi and Amman Vazhi worshippers when they come home after festivals in the temple. These are some symbols that bear witness to multiple religious belonging at the grassroots. The tradition that Muthukutti, the founder of Ayya Vazhi tradition, was a sexton in the nearby CSI church is a popular tradition prevalent in Gramam and in the district, indicating that Christians and Ayya Vazhi are related and therefore implying a degree of amity. I have discussed similar oral traditions in the district in Chapter 8.

These traditions do not concern singular religious identity, but they reveal how multiple religious identities are exercised. After all, in a single family there is multiple religious belonging. In my own family, seven of us go to church and two go to temple, and the symbolic materials from each religion (such as the Bible, or *pooja* materials) are placed in our house which are seen, touched and used by each other. As I discussed in detail in Chapter 5, these multiple religious identities also have been researched by Peter Gottschalk who has worked on and theorized multiple religious identities in a North Indian village and argued that for people in villages, crossing their respective religious identities is so normal that not to do so would seem unusual.[14]

Third, in addition to intra-religious identities and multiple religious identities, people live with other identities that cross religious identities. Caste, education, gender, profession, occupation, age, friendship and many other identities also are used in everyday life. This is not to say that people do not use religious identities at all – they do, depending upon contexts – but their normal way of life is influenced not by fixed religious identities but rather by multiple identities, on which Amartya Sen has worked in his acclaimed work *Identity and Violence*.[15] Pointing to people's multiple identities, he says,

> While religious categories have received much airing in recent years, they cannot be presumed to obliterate other distinctions, and even less can they be seen as the only relevant system of classifying people across the globe.[16]

Criticizing the act of categorizing people into boxes such as 'Hindu civilization' or 'Islamic civilization' and calling it a reductionist view, Sen says that this overlooks

> first, the extent of *internal* diversities within these civilizational categories, and second, the reach of influence of *interactions* – intellectual as well as material – that go right across the regional borders of so-called civilizations.[17]

Noting that he as an individual has a number of identities at the same time, Sen speaks about the importance of the context for exercising our identities and how people move between choosing one or other identity. He says thus:

> Belonging to each one of the membership groups can be quite important, depending on the particular context. When they compete for attention and priority over each other … the person has to decide on the relative importance to attach to the respective identities, which will, again, depend on the exact context. There are two distinct issues here. First, the recognition that identities are robustly plural, and that the importance of one identity need not obliterate the importance of others. Second, a person has to make choices – explicitly or by implication – about what relative importance to attach, in a particular context, to the divergent loyalties and priorities that may compete for precedence.[18]

Thus Sen raises a strong voice for multiple identities and also for the fact that we constantly make choices 'about priorities to be attached to our different affiliations and associations'.[19] This issue of people choosing their identities has also been studied by others in different contexts. In the context of social and economic life in society, Albert O. Hirschmann, an acclaimed economist of the last century, has investigated the issue of people moving from involvement in one thing to another.

Concerned with why people move between public involvement and individual improvement especially in Western societies,[20] Hirschmann sets the basis of his problem: 'how to account for preference change, not just from private-oriented to public-oriented activity and vice versa, but quite generally from commodity A to commodity B or from activity A to activity B.'[21] Calling these preference changes 'shifting involvements', he points out the importance of understanding 'people's critical appraisals of their own experiences and choices as important determinants of new and different choices'.[22] For him, 'In this manner, human perception, self-perception, and interpretation should be accorded their proper weight in the unfolding of events.'[23] According to him, the shifting involvements of people appear mainly due to personal disappointment, which goes up and down.[24] Despite the fact that Hirschmann's work was carried out within a different field, his idea of shifting involvements can be extended to talk about the identities in relationships between people who do not just function in the static identities attributed to them but change due to many reasons, one of which is personal benefit.

How people of different religions should be or are relating with each other is a concern for those involved in dialogue, but the solution they offer in terms of theological approaches is only one of many. People relate with each other within and between their religions in their own way and not by following the models set by theologians and religious leaders, and they also relate to each other in their own ways according to context. These realities suggest that religious plurality does not work as dialogue or as theologians assume it to do. Also, multiple identities are usual for all people, a religious or theological platform alone being sufficient for none. Moreover – and this may be more relevant in rural than urban and in grassroots than elite contexts – religion should not be seen as a separate part in life, but has to be understood holistically, mingled and integrated with all aspects of life. Singling out religion as a separate good thing in an otherwise bad society (or as others do, a bad thing in a good secular society) does not help here.

(b) Religious Conflicts to Real-Life Conflicts

Another aspect of the proposed model is the necessity to move beyond accepting religious conflicts to understanding conflicts in the real-life contexts. My purpose in this book has not been to critique the intention of dialogue activists in attempting to reduce tensions and conflicts among people: these must be lessened to avoid large-scale communal violence. My own involvement in dialogue was influenced from this perspective. But my observations have been that in dialogue, conflicts are misunderstood or misrepresented, relating religion to conflict in one way or another since it accepts either the 'religion is prone to violence' or the 'religion as instrument for violence' or 'the potentials of religion for overcoming violence' models. My critique lies here, and my argument is that when conflicts among people are looked at not through dialogical approaches but through multiple identities of people, they can be understood and addressed much better in the light of their wider circumstances, causes and results. This can also help those who are engaged in research on conflict resolution and peace-building.

'Conflicts come first, and then comes religion,'[25] was the response from one of interviewees from Gramam, which no one in the focus-group interview denied; rather, they used it in their ongoing discussion. As discussed in Chapter 8, people at the grassroots approach conflict in society differently from dialogue activists. Especially when the Mandaikadu clashes occurred, people in Gramam never saw it as Hindu–Christian, and all Hindus, Christians and Muslims stood together to protect *their village* when there were apprehensions that *their village* was going to be attacked. Moreover, grassroot people root the prime cause of conflicts in not only those who seek political power but also those who try to gain other kinds of domination over others, including religious leaders who exploit tense situations for their advantage, and in personal issues among people.[26] More importantly ordinary people do not simply accept that conflicts are religious, as I have recorded above, and there are various factors such as caste, region, language and others involved. This understanding is very important, given the efforts of many, including dialogue activists, to find the causes of conflicts between singular fixed identities or established structures or imagined communities based primarily on religion. Moreover, and often in elite academic circles, the understanding of personal issues behind conflicts such as jealousy and survival concerns are taken as simplistic and narrow explanations of conflicts and are distanced from academic theorization: the causes of conflicts are sought in established structures. But ordinary people are aware of and talk about the multiple factors involved in what are called religious conflicts.

The issue of understanding conflicts using available structures in the conventional understanding has been critiqued in the contemporary context, as the world is increasingly witnessing genocides, pogroms and mass killings. Insights from these studies based on sociological, anthropological and psychological approaches have relevance to interpreting religious conflicts, and they are based on the experiences of people who look at conflicts beyond any established structure. I have already discussed William Cavanaugh, who has critiqued Mark Juergensmeyer and Charles Kimball for their 'religion is prone to violence' approach. Questioning this approach and calling it a myth, he says that it

> is the idea that religion is a transhistorical and transcultural feature of human life, essentially distinct from 'secular' features such as politics and economics, which has a peculiarly dangerous inclination to promote violence. Religion must therefore be tamed by restricting its access to public power. The secular nation-state then appears as natural, corresponding to a universal and timeless truth about the inherent dangers of religion. … The myth of religious violence helps to construct and marginalize a religious Other, prone to fanaticism, to contrast with the rational, peace-making, secular subject. This myth can be and is used in domestic politics to legitimate the marginalization of certain types of practices and groups labeled religious, while underwriting the nation-state's monopoly on its citizens' willingness to sacrifice and kill.[27]

Moreover, James Waller, an American social psychologist, has done an outstanding study on how ordinary people are involved in violence. Emphasizing that instead of seeking explanations for genocides in terms of community identities based on culture, society, nation, ideology, historical prejudice and ethnicity, he invites everyone to 'understand the ordinariness of extraordinary evil'[28] and asserts that we cannot simply blame the powerful, such as political leaders, because there are many ordinary people involved in genocides and mass killing.[29] Affirming that ordinary people are transformed into perpetrators of violence, Waller notes that there are always multiple issues behind this. He says thus:

> Indeed, the multiplicity of variables that lead an ordinary person to commit genocide and mass killing is difficult to pin down. It is impossible to establish general 'laws' that apply to all individuals in all contexts and at all times.[30]

Waller's words may serve as a warning for those who attempt to understand conflicts and violence in society only within the framework of a clear single factor. He goes on to argue that

> the process [of violence] is far too complex to be reduced to one factor alone, such as the nature of the collective; the influence of an extraordinary language; psychopathology; a common, homogenous extraordinary personality; or the elaborate creation of a divided self.[31]

Believing that they each may have their share, Waller argues that 'it is not that all of the existing theories are completely *wrong*; rather each of them is *incomplete*'.[32] For him the incomplete part is to do with missing out the ordinariness of mass killing. As a psychologist, of course, he bases his understanding within human nature where the ultimate influence to kill should be found – which reveals that 'we are all *capable* of committing evil',[33] but lists three proximate influences, namely, cultural construction of the world view where collective values, authority orientation and social dominance are responsible; psychological construction of the 'Other' where us-them thinking, moral disengagement and blaming the victims involved for the violence meted out to them are responsible; and social construction of cruelty where professional socialization, group identification and binding factors of the group are responsible.[34] While I am not elaborating these aspects here, my point is to say that Waller's arguments challenge the act of interpreting conflicts through structures, especially in elite discourses, and conform to the common understanding of conflict among people.[35]

Another recent work, *Genocides by the Oppressed*,[36] also challenges any fixed notions of conflicts in general and the tendency to attribute violence and mass killing only to the dominant groups in particular. Asserting that 'even where definitions of genocide are not conditioned on state power, they exude a strong sense that genocide is something socially and politically dominant groups inflict on subordinate ones', the editors of this volume invite the readers to understand genocide and violence in their wider context.[37] For them, what is often missed out in studying conflicts among people is the participation of ordinary masses even in the elite-initiated conflicts. Pointing to the popular participation in genocides in Cambodia and Rwanda, the authors of this work say that it is at the 'level of popular involvement that the element of subaltern genocide is most powerfully evident'.[38] Thus, the reality of popular participation in conflicts can help to understand conflicts in the light of multifarious factors involved. Further, how identities are constructed and stereotyped during conflicts also needs attention. Citing the example of the representatives of previously Nazi-occupied populations unleashing large-scale violence and dispossession on ethnic Germans between 1945 and 1947, Jones and Robins argue that 'many victims of subaltern genocide are subsumed, by perpetrators' imputation, into a wider group identity – usually – ethnically or religiously stereotyped'.[39] Thus, the people who were once dominated by Nazi rulers 'selected their victims because of the ethnic attributes they shared with their former oppressors. No attempt was made to ascertain whether particular members of those populations had collaborated with Nazi occupation forces; the collectivity was simply targeted en masse.'[40]

Even though all these works that study and research conflicts and violence are from different cultural contexts, and many of their findings will be debated, my point is that they all insist on one point: conflict is complex, and it cannot be confined to any singular collectivity or single reason. With regard to the themes under discussion in this book, they bring challenges for understanding conflict through the single lens of religion and religious identities.

Thus one has to move beyond religious conflicts to understand the real-life conflicts in their multiple causes, processes and means. We cannot simply speak of the 'religion is prone to violence' or 'religion as instrument in violence' hypothesis. Nor can one say that religion is not violent but secularism is, or vice versa. If the approach to conflict is misguided – either as religion being responsible for conflict or secularism, as anti-religion, being responsible – it can lead to more unrest and more problems. Hence understanding the multiple factors behind conflicts is important. The factors may range from personal envy, jealousy or revenge attitude to caste to ethnic, regional, professional and any other differences. In such a context, what is needed is a 'context-specific participatory approach' whereby those involved in conflict resolution should understand the nature of conflicts through participation – listening to and understanding how the people at the grassroots view a particular conflict – and should help to understand the conflicts in their contexts, bearing in mind that it is not always feasible to challenge power holders openly even when their actions underlie the problem.

(c) Elite Dialogue to Relations based on Multiple Identities

A dialogical approach to religions has influenced many people in the past few decades to accept dialogue as a good thing, imperative and urgent – the overwhelming amount of literature produced is evidence for this. Perhaps, dialogue as an intellectual exercise might have helped to develop theoretical and theological reflections on the topic. However, how far the theories, theologies and concepts around it appeal to people at the bottom of society is the question that drives the critique of the elite nature of dialogue. Of particular concern is how the elite dialogue proponents perceive and theorize the world outside dialogue. Their assumption, predominantly, is that many parts of society, especially the poor, lack dialogue which dialogists can provide. Hence elite theologians, religious leaders and dialogue activists want to take dialogue as a pre-packaged gift to ordinary people. The insights grassroot people offer are most often undermined. In other words elite dialogue assumes that it is there to *give* something to the grassroots, and not to learn from them. Here lies the most crucial problem of dialogue. This suggests that there should be a shift from telling people *how to dialogue* to learning and understanding *how do people relate*. The framework of multiple identities of common people in the ordinariness of the everyday life experiences rather than dialogue can help here in a much better way.

'We meet each other on the road, in markets, and almost every day,'[41] an interviewee said when asked about how religious neighbours in his village meet with each other. As I have shown, relating and negotiating, including at the level of religious identity, is part of everyday life among people. Helping and meeting each other happens daily, and this improves relationships and curtails conflict. In a formal dialogue programme, such meetings would not be called dialogue, but they help in achieving what is fundamentally the purpose of dialogue: peace, harmony and better relationships in society. In such a context, what is needed is to listen and learn from the common people, instead of declaring 'dialogue should be taken to', and then to encourage them in what they do and not consider them as insignificant or trivial.

The two issues mentioned above concerning elite dialogists – their scanty perceptions of everyday grassroot realities and relationships as well as problems and their emphasis on 'taking dialogue to the grassroots' – stem from the typical elite ways of theorization and conceptualization about grassroots realities. The problems arise when such theorizations take place sophisticatedly ignoring multiple and complex factors associated with everyday relationships among people that cannot be put into neatly framed categories. I have already noted how the various researches undertaken by the Subaltern Studies Collective for the last three decades or so have significantly highlighted the issues and nuances involved in theorizing the lives of ordinary people, the subaltern. Studying history from a subaltern perspective, Gyanendra Pandey, a member of the Subaltern Studies Collective, has recently worked on the issue of un-archived histories.[42] Commenting on the archive which is an important part of history writing, he says that 'the very process of archiving is accompanied by a process of "un-archiving": rendering many aspects of social, cultural, political relations in the past and the present as incidental, chaotic, trivial, inconsequential, and therefore unhistorical'.[43] The archive also has boundaries, and one of the boundaries is to keep away 'the ordinary, the everyday, the ever-present, yet trivialized or trifling: conditions, practices, relationships, expectations and agendas so common as to not even to be noticed'.[44] Nevertheless he emphasizes the importance of examining 'signs, traces, evidence of human activities and relationships – the body as a register of events; inchoate dreams; gestures, pauses, gut-reactions; feelings of ecstasy, humiliation, pain – that cannot easily be articulated or read, let alone archived, but that nevertheless, call out for attention.[45] Pandey's observations and remarks have relevance for talking about grassroots relationships in the context of dialogue. Seen as ambiguous, inchoate and scrappy by too many elite dialogue activists, everyday realities need to be taken into consideration when action programmes are devised by outsiders.

In a very fascinating study, M. S. S. Pandian argues for how theorists should write ordinary lives – he focuses on Dalits in his essay.[46] For me, some of the suggestions Pandian makes for his fellow social scientists can challenge the elite dialogue activists to know and understand the problems and weaknesses in their theorizing and conceptualizing of the grassroots realities and everyday life experiences of ordinary people. Pandian starts his essay citing Gopal Guru, who says that

> social science discourse in India is being closely disciplined by self-appointed juries who sit in the apex court and decide what the correct practice according the canons is. These juries decide what is theory and what is trash. … [This] apex court … keeps ruling out subaltern objections as absurd and idiosyncratic at worst and emotional, descriptive-empirical and polemical at best.[47]

Noting that the issues Guru and similar thinkers raise are the questions of 'the privilege of theory over the empirical in social sciences and the consequent problem of hierarchies of knowledge within social science practices',[48] Pandian says that

> it is time to recognise that the domain of theory-making or the wider field of social sciences is constrained by its own ground rules which often come in the way of producing morally and politically enabling knowledge(s) about dalits and other subaltern groups. Instead, those narrative forms … [such] as 'raw empiricism' or what the gate-keepers of social science theory describe as 'emotional, descriptive-empirical and polemical,' can in most instances enable such knowledges.[49]

He argues that narratives available among the subaltern people (such as Dalits, grassroots) could be

> a compensation for and/or a challenge to the deficiencies of dominant modes of theory-making in the social sciences. Not bound by the evidentiary rules of social science, the privileged notion of teleological time, and claims to objectivity and authorial neutrality, these narrative forms can produce enabling descriptions of life-worlds and facilitate the re-imagination of the political.[50]

Pandian goes on establishing his points by studying two Dalit texts in Tamil which bring out the situation of being Dalit and experiencing untouchability. Such texts *from* the casteless, rather than writings *on* caste and castelessness, speak louder than that of, for example, the eminent sociologist M. N. Srinivas, who offered a Sanskritized understanding of caste, through an act of what Pandian calls a 'multiple distancing.'[51] He finds at least two instances of such multiple distancing in Srinivas – one is distancing himself from the language of affect which does not have place in social science because 'this violates the criteria of neutrality and objectivity,'[52] and the other is 'the practice of the differentiating the so-called "real" from "appearances".'[53] Pandian continues:

> That is, what is being studied needs to be made sense of and explained. *There is no space for incomprehension or astonishment in social science practice.* This is perhaps why in Srinivas's theorisation, caste has to be dealt with not on its own terms but reduced to other variants such as efficiency and development. Significantly this is precisely the moment in his theorisation at which the everyday and the ordinary are shown the door.[54]

Pandian concludes that 'thus theory, as an act of multiple distancing, and the dalit texts, that capture the world of the everyday, of affect and incomprehension, differ radically in their intensions and methods.'[55] Using Stanley Tambiah's distinction between the 'discourse of causality', 'which is framed in terms of distancing, neutrality, experimentation, and the language of analytic reason' and 'stresses the rationality of instrumental action and the language of cognition,'[56] and 'the discourse of participation', which 'can be framed in term of sympathetic immediacy, performative speech acts, and ritual action ... [and] emphasizes sensory and affective communication and the language of emotion,'[57] Pandian says that 'while social science practices and theory-making belong to the discourse of causality, the dalit texts belong to the "discourse of participation".'[58] Citing Bruno Latour who says that for some, 'the ozone hole above our heads, the moral law in our hearts, the autonomous text, may each be of interest, but only separately' and 'that a delicate shuttle should have woven together the heavens, industry, texts, soul and moral law – this remains uncanny, unthinkable, unseemly,'[59] Pandian opines that 'what remains uncanny, unthinkable and unseemly for theory and social sciences is precisely what is possible' for subaltern texts as 'they can weave together "heavens, industry, texts, soul and moral law" and produce an ethical and political appeal that theory, as it is practiced, simply cannot.'[60]

These may illustrate why those multiple realities found among ordinary people which cannot be put into obvious frames are ignored, or patronizingly called 'simple faith' in dialogue circles. As already mentioned, when saying to a dialogue activist involved in Kanyakumari district that I was going to Gramam to do research on dialogue, the immediate answer was 'Why are you going to them? *What do those people know about dialogue?*' The underlying notion was that they know nothing and must be taught. I too have pointed out that Gramam people had little if any knowledge of dialogue, but I have shown how they *live* it in their simple and ordinary everyday life. But those engaged in dialogue fail to learn from them about how relating and negotiating with people of other faiths is an everyday activity, not primarily informed by religious affiliation. Dialogue in its one-sided endeavour to impart knowledge to common people fails to learn and understand from them about their actual living experiences.

This chapter has raised three basic questions: whether *inter*religious dialogue is *helpful* to address the issue of religious conflicts when there are many issues behind conflicts among people, not only religious identities; whether interreligious *dialogue* is a *necessity* when there are relationships among people who live with multiple identities, not only religious, and who make many efforts in their everyday life to see that they solve problems; and whether inter*religious* dialogue is *possible* at all when the very idea of religion as a separate category and the idea of many world religions which is fundamental for any interreligious dialogue is questionable.

This chapter also has attempted to show that multiple identities can be explored to offer a framework to challenge world religions and the dialogue that is based on this category. It offers a better framework to look at the plurality of identities and conflicts in their wider aspects and to study and understand the different ways in which ordinary people perceive and practice religion and relate and negotiate with each other. On the contrary what dialogue and world religions are attempting to do is only what Pandian calls a 'multiple distancing'. The category of 'world religions' has led to the distancing of religion from the other aspects of life and of one 'world religion' from another 'world religion'. Dialogue that claims to make better relationships between religions in fact only furthers the distancing since it retains the same category of 'world religions' in its concept and practice. In a similar way, the multiple distancing by dialogue can be also seen in its reducing conflicts to religious conflicts or 'making religion to work for the betterment of society'. And multiple distancing can be also seen in elite dialogue's ignoring and undermining of the ordinary people's ways of religious practice, identity matters and relationships. Thus what dialogue and world religions have offered is only multiple distancing through the forms of reduction, essentialization and elitism. As discussed above, explorations of multiple identities as well as relations based on multiple identities of common people in the ordinariness of everyday life can challenge the multiple distancing of the 'world religions' category and that of dialogue, and can offer a better framework to understand and interpret how religion, identities and relations among common people are found.

Notes

1 Interestingly, during my research for this book, when someone knew I was working on interreligious dialogue, the immediate question placed before me was 'Dialogue between which two religions?' This is a simple example of how dialogue is strongly related to such an understanding of the world religions category.

2 Many of the Indian writings on secularism follow this view. For instance, see Rajeev Bhargava, *Secularism and Its Critics* (New Delhi: Oxford University Press, 1998). See also Anuradha Dingwaney Needham and Rajeswari Sunder Rajan, *Crisis of Secularism in India* (New Delhi: Permanent Black, 2007); and Shabnum Tejani, *Indian Secularism: A Social and Intellectual History 1890–1950* (New Delhi: Permanent Black, 2007).

3 Michael Hames-Garcia, *Identity Complex: Making the Case for Multiplicity* (Minneapolis: University of Minnesota Press, 2011), ix.

4   Sigrid Norris, *Identity in (Inter)action: Introducing Multimodal (Inter)action Analysis* (Berlin: De Gruyter Mouton, 2011), xiii.

5   Norris, *Identity in (Inter)action*, xiii.

6   Parvathi, Interview.

7   Catherine Cornille, ed., *Many Mansions? Multiple Religious Belonging and Christian Identity* (Eugene, OR: WIPF & STOCK, 2010).

8   Catherine Cornille, 'Introduction: The Dynamics of Multiple Belonging,' in *Many Mansions? Multiple Religious Belonging and Christian Identity*, ed. Catherine Cornille (Eugene, OR: WIPF & STOCK, 2010), 3.

9   Cornille, 'Introduction,' 5.

10 Ibid.

11 Ibid., 6.

12 Harun, Interview, Gramam, 8 July 2008.

13 Jacob, Interview, Gramam, 24 June 2008.

14 Gottschalk, *Beyond Hindu and Muslim*.

15 Amartya Sen, *Identity and Violence: The Illusion of Destiny* (London: Penguin Books, 2006).

16 Sen, *Identity and Violence*, 10–11.

17 Ibid., 11. Emphasis original.

18 Ibid., 19.

19 Ibid., 30.

20 Albert O. Hirschman, *Shifting Involvements: Private Interest and Public Action* (Princeton: Princeton University Press, 2002), 3.

21 Hirschman, *Shifting Involvements*, 8.

22 Ibid., 6.

23 Ibid.

24 Ibid., 8.

25 Mohammad, Focus-group Interview.

26 As I already mentioned, one of my interviewees, asking for confidentiality, said that during the Mandaikadu clashes, the local church administration arranged for a procession carrying the bodies of six fisherfolk Christians who were killed in police firing, which increased tensions in the district.

27 William T. Cavanaugh, *The Myth of Religious Violence* (Oxford: Oxford University Press, 2009), 3–4.

28 James Waller, *Becoming Evil: How Ordinary People Commit Genocide and Mass Killing*, 2nd ed. (Oxford: Oxford University Press, 2007), xvii.

29 Waller, *Becoming Evil*, 8. Studying the Holocaust, he makes this finding,

30 Ibid., 137.

31 Ibid., 137–8.

32 Ibid., 138. Emphasis original.

33 Ibid., 171. Emphasis original.

34 Ibid., 138; chapters 6–8.

35 See also an article by James Waller, 'The Ordinariness of Extraordinary Evil: The Making of Perpetrators of Genocide and Mass Killing,' in *Ordinary People as Mass Murderers: Perpetrators in Comparative Perspectives*, ed. Olaf Jensen (New York: Palgrave Macmillan, 2008), 145–64; also in the same book *Harald Welzer*, 'On Killing and Morality: How Normal People Become Mass Murderers,' 165–84.

36 Nicholas A. Robins and Adam Jones, eds, *Genocides by the Oppressed* (Bloomington: Indiana University Press, 2009).

37 Adam Jones and Nicholas A. Robins, 'Introduction: Subaltern Genocide in Theory and Practice,' in *Genocides by the Oppressed*, ed. Nicholas A. Robins and Adam Jones (Bloomington: Indiana University Press, 2009), 4.

38 Jones and Robins, 'Introduction,' 6.

39 Ibid., 12.

40 Ibid.

41 Samuel, Interview, Gramam, 8 July 2008.

42 Gyanendra Pandey, 'Un-archived Histories: The "Mad and the Trifling,"' *Economic and Political Weekly* XLVII, no. 1 (7 January 2012): 37–41.

43 Pandey, 'Un-archived Histories,' 38.

44 Ibid.

45 Ibid.

46 M. S. S. Pandian, 'Writing Ordinary Lives,' in *Subaltern Citizens and Their Histories: Investigations from India and the USA*, ed. Gyanendra Pandey (London: Routledge, 2010), 96–108.

47 Gopal Guru, 'How Egalitarian are the Social Sciences in India?,' *Economic and Political Weekly*, xxxvii, no. 50 (14 December 2002): 5006; cited in Pandian, 'Writing Ordinary Lives,' 96.

48 Pandian, 'Writing Ordinary Lives,' 96.

49 Ibid., 97.

50 Ibid.

51 Ibid., 103.

52 Ibid., 105.

53 Ibid.

54 Ibid. Emphasis original.

55 Ibid.

56 Stanley J. Tambiah, *Magic, Science, Religion, and the Scope of Rationality* (Cambridge: Cambridge University Press, 1990), 108.

57 Tambiah, *Magic Science, Religion*, 108.

58 Pandian, 'Writing Ordinary Lives,' 106.

59 Bruno Latour, *We have Never Been Modern*, trans. Catherine Porter (Cambridge, MA: Harvard University Press, 1993), 5, cited in Pandian, 'Writing Ordinary Lives,' 106.

60 Pandian, 'Writing Ordinary Lives,' 106.

CONCLUSION

This book has attempted to offer an evaluation of interreligious dialogue in contemporary India. The awareness of interreligious dialogue is said to be increasing in the global context today as in India, as is the enthusiastic involvement in interreligious dialogue by many followers of religions. On the one hand, many advocates of interreligious dialogue earnestly promote it through various means and encourage people to take part in dialogue in order to maintain peace and harmony in society. On the other hand, it is claimed, there is also an overwhelming reaction to dialogue as many people are willing to participate in it in order to gain mutual understanding of religions which for them would lead to better relationships among religious adherents. Both in the religious circles and in the administrative affairs of governments in several countries, interreligious dialogue is advocated with the hope that it will help to create a peaceful situation among people. In a nutshell, dialogue is presented as a good thing for society that every member has to embrace. In the light of interreligious gatherings, meetings and various dialogue programmes, dialogue is presented as successful endeavour and the necessity for our time.

Yet, as this book has argued, the foundations on which interreligious dialogue stands seem to be dubious. The basic ingredients in dialogue are religion, religions and world religions, but the existence of these aspects can be questioned from postcolonial and subaltern perspectives. Categorizing people primarily through religion and religious identities, which has been much influenced by the West and by European colonialism, has serious limitations and must be critiqued in the light of the reality of multiple identities operating among people. The central stated purpose of dialogue is creating better understanding and better relationships between religious adherents in the context of religious conflicts. However, most often, the notion of 'religious conflicts' can be shown to be a myth, given the multiple factors involved in conflicts, including caste, poverty and other issues. Hence conflicts need to be understood in their actual and real-life contexts. Further, the nature and process of dialogue is elitist dialogue often being presented as a top-down process done by elite people to people at the grassroots. This can be challenged, as this book has attempted, in the light of the everyday experiences of people at the grassroots who relate and negotiate with each other, have multiple identities in ordinary life situations and have established ways of avoiding and ameliorating conflicts.

These realities in ordinary life challenge the limitations of dialogue, and theorizing them can help to continue questioning the notion of world religions that has been taken for granted for centuries in the field of religious studies. They raise disturbing questions regarding the usefulness, necessity and the possibility of dialogue. The failure of dialogists to understand the way in which power works in the fundamentals of dialogue such as religion, religious conflicts and dialogue actually sets limitations for the stated commitment of dialogists to create and maintain peace and harmony in society.

The efforts of dialogists in creating a better society with the values of peace and harmony are also challenged by their failure to understand how the reality of power operates in determining relationships among people in society. Dialogists fail to understand the operation of power in the creation of religion as a distinct entity, religion-secularism distinctions, world religions category and the application of these categories to the identities of people in the colonized territories, the role of native elites in appropriating and manipulating these colonially constructed religious identities and the subtle and overt ways in which power operates in naming and interpreting conflicts among people as primarily religious. Yet they also fail to realize how power and domination function even through interreligious dialogue where the relationships among the non-participants of dialogue – mostly people at the grassroots – are neglected as deemed inadequate or absent. It may be in challenging these power structures that the basic goals to create peace and harmony in society may be realized, rather than in picking up commonalities or similarities between religions as starting points for dialogue, insisting on the role of religion in secular society, bringing different religions together to eliminate religious conflicts or making interreligious dialogue imperative for everyone by inviting them to participate in dialogue.

These characteristics that limit the value of interreligious dialogue in India are relevant to many other parts of the world today where it is likewise seen as a successful enterprise. There are attempts to talk about the global nature of dialogue or global dialogue in terms of dialogue between religions. Various international organizations committed to dialogue are involved in promoting global dialogue in what is understood to be the increasingly globalized nature of our society today. With the rise of concepts such as globalization and multiculturalism, and more recently 'glocalism' (combining and balancing the global and local aspects of life), interreligious dialogue is proposed as a way of life in many countries. In such contexts one finds similar issues: religious − secular distinctions and world religions category are accepted, as is the idea that people are divided by religion, together with the assumption that ordinary people need to learn dialogue. Personally, in the United Kingdom and elsewhere, when I was sharing about my research for this book and presenting papers on relationships between people at the grassroots based on my field research, many participants used to draw parallels to their context regarding how dialogue in their context too is happening among elite religious leaders and theologians and how these elites ponder over religious conflicts and religious divisions whereas ordinary people understand better about the conflicts and deal with them and relate between themselves well.[1] As in India, dialogists elsewhere ignore how people in everyday life relate to each other. As in

India, the spreading of interreligious dialogue organized by elites is seen as vital for local harmony.

Thus both in the Indian context and elsewhere, apparently 'successful' interreligious dialogue is based on false assumptions about religion, world religions and religious conflicts and by the exercise of dominance over ordinary people who live in generally amicable or at least manageable relationships. In such a context the question about the usefulness, necessity and the possibility of interreligious dialogue should receive greater importance. In light of the arguments presented in this book, I have raised and discussed three questions: first, the helpfulness or usefulness of interreligious dialogue in dealing with what are considered to be religious conflicts; secondly, the necessity of interreligious dialogue in the context where people in ordinary life situations work out their own resources to relate and negotiate with their neighbours; and finally, the possibility of doing interreligious dialogue in the present context when the notions of world religions and plurality of religions are increasingly shown to be problematic and inadequate.

It is against such a context I have discussed the possibility of exploring multiple identities based on everyday living situations of ordinary people as a challenger to interreligious dialogue as well as the world religions category on which dialogue is rooted. Exploring and theorizing multiple identities in the light of actual everyday living invites one to think about plurality of identities and relations rather than strictly religious plurality, comprehend conflict in the real-life situations rather than simply buying into the notions of religious conflicts or religious violence whereby the many vested power interests behind such discourses are not considered seriously, and to move from patronizing elitist dialogues to understand and appreciate how ordinary people in everyday life situations develop their resources relating to each other.

In conclusion, I must say that my proposals are not without their limitations. First, there may be some unavoidable ambiguities in my proposals and few fixed answers, for changing situations demand flexibility. But the alternative, using concrete structures to define relationships, is inadequate. Second, questions may be raised regarding the place of religion in the proposals. What would be the place of religion in a model that calls to explore 'multiple identities of common people in the ordinariness of everyday life experiences' rather than interreligious dialogue? Does it have place at all? The answer is yes, religion does have a place, but as it is understood and interpreted by the varied people on the ground, and not in terms of world religions or religion as a separate category distinct from other aspects and not just by the elites – and this does not mean talking of 'folk religion', or the 'religion of the ignorant', but working with people's perception and praxis as it is. Third, the authors, whom I have used to draw insights to support my proposals, are obviously elites – as am I – who attempt to understand relationship issues in rural areas. But I am conscious of the fact that the insights of these theorists challenge the conventional understanding of everyday life – the understanding in which each element of life is compartmentalized – and insist on the significance of the ordinary and interlinked or integrated nature of everyday life. More importantly they are theorists, but they do not theorize realities on the basis of the ground rules of their discipline or perspective, imposing theories onto the subaltern, but examine and learn from grassroots realities and thereby challenge the ground rules of their disciplines. There is still the issue of who is decoding and deciding what those marginalized realities are, and to that extent elite control is still almost inevitably being exercised. But it is a start if the rural farmer or fisherman is assumed to have valuable knowledge, capacity and agency about religion, identities and relations, without which any attempt to study and interpret religion and relationships or to work for conflict resolution and peace-building in a society is liable to be superficial, irrelevant or an unintentional exercise of yet more power. Fourth, I am not of the opinion that theology or theologies of religions have no relevance at all. They have helped greatly with the various theological issues that arise in the context of relationships between religious adherents, and continue to influence elites and the theologically educated especially in challenging the superior attitudes and religious fanaticism. But my difficulty is to do with the elites' detachment from the ordinary people's understanding of God, religion and religious life in their theological formulations of dialogue. Fifth, what seems to be the case in Kanyakumari district may be also true of the lives of other people, even those elites who reflect and express those concerns. Nevertheless, my argument is that elite discourses often have their own ground rules, as Pandian mentions, which commonly avoid bringing everyday life issues, such as survival, into public discourse.

I must admit that this was true for me as well, and indeed the research undertaken for this book has been a very personal challenge. I initially struggled to put into theories and writing the everyday experiences of people in relating and negotiating with each other that I witnessed in the district, and my observations of them, wondering whether they were really worth putting to paper. However, as I progressed with my work I started to realize how important it is to observe and interpret everyday religious experiences and relationships as they are lived and expressed, rather than to interpret them on the basis of the ground rules set by dialogists. I do not claim to have achieved this fully, for there may be much of my own experience in the field, on several levels, which will hopefully become clearer over time as I continue to struggle with understanding and theorizing these issues.

The arguments in and insights from this research may be tested or used in other similar contexts where conflicts and violence are to be understood and comprehended or where interreligious dialogue works with the similar limitations I have discussed in this book. It is possible that research in different contexts, for instance a different demographic makeup, may bring similar or different outcomes. But while I do not rush to generalize, I must say that interreligious dialogue that is based on the world religions category, that propagates the myth of religious conflicts and that retains and promotes elitist forms of interactions, ignoring relations and negotiations in everyday and ordinary life situations, is limited for any context today. That religion, multiple identities and the everyday relations of people from the bottom need to be learnt and understood by those at the top rather than delivered in the reverse direction through elite discourses such as dialogue based on world religions is my succinct conclusion.

Note

1 Between 2007 and 2009 I presented this theme in meetings in the Methodist churches in Edinburgh, in the Church of Scotland and also in seminars arranged by the Fellowship of St Thomas in Scotland and in the University of Edinburgh. In June 2010 I presented it in the Global Institute of Theology in Chicago and Grand Rapids where reformed Christians from different countries all over the world gathered. In all these presentations I could hear from people about the elite nature of dialogue in their own contexts.

BIBLIOGRAPHY

Books and Articles

Abhishiktananda, Swami. *Hindu-Christian Meeting Point*. Rev. edn. Delhi: ISPCK, 1976.

Abhishiktananda, Swami. 'The Way of Dialogue.' In *Interreligious Dialogue*, edited by Herbert Jai Singh, 78–103. Bangalore: CISRS, 1967.

Abhishiktananda, Swami. *Saccidananda: A Christian Experience of Advaita*. London: SPCK, 1974.

Abraham, K. C. 'Dialogue in the Context of Indian Life.' In *Christian Concern for Dialogue in India*, edited by C. D. Jathanna, 48–63. Bangalore: The Gubbi Mission Press, 1987.

Abraham, K. C. 'Inter-faith Dialogue for Humanization.' *Religion and Society* 46, no. 1/2 (1999): 65–76.

Agur, C. M. *Church History of Travancore*. 1903. Reprinted. New Delhi: Asian Educational Services, 1990.

Aleaz, K. P. 'Pluralistic Inclusivism – Viable Indian Theology of Religions.' *Asian Journal of Theology* 12, no. 2 (1998): 265–88.

Aleaz, K. P. *Christian Thought through Advaita Vedanta*. Delhi: ISPCK, 1996.

Aleaz, K. P. *Dimensions of Indian Religion*. Calcutta: Punthi Pustak, 1995.

Aleaz, K. P. *From Exclusivism to Inclusivism: The Theological Writings of Krishna Mohun Banerjea*, vols 1 and 2. Delhi: ISPCK, 1998.

Aleaz, K. P. 'Christian Dialogues with Hinduism.' In *Interfaith Relations after Hundred Years: Christian Mission among other Faiths*, edited by Marina Ngursangzeli Behera, 79–104. Oxford: Regnum Books International, 2011.

Aloysius, G. *Religion as Emancipatory Identity: A Buddhist Movement among the Tamils under Colonialism*. Bangalore: CISRS, 1998.

Amaladass, Anand. 'Dialogue between Hindus and the St. Thomas Christians.' In *Hindu-Christian Dialogue: Perspectives and Encounters*, edited by Harold Coward, 13–27. Maryknoll, New York: Orbis Books, 1989.

Amaladoss, Michael. 'The Pluralism of Religions and the Significance of Christ.' In *Asian Faces of Jesus*, edited by R. S. Sugirtharajah, 85–103. London: SCM Press, 1993.

Amaladoss, Michael. 'Liberation as an Interreligious Project.' In *Leave the Temple: Indian Paths to Human Liberation*, edited by Felix Wilfred, 158–74. Maryknoll, New York: Orbis Books, 1992.

Amaladoss, Michael. *Making Harmony*. Delhi: ISPCK, 2003.

Amalorpavadoss, D. S., ed. *Research Seminar on Non-Biblical Scriptures*. Bangalore: NBCLC, 1975.

Amalorpavadoss, D. S. 'The Bible in Self-renewal and Church-renewal for Service in Society.' In *Voices from the Margin: Interpreting the Bible in the Third World*, edited by R. S. Sugirtharajah, 316–29. Maryknoll, New York: Orbis Books, 1991.

Appasamy, A. J. *An Indian Interpretation of Christianity*. Madras: CLS, 1924.

Ariarajah, S. Wesley. *The Bible and People of Other Faiths*. Geneva: WCC, 1985.

Ariarajah, S. Wesley. 'A World Council of Churches' Perspective on the Future of Hindu-Christian Dialogue.' In *Hindu-Christian Dialogue: Perspectives and Encounters*, edited by Harold Coward, 251–61. Maryknoll, New York: Orbis Books, 1989.

Ariarajah, S. Wesley. *Hindus and Christians: A Century of Protestant Ecumenical Thought.* Grand Rapids, MI: William B. Eerdmans Publishing Company, 1991.

Ariarajah, S. Wesley. *Not without my Neighbour: Issues in Interfaith Relations.* Geneva: WCC, 1999.

Arokiasamy, S. 'Theology of Religions from Liberation Perspective.' In *Religious Pluralism: An Indian Christian Perspective*, edited by Kuncheria Pathil CMI, 300–23. New Delhi: ISPCK, 1999.

Asad, Talal. *Genealogies of Religion: Disciplines and Reasons of Power in Christianity and Islam.* London: John Hopkins University Press, 1993.

Ashcroft, Bill, Gareth Griffiths and Helen Tiffin, eds. *The Post-Colonial Studies Reader.* London and New York: Routledge, 1995.

Ayrookuzhiel, A. M. Abraham. 'The Religious Factor in Dalit Liberation: Some Reflections.' In *Culture, Religion and Society*, edited by S. K. Chatterji and Hunter P. Mabry, 212–26. Bangalore: CISRS, 1996.

Ayrookuzhiel, A. M. Abraham. *Essays on Dalits, Religion and Liberation.* Bangalore: CISRS, 2006.

Ayrookuzhiel, A. M. Abraham. 'The Living Hindu Popular Religious Consciousness and Some Reflections on it in the Context of Hindu-Christian Dialogue.' *Religion and Society* XXVI, no. 1 (1979): 5–25.

Baago, Kaaj. *Pioneers of Indigenous Christianity.* Bangalore: CISRS & Madras: CLS, 1969.

Bage, M., R. Hedlund, P. B. Thomas, Martin Alphonse and George David. *Many Other Ways: Questions of Religious Pluralism.* Delhi: ISPCK, 1992.

Balagangadhara, S. N. *'The Heathen in His Blindness': Asia, the West and the Dynamic of Religion.* Leiden: E. J. Brill, 1994.

Balasundaram, Franklyn J. 'Dalit Theologies and Other Theologies.' In *Frontiers of Dalit Theology*, edited by V. Devasahayam, 251–69. Delhi and Madras: ISPCK and Gurukul, 1997.

Banerjea, K. M. *The Arian Witness: or Testimony of Arian Scriptures in Corroboration of Biblical History and the Rudiments of Christian Doctrine, including Dissertations on the Original Home and Early adventures of Indo-Arians.* Calcutta: Thacker, Spink & Co., 1875.

Banerjea, K. M. *Dialogues on the Hindu Philosophy.* London and Madras: CLS, 1903.

Barrows, John Henry, ed. *The World's Parliament of Religions: An Illustrated and Popular Story of the World's First Parliament of religions, Held in Chicago in Connection with the Columbian Exposition of 1893*, vols I and II. London: 'Review of Reviews' Office, 1893.

Basham, A. L. *The Wonder that was India*, Fantona Ancient History, Delhi: Rupa & Co., 1975.

Basu, Shamita. *Religious Revivalism as a Nationalist Discourse: Swami Vivekananda and New Hinduism in Nineteenth Century Bengal.* New Delhi: Oxford University Press, 2002.

Baviskar, Amita, and Rakay Ray. *Elite and Everyman: The Cultural Politics of the Indian Middle Classes.* New Delhi: Routledge, 2011.

Bayly, C. A. *Indian Society and the Making of the British Empire.* Cambridge: Cambridge University Press, 1988.

Bayly, C. A. 'The Pre-History of "Communalism?"' *Modern Asian Studies* 19, no. 2 (1985): 177–203.

Bayly, Susan. 'Christians and Competing Fundamentalisms in south Indian Society.' In *Accounting for Fundamentalisms*, vol. 4, edited by Martin E. Marty and R. Scott Appleby, 726–69. Chicago: The University of Chicago Press, 1994.

Behera, Marina Ngursangzeli, ed. *Interfaith Relations after Hundred Years: Christian Mission among other Faiths.* Oxford: Regnum Books International, 2011.

Bender, Courtney and Pamela E. Klassen, eds. *After Pluralism: Reimagining Religious Engagement.* New York: Columbia University Press, 2010.

Bhargava, Rajeev, ed. *Secularism and Its Critics.* New Delhi: Oxford University Press, 1998.

Bhatt, Chetan. *Hindu Nationalism: Origins, Ideologies and Modern Myths.* New York and Oxford: Berg, 2001.

Bloch, Esther, Marianne Keppens and Rajaram Hegde. *Rethinking Religion in India: The Colonial Construction of Hinduism.* New Delhi: Routledge, 2011.

Boyd, Robin. *An Introduction to Indian Christian Theology.* Rev. edn. Delhi: ISPCK, 1975.

Brass, Paul R. *The Production of Hindu-Muslim Violence in Contemporary India.* New Delhi: Oxford University Press, 2003.

Braybrooke, Marcus. *Interreligious Organizations, 1893–1979: An Historical Directory.* New York and Toronto: The Edwin Mellen Press, 1980.

Braybrooke, Marcus. *Pilgrimage of Hope: One Hundred Years of Global Interfaith Dialogue.* London: SCM Press, 1992.

Caldwell, Robert et al. *Christianity Explained to a Hindu, Or, Hinduism and Christianity Compared.* Madras: CLS, 1893.

Cavanaugh, William T. *The Myth of Religious Violence.* Oxford: Oxford University Press, 2009.

Cavanaugh, William T. 'Colonialism and the Myth of Religious Violence.' In *Religion and the Secular: Historical and Colonial Formations,* edited by Timothy Fitzgerald, 241–62. London and Oakville: Equinox Publishing Ltd., 2007.

Chandran, J. Russell. 'The Importance of Interreligious Dialogue Today: A Theological and Ethical Perspective.' In *Dialogue in India: Multi-religious Perspective and Practice,* edited by K. P. Aleaz, 1–11. Calcutta: Bishop's College, 1991.

Chandran, J. Russell. 'The Significance of the Study of Other Religions for Christian Theology.' In *The Multi-faith Context of India,* edited by Israel Selvanayagam, 17–23. Bangalore: BTTBPSA, 1993.

Chenchiah, P. 'Jesus and Non-Christian Faiths.' In *Rethinking Christianity in India,* edited by A. N. Sudarisanam. Madras: A. N. Sudarisanam, 1938.

Cherian, M. T. 'Public Dialogue and Dialogical Theology.' In *Jesus Christ: The Light of the World,* edited by Solomon Rongpi and Wati Longchar, 133–44. Nagpur: NCCI, 2011.

Chidester, David. 'Real and Imagined: Imperial Inventions of Religion in Colonial Southern Africa.' In *Religion and the Secular: Historical and Colonial Formations,* edited by Timothy Fitzgerald, 153–75. London and Oakville: Equinox Publishing Ltd., 2007.

Chidester, David. *Savage Systems: Colonialism and Comparative Religion in Southern Africa.* Charlottesville: University of Virginia Press, 1996.

Chokkalingam, C. *Matham, Panbaadu: Sila Maruthedalhal* [*Religion and Culture: Some Re-searches*]. Nagercoil: Thinnai Publishers, 2000.

Christudas, D. *Impact of Lutheran Mission among Sambavars in South Travancore from 1907 to 1956.* New Delhi: ISPCK, 2008.

CISRS. *A Catalogue of CISRS Publications: A Complete Listing of CISRS Publications 1953–2006.* Bangalore: CISRS, 2007.

Clarke, Sathianathan. *Dalits and Christianity.* New Delhi: Oxford University Press, 1998.

Cornille, Catherine, ed. *Many Mansions? Multiple Religious Belonging and Christian Identity.* Eugene, OR: WIPF & STOCK, 2010.

Cornille, Catherine. 'Introduction: The Dynamics of Multiple Belonging.' In *Many Mansions? Multiple Religious Belonging and Christian Identity,* edited by Catherine Cornille, 1–6. Eugene, OR: WIPF & STOCK, 2010.

Cornille, Catherine. *The Wiley-Blackwell Companion to Inter-religious Dialogue.* Malden, MA: Wiley-Blackwell, 2013.

Coward, Harold. 'Introduction.' In *Hindu-Christian Dialogue: Perspectives and Encounters*, edited by Harold Coward, 1–9. Maryknoll, New York: Orbis Books, 1989.

Coward, Harold. 'The Experience of Scripture in Hinduism and Christianity.' In *Hindu-Christian Dialogue: Perspectives and Encounters*, edited by Harold Coward, 230–50. Maryknoll, New York: Orbis Books, 1989.

Cox, James L. 'Faith and Faiths: The Significance of A.G. Hogg's Missionary Thought for a Theology of Dialogue.' *Scottish Journal of Theology* 32, no. 3 (1982): 241–56.

Cuttat, Jacques-Albert. *The Encounter of Religions: A Dialogue between the West and the Orient with an Essay on the Prayer of Jesus*. New York: Desclee Company, 1960.

Cuttat, Jacques-Albert. *The Spiritual Dialogue of East and West*. New Delhi: Max Muller Bhavan, 1961.

D'Costa, Gavin. *Christian Uniqueness Reconsidered*. Maryknoll, New York: Orbis Books, 1990.

D'Souza, Andreas. 'Theology of Relationship.' *The Forum In-Focus* 14 (2002–3): 1–8.

D'Souza, Andreas. 'Reconciliation in Practice: The Indian Experience.' *Journal of the Henry Martyn Institute* 21, no. 2 (2002): 94–6.

D'Souza, Diane. *Evangelism, Dialogue, Reconciliation: The Transformative Journey of the Henry Martyn Institute*. Hyderabad: Henry Martyn Institute, 1998.

Dalmia, Vasudha. *The Nationalization of Hindu Traditions*. New Delhi: Oxford University Press, 1997.

Das, Veena, ed. *Mirrors of Violence: Communities, Riots and Survivors in South Asia*. New Delhi: Oxford University Press, 1990.

David, A. Maria. *Beyond Boundaries: Hindu-Christian Relationship and Basic Christian Communities*. Delhi: ISPCK, 2009.

Davie, Grace. 'Vicarious Religion: A Methodological Challenge.' In *Everyday Religion: Observing Modern Religious Lives*, edited by Nancy T. Ammerman, 21–37. New York: Oxford University Press, 2006.

Davie, Grace. *Religion in Britain since 1945: Believing without Belonging*. Oxford: Blackwell, 1994.

Davies, Charlotte Aull. *Reflexive Ethnography: A Guide to Researching Selves and Others*. London and New York: Routledge, 2008.

Day, Abby. *Believing in Belonging: Belief and Social Identity in the Modern World*. New York: Oxford University Press, 2011.

Day, Abby. 'Believing in Belonging: An Ethnography of Young People's Constructions of Belief.' *Culture and Religion* 10, no. 3 (2009): 263–78.

Devanandan, P. D. 'Called to Witness.' *Ecumenical Review* 14, no. 2 (1962): 154–63.

Devanandan, P. D. *Christian Issues in Southern Asia*. Bangalore: CISRS, 1959.

Devanandan, P. D. *Christian Concern in Hinduism*. Bangalore: CISRS, 1961.

Devanandan, P. D. *Cultural Foundations of Indian Democracy*. Bangalore: Literature on Social Concerns, 1955.

Devanandan, P. D. *The Gospel and the Hindu Intellectual: A Christian Approach*. Bangalore: CISRS, 1958.

Devanandan, P. D. *Human Person, Society and State*. Bangalore: Literature on Social Concerns, 1957.

Devanandan, P. D. and M. M. Thomas, eds. *Christian Participation in Nation Building*. Bangalore: CISRS, 1960.

Devanandan, P. D. and M. M. Thomas, eds. *Problems of Indian Democracy*. Bangalore: CISRS, 1962.

Devanandan, Nalini, and M. M. Thomas, eds. *Preparation for Dialogue: A Collection of Essays on Hinduism and Christianity in New India by Dr P. D. Devanandan*, Devanandan Memorial Volume 2. Bangalore: CISRS, 1964.

Dhasan, Samuel. *Samaya Amaippukkalum Samuthaya Pracchnaikalum* [*Religious Organizations and Social Problems*]. Kanyakumari: Centre for Peace and Justice, n.d.

Engineer, Asghar Ali, ed. *Communal Riots in Post-Independence India*. Hyderabad: Sangam Books, 1991.

Engineer, Asghar Ali. 'Some Thoughts on Interfaith Dialogue.' *Interreligious Insight* 8, no. 1 (2010): 49–52.

England, John C., et al., eds. *Asian Christian Theologies: A Research Guide to Authors, Movements and Sources, Vol. 1: Asian Region, South Asia, Austral Asia*. Maryknoll, New York: Orbis Books, 2002.

Farquhar, J. N. *The Crown of Hinduism*. London: Oxford University Press, 1913.

Fernandes, Edna. *Holy Warriors: A Journey into the Heart of Indian Fundamentalism*. Revised and updated ed. New Delhi: Penguin Books, 2006.

Fernandes, Walter. 'A Socio-Historical Perspective for Liberation Theology in India.' In *Leave the Temple: Indian Paths to Human Liberation*, edited by Felix Wilfred, 9–34. Maryknoll, New York: Orbis Books, 1992.

Fitzgerald, Timothy. *Discourse on Civility and Barbarity*. New York: Oxford University Press, 2007.

Fitzgerald, Timothy. *The Ideology of Religious Studies*. New York: Oxford University Press, 2000.

Fitzgerald, Timothy. 'Hinduism and the "World-religion" Fallacy.' *Religion* 20, no. 2 (1990): 108–18.

Fitzgerald, Timothy. 'Encompassing Religion, Privatized Religions and the Invention of Modern Politics.' In *Religion and the Secular: Historical and Colonial Formations*, edited by Timothy Fitzgerald, 211–40. London and Oakville: Equinox Publishing Ltd., 2007.

Forward, Martin. *Interreligious Dialogue: A Short Introduction*. Oxford: Oneworld, 2007.

Francis, Dayanandan. *Reflections on Inter-faith Themes*. Delhi: ISPCK, 2007.

Freire, Paulo. *Pedagogy of the Oppressed*. 1970. Reprinted. New York: Continuum, 2003.

Gaborieau, Marc. 'From Al-Beruni to Jinnah: Idiom, Ritual and Ideology of the Hindu-Muslim Confrontation in South Asia.' *Anthropology Today* 1, no. 3 (1985): 7–14.

George, Geomon K. *Religious Pluralism: Challenges for Pentecostalism in India*. Bangalore: Centre for Contemporary Christianity, 2006.

Ghosh, Partha S. *BJP and the Evolution of the Hindu Nationalism: From Periphery to Centre*. New Delhi: Manohar, 2000.

Gilmartin, David and Bruce B. Lawrence. *Beyond Turk and Hindu Rethinking Religious Identities in Islamicate South Asia*. Gainesville: University of Florida Press, 2000.

Giordan Giuseppe and Enzo Pace, eds. *Religious Pluralism: Framing Religious Diversity in the Contemporary World*. Heidelberg: Springer International Publishing, 2014.

Gladstone, J. W. *Protestant Christianity and People's Movements in Kerala 1850–1936*. Kannamoola, Trivandrum. The Seminary Publications, Kerala United Theological Seminary, 1984.

Gnanadason, Joy. *Oru Marakkappatta Varalaru* [*A Forgotten History*]. Madurai: Indian Kalvi Kazhagam, 1998.

Gnanakan, Ken. *The Pluralistic Predicament*. Bangalore: Theological Book Trust, 1992.

Gnanakan, Ken. *Proclaiming Christ in a Pluralistic Context*. Bangalore: Theological Book Trust, 2002.

Gopalakrishnan, M., ed. *Gazatteers of India, Tamil Nadu State: Kanyakumari District*. Madras: Government of Tamil Nadu, 1995.

Gottschalk, Peter. *Beyond Hindu and Muslim: Multiple Identity in Narratives from Village India*. New Delhi: Oxford University Press, 2001.

Grant, Sara. 'The Contemporary Relevance of Christian Ashrams: Reflections in the Light of Ecumenical Experience.' In *Culture, Religion and Society*, edited by S. K. Chatterji and Hunter P. Mabry, 111–30. Bangalore: CISRS, 1996.

Gregorios, Paulose Mar. 'Hermeneutical Discussion in India Today.' *Indian Journal of Theology* 31, no. 314 (1982): 153–5.

Gregorios, Paulose Mar. *Religion and Dialogue*. Delhi: ISPCK, 2000.

Griffiths, Bede. *Christ in India: Essays towards a Hindu-Christian Dialogue*. Bangalore: Asian Trading Corporation, 1986.

Griffiths, Bede. *Christian Ashram*. London: Darton, Longman & Todd, 1966.

Guha, Ranajit, ed. *A Subaltern Studies Reader 1986–1995*. New Delhi: Oxford University Press, 1997.

Guha, Ranajit, Partha Chatterjee, Gyanendra Pandey, David Arnold, David Hardiman, Sahid Amin, Dipesh Chakrabarty, Gautam Bhadra, Gyan Prakash and Susie Tharu, eds. *Subaltern Studies I-X: Writings on South Asian History and Society*. New Delhi: Oxford University, 1982–99.

Guru, Gopal. 'How Egalitarian are the Social Sciences in India?' *Economic and Political Weekly* xxxvii, no. 50 (14 December 2002): 5003–9.

Gurumoorthy, Sitaram. *Kanniyakumari Maavatta Tholliyal Kaiyedu* (The Archaeological Handbook for Kanyakumari District]. Chennai: Department of Archaeology of Government of Tamil Nadu, 2008.

Halbfass, Wilhelm. *India and Europe: An Essay in Understanding*. Albany: State University of New York Press, 1988.

Hames-Garcia, Michael. *Identity Complex: Making the Case for Multiplicity*. Minneapolis: University of Minnesota Press, 2011.

Hardy, Friedhelm. 'A Radical Reassessment of Vedic Heritage: The *Acaryahrdayam* and Its Wider Implications.' In *Representing Hinduism: The Constructions of Religious Traditions and National Identity*, edited by Vasudha Dalima and H. Von Stietencron. New Delhi: Sage Publications, 1995.

Harrison, Peter. *Religion and the Religions in the English Enlightenment*. Cambridge: Cambridge University Press, 1990.

Harvey, Graham. *Food, Sex and Strangers: Understanding Religion as Everyday Life*. Durham: Acumen, 2013.

Hashima, Abu. *Pettagam: Kumari Mavatta Muslimkalin Varalaattru Pokkisham* [*Box: The Historical Treasure of the Muslims of Kanyakumari District*]. Nagercoil: Rahmaniya Society, 2001.

Heim, Mark. *Salvations*. Maryknoll, New York: Orbis Books, 1995.

Hick, John, and Paul Knitter, eds. *The Myth of Christian Uniqueness*. 7th imprint. Maryknoll, New York: Orbis Books, February 1998.

Hirschman, Albert O. *Shifting Involvements: Private Interest and Public Action*. Princeton: Princeton University Press, 2002.

Hocking, William Ernest. *Rethinking Missions: A Laymen's Inquiry After One Hundred Years*. New York and London: Harpers & Brothers Publishers, 1932.

Hogg, A. G. *Christian Message to the Hindu*. London: SCM Press, 1947.

Hogg, A. G. *Karma and Redemption: An Essay Toward the Interpretation of Hinduism and the Restatement of Christianity*. Madras: CLS, 1970.

Hornung, Maria. 'Conclusion: Making Dialogue Real.' In *Interfaith Dialogue at the Grassroots*, edited by Rebecca Kratz Mays, 97–108. Philadelphia: Ecumenical Press, 2009.

Immanuel, M. *The Dravidian Lineages – A Socio-Historical Study: The Nadars through the Ages*. Nagercoil: Historical Research & Publications Trust, 2002.

Immanuel, M. *Kanniyakumari: Aspects and Architects*. Nagercoil: Historical Research & Publications Trust, 2007.

Inden, Ronald. *Imagining India*. Bloomington: Indiana University Press, 1990.

Inden, Ronald. 'Orientalist Constructions of India.' *Modern Asian Studies* 20, no. 3 (1986): 401–46.

International Missionary Council. *The Christian Life and Message in Relation to Non-Christian Systems: Report of the Jerusalem Meeting of the International Missionary Council, March 24th–April 8th, 1928*. London: Oxford University Press, 1928.

Irudhayaraj, Xavier, ed. *Liberation and Dialogue*. Bangalore: Claretian Press, 1989.

Jathanna, O. V. 'Religious Pluralism: A Theological Critique.' *Bangalore Theological Forum* XXXI, no. 2 (1999): 1–18.

Jathanna, O. V. 'The Madras Rethinking Group and Its Contributions to the Development of Indian Christian theology.' *Religion and Society* 44, no. 3 (1997): 74–97.

John, Matthew P. 'The Biblical Bases of Dialogue.' In *Inter-Religious Dialogue*, edited by Herbert Jai Singh, 65–77. Bangalore: CISRS, 1967.

Jones, Adam and Nicholas A. Robins. 'Introduction: Subaltern Genocide in Theory and Practice.' In *Genocides by the Oppressed*, edited by Nicholas A. Robins and Adam Jones, 1–24. Bloomington: Indiana University Press, 2009.

Juergensmeyer, Mark. *The New Cold War?: Religious Nationalism Confronts the Secular State*. Berkeley, CA: University of California Press, 1993.

Juergensmeyer, Mark. *Terror in the Mind of God: The Global Rise of Religious Violence*. New Delhi: Oxford University Press, 2000.

Kaspar, Jegat. *Intha Mann Mathaveriyai Vellum [This Land will Do Away with Religious Extremism]*. Kanyakumari: Naalai Publication, 1995.

Kaur, Ravinder. 'Mythology of Communal Violence: An Introduction.' In *Religion, Violence and Political Mobilisation in South Asia*, edited by Ravinder Kaur, 19–45. New Delhi: Sage, 2005.

Kimball, Charles. *When Religion Becomes Evil*. San Francisco, CA: HarperSanFrancisco, 2002.

King, Richard. *Orientalism and Religion: Postcolonial Theory, India and 'The Mystic East.'* London and New York: Routledge, 1999.

Kishwar, Madhu. *Religion at the Service of Nationalism*. New Delhi: Oxford University Press, 1998.

Klostermaier, Klaus K. 'Hindu-Christian Dialogue.' In *Dialogue between Men of Living Faiths*, edited by Stanley J. Samartha, 11–20. Geneva: WCC, 1971.

Klostermaier, Klaus K. *Hindu and Christian in Vrindaban*. London: SCM Press, 1969.

Klostermaier, Klaus K. 'The Future of Hindu-Christian Dialogue.' In *Hindu-Christian Dialogue: Perspectives and Encounters*, edited by Harold Coward, 262–74. Maryknoll, New York: Orbis Books, 1989.

Klostermaier, Klaus K. *Indian Theology in Dialogue*. Madras: CLS, 1986.

Klostermaier, Klaus K. 'Dialogue – the Work of God.' In *Interreligious Dialogue*, edited by Herbert Jai Singh, 118–26. Bangalore: CISRS, 1967.

Klostermaier, Klaus K. *A Survey of Hinduism*. New York: State University of New York Press, 1989.

Knitter, Paul F. 'Cosmic Confidence or Preferential Option?' In *The Intercultural Challenge of Raimon Panikkar*, edited by Joseph Prabhu, 177–91. Maryknoll, New York: Orbis Books, 1996.

Knitter, Paul F. 'Toward a Liberation Theology of Religions.' In *The Myth of Christian Uniqueness: Toward a Pluralistic Theology of Religions*, 7th imprint, edited by John Hick and Paul Knitter, 178–218. Maryknoll, New York: Orbis Books, February 1998.

Knitter, Paul F. *No Other Name? A Critical Survey of Christian Attitudes toward World-religions*. Maryknoll, New York: Orbis Books, 1985.

Knitter, Paul F. *One Earth Many Religions: Multifaith Dialogue and Global Responsibility*. Maryknoll, New York: Orbis Books, 1996.

Knitter, Paul F. 'Responsibilities for the Future: Toward and Interfaith Ethic.' In *Pluralism and the Religions: The Theological and Political Dimensions*, edited by John D'Archy May, 75–99. London: Cassell, 1998.

Koepping, Elizabeth. 'Family, State and Religious Conversion: Multiple Discourses from Malaysia and South Australia.' *Bulletin of the Royal Institute for Inter-Faith Studies* 2, no. 2 (2000): 141–66.

Koepping, Elizabeth. *Food, Friends and Funeral: On Lived Religion*. Berlin: LIT Verlag, 2008.

Komulainen, Jyri. *An Emerging Cosmotheandric Religion? Raimon Panikkar's Pluralistic Theology of Religions*. Helsinki: University of Helsinki, 2003.

Kooiman, Dick. 'Who is to Benefit from Missionary Education? Travancore in the 1930s.' In *Missionary Encounters: Sources and Issues*, edited by Robert A. Bickers and Rosemary Seton, 153–73. Surrey: Curzon Press, 1996.

Kuttianimattathil, Jose. *Practice and Theology of Interreligious Dialogue*. Bangalore: Kristy Jyoti College, 1998.

Lande, Aasulv. 'Recent Developments in Interreligious Dialogue.' In *The Concept of God in Global Dialogue*, edited by Werner G. Jeanrond and Aasulv Lande, 32–47. Maryknoll, New York: Orbis Books, 2005.

Latour, Bruno. *We have Never Been Modern*. Translated by Catherine Porter. Cambridge, MA: Harvard University Press, 1993.

Lipner, Julius and George Gispert-Sauch. *The Writings of Brahmabandhab Upadhyay*, vols I and II. Bangalore: UTC, 2002.

Lorenzen, David N. *Kabir Legends and Ananta-das's Kabir Parachai*. Albany, New York: State University of New York Press, 1991.

Ludden, David. *Making India Hindu: Religion, Community, and the Politics of Democracy in India*. New Delhi: Oxford University Press, 1996.

Manickam, S. *Slavery in the Tamil Country: A Historical Overview*. Madras: CLS, 1982.

Massey James. 'Guru Nanak Devji's Teachings in the Context of Inter-faith Dialogue.' In *From Truth to Truth*, 106–12. Delhi: Centre for Dalit Studies, 2008.

Matthew, George. 'Hindu Christian Communalism: An Analysis of Kanyakumari Riots.' *Social Action* 33, no. 3/4 (1983): 49–66.

Matus, Thomas. *Jules Monchanin (1895-1957) as Seen from East and West*, 2 vols. Delhi: ISPCK, 2001.

Mays, Rebecca Kratz. *Interfaith Dialogue at the Grassroots*. Philadelphia: Ecumenical Press, 2009.

McCutcheon, Russell. *Manufacturing Religion: The Discourse on Sui Generis Religion and the Politics of Nostalgia*. New York: Oxford University Press, 1997.

Menon, P. Shungoony. *History of Travancore from the Earliest Times*. 1878 Reprinted. New Delhi: Asian Educational Services, 1985.

Mills, C. Wright, and Alan Wolfe. *Power Elite* [1956]. New edn. New York: Oxford University Press, 2000.

Mojzes, Paul, ed. *Christian Mission and Interreligious Dialogue*. New York: Edwin Mellen Publishers, 1991.

Mozoomdar, P. C. *The Life and Teachings of Keshub Chunder Sen*. Calcutta: Baptist Mission Press, 1887.

Muller, F. Max. *Introduction to the Science of Religion*. London: Longmans, Green, 1873.

Muzzafar, Chandra, ed. *Universalism of Islam*. Penang: Aliran, 1984.

Narcheesan, S. R. *Kumari Kristhavargalin Payana Paathai* [*The Journey of Christians in Kanyakumari*]. Nagercoil: Nanjil Publishers, 2000.

Needham, Anuradha Dingwaney and Rajeswari Sunder Rajan. *Crisis of Secularism in India*. New Delhi: Permanent Black, 2007.

Newbigin, Lesslie. *The Gospel in a Pluralist Society*. London: SPCK, 1991.

Nirmal, Arvind P. *Heuristic Explorations*. Madras: CLS, 1990.

Norris, Sigrid. *Identity in (Inter)action: Introducing Multimodal (Inter)action Analysis*. Berlin: De Gruyter Mouton, 2011.

Oddie, Geoffrey A. *Imagined Hinduism: British Protestant Missionary Constructions of Hinduism, 1793–1900*. New Delhi: Sage Publications, 2006.

Oddie, Geoffrey A. "'Orientalism' and British Protestant Missionary Constructions of India in the 19th Century." *South Asia* 17, no. 2 (1994): 27–42.

Oldmeadow, Harry. *A Christian Pilgrim in India: The Spiritual Journey of Swami Abhishiktananda (Henri Le Saux)*. Bloomington: World Wisdom Inc., 2008.

Openshaw, Jeanne. 'The Web of Deceit: Challenges to Hindu and Muslim "Orthodoxies" by "Bauls" of Bengal.' *Religion* 27, no. 4 (1997): 297–309.

Openshaw, Jeanne. *Seeking Bauls of Bengal*. Cambridge: Cambridge University Press, 2004.

Openshaw, Jeanne. *Writing the Self: The Life and Philosophy of a Dissenting Bengali Baul Guru*. New Delhi: Oxford University Press, 2009.

Padmanabhan, S. *The Contribution of Kanyakumari to the Tamil World*. Nagercoil: Kumaran Pathippagam, 1981.

Padmanabhan, S. *Temples in Kanyakumari District*. Nagercoil: Kumaran Pathippagam, 1980.

Painadath, Sebastian, and Jacob Parappally, eds. *A Hindu-Catholic: Brahmabandhab Upadhyay's Significance for Indian Christian Theology*. Bangalore: ATC, 2008.

Pandey, Gyanendra. *The Construction of Communalism in Colonial North India*. 2nd edn. New Delhi: Oxford University Press, 2006.

Pandey, Gyanendra. 'Un-archived Histories: The "Mad and the "Trifling."' *Economic and Political Weekly* XLVII, no. 1 (7 January 2012): 37–41.

Pandian, M. S. S. 'Writing Ordinary Lives.' In *Subaltern Citizens and Their Histories: Investigations from India and the USA*, edited by Gyanendra Pandey, 96–108. London: Routledge, 2010.

Panikkar, Raimundo. 'Foreword: The Ongoing Dialogue.' In *Hindu-Christian Dialogue: Perspectives and Encounters*, edited by Harold Coward, ix–xviii. Maryknoll, New York: Orbis Books, 1989.

Panikkar, Raimon. 'A Self-Critical Dialogue.' In *The Intercultural Challenge of Raimon Panikkar*, edited by Joseph Prabhu, 247–63. Maryknoll, New York: Orbis Books, 1996.

Panikkar, Raimundo. *The Intrareligious Dialogue*. New York: Paulist Press, 1978.

Panikkar, Raimundo. 'Indic Theology of Religious Pluralism from the Perspective of Interculturation.' In *Religious Pluralism: an Indian Christian Perspective*, edited by Kuncheria Pathil, 252–99. Delhi: ISPCK, 1999.

Panikkar, Raimundo. 'The Invisible Harmony: A Universal Theory or a Cosmic Confidence?' In *Toward a Universal Theology of Religion*, edited by Leonard Swidler, 118–53. Maryknoll, New York: Orbis Books, 1987.

Panikkar, Raymond. *The Trinity and World Religions: Icon-Person-Mystery*. Madras: CLS/CISRS, 1970.

Panikkar, Raimundo. *The Unknown Christ of Hinduism: Towards an Ecumenical Christophany*. London: Darton, Longman & Todd, 1964.

Parekh, Manilal C. *Brahmarshi Keshub Chunder Sen.* Bombay: Vaibhav Press, 1926.

Parekh, Manilal C. *The Brahma Samaj: A Short History.* Rajkot: Oriental Christ House, 1929.

Parry, John. *The Word of God is Not Bound: The Encounter of Sikhs and Christians in India and the United Kingdom.* Bangalore: Centre for Contemporary Christianity, 2009.

Patrick, G. *Religion and Subaltern Agency: A Case Study of Ayya Vali – A Subaltern Religious Phenomenon in South Tiruvitankur.* Chennai: Department of Christian Studies, University of Madras, 2003.

Pennington, Brian K. *Was Hinduism Invented?: Britons, Indians, and the Colonial Construction of Religion.* New York: Oxford University Press, 2007.

Perumal, A. K. *Then Kumariyin Kathai [The Story of Kanyakumari].* Chennai: United Writers Publishers, 2003.

Peter, Ivee, and D. Peter. *Malayali Aathikkamum Thamizhar Viduathalayum: Odukkappatta Oru Samuthaayatthin Samuga Porulaathaara Arasiyal Viduthalai Varalaaru [The Domination of Malayalis and the Liberation of Tamils: The Socioeconomic and Political Liberation History of an Oppressed Community].* Nagercoil: Kanyakumari Institute of Development Studies, 2002.

Peter, Ivee, and D. Peter. *Samaya Thondargalum Samudhaaya Marumalarchiyum [Religious Leaders and Social Reformation].* Nagercoil: Kanyakumari Institute of Development Studies, 1999.

Philip, Matthew. *The Unique Christ: Dialogue in Missions.* Bangalore: Centre for Contemporary Christianity, 2006.

Pieris, Aloysius. *An Asian Theology of Liberation.* Edinburgh: T&T Clark, 1988.

Pinch, William R. *Warrior Ascetics and Indian Empires.* Cambridge: Cambridge University Press, 2006.

Ponnu, R. *Thenkodiyil Oru Samuthaya Puratchi [A Social Revolution in Southern End].* Nagercoil: Thenkumari Publishers, 1987.

Porter, Andrew. *Religion Versus Empire? British Protestant Missionaries and Overseas Expansion, 1700–1914.* Manchester and New York: Manchester University Press, 2004.

Purohit, B. R. *Hindu Revivalism and Indian Nationalism.* Sagar: Sathi Prakashan, 1965.

Pushparajan, A. *From Conversion to Fellowship: The Hindu-Christian Encounter in the Gandhian Perspective.* Allahabad: St Paul Press, 1990.

Puthiadam, Ignatius. 'Theology of Religions in the Indian Context.' In *Religious Pluralism: An Indian Christian Perspective,* edited by Kuncheria Pathil, CMI, 191–228. New Delhi: ISPCK, 1999.

Race, Alan. *Christians and Religious Pluralism.* Maryknoll, New York: Orbis Books, 1983.

Raj, M. C. *Dalitology.* Tumkur: Ambedkar Resource Centre, 2001.

Rajamony, C. 'Dialogue in Kanyakumari in the Context of Mission.' *Religion and Society* XXVI, no. 1 (1979): 78–87.

Rajamony, C. *Samaya Panmayum Suthanthiramum [Freedom of Religion and Pluralism].* Nagercoil: Pushba Publishers, 1993.

Rao, K. L. Seshagiri. 'Human Community and Religious Pluralism: A Hindu Perspective.' In *Dialogue in Community,* edited by C. D. Jathanna, 161–6. Mangalore: The Karnataka Theological Research Institute, 1982.

Rayan, Samuel. 'Spirituality for Inter-faith Social Action.' In *Liberation and Dialogue,* edited by Xavier Irudayaraj. Bangalore: Claretian Publications, 1989.

Robins, Nicholas A., and Adam Jones, ed. *Genocides by the Oppressed.* Bloomington: Indiana University Press, 2009.

Robinson, Gnana. 'Why is Fundamentalism a Problem Today?' In *Fundamentalism and Secularism*, edited by Andreas Nehring, 9–15. Madras: Gurukul, 1994.

Robinson, Gnana. 'From Apartheid to Dialogical Living in India: The Need of the Hour.' *Religion and Society* 46, no. 1/2 (1999): 82–96.

Robinson, Gnana. 'India, the Great Nation, Whose Pride is at Stake: The Context of the National Convention.' In *Unite to Serve: Papers Presented at the National Convention on Communal Harmony at Kanyakumari on August 25–28, 2000*, edited by Gnana Robinson, 2–9. Kanyakumari: Kanyakumari Justice & Peace Publications, 2002.

Rodrigues, Valerian. *The Essential Writings of B. R. Ambedkar*. New Delhi: Oxford University Press, 2002.

Rogers, Murray. 'Hindu-Christian Dialogue Postponed.' In *Dialogue between Men of Living Faiths*, edited by Stanley J. Samartha. Geneva: WCC, 1971.

Rogers, Murray. 'Hindu and Christian – a Moment Breaks.' In *Interreligious Dialogue*, edited by Herbert Jai Singh, 104–17. Bangalore: CISRS, 1967.

Royston, Helen. *Christian Ashrams*. Lewiston: New York: Edwin Mellen Press, 1987.

Said, Edward. *Orientalism*. New York: Pantheon, 1978.

Samartha, Stanley J. 'Inter-Religious Relationships in the Secular State.' In *Asian Expressions of Christian Commitment*, edited by Dayanandan Francis and Franklyn Balasundaram, 128–36. Madras: CLS, 1992.

Samartha, Stanley J. 'The Cross and the Rainbow: Christ in a Multireligious Culture.' In *Asian Faces of Jesus*, edited by R. S. Sugirtharajah, 104–23. London: SCM Press, 1993.

Samartha, Stanley J. *Between Two Cultures: Ecumenical Ministry in a Pluralist World*. Bangalore: Asia Trading Corporation, 1997.

Samartha, Stanley J. 'Christian Concern for Dialogue in India.' In *Christian Concern for Dialogue in India*, edited by C. D. Jathanna, 1–19. Madras: The Theological Commission of the Synod of the Church of South India, 1987.

Samartha, Stanley J. *Courage for Dialogue: Ecumenical Issues in Inter-religious Relationships*. Geneva: WCC, 1981.

Samartha, Stanley J., ed. *Dialogue Between Men of Living Faiths: Papers Presented at a Consultation held at Ajaltoun, Lebanon, March 1970*. Geneva: WCC, 1971.

Samartha, Stanley J., ed. *Faith in the Midst of Faiths: Reflections on Dialogue in Community*. Geneva: WCC, 1977.

Samartha, Stanley J. *The Hindu Response to the Unbound Christ*. Madras: CLS, 1974.

Samartha, Stanley J., ed. *Living Faiths and the Ecumenical Movement*. Geneva: WCC, 1971.

Samartha, Stanley J., ed. *Living Faiths and Ultimate Goals: A Continuing Dialogue*. Geneva: WCC, 1973; Maryknoll, New York: Orbis Books, 1974.

Samartha, Stanley J. 'Dialogue in a Plural Society.' In *The Multi-faith Context of India*, edited by Israel Selvanayagam, 1–16. Bangalore: The Board for Theological Text Books Programme of South Asia, 1993.

Samartha, Stanley J. 'The Temper of Crusades and the Spirit of Dialogue.' *NCC Review* 104, no. 9 (1984): 474–8.

Samartha, Stanley J. *One Christ – Many Religions: Towards a Revised Christology*. 3rd edn. Bangalore: South Asia Theological Research Institute, 2000.

Samartha, Stanley J. *The Search for New Hermeneutics in Asian Christian Theology*. Bangalore: Board of Theological Education of the Senate of Serampore College, 1987.

Samartha, Stanley J., ed. *Towards World Community: The Colombo Papers*. Geneva: WCC, 1975.

Samartha, Stanley J., and Nalini Devanandan, eds. *I Will Lift Mine Eyes Unto The Hills: Selected Sermons and Bible Studies of P. D. Devanandan*, Devanandan Memorial, vol. 1. Bangalore: CISRS, 1963.

Scott, David C. *Keshub Chunder Sen*. Bangalore: CLS/UTC, 1979.

Selvanayagam, Israel, ed. *Biblical Insights on Inter-faith Dialogue*. Bangalore: Board of Theological Education of the Senate of Serampore College, 1995.

Selvanayagam, Israel. *A Dialogue on Dialogue: Reflections on Interfaith Encounters*. Madras: Christian Literature Society, 1995.

Selvanayagam, Israel. *Evangelical and Dialogical: Healthy Balance in a Multi-faith Context*. Delhi: ISPCK, 2012.

Selvanayagam, Israel. *Evangelism and Inter-faith Dialogue*. Tiruvalla: CSS, 1993.

Selvanayagam, Israel. *Relating to People of Other Faiths*. Tiruvalla: CSS, 2004.

Selvanayagam, Israel. *A Second Call: Ministry and Mission in a Multifaith Milieu*. Madras: CLS, 2000.

Sen, Amartya. *The Argumentative Indian: Writings on Indian History, Culture and Identity*. New York: Farrar, Straus and Giroux, 2005.

Sen, Amartya. *Identity and Violence: The Illusion of Destiny*. London: Penguin Books, 2006.

Sharpe, Eric J. *Comparative Religion: A History*. London: Duckworth, 2003 (1975).

Sharpe, Eric J. 'Hindu-Christian Dialogue in Europe.' In *Hindu-Christian Dialogue: Perspectives and Encounters*, edited by Harold Coward, 100–15. Maryknoll, New York: Orbis Books, 1989.

Sharpe, Eric J. *Not to Destroy but to Fulfil: the Contribution of J. N. Farquhar to Protestant Missionary Thought in India before 1914*. Uppsala: Gleerup, 1965.

Sharpe, Eric J. 'The Goals of Inter-religious Dialogue.' *Truth and Dialogue: The Relationships between World Religions*, edited by John Hick, 77–95. London: Sheldon Press, 1974.

Singh, Godwin R. 'Inter-religious Dialogue between Sikhism and Christianity.' In *Fundamentalism and Secularism*, edited by Andreas Nehring, 298–309. Madras: Gurukul, 1994.

Singh, Herbert Jai. 'Preparation for Dialogue.' In *Inter-Religious Dialogue*, edited by Herbert Jai Singh, 41–54. Bangalore: CISRS, 1967.

Singh, Herbert Jai. *My Neighbours: Men of different Faiths*. Bangalore: CISRS, 1965.

Slater, T. E. *The Higher Hinduism in Relation to Christianity: Certain Aspects of Hindu Thought from the Christian Standpoint*. London: Elliot Stock, 1902.

Smith, Jonathan Z. *Imagining Religion: from Babylon to Jonestown*. Chicago: University of Chicago Press, 1982.

Smith, W. C. *The Meaning and End of Religion: A Revolutionary Approach to the Great Religious Traditions*. London: SPCK, 1978.

Spendlove, Gregory Blake. *A Critical Study of the Life and Thought of Brahmabandhab Upadhyay*. Deerfield: Trinity International University, 2005.

Srinivas, M. N. *Social Change in Modern India*. New Delhi: Orient Longman, 1995.

Stack, Trevor. 'A Higher Ground: The Secular Knowledge of Objects of Religious Devotion.' In *Religion and the Secular: Historical and Colonial Formations*, edited by Timothy Fitzgerald, 47–69. London and Oakville: Equinox Publishing Ltd., 2007.

Sudarisanam, A. N., ed. *Rethinking Christianity in India*. Madras: A. N. Sudarisanam, 1938.

Sugirtharaja, Sharada. *Imagining Hinduism: A Postcolonial Perspective*. London: Routledege, 2004.

Sugirtharajah, R. S. 'Inter-faith Hermeneutics: An Example and Some Implications.' In *Voices from the Margin: Interpreting the Bible in the Third World*, edited by R. S. Sugirtharajah, 352–63. Maryknoll, New York: Orbis Books, 1991.

Sukumaran, Ilanthottam. *Kumari Sirpi Nesamonyum Thenkumari Thamizh Makkalum* [*Kanyakumari Maker Nesamony and the Tamil People of South Kanyakmuari*]. Nagercoil: Sandini Publishers, 2004.

Sukumaran, K. *Cherar Varalaarum Makkal Vaazhviyalum* [*The History and Life of Cheras*]. Nagercoil: Santhini Publishers, 2005.

Sweetman, Will. 'Colonialism all the Way down? Religion and the Secular in Early Modern Writing on South India.' In *Religion and the Secular: Historical and Colonial Formations*, edited by Timothy Fitzgerald, 117–34. London and Oakville: Equinox Publishing Ltd., 2007.

Swidler, Leonard. *After the Absolute: The Dialogical Future of Religious Reflection*. Minneapolis: Augsburg Fortress Publishers, 1990.

Tambiah, Stanley. *Magic, Science, Religion, and the Scope of Rationality*. Cambridge: Cambridge University Press, 1990.

Taylor, Richard. 'Current Hindu-Christian Dialogue in India.' In *Hindu-Christian Dialogue: Perspectives and Encounters*, edited by Harold Coward, 119–28. Maryknoll, New York, Orbis Books, 1989.

Taylor, Richard. 'The Meaning of Dialogue.' In *Inter-Religious Dialogue*, edited by Herbert Jai Singh, 55–64. Bangalore: CISRS, 1967.

Tejani, Shabnum. *Indian Secularism: A Social and Intellectual History 1890–1950*. New Delhi: Permanent Black, 2007.

Tennent, Timothy C. *Building Christianity on Indian Foundations: The Legacy of Brahmabhandhav Upadhyay*. Delhi: ISPCK, 2000.

Tennent, Timothy C. *Christianity at the Religious Roundtable*. Grand Rapids, MI: Baker Academic, 2002.

Thambi, Vikraman, and Shenbaga Perumal. *Varalatril Mandaikadu* [*Mandaikadu in History*]. Kanyakumari: Triveni Publishers, 1988.

Thangamani, C., ed. *Kanyakumari Maavattam: Arasiyal-Samuga Varalaru* [*Kanyakumari District: Political-Social History*]. Chennai: Kanyakumari District Historical Council, 2005.

Thangaraj, M. Thomas. *Christian Witness in the Multi-religious Context*. Bangalore: CISRS, 2011.

Thangaraj, M. Thomas. *The Common Task: A Theology of Christian Mission*. Nashville: Abingdon Press, 1999.

Thangaraj, M. Thomas. *The Crucified Guru: An Experiment in Cross-Cultural Christology*. Nashville: Abingdon Press. 1994.

Thangaraj, M. Thomas. 'Hindu Universalism and Christian Catholicity.' In *Influence of Hinduism on Christianity*, edited by Gnana Robinson, 1–14. Madurai: TTS, 1980.

Thangaraj, M. Thomas. *Relating to People of Other Religions: What Every Christian Needs to Know*. Nashville: Abingdon Press, 1997.

Thomas, M. M. *The Acknowledged Christ of Hindu Renaissance*. Bangalore: CISRS, 1970.

Thomas, M. M. *Christian Participation in Nation-Building*. Bangalore: NCCI & CISRS, 1960.

Thomas, M. M. 'The Significance of the Thought of Paul D. Devanandan for a Theology of Dialogue.' In *Inter-Religious Dialogue*, edited by Herbert Jai Singh, 1–37. Bangalore: CISRS, 1967.

Thomas, M. M. *Man and the Universe of Faiths*. Bangalore: CISRS, 1975.

Thomas, M. M. 'Inter-religious Conversion.' In *Religion, State & Communalism: A Post-Ayodhya Reflection*, edited by J. John and Jesudhas Athyal, 95–131. Madras: The Academy of Ecumenical Indian Theology and Church Administrations, 1994.

Thomas, M. M. *Risking Christ for Christ's Sake: Towards an Ecumenical Theology of Pluralism* [1987]. Geneva: ECC Publications (Indian Edition), 1999.

Thomas, M. M. *Salvation and Humanisation*. Bangalore: CISRS, 1971.

Thomas, M. M. *Salvation and Humanisation: Some Crucial Issues of the Theology of Mission in Contemporary India*. Madras: CLS, 1971.

Thomas, M. M. *The Secular Ideologies of India and the Secular Meaning of Christ*. Madras: The Christian Literature Society, 1976.

Thomas, M. M. *Some Theological Dialogues*. Bangalore: CISRS, 1977.

Thomas, M. M. 'The World in which we Preach Christ.' In *Witness in Six Continents: Records of the Meeting of the Commission on World Mission and Evangelism of the World Council of Churches, held in Mexico City, December 8th to 19th, 1963*, edited by Ronald K. Orchard, 11–19. London: Edinburgh House Press, 1964.

Thumma, Anthoniraj. *Breaking Barriers: Liberation of Dialogue and Dialogue of Liberation*. Delhi: ISPCK, 2000.

van der Veer, Peter. *Gods on Earth: The Management of Religious Experience and Identity in a North Indian Pilgrimage Centre*. London: Athlone, 1988.

van der Veer, Peter. *Religious Nationalism: Hindus and Muslims in India*. Berkeley: University of California Press, 1994.

Varma, Pavan K. *The Great Indian Middle Class*. New Delhi: Penguin, 2007.

Veliath, Dominic. 'Jesus Christ and the Theology of Religions: A Conspectus of Models.' In *Religious Pluralism: An Indian Christian Perspective*, edited by Kuncheria Pathil CMI, 156–90. New Delhi: ISPCK, 1999.

Verghese, Paul. 'Dialogue with Secularism.' In *Interreligious Dialogue*, edited by Herbert Jai Singh, 225–37. Bangalore: CISRS, 1967.

Verghese, Paul. 'Christ and All Men.' In *Living Faiths and the Ecumenical Movement*, edited by S. J. Samartha, 159–64. Geneva: WCC, 1971.

Vincent, Maria. *Urayadal Vazhi Uravai Valarppom [Let Us Improve Our Relationships through Dialogue]*. Nagercoil: Nanjil, 2000.

Vineeth, Francis. 'Theology of Religions from the Perspective of Inter-religious Dialogue.' In *Religious Pluralism: an Indian Christian Perspective*, edited by Kuncheria Pathil, 229–51. Delhi: ISPCK, 1999.

Voas, David, and Alasdair Crockett. 'Religion in Britain: Neither Believing nor Belonging.' *Sociology* 39, no. 1 (2005): 11–28.

Wagner, Melinda Bollar. 'The Study of Religion in American Society.' In *Anthropology of Religion: A Handbook*, edited by Stephen D. Glazier, 85–101. Westport, CT and London: Praeger, 1997.

Waller, James. *Becoming Evil: How Ordinary People Commit Genocide and Mass Killing*. 2nd ed. Oxford: Oxford University Press, 2007.

Waller, James. 'The Ordinariness of Extraordinary Evil: The Making of Perpetrators of Genocide and Mass Killing.' In *Ordinary People as Mass Murderers: Perpetrators in Comparative Perspectives*, edited By Olaf Jensen, 145–64. New York: Palgrave Macmillan, 2008.

Webster, John C. B. 'Gandhi and the Christians: Dialogue in the Nationalist Era.' In *Hindu-Christian Dialogue: Perspectives and Encounters*, edited by Harold Coward, 80–99. Maryknoll, New York: Orbis Books, 1989.

Welzer, Harald. 'On Killing and Morality: How Normal People Become Mass Murderers.' In *Ordinary People as Mass Murderers: Perpetrators in Comparative Perspectives*, edited By Olaf Jensen, 165–84. New York: Palgrave Macmillan, 2008.

Wietzke, Joachim. *Paul D. Devanandan*, vols I and II. Madras/Bangalore: CLS/UTC, 1983 and 1987.

Wilfred, Felix. 'Inter-religious Dialogue as a Political Question.' In *Christian Witness in Society*, edited by K. C. Abraham, 187–202. Bangalore: Board of Theological Education of the Senate of Serampore College, 1998.

Wilfred, Felix, ed. *Leave the Temple: Indian Paths to Human Liberation*. Maryknoll, New York: Orbis Books, 1992.

Wilfred, Felix. 'Dialogue Gasping for Breath? Towards New Frontiers in Interreligious Dialogue.' In *Living and Working with Sisters and Brothers of Other Faiths*, 68–86. Hong Kong: Christian Conference of Asia, 1989.

Wilfred, Felix. 'Our Neighbours and Our Christian Mission: Deconstructing Mission without Destroying the Gospel.' In *The People of God among All God's People*, edited by Philip L. Wickeri, 78–100. Hong Kong: Christian Conference of Asia, 2000.

Wilkinson, Steven I. *Votes and Violence: Electoral Competition and Communal Riots in India*. Cambridge: Cambridge University Press, 2005.

Winter, Michael, and Christopher Short. 'Believing and Belonging: Religion in Rural England.' Review. *The British Journal of Sociology* 44, no. 4 (1993): 635–51.

World Council of Churches. *Ecumenical Considerations for Dialogue and Relations with People of Other Religions*. Geneva: WCC, 2003.

World Council of Churches. *Guidelines on Dialogue with People of Living Faiths and Ideologies*. Geneva: WCC, 1979.

World Council of Churches. *Religious Resources for a Just Society: A Hindu-Christian Dialogue*. Report of the Rajpur Meeting, Geneva: WCC, 1981.

Yesudhason, V. and R. Isaac Jayadhas. *History of Tamil Society and Culture since 1336*. Villukiri. Kanyakumari District: MCL Roy Publications, 2002.

Young, Richard F. 'Francis Xavier in the Perspective of the Saivite Brahmins of Tiruchendur Temple.' In *Hindu-Christian Dialogue: Perspectives and Encounters*, edited by Harold Coward, 64–79. Maryknoll, New York: Orbis Books, 1989.

Young, Richard Fox. *Resistant Hinduism: Sanskrit Sources on Anti-Christian Apologetics in Early Nineteenth-Century India*. Vienna: Institüt für Indologie der Universität Wien, 1981.

Young, Robert J. C. *Postcolonialism: A Very Short Introduction*. New Delhi: Oxford University Press, 2003.

Ziolkowski, Eric J., ed. *A Museum of Faiths: Histories and Legacies of the 1893 World's Parliament of Religion*. Atlanta, Georgia: Scholars Press, 1993.

Theses, Reports and Magazine News

Daily Thanthi (a Tamil Newspaper), 31 May 2008.

Dinakaran (a Tamil Newspaper), 10 June 2009.

Election Commission of India, *Statistical Report on General Election, 1980 to the Legislative Assembly of Tamil Nadu*. New Delhi: ECI, 1980.

Election Commission of India, *Statistical Report on General Election, 1984 to the Legislative Assembly of Tamil Nadu*. New Delhi: ECI, 1984.

Elections Commission of India, *Statistical Report on General Election, 1989 to the Legislative Assembly of Tamil Nadu*. New Delhi: ECI, 1989.

Elections Commission of India, *Statistical Report on General Election, 1991 to the Legislative Assembly of Tamil Nadu*. New Delhi: ECI, 1991.

Government of India, *Liberhan Commission Report*, 2009.

Government of Tamil Nadu, *Venugopal Commission Report*. Madras: Tamil Nadu Government, n.d.

Muthuraj, S. *The Contributions of Peace Trust in Interreligious Relations in Kanyakumari District*. BD Thesis, United Theological College, Bangalore, 2001.

Richard, D. Austin Edwin. *A Research on Mandaikadu*. BD Thesis, Tamil Nadu Theological Seminary, Madurai, 1986.
State Planning Commission. *District Human Development Report: Kanyakumari District*. Madurai: Dhan Foundation, 2011.

Interviews

Brahma, Interview, Gramam, 29 June 2008.
Balarasu, Interview, Swamithoppu, 2 July 2008.
Chokkalingam, C., Interview, Nagercoil, 4 July 2008.
Chokkalingam, Kasthooori, Interview, Kottaram, 28 June 2008.
Dhasan, Samuel, Interview, Kottaram, 26 June 2008.
Focus-group Interview, Gramam, 23 June 2008.
Fatima, Interview, Gramam, 6 July 2008.
Focus-group Interview, Gramam, 8 July 2008.
Harris, Arthur J., Interview, Marthandam, 10 July 2008.
Harun, Interview, Gramam, 8 July 2008.
Jacob, Interview, Gramam, 24 June 2008.
Jayaraj, Interview, Kanyakuamari, 6 July 2008.
Khan, Ahmad, Interview, Nagercoil, 3 July 2008.
Mohammed, Interview, Gramam, 6 July 2008.
Mohammed, Interview, Gramam, 8 July 2008.
Murugan, Interview, Gramam, 15 June 2008.
Nagalingam, P., Interview, Nagercoil, 12 July 2008.
Narayana, Interview, Gramam, 8 July 2008.
Narayana, Interview, Gramam, 23 June 2008.
Parvathi, Interview, Gramam, 8 July 2008.
Perumal, Shenbaga Interview, Mandaikadu, 13 July 2008.
Ponneelan, Interview, Nagercoil, 11 July 2008.
Rajamony, C., Interview, Nagercoil, 10 July 2008.
Rajamony, C., Interview, Nagercoil, 13 July 2008.
Salaam, Abdul, Interview, Nagercoil, 13 July 2008.
Samuel, Interview, Gramam, 8 July 2008.
Sukumaran, K., Interview, Nagercoil, 3 July 2008.
Tobias, Antony, Interview, Nagercoil, 22 June 2008.
Velan, Interview, Kanyakumari, 12 July 2008.
Vincent, Maria, Interview, Thuckalay, 9 July 2008.
Vincent, Panivanban, Interview, Kanyakumari, 24 June 2008.
Vishnu, Interview, Gramam, 2 June 2008.

Website Sources

1. http://www.interfaith.cam.ac.uk/.
2. http://eci.nic.in/eci_main/CurrentElections/eci2011.html.
3. http://election.rediff.com/slide-show/2009/may/12/slide-show-1-constituency-profile-kanyakumari.htm.

4. http://election.rediff.com/slide-show/2009/may/12/slide-show-1-constituency-profile-kanyakumari.htm.
5. http://india.gov.in/knowindia/state_uts.php.
6. http://www.chennai.tn.nic.in/chndistprof.htm#loc.
7. http://www.csi-kanyakumari.org/About.htm.
8. http://www.hmiindia.com/history.html.
9. http://www.kanyakumari.tn.nic.in/.
10. http://www.presenceandengagement.org.uk/pdf_lib/6_Inter_Faith_relations_guidelines.pdf.
11. http://www.sedos.org/english/amaladoss1.html.
12. http://www.tcd.ie/ise/study/http://institute.jesdialogue.org/programmes/temple/graduate/.
13. http://www.tn.gov.in/districts.htm.
14. http://www.travelindia-guide.com/assembly-elections/tamil-nadu/kanniyakumari-constituencies/.
15. http://sedosmission.org/old/eng/amaladoss1.html.

INDEX

Advaita   87, 89, 99, 106
ahimsa   100
ashram(s)   1, 6, 26–8, 57, 148, 153

Cicero   74
colonialism   7, 72–3, 76, 78, 83–4, 87,
    101, 188, 206
colonization   ix, 72, 77, 80
colonial Christianity   140
colonial construction(s) of religion   72,
    81, 83, 85, 86, 94
common humanity   26, 94, 97,152
communal   35, 84, 104, 115–16,
    118–19, 121
    conflict   8, 94, 103, 110, 118–19,
      121, 171
    harmony   7, 8, 12, 14, 38, 56–61, 105,
      130, 156
    identity   103
    riots   115–17, 121
    tensions   15, 176, 177
    violence   38–9, 117–18, 121, 196
communalism   83, 113, 116–19
comparative religion   8, 28, 80–2, 87, 96,
    99, 155
conflict resolution   39, 196, 199, 209

Dalit(s)   36–8, 86, 99–100, 147, 201
    movements   37
    religion   37
    texts   201–2
    theology   23, 36–7, 147
deconstruction
    of evangelism and mission   32
    of religion and identity   73, 105
dialogical   23–4, 29, 34–5, 38, 58, 61, 132,
    150–1, 154–5, 157, 175
    activities   x, 12, 24, 62
    approach   31, 40, 150–1, 190, 192,
      196, 199
    dialogue   30

    discourses   16, 125, 141, 185
    elitism   15, 146, 186
    hegemony   186
    models   152, 190

Ecumenical movements   28, 31, 56
elite/elitist
    dialogue   163, 178, 208
    discourses   xiii, 169, 198, 209
    theologians   200
encompassing religion   77
Enlightenment
    European   72–4, 76–8, 82, 94–5, 188–9
    Western   ix, 7, 14, 76, 85, 98
exclusivism   29, 30, 32, 35, 75, 114,
    150–1, 192
    disguised   30
exclusivist(s)   ix, 40, 54, 71, 112, 131,
    155, 175, 179, 190

fanaticism, religious   35, 38, 117, 133,
    197, 209
formal/formalized dialogue   4–6, 9, 15,
    16, 24, 35, 59, 145–6, 148, 149,
    151–4, 163, 174, 176, 200
Friere, Paulo   9

genocide(s)   184, 197–9

hermeneutics   33, 34, 194
Hindu
    extremist(s)   86, 131, 137
    gods/goddesses   13, 88
    identity/identities   83, 86–7, 117, 134,
      136, 166–8
    nationalism   39, 116–17, 138–9
    nationalist(s)   50, 82, 86, 100, 117,
      129, 136, 138–9
    reformation/renaissance   100
    reformers/revivalists   5, 86, 89
    tolerance, critique of   100

Hinduism
  (colonial) construction/invention
    of 8, 81, 82, 99, 100, 188
  differentiation with Hindutva 39
  dominant traditions within 23, 35–6,
    38, 87, 89, 99, 100–1, 106, 147,
    154–5, 188
  and multiple/plural traditions within
    it 106
  as the religion of India 87, 99, 188
  renascent/resurgent 25, 100
  as a single/unified religion 14, 100,
    106–7
  as a Western Christian idea of
    religion 74, 82, 189
  as a world religion 8
Hinduized Christianity 88, 89
Hindus
  mobilization of 116–18, 121, 124,
    129, 136–8
Hindutva 39, 86, 100–1, 106,
    116–18, 121–2, 129, 136–40, 167,
    169, 186
  ideology/ideologues 55, 100–1
  organizations 117, 124, 136

identity/identities
  fixed religious x, 1, 14, 15, 31, 71, 73,
    83, 85, 101–2, 105–6, 110–11, 113,
    128, 140, 166, 168–71, 173, 182,
    192–5, 198
  monolithic 16
  multiple ix–xii, 2, 15–16, 61, 102,
    103, 104, 106, 121, 122, 128, 147,
    148, 166, 169, 175, 179, 183, 189,
    190, 191, 192, 193, 195, 196, 199,
    203, 206, 208, 209
imperative dialogue 5, 14–15, 148, 186,
    199, 207
inclusivism 29, 30, 40, 150, 192
inculturation 33, 36, 87–9

Lactantius 75
liberation theology/theologies 23, 26, 35,
    36–8, 99, 147

missionaries
  European 5, 73

Christian 7, 39, 72, 79–82, 87, 169
Jesuit- 87
multireligious 2, 10, 34, 54, 58, 61, 71,
    101, 157, 163–5, 188
  celebration of festivals 2–3, 61
  context 34, 58, 149, 153–4, 157
  groups 58, 61

ordinariness
  of everyday life 16, 190–2, 200,
    203, 208
  of violence/evil 198–9
Orientalism 72, 79–80, 87, 101
orientalist(s) 7, 30, 72–3, 79–83, 85–7,
    99, 102, 188

postcolonial/postcolonialism 14, 72–3,
    80, 206
post-pluralism 30
public dialogue 39

radical pluralism 30
radical reflexivity 10
reconciliation 23, 38, 39, 57, 117
reflexive ethnography 10
relativism 6, 15, 30, 155–7, 174, 178–9,
    186–94
religion-secular distinctions 14, 35,
    71–2, 76–8, 94–5, 98, 110, 183,
    189, 207
religious fundamentalism/
    fundamentalist(s) ix, 6, 38–9, 54,
    112, 114, 116, 130–2, 140, 186
religious identity ix, 49, 55, 81, 85, 94,
    101–7, 115, 117, 118, 120, 122, 123,
    125, 146, 157, 166–74, 176–8, 189,
    192, 194
religious violence xi–xii, 8, 38, 110,
    112–13, 117, 133, 136–8, 140–1,
    157, 178, 197, 208
Roman Catholic
  Christians 26, 131, 134, 168
  Church 6, 7, 12, 14, 57, 129, 130, 135

Sanskritization 36, 38
  of theology 35, 36, 37
secular
  elites/intellectuals xi, 76, 78

ideologies   26, 34, 78, 94–8, 111
society   34, 77, 95–7, 189, 196, 207
West   30
secularism   ix, 23, 30, 35, 50, 77, 78, 87, 94, 96, 97, 98, 189, 199
secularist   94, 95, 111–12, 116, 184, 189
secularization   34–5, 78, 94–5, 97–8
slavery   49
subaltern
approach   73, 147, 206
genocide   199
method   147
Studies Collective   102, 147, 200
texts   202

symbols
cultural   177
religious   117, 141
syncretism   6, 15, 31, 155–7, 178, 179, 186, 194

terrorism   8, 38
theology of religion(s)   29, 30, 33, 37–8, 71, 151, 192
Trinity   150, 154

Vatican II   7, 23, 28, 29, 56

Xavier, Francis   53

Lightning Source UK Ltd.
Milton Keynes UK
UKOW06f0129210917
309597UK00003B/145/P

9 781350 048591